2 Jansenism

Black Robes in Paraguay

The Success of the Guaraní Missions Hastened the Abolition of the Jesuits

WILLIAM F. JAENIKE

Kirk House Publishers
Minneapolis, Minnesota

Black Robes in Paraguay

The Success of the Guaraní Missions Hastened the Abolition of the Jesuits

by William F. Jaenike

Publisher's Cataloging-In-Publication Data
(Prepared by The Donohue Group, Inc.)

Jaenike, William F.
    Black robes in Paraguay : the success of the Guaraní missions hastened the abolition of the Jesuits / William F. Jaenike.

      p. : maps ; cm.

    Includes index.
    ISBN-13: 978-1-933794-04-4
    SBN-10: 1-933794-04-6

1. Jesuits—Paraguay—History. 2. Guaraní Indians—Missions—Paraguay—History. 3. Missionaries—Paraguay—History. I. Title.

BX3714.P2 J34 2007
271./53/0892   2007923825

Cover: Ruins of the great mission of San Miguel and a medallion, described in chapter 18, commemorating the abolition of the Jesuit order.

Kirk House Publishers, PO Box 390759, Minneapolis, MN 55439
Manufactured in the United States of America

In memory of the many hundreds
of unsung Jesuit fathers and brothers
who labored and died in the old *Paraquaria*
and to the hundreds of thousands of Guaraní,
nameless and faceless,
who lived and died in their care.

Table of Contents

PART TWO:
Jesuits Are Expelled from Europe and South America

Santarelli Treatise Fiasco—Louis XIV Persecutes Huguenots, Builds Versailles, Drains the Treasury—Louis XV Reigns During the Enlightenment—*Philosophes'* Predecessors and Christian Humanism, Erasmus and the Philosophy of Christ—*Philosophes* of the Enlightenment Rise, Disparage Jesuits; Voltaire Dominates the Scene—Diderot Publishes *L'Encyclopédie*—Rousseau Influences Revolutionaries, Declaration of Independence—Attempted Assassination of Louis XV Blamed on Jesuits—Jesuit Financial Scandal Enrages Paris Parlement—French Jesuits Surrender, Pope Reacts Rudely—Expulsion from Paris and then France

Spain's Favorite Sons—Louis XIV's Grandson Becomes Philip V of Spain (1700)—War of the Spanish Succession—What Charles III's Early Years Were Like—Charles Marries María Warburg—Queen Maria Amalia Dies at Thirty-six—Charles in Naples Protests the Treaty of Madrid (1750)—Charles Ascends the Throne—Madrid Riots Threaten Monarchy—Charles Appoints Aranda as Prime Minister—Charles' Anti-Jesuit Feelings Grow, the Teaching of Suarez and the Palafox Case—Charles Angry at Vatican over Censorship—Fallout Lingers from Charles' Rescinding the Treaty of Madrid—Aranda Takes Charge—Ricci's Letter Alleges Charles' Illegitimacy—Aranda Initiates the Secret Trial of the Jesuits—Court Issues Formal Charges, Paraguay Jesuits Singled Out—Trial Finds Jesuits Guilty—Charles Expels Jesuits—Expulsion Is Carried Out—Pope Rejects the Jesuits, They Become Refugees Stuck at Sea—Jesuits Finally Land in Italy—History Judges the Expulsion, the Aftermath—Aranda Dies, Charles Dies

Anti-Jesuit Governor Bucareli Arrives in Buenos Aires—Bucareli Arrests Buenos Aires Jesuits—Jesuit College of Córdoba Closed—Córdoba Jesuits Expelled New—New Jesuits Arrive, Are Imprisoned, Expelled—Bucareli Afraid to Attack the Missions, Fears "Clouds" of Guaraní Warriors—Bucareli Finally Invades the Republic of the Guaraní, Jesuits Surrender Peacefully—Other Tribes Resist—Old, Sick Jesuits Trek Long Distances into Exile—Brazilian Jesuits Expelled to Portugal

Prologue

This is the true story of a sad and shameful part of an epic struggle played out almost entirely within the Roman Catholic Church of the eighteenth century. Ultimately the contest was over government control of the Church in Europe and the abolition of the Society of Jesus—the Jesuits.

The main combatants in our story were Jesuit missionaries armed only with their intellects, guts, and the message of Christ aligned against the governments of Spain and Portugal as well as the Roman Catholic Church's hierarchy. With a weakened papacy, the Church attempted to appease those monarchs. Back in Europe, France would eventually join the fray.

The setting in early seventeenth century colonial Spanish South America was called *Paraquaria* or the Jesuit Province of Paraguay. Initially, it was almost two million square miles or thirty percent of the continent. Spain gradually subdivided *Paraquaria* and rearranged its borders so that, by the middle of the eighteenth century when the Jesuits were expelled, it was greatly reduced to consist of much of today's northern Argentina, Paraguay, southern Bolivia, southern Brazil, and northern Uruguay.

The principal focus of this book is on that part of *Paraquaria* called the "Jesuit Republic of the Guaraní" or the "Guaraní Republic." Actually, it was no republic at all, nor was it any sort of legal entity. Rather, it was a loose confederation of semi-independent missions which gathered the Indians in the region into a protective, paternalistic society. The term "republic" was concocted by an unlikely combination of quixotic historians and contemporary commentators: on the one hand, philosophers and poets, who saw it as the ideal society, a Plato's *Republic* or a More's *Utopia*, and on the other, by anti-Jesuit forces who claimed that the Jesuits were trying to set up a state independent of the Spanish crown.

At stake was the spiritual and material welfare of hundreds of thousands of Indians, members of a loosely defined Tupí-Guaraní people—more commonly called the Guaraní. The Guaraní inhabited much of South America east of the Inca-dominated Andes, stretching

Original "Province of Paraquaria of the Company of Jesus" circa 1625

Thirty missions of the Republic of the Guaraní Pre-1750

SOUTH AMERICA.
1875

from northern Brazil down to central Argentina. In total there were probably several million of them living on the continent.

The Catholic Church at the time was riven by internal and external forces with which it would not or could not deal. Among those forces were an inflexible, beleaguered papal leadership resisting inevitable changes that were sweeping over Europe, especially the evolution of nationalism and nation-states which threatened the existing transnational quasi-government—the Holy Roman Empire of the Middle Ages and the early Renaissance; humanism, first Christian humanism, then its progeny the more irresistible secular humanism with its Enlightenment; the revelations of science and astronomy and their effect on traditional beliefs in Scripture and Church teachings; Protestant reforms sweeping down from the north; interminable, bloody, sectarian wars among Christian sects each convinced it alone had the one true faith; and a race for hegemony over territory, trade, and wealth.

The Jesuits

In the sixteenth, seventeenth, and eighteenth centuries the Society of Jesus—Jesuits for short—became popular among gifted, intellectual, often professional, committed Catholic men from all over Europe. This order acquired a mystique, helping it to recruit the most outstanding priests and brothers—those with total dedication, irrepressible optimism, unfaltering obedience, and a record of accomplishments. No other order could match it. It became a virtuous circle with success, allowing it to recruit the best people who, in turn, caused more success. Their achievements attracted attention everywhere in Europe, Asia, and the Americas. These men gave up their careers, their creature comforts, and even their lives to serve God and humanity. In this narrative, they did it in a remote, subtropical rainforest in South America, centered in what came to be called the Jesuit Republic of the Guaraní (the Republic)—a small part of eastern *Paraquaria* accounting for perhaps three percent of South America's total land area. They labored for over 150 years to bring the souls of the Guaraní to Christ and to create a better, safer life for them in this world.

Although the Jesuits also worked with Indians throughout *Paraquaria* and other lands of the Americas as far away as French Canada, this account is mainly about the Republic and nearby areas stretching from Buenos Aires, Argentina, to Asunción, Paraguay. The narrative describes the physical, military, political, religious and social environment in which these Jesuits of the Republic worked.

Most importantly, this book shows how and why the Jesuits' labors among the Guaraní became a factor in the religious intrigues and geopolitics of the French, Portuguese, and Spanish Catholic monarchs and the papacy, ultimately leading to a catastrophe—the pope's abolition of the Jesuit order. This account also focuses on the conflicts the Jesuits had at the time with the monarchs of Spain, Portugal, and France. When the problems the Jesuits "caused" in their Republic were added to those that they were already having in Europe with those same monarchs, the catastrophe resulted.

The Jesuit order had grown exponentially after its founding in 1534 by six Spanish and one Portuguese priest in Montmartre, Paris, where they had attended university together. (The order was formally approved by Pope Paul III in 1540.) The founders included the charismatic Ignatius of Loyola, the titular founding father, and Francis Xavier, the globe-trotting evangelist responsible for countless thousands in Asia being converted to Catholicism. Along the way, the Jesuits' reputation for excellence in everything they undertook, especially teaching and becoming advisors and confessors to nobility, bred jealousy and discord with older orders of priests and brothers and with diocesan bishops and their parish clergy. The conflicts with the monarchs boiled over to irritate the very popes whom the Jesuits were sworn to serve. The popes' energies were already taxed by the forces described earlier. Additional conflicts with the Spanish and Portuguese monarchs, thrust upon the popes from the Jesuits' activity in South America, were the last thing the papacy needed.

The European Monarchs

The antagonists were the evolving nation-states of Spain, Portugal, and France. They came to view the Jesuits with hostility for their perceived intractability in remaining so loyal to those same popes and for not bending to the political demands of their governments.

For over a century, the papacy had been obstructing the monarchs' desires to modernize their countries unfettered by meddling religious authorities. As monarchial power increased, the papacy gradually became more and more impotent. In too many cases, the popes' personal behaviors led to their diminishing moral authority. Pope Clement XIII's appeals to Spain's powerful King Charles III, in response to the king's expulsion of the Jesuits from Spain in 1767, and the pope's personal agony over the matter, show how powerless the papacy had become. Clement XIII could not save the Jesuits in Spain and soon after he suffered a fatal heart attack or stroke. Perhaps if there had been a meaningful separation of Church and state much earlier, the kings would not have had the same leverage over the papacy and the Jesuits. On the other hand, if that were so, the Guaraní mission system would have been different, perhaps impossible.

The Guaraní

At the center of the struggle were the Guaraní Republic and the Guaraní people, a primitive, generally sedentary though sometimes nomadic, mostly forest-dwelling, hunter-gatherer, frequently cannibalistic people.

Unlike most New World Indians, the Guaraní willingly, often eagerly embraced the Jesuits' new society with its improved quality of life. Acceptance was never under threat or force by the missionaries, which the Jesuits, given their observations of Indian conversions elsewhere in Hispanic-America, knew to be both un-Christian and counter-productive. However, the Indians' motivation was not all positive. The fear of enslavement by Spanish settlers and Portuguese invaders drove many Guaraní to flee to the protection afforded by the missions.

The Missions

The Republic missions were equivalent to self-sufficient towns, clustered near the mighty Paraná river and its smaller Uruguay tributary. Fifteen were in northern Argentina, eight in southern Paraguay, and seven in southern Brazil. The fathers at these missions and others nearby came to be called "the Jesuits of Paraguay." Each mission had a *templo*, or church building, as its centerpiece. The few remaining ruins show that the larger *templos*, built in the Republic's latter years, were truly monumental—rivaling the size of some American cathedrals today. Each *templo* was hand crafted over a number of years by Guaraní eager to showcase their artistic talents for visitors and to compete with other missions for having constructed the most imposing and beautiful buildings.

For two centuries the Jesuits' European-based culture interacted, combined, and thrived with that of the Guaraní in their Republic, elsewhere in *Paraquaria*, or in many Jesuit missions in Brazil in a most felicitous way. What resulted in the Republic was a unique society with hugely profitable farming, ranching, skilled trades, and light industry, all isolated from the predations of the neighboring Spanish and Portuguese colonial society—plantation owners, settlers, and soldiers.

The missions were often likened to early Christian communism. All assets and income were shared. All worked for the benefit of the community. These attributes were almost universally applauded among intellectuals, especially by France's *philosophes* of the Enlightenment such as Voltaire, who otherwise had little use for religion in general and much less for Catholicism or for Jesuits outside of Paraguay.

The Protestant Poet Laureate of England Robert Southey, in his mammoth three-volume, 1,500-page *History of Brazil* written between 1810 and 1819 and his famous 2,198-line epic poem "Song of Paraguay," describes better than anyone else writing in English what these priests faced. He wrote:

> Among the numberless calumnies with which (these) Jesuits have been assailed. . . was . . . that they lived like princes in their empire of Paraguay; and gave free scope to themselves in all of those sensualities from which their converts [Indians] were [prohibited].

> Nothing in the romances of Catholic [legends of the saints] . . . is more monstrous than it would be to believe that these missionaries were influenced by any other motives than those of duty towards God and man. . . . The life of the missionary, after he began his labors in seeking out the wild Indians, was spent in the most arduous toils, the severest privations, and the greatest dangers, which were frequently terminated by untimely death.

Southey's staunchly pro-Paraguay Jesuit writings, when contrasted with his ridicule of the papacy and Catholicism with its sacraments and rituals, testify to those missionaries' humanism as they knowingly and eagerly entered the forest primeval, prepared for the worst (some of them viewed it as the best) outcome, that of martyrdom or other "untimely death."

Another Protestant author, the Scot R. B. Cunninghame-Graham, in his *A Vanished Arcadia* exalted the Jesuits there in the most lofty and moving prose for their unceasing labors and commitment to justice for the Indians. Cunninghame-Graham was a founder of the British Labour Party and had lived in the area of Paraguay for twenty-five years toward the end of the nineteenth century. Ironically, the few critics of the Paraguay mission endeavors seem to have been mostly disaffected Jesuits who had been expelled by their society.

The Jesuits: Finally Expelled and Abolished

Then, at the very peak of the Jesuits' success, with many new missions radiating outward from the core, all of their efforts came to a crashing halt. First the Jesuits were expelled from Portugal in 1759, then dissolved in France in 1764, and most importantly expelled from the globe-girdling Spanish empire of 1767.

Six years after Spain expelled its Jesuits, the entire Jesuit order was liquidated (euphemistically referred to as the "Suppression") by an intimidated Pope Clement XIV who was acting under pressure, mainly from the Spanish king. Clement had 70-year-old Jesuit General Lorenzo Ricci arrested and placed in solitary confinement in the papal prison, Castel Sant'Angelo, until Ricci's death there in 1775. Those who had so faithfully and energetically served the popes and the Catholic Church for 233 years were scattered throughout Europe as refugees.

It was equally tragic for the Guaraní. Without the protection of the Jesuits, the slavers who had constantly threatened the Guaraní in the missions for a century and a half were no longer constrained. Some mission Indians were hauled off to Brazil, where slavery was tolerated. Others fled back into the jungle, retaining the Jesuits' liturgy and religious festivals, trying to keep a grip on their happier days in the missions. A smaller number returned to the jungle and their pre-mission ways.

Gradually the missions, monuments to God, the Jesuits' vision and the Guaraníes' labor were abandoned or battered by invaders. Their adobe structures were literally dissolved by tropical rains. People living near missions pilfered construction materials, especially stone foundations and wood beams, for their own dwellings. Other mission buildings were badly damaged or leveled during an insane, ruinous war in the nineteenth century when little Paraguay took on Argentina, Brazil, and Uruguay simultaneously. Most of the thirty core missions remain in various states of ruin as the photos in this book, taken in July 2003, illustrate.

Longstanding disputes between Spain and Portugal over the Guaraní missions contributed to the Jesuits' downfall. The first thirteen chapters, Part I, of this book are mainly about these and related events in South America. Part II, with six chapters, describes the jealousy, greed, intrigues, lies, bribery, manipulations, and even illicit sex that were so prevalent at the time in the courts of Europe and even in the Vatican.

These chapters show how this abhorrent behavior also contributed to the Jesuits' demise.

By covering in some detail the kings and popes, their ministers and courtiers, and the philosophical upheaval in Europe, I have tried to give the reader a look inside their minds to see how and why they came to their decisions affecting the Jesuits. I also hope to show that evil consequences derived from their actions progressed Mao-like, one step at a time, until the centuries-long journey was completed in 1773. Some of these stories and the people behind them, though only tangential to the Jesuits themselves, are included because they help illustrate the political and religious climate of the times.

While the Guaraní missions were a convenient weapon for the monarchs of Spain and Portugal to use against the Jesuits, the struggle between nationalism and the Catholic Church in Europe probably would have led to the Jesuits' downfall in any event. That downfall was, however, hastened by the 1750 Treaty of Madrid, under which seven of the most flourishing missions in the eastern Republic were forcedly transferred from Spain to Portugal. The treaty was a catalyst that sparked the catastrophe of the Guaraní War—what Jesuit historian William Bangert aptly calls a "kind of Sarajevo," for the monarch—Jesuit conflict. The triumph of the monarchs over the Jesuits was short-lived. It was followed a generation later by cataclysmic European social upheaval, revolution, and war that swept away the monarchies themselves. The Jesuit order was reestablished a generation later thanks in part to their rescue by two "heretics," Frederick the Great of Prussia and especially Catherine the Great of Russia whose role was recognized in the papal Bull of restoration.

The Politically Correct View

Today many sociologists, including religious writers, take a more politicized view—some call it a "nuanced" view—of this epoch, arguing that a whole indigenous society and its culture and system of beliefs were lost due to the Jesuits' efforts. The question of what was gained by these native peoples versus what was lost when they gave up their old, pre-Columbian ways is a classic debate among political historians that will be argued for many years. One simple fact becomes obvious however: Leaving the Guaraní in their natural habitat, untouched by European civilization, was not an option. The slavers would have captured virtually all of them, and they would have been exterminated. The Jesuits understood this and made the Hobson's choice, throwing up a misunderstood, insulating, but protective wall around them.

If there is anything negative one can say about the Jesuits' efforts among the Guaraní, it is that the fathers kept their charges in tutelage—in *statu pupillae*—too long. Southey deals with this accusation:

> [The Indians] were kept in a state of moral inferiority . . . nothing [was done] that could tend to political and intellectual emancipation. The enemies of the Company [of Jesus] were thus provided with a fair cause of accusation: Why . . . was no attempt made to elevate the Indians into free agents? . . . Why, it is asked, will not the Jesuits recruit themselves from the Indians who are born and bred among them, when it is so difficult to procure missionaries from Europe, so expensive to transport them, and impossible to obtain them in sufficient numbers?

Southey answers his own question:

> . . . their superiors [in Europe] had determined otherwise . . . that things were well as they were; the object was accomplished; the Indians were brought to a state of Christian obedience, Christian virtue, and Christian happiness . . . their welfare here and hereafter was secured. To those who look forward for that improvement of mankind and that diminution of evil in the world which human wisdom and divine religion both authorize us to expect, the reply will appear miserably insufficient: But the circumstances of the surrounding society into which it was proposed that the Indians should be incorporated must be considered, and when the reader shall have that picture before him he will hold the Jesuits justified.

It's arguable.

Faced with the sudden expulsion of the Jesuits in 1767 and 1768, the Indians were ill-equipped to survive on their own in the materialistically Darwinian, still racist, exploitational late eighteenth century colonial society. Yet in their defense the fathers, at least those living among the Guaraní and so far removed from the main event in Catholic Europe, could not have foreseen the disaster coming. Perhaps they thought that their energies should be directed at expanding the frontiers of their successes. Perhaps they felt they could develop the Guaraní to be totally self-sufficient at a later time, after they had achieved greater maturity in business and governance, when the surrounding society was willing to accept them as equals. (This was two centuries before the United States decided it was necessary to pass the 1964 Civil Rights Act. Today they are accepted as equals—ninety-eight percent of the people of Paraguay are indigenous [twenty percent] and mestizo [seventy-eight percent], and their long reigning president dictator, Alfredo Stroessner, was the son of a German immigrant and a Guaraní peasant woman.)

Perhaps the Jesuits felt they had achieved the "best civilization possible" as their champions in the Enlightenment said they had. Perhaps they and their superiors in Rome did not view these subtle and complex questions with one mind. We will probably never know.

Foreword

This account is written for those amateur historians with a curious and open mind about the interaction of European missionaries and the indigenous peoples of the Americas during the time of conquest, conversion, and colonization. Those interested in a more complete and detailed understanding of various aspects of these events can consult the Bibliography and its list of frequently used sources. Those wanting simply to be entertained by the subject can watch the highly acclaimed 1986 movie, *The Mission,* starring Robert DeNiro and Jeremy Irons and directed by Roland Joffe, a historical fiction that provides some feel for the South American part of this story.

In writing this narrative I had to depend almost entirely on books, documents, and a few carefully selected internet articles in English. It was disconcerting to find so many conflicting reports on matters of "fact." While documenting the conflicts would have made for scholarly completeness, the story would have become unwieldy. Instead, I tried to resolve them by comparing multiple sources, giving appropriate weight based on each source's credibility. I suspect many of the differences arose from oral histories related in casual situations where raconteurs, both Europeans and Indians, wanted to entertain their listener with a good story or to make themselves the center of attention. There are a few documented cases where this was certainly so.

I would like to assure readers that this book is not an apologia for the Jesuit order as a whole. The order's reluctance to admit Jewish and Muslim converts into its ranks for over three centuries, starting in 1593, well after the pro-Jewish founders had died, is pathetic and shameful. The order made a concession to bigotry. The Jesuits' possession of African slaves in some parts of South America—10,000 or more spread around the continent, regardless of how well they were reportedly treated and what good works came from their labor—is nothing less than bizarre. Even the Jesuits in the Province of Paraguay kept African slaves at their nine colleges, especially the more renowned ones at Córdoba and Asunción. But there were no slaves of any kind in the Jesuit Republic of the Guaraní. There was bigotry among some outspoken Jesuits against Native Americans being ordained to the priesthood. These attitudes and practices were incompatible with the beliefs and teachings of the fathers in Paraguay and of the Company itself. Those anomalies are for another book.

I have tried to put aside my own opinions developed from what I learned about the strengths and weaknesses of the Jesuits generally, and of their men in Paraguay in particular. By doing so, I hoped to maintain objectivity and to report only the facts so that readers can form their own conclusions about them. Nevertheless, the deeper I got into the research, the more difficult it became not to admire these *Paraguayan* missionaries and feel sympathy for the lost Guaraní. I was especially moved by visits to the mission ruins of the Republic. Many ruins in the jungle are so badly eroded and overgrown with vegetation that they are no longer recognizable, even as parts of buildings. Others are barely discernable as structures. A few are restored, still ruins, however, that give the visitor a sense of the masterpieces they once were. One was reclaimed from the jungle by a group of Italian volunteers but not actually restored; it was purposely left in its collapsed condition, with the jungle's overgrowth cleared away.

After two and a half centuries, the few missions that have been re-claimed are towering, ghostly sentinels, silently testifying to the goodness as well as the folly of man. A visitor, standing inside the massive shell of a roofless church building at one of these remote and lonely sites, can almost hear the mournful hymns of the mission's five thousand long-gone Guaraní, whispering through the sad remains.

Finally, I have become convinced that these Jesuits could not have been more benevolent, virtuous, or effective guardians of these primitive Indians during the era of the Jesuit Republic of the Guaraní.

Chronology of Events

DATE	AMERICAS	EUROPE
1325	Mexico City founded by Aztecs	
1491		Ignatius of Loyola born
1492	Columbus discovers New World	
1494		Treaty of Tordesillas (first version) divides globe between Portugal and Spain
1497	Columbus reaches South America	
1515	Díaz discovers Río de La Plata	
1518	Cabot explores Brazil and Argentina coast	More's Utopia
1519	Cortés invades Mexico	
1521		Luther's Diet of Worms
1525	Brazil colonization starts Portugal's king approves Indian slavery	
1533-1535	Pizarro conquers Inca	
1534	Mendoza founds Buenos Aires	
1536		Erasmus' Christian humanism
1537	Asunción founded	
1540		Society of Jesus formally founded
1549	Jesuits arrive in Brazil	
1561-1565	Portuguese defeat Dutch and French in Brazil	
1562-1598		Wars of Religion in France
1572		St. Bartholomew's Day Massacre
1580		Spain absorbs Portugal
1587	First Jesuits arrive in Paraguay	
1588		Spanish Armada
1589		Monk assassinates Henry III
1594		Jesuits expelled from Paris for regicide
1598		Edict of Nantes brings French Huguenot equality

DATE	AMERICAS	EUROPE
1607	English found Jamestown	
1609	First Jesuit missions in Paraguay	
1610		Henry IV assassinated – Jesuits blamed
1618-1648		Thirty Years' War over religion and hegemony
1622		Richelieu begins his rule in France
1629	Mamelucos slavers invade Guayrá – Ruíz de Montoya and Guaraní escape	
1640	Spain arms Guaraní	Portuguese Revolution – Break with Spain Beginning of Jansenism
1641	Armed Guaraní wipe out Mamelucos	
1643		Louis XIV, king of France at age 4
1649	Cárdenas expels Jesuits from Asunción	
1650	Cárdenas defeated, Jesuits restored	
651-1721	Golden Years of the Jesuit Republic of the Guaraní	
1721-1736	Civil War and Communist Revolt in Paraguay	
1750		Treaty of Madrid sells out seven Guaraní missions in the Guayrá
1751-1772		Diderot publishes *L'Encyclopédie*, the Enlightenment reaches zenith
1752	Jesuits in Paraguay rebel against their own hierarchy, reject Treaty of Madrid	
1754	Guaraní War starts	
1756	Spanish-Portuguese army annihilates the Guaraní	
1759	Jesuits exiled from Brazil	Charles III becomes King of Spain; annuls Treaty of Madrid Pombal liquidates Jesuit order in Portugal Voltaire's *Candide*
1760		Pombal *de facto* leader of Portugal
1762		Paris Parlement expels Jesuits. Charles III annuls Treaty of Madrid
1763		Treaty of Paris rearranges colonies world-wide
1764		Louis XV liquidates Jesuit order

DATE	AMERICAS	EUROPE
		throughout France and its possessions
1767		Charles III expels Jesuits from Spain and its colonies
1768	Last of Jesuits leave Paraguay	
1773		Pope Clement XIV liquidates Jesuit order, imprisons Jesuit General Ricci
1775		Pope Clement XIV dies, Jesuit General Ricci dies in prison
1776	Declaration of Independence	
1773-1801		Frederick the Great and Catherine the Great rescue many Jesuits
1789		French Revolution
1800	Republic's missions virtually abandoned	
1801	The Guayrá annexed by Portugal	
1802-1805		Jesuit Vicar-General in St. Petersburg is *de facto* head of Jesuits
1814		Napoleon abdicates. Pope Pius VII reestablishes the Jesuit order world-wide
1817-1819	Luso-Brazilian General Chargas destroys many missions with artillery	
1820-1980s	Missions melt into ruins	
1860s-1880s	Cunninghame-Graham lives in Paraguay area	
1980s	Restoration starts on a few missions	
1983	UNESCO declares São Miguel a World Heritage site	

PART ONE

The Scene in South America; the Jesuits' Founding

CHAPTER 1

Why the Europeans Went to the Land of the Guaraní

Díaz de Solís Butchered at Río de La Plata

It was 1515 when Spain's King Ferdinand dispatched the renowned forty-five-year-old navigator Juan Díaz de Solís to find an all-water route from the South Atlantic west to the Pacific. Little did the king or Díaz de Solís suspect that this was to be a one-way journey for the explorer, ending in horror.

Díaz de Solís was widely acclaimed as the most skillful navigator alive. The king had awarded him the supreme honorific title of pilot-major, a highly paid position, previously held by none other than the explorer Amerigo Vespucci, after whom America is named.

Sailing along the South American east coast with several ships, he discovered an estuary that today is called Río de La Plata, on the south bank of which is now Buenos Aires. Might it be a route to the Pacific? On the north bank of the estuary's mouth near today's Montevideo, Uruguay, he spied a band of Charrua Indians who waved him ashore. Leaving the safety of his ships, he landed with some of his crew in a small boat, intending to capture one of the Charruas to take back to Spain. However, the Charruas were wily and fierce. They had other ideas. Staging an ambush, they seized the boat with its crew and clubbed every man to death (save one who survived and joined them) including Díaz de Solís. Then, taking their victims to a spot beyond reach of the Spaniards' guns but in plain sight, they dismembered the bodies, roasted the remains on great fires, and devoured them. All this was done with insulting gestures and taunts to the horrified ships' crews.

Thus was the land and the people to whom the Jesuit missionaries would bring the message of Jesus Christ a century later.

Díaz de Solís' ships, loaded earlier with valuable Brazil wood, returned to Spain with their crews' vivid description of what this new land had to offer. The expedition also produced the first of never-ending quarrels between Spain and Portugal since the latter claimed, probably correctly but to no avail, that Díaz de Solís had poached the wood from territory both had agreed was Portugal's under the 1494 Treaty of Tordesillas.

But we are getting ahead of our story. It should begin with Columbus and why Spain funded his search for a westward route to Asia.

Spain Seeks a Passage to Asia, Columbus' Third Trip

During the second half of the fifteenth century Portugal and, to a much lesser extent, Spain led the way in exploration. Spain's main interest was to find a *westward* route to Asia and its treasures, especially the spices and silk of India, China, and that portion of the East Indies known as the Spice Islands in today's Indonesia. For Spain a westward route was suspected of being a short one. The circumference of the globe was grossly underestimated by most cartographers and navigators, in part because longitude was an inexact science, little used or understood. The long route—taking a year or more—around Africa's Cape of Good Hope was expensive and dangerous, because Muslim corsairs preyed upon merchant vessels following Africa's east coast and crossing the Indian Ocean. Besides, Portugal had established a number of forts and plantations along Africa's west coast, thus supporting its merchant ships sailing this route. Spain had virtually none.

Enter Christopher Columbus.

Sponsored by King Ferdinand and Queen Isabella, Columbus' westward route during his first two trips had taken him to the Bahamas and the islands of the Caribbean. Were they outlying islands of Asia? Uncertain, but suspecting that the mother lode of the East might be just on the other side of the western Caribbean, he launched his third voyage in 1498. Sailing on a more southern route than before, he came upon Trinidad and the northern coast of Venezuela and, most notably, its Orinoco river. Judging by the size of the river—larger than any other he or his crew had ever seen—he suspected that it led back into nothing less than a continent. On his star-crossed fourth and final trip he explored the Caribbean coast of Honduras and Panama and learned from Indians that there was a great sea not far away on the other side of the isthmus. For him, it was a possible sea-land-sea short route to Asia.

Upon returning to Spain in September 1504, he found that his principal sponsor, Isabella, was gravely ill. She would die two months later at age fifty-three. His own health was failing rapidly. He had taken his last voyage. In 1506, this "Admiral of the Ocean Sea," a title he inveigled from the king and queen, would die himself at fifty-five. Columbus had only a sketchy idea of where he had been and what he had found. Now as the sixteenth century unfolded it was time for others to discover where the coast of South America might take them.

Meanwhile, by 1494 the westward route to Asia had taken on a new urgency for Spain. That year, under the Treaty of Tordesillas, it had ceded much of the South Atlantic, Africa, the Indian Ocean, and a sliver of yet-to-be-discovered eastern South America to Portugal. Thus, Spanish ships were not allowed to use the eastward route around Africa to reach Asia.

The Treaty of Tordesillas, Popes Divide the Globe to Limit Competition

In 1493, just months following Columbus' return from his maiden voyage, the Spanish-born Pope Alexander VI, after discussions with the crowns of Spain and Portugal, had the foresight (and hubris) to divide what might be discovered to the south during future expeditions so that it could be explored and exploited with the least contention possible between these two growing nautical powers. Pope Alexander, Rodrigo Borja, became known as the "Borgia" pope (Italian for the Spanish "Borja"). He was handsome, eloquent, and charming, but also tough and shrewd, an unprincipled, philandering embarrassment to the Catholic Church. He was also the ultimate nepotist, appointing his second son to be an archbishop at seventeen and cardinal at eighteen; four other family members received the "red hat" from him. The only problems with his division were that the existence of these lands was pure speculation and other countries with imperial ambitions were excluded. France had neglected to seek a place at the table; it was not offered one. The French were preoccupied with internal, emerging heresies, especially Calvinism (in the form of France's Huguenots), and the centuries-long rivalry with England. Most of France's colonial energies were being directed to the Far East. Only decades later did France awaken to the potential of the Americas. England and Holland, more geographically and ethnically distant, though still Catholic, did not figure in Alexander's plan. The pope's reputation and his Spanish origin would not be helpful later on, when other powers considered his division of South America.

Alexander divided up South America by decreeing that all lands west of what was to be the 38th meridian were to be Spanish; east of it, Portuguese. The 38th meridian line gave Portugal the African conti-

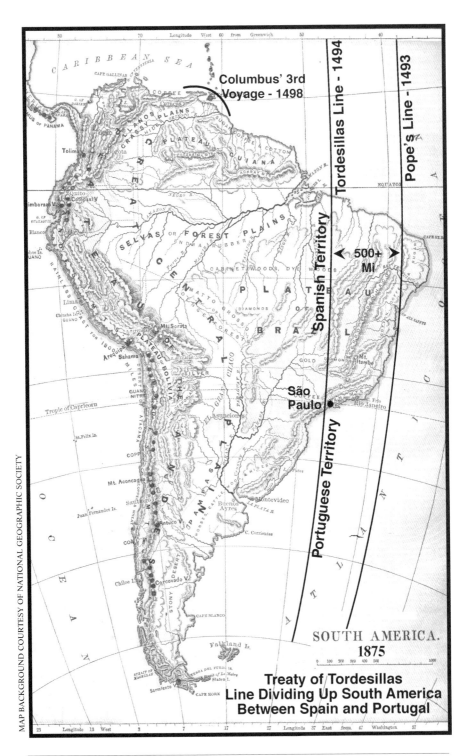

Columbus' 3rd Voyage - 1498

Tordesillas Line - 1494

Pope's Line - 1493

Spanish Territory

◄ 500+ Mi ►

Portuguese Territory

São Paulo ●

SOUTH AMERICA.
1875

Treaty of Tordesillas
Line Dividing Up South America
Between Spain and Portugal

nent that it had explored for almost a century under Henry the Navigator. Africa's coasts, especially the west coast with its Portuguese forts and colonies, were now Portugal's and not to be contested, at least by Spain.

South America was a different story. Its existence was largely a guess. Columbus would not discover it for another four years and even then he had only an inkling of what he had found. With South America divided up so blindly, the pope wound up giving only a miniscule tip of the eastern part of the continent (i.e., a tiny slice of eastern Brazil) to Portugal. Portugal, from its African and Asian exploration and from the tales of Arab traders and others in the Indian Ocean, understood the unintended benefits to them from the pope's line on the unknown side of the globe. After all, a meridian circles the globe, and the pope had handed Portugal much of the East Indies, especially the Spice Islands and the fabulous trading prizes of India. No one fully appreciated this at the time. It was largely serendipity. This meridian might give Spain too much of any South America lands as far as Portugal was concerned. Only Portugal knew enough about the East Indies to know it could probably afford to give up the most eastern part of them to Spain if it could get more of the unexplored western hemisphere. That could be done by moving the dividing line westward from the 38th meridian. That is what happened next.

In May 1494 negotiations began between agents of Portugal's John II (João II) and Spain's Ferdinand and Isabella to move Alexander's line westward. The negotiations were a mismatch. Portugal's representatives were accomplished navigators and explorers, especially of Africa's coast. Spain appointed grandees unencumbered by any knowledge of Africa or the Atlantic. One of them, Enrique Enríquez, was on Spain's team only because he was the father-in-law of one of Pope Alexander's sons. None of the Spaniards consulted Columbus, although he could not have helped much at that time. The negotiators met in a convent in Tordesillas near Valladolid, the Spanish capital, in Castile. In June the Treaty was signed moving the pope's 38th meridian line some 500 miles westward to 370 leagues—about 1100 miles—west of the most westerly of the Cape Verde Islands, or roughly the 47th meridian. (Longitude could only be approximated at that time.) This would give Portugal a bigger slice of the western hemisphere while leaving it the most valuable part of the East Indies and all of the Indian Ocean. These were no doubt John's objectives. Ferdinand and Isabella's motives for giving up so much are obscure.

Portugal and Spain continued to argue over the matter until 1506, when they were formally "reconciled" to their monarchs' satisfaction by a Bull from Pope Julius II. By then, Portugal had gotten a better idea of Brazil's geography. In 1500 Portuguese nobleman and explorer Pedro Álvares Cabral was en route to India with his fleet of thirteen ships. Navigating south on the Atlantic for the African cape, he took advantage of favorable winds and made such a wide arc around Africa's west coast that he came upon the eastern tip of Brazil. Putting ashore for ten days, he claimed the land for Portugal and learned something of it and its people before he continued around Africa's Cape of Good Hope and the rest of his journey to India. While he lost nine of his ships to storms, shipwrecks, and an attack by Muslim traders in India, he made it back to Portugal in June 1501 with four cargoes of such valuable spices that his losses were financially justified.

Pope Julius was another temporal embarrassment, known to the Italians as *"il Terrible."* The first Mèdici pope, he was irascible, ambitious, and warlike, personally directing campaigns against the Borgias and others over Papal State territory. His main objective was the temporal grandeur of the papacy. He built palaces and forts with benefices (revenues) from his ecclesiastic posts, while using some of the money to bribe other cardinals to elect his puppet and predecessor, Pope Innocent VIII. As a cardinal-priest he fathered three daughters and continued to have relations with their mother during his papacy.

For some 160 years, the Treaty of Tordesillas provided a dividing line between Portugal's Brazil with its officially outlawed but rampant quasi-legalized slavery and Spain's lands to the west of the Tordesillas line where slavery was outlawed by repeated and forceful royal decrees. There, the decrees were often observed, at least in southern South America. This line could have played an important role in the Jesuits' struggle to protect their missions and the Guaraní Indians from Portuguese slavers, but only if the line had been respected by Portugal. In that case, the history of the Jesuit Republic of the Guaraní and, indeed, all of Brazil would have turned out much differently. If only.

Europeans Compete for Hegemony over South America

To understand the Jesuits' 175-year struggle for the Guaraníes' souls and their earthly welfare, we must start with another, concurrent struggle: the evolving battle for hegemony over world trade and colonial possessions among the European powers, not just Spain and Portugal. Leopold von Ranke, the nineteenth century German historian and doyen of the study of statecraft, portrayed European history as an incessant struggle for mastery in which a balance of power was possible only through recurrent conflict. That struggle for mastery in the Americas began on the Brazilian coast. It was no coincidence that the Brazilian coast is also where the Jesuits first built their missions.

Competition among European nations was the globalization issue of its time—the sixteenth, seventeenth, and eighteenth centuries. Initially, the Asian silk and spice trade was the grand prize. The competitors and often bitter combatants were, in order of influence, imperial Spain, England, Portugal, France and Holland, although that order changed from time to time. This part of the story focuses on one isolated but dramatic part of that bloody struggle: the contest for control of the eastern South America coast, a wild part of the continent thinly populated by stone-age peoples. The outcome would profoundly affect the Jesuits and their missions in Paraguay.

David Davis writes that the race towards globalization was made possible by two technological innovations in Europe: the caraval (a fast, maneuverable sailing ship) and navigational instruments including the compass which came from China via the Arabs and the quadrant which permitted celestial navigation. Portugal, with its Jewish cosmographers and well-known historical figures like Prince Henry the Navigator and Vasco da Gama, became the technology and exploration leader.

South America and Globalization, Colonization, and Trade

By the middle of the sixteenth century it was clear that Spain considered South America an obstacle in the way of the Pacific and the East Indies. In 1520 Magellan had shown that the only certain all-water route to the Pacific was long and dangerous—especially for him; he never made it home, dying in combat with Philippine natives. Spain's energies became focused mainly on the easy wealth taken from the Aztec and Inca civilizations. Colonization in other regions took a back seat. Not so for Portugal. Its vision was more strategic. It had already developed a relatively efficient route to the Indies. Portugal, locked out of the Mexican and Peruvian gold and silver bonanza, placed a big bet on the east coast of South America by investing huge resources there, both people and treasure. As a small trading nation it had already developed well before Columbus' trips ingenuity and entrepreneurial skills, especially on the islands off the west coast of Africa. Its expeditions had gone there to find wheat and barley, as well as the sources of gold and pepper on the coast south of Mali. Soon they discovered the

Southern South American
Cities and Towns Noted In Text

1 in = 90 mi

value of "black gold," slaves from the coast that could labor so effectively on sugar plantations. By 1492 these had evolved into what Davis
calls a "sugar monoculture" that was so successful that the Madeiras,
Portuguese islands off the African coast, produced more sugar than all
of the Mediterranean.

Columbus, having lived for over ten years near Madeira, had the
foresight to take sugar cane with him to the New World on his second
voyage. That initiated a long, painful relationship of sugar, slavery, and
rum in the Caribbean, but Portugal had the strategic vision to transfer
its commercial experience and skills from Africa to Brazil. Today we
call it "globalization." By the mid-sixteenth century, Brazilian sugar
plantations, manned by Indian slaves, were developing rapidly. This
industry was becoming the economic driving force behind a century-
long, hegemonic struggle among Portugal, France, and Holland over

Southern South American Cities and Towns Noted In Text

1 in = 90 mi

2,000 miles of Brazilian coastline. The fighting and slavery that coincided with it would eventually spill over into Spanish *Paraquaria*, the locus of this story, in the seventeenth and eighteenth centuries.

The second quarter of the sixteenth century saw the Portuguese settlements on the Brazilian coast prosper under its slave-labor plantation economy. The experience with Indian slaves was largely a failure, as the Indian life-span under slavery was horrifically short. Exposed to European diseases, the Indians suffered terribly from smallpox and measles. Diseases combined with a temperament built on an unfettered jungle life produced a death rate that required a never-ending re-supply of Indians. The cost of re-supply would eventually eclipse that of importing Africans, more temperamentally adaptable and disease-resistant. It also helped that Portugal's African possessions were geographically close to eastern Brazil which juts out toward Africa, making the trans-Atlantic trip for slave ships a short one.

Portugal's colony would gradually evolve into a coastal strip running 2,000 miles from the Amazon river to below São Paulo, never more than a hundred miles wide. Davis writes that the Portuguese investment came "closer to resembling an agribusiness" than the feudal European farming known to its settlers. By 1600, Brazilian sugar produced greater profits for Portugal "than the fabled Asian spice trade." Large quantities of gold were discovered in Brazil at the end of the seventeenth century, and diamonds soon thereafter. When added to its sugar successes, Portugal's return on investment in Brazil would prove to be spectacular.

Portuguese Jesuits Arrive in Brazil, Make a Mark for Their Country

Jesuit missionaries arrived in Brazil thirty-eight years before their brethren came to Paraguay. They were almost all Portuguese, dispatched by Portugal's King John III (João III), a devout Catholic, a great benefactor of the Jesuits, "their first, steadiest and most useful friend," and a clever strategist on the international political stage. John clearly understood the value of missionaries in pacifying conquered peoples, thus strengthening Portugal's foothold in its developing colonies and solidifying Portugal's claims to those lands against rival European powers. The strategy was working in Africa and in south Asia where its adversaries were sometimes Muslims who intimidated Hindu India. The Jesuits would be a useful tool in converting and subjugating the South American native people.

In 1549, John ordered the first large settlement, Cidade do São Salvador, to be built about mid-point on Brazil's coast at Baía de Todos os Santos (City of the Holy Savior in All Saints' Bay) by Tomé de Sousa whom John appointed to be its first governor. Six Jesuits including Manoel de Nóbrega, the most famous of Brazilian Jesuits, and his deputy José de Anchieta, both appointed by the king and Ignatius of Loyola, were in the founding party of a thousand colonists, exiles, soldiers, sailors, and government functionaries. Within four months they had built a hundred houses and established sugar plantations in the outlying areas. The city was only a tenuous foothold, and good relations with the surrounding Indians were vital to its survival. The local tribes were part of an overall group known as the Tupí-Guaraní, a people who stretched from today's Guyanas north of the Amazon to the pampas of Argentina—some two million Indians inhabiting almost all of South America east of the Andes.

Those good relations were due in large part to a friendly old Tupinamba Indian chief. Nevertheless, the Portuguese and the Tupinamba were wary of each other. As was typical during the formative years of these settlements, not only in Brazil but also throughout the New World, there was an incident that could have been blown up enough to destroy the developing European settlements while their foothold was still so slender: A Tupinamba murdered a colonist a few miles outside São Salvador. Governor Sousa was caught in a bind. He could not ignore the offense; that would have emboldened all natives still "hostile." However, if he demanded that the murderer be handed over and the natives did not comply, he would have to take military action or lose face. He was ill-prepared for that option, given the relative number of Indians and colonists. Fortunately, guilt was clearly established to the chief's and his tribe's satisfaction, and the culprit was surrendered. To demonstrate the awesome power of Portuguese weaponry and leave a lasting impression on the Tupinamba, Sousa had the murderer tied to the mouth of a cannon and blown to pieces in front of a large crowd. Things proceeded happily after that. Many gifts were routinely exchanged with the Indians who worked willingly, or so it was said, on Portuguese construction projects.

Brazil was on its way to being the jewel in the crown of Portugal. But the Portuguese would have to deal with the French and Dutch first. By now both of them had learned enough about the potential of this mysterious continent to have their appetites whetted regardless of what some distant, presumptuous pope might have promised to Portugal and Spain.

CHAPTER 2

Who *Were* These Jesuits?

The famous Scottish Protestant chronicler of the Guaraní Republic, R. B. Cunninghame-Graham, once wrote, "Your Jesuit is . . . the most tremendous wild-fowl that the world has known." He should know. He studied the Jesuits of Paraguay for much of the quarter century he spent there.

How Did the Jesuits Get Started?

The Society of Jesus, a Roman Catholic religious order of priests and brothers, was founded by Ignatius of Loyola in 1534 to do apostolic work. They were to follow a religious rule and a life of poverty, chastity, and obedience while relying on alms for their support. Ignatius, a Basque of minor nobility, led a dissolute life until, as a twenty-nine-year-old soldier, he was severely wounded with his right leg shattered by a cannonball in a battle with French invaders at Pamplona. During a long and painful recuperation he had a spiritual awakening and committed himself to an ascetic, devotional life. In 1528 he entered the University of Paris where by 1534 in a chapel in Montmartre he collaborated with six fellow students, one Portuguese and five Spaniards, to form the *Compañía de Jesús* or Company of Jesus dedicated to his service. The name of this Company reflected Ignatius' military background and his approach to the governance of his group. Ignatius would choose *"Ad Majorem Dei Gloriam"* (To the greater glory of God) as the Company's motto. Its head, chosen for a life term by a congregation of its membership, was and still is called their "general." While sounding rigid and military, the group developed its humanistic tendencies in Paris, the philosophically open capital of the broad-minded, clever and irreverently witty King Francis I. This group included Francis Xavier who was to become the most famous Christian missionary since St. Paul.

Jesuits Formally Founded in 1540

Six years later in 1540 Pope Paul III (formerly Alessandro Farnese, a typical Renaissance pope who was self-indulgent, urbane, nepotistic, and given to lavish banquets, but with a keen eye for talent) sanctioned the *Societatis Iesu*, known in English as the Society of Jesus. This would be a body of priests organized to carry on the work of the Apostles while "following a religious rule" of chastity, poverty, and obedience and "relying on alms for their support." Its general would report directly to the pope. Even Paul's papal Bull establishing the order had a military ring to it, *Regimini Militantis Ecclesiae* (To the Ranks of the Church Militant). Ignatius' Company grew rapidly in prominence and numbers, eclipsing in several ways well-known orders of the time—Augustinians, Benedictines, Capuchins, Dominicans, Franciscans, Mercedarians, and others who had been around for centuries. These orders had often become introspective, emphasizing prayer, penance, passivity, and repose in a more contemplative spiritual life often inside a monastery. They were populated primarily by more simple, change-resistant, and complacent men, though no less devout, sincere, or well-intentioned. They were unlike the more driven Jesuits —men who were known as vibrant, liberal, open-minded, provocative, and even heretical to some powerful conservative churchmen. On the left, one contemporary Protestant critic said, "The most troubling thing about Loyola's scoundrels was that they had 'left the shade of ancient sloth and inactivity, in which other monks had grown grey' and come forth to engage in toils." A backhanded compliment?

Archibald Bower in his *History of the Popes* wrote:

> It may be said with truth that this order alone has contributed more than all the other orders together to confirm the waver-ing nations in the faith of Rome, to support the tottering authority of the high pontiff, to check the progress of the Reformation, and to make amends for the losses their holiness had sustained in Europe by propagating the gospel and with it a blind submission to the Holy See among the African, Ameri-can, and Indian infidels.

That was written seven years before the liquidation of "this order" by the "Holy See."

In the 1950s German Jesuit Peter Limpert wrote that there was always "a loneliness—the loneliness of the gathering storm" about the Jesuits. Mitchell writes that the excitement of playing a lone hand may help explain the cloak-and-dagger appeal of this most controversial and mythologized of Christian orders.

The term "Jesuit" was first heard as referring to the order in 1544. It was applied scornfully by adversaries. It had been used in the prior century, well before the order's founding, to describe someone who cantingly interlarded his speech with repetitions of Jesus' name. Before long its supporters felt it could be used in a positive sense, and they adopted it.

Catholic Church Threatened by the Reformation

The Jesuits were born into the raging religious and political strife of sixteenth century Europe, a time of the greatest crisis in Catholic Church history. The Church at the time was being assaulted from many directions, both internal and external, and had in fact been severely dismembered by Protestantism. Strong, fresh winds of reform were blowing from the north—Lutheranism, Calvinism, and the Anglican schism initiated by Henry VIII to assure that he would be the head of the Church of England. The Reform movement had mass appeal for disillusioned Catholics who were learning to think for themselves, in large part thanks to Gutenberg, after the oppressive, stifling doctrine and widespread corruption of medieval Catholicism. Within the Roman Catholic Church, Jansenism, with its extreme interpretation of St. Augustine's teaching on the role of grace in salvation, led to a belief in a sort of predestination that undervalued the role of good works in salvation. It held sway in influential Catholic quarters. Many in those quarters were finding a theological home among Reformed Protestants especially Calvinists whose beliefs related to predestination were shared by Jansenists.

The Roman Catholic Church's Council of Trent met intermittently in northern Italy from 1545 to 1563 (coinciding with the earliest years of the Society of Jesus) to introduce defensive reforms against Protestantism. These turned out to be long on theory but short on implementation. A half-century later Galileo's proof of Copernicus' helio-centric solar system was condemned by the papacy. Simony (the sale of Church positions) and the sale of indulgences, causing major, influential objections from an Augustinian monk named Martin Luther, were still practiced as late as the seventeenth century. Corruption was such a force that even the inner sanctum, the papal Curia of senior clergymen surrounding and advising the pope, could be bought. Incredibly, there was bribing of the Curia even in support of the 1773 liquidation of the Society of Jesus! Some historians believe that the Jesuits were founded primarily to lead a charge, initiated by the Council of Trent, against the

Reformation—a Jesuit counter-reformation. The fact is that the Jesuits saw the Reformation for what it was: a symptom of widespread spiritual malaise and moral crisis. Combating these would be their main *raison d'être*.

Jesuits Come From All Over, Have Special Talents

The Jesuits came from the cream of the emerging middle and professional classes and even the aristocracy of the world's most advanced and dynamic societies. They were university professors and other teachers, scientists, architects, engineers, builders, artisans, soldiers, and musicians. Sometimes several siblings in large families of professionals joined the order when the parents could leave the family assets to only one of the children.

More than other orders, the Jesuits were outward-looking and open to the beliefs and religious practices of other societies and cultures—an approach that often brought them into conflict with the conservative, often reactionary Church hierarchy, the Curia and the pope. Indeed, in China in the late 1500s Portuguese Jesuit Matteo Ricci, "sporting pigtails, dressed as a Confucian scholar, and proficient in the Confucian classics, [wooed] the empire's intellectual elites...with [his] knowledge of mathematics, geography and science, seeking ways to adapt his message." Had the missionary Jesuits in the Far East not been censured by the papacy for their accommodation of local cultural traditions—in particular the rites of ancestor veneration and Confucius reverence of the Chinese and Indians—those huge countries might have become Catholic.

The men who were to become missionaries, especially in the wild lands of South America, needed physical vitality, stamina, personal courage, and a commitment to persevere in the face of extreme hardship, danger, and disheartening setbacks in their labors among the Guaraní. It is remarkable how prescient their superiors were, to be able to see how these traits would be demonstrated by almost all of the Jesuits, both priests and brothers, selected to serve in Paraguay.

Early on, the order gained a reputation for excellence in analytical thought, writing, and argument as well as philosophy and the sciences, leading to their Europe-wide reputation as superior educators, notwithstanding the controversy over their spiritual and philosophical leanings. These abilities were valued in defending a Catholicism that had lost the edge. Other Catholic orders did not have the same charisma, magnetism, intellectual firepower, or fire-in-the-belly. The best men wanted to be with the best organization, the one where they would be with peers and where the action was. Dynamic young intellectuals from all over the Catholic world joined in great numbers. Its broad base among different nationalities, cultures, languages, politics, philosophies, and achievements had a cross-fertilizing effect. Morale was the highest of any sect or order in Christendom. All of this had the unintended though predictable effect of arousing jealousy among other orders, leading some of their most prominent hierarchy to oppose and even attack the Society in its days of mortal peril in 1773. It was particularly irksome to the other orders that the monarchs of Catholic Europe, especially the Bourbons, often chose Jesuits to be their confessors. This choice would be an easy one given the spiritual and intellectual malaise and mediocrity that infected so much of the rest of the Church. The monarchs no doubt took special comfort in absolution from such exceptional minds. The monarchs' religious serenity must have been further enhanced by the thought that the abler of the Jesuit generals "occasionally kept the popes in mental servitude," thus holding St. Peter's keys to the kingdom. This had to grate on the nerves of other religious orders.

Besides the variety and quality of the Jesuits' activities, what also brought them to the forefront of public attention was the publicity they spread about their labors around the world. Today this would be well received and considered good business. No other order was as accomplished at report writing, especially the annual reports (called *cartas anuales* in Spanish Jesuit mission regions) colleges and provinces were expected to prepare. Initially these were published quarterly, with the first one in Paraguay published in 1609. However, their preparation became a burden, and they were prepared annually. In Paraguay they typically included plans for new mission buildings, overcoming poverty and developing light manufacturing, increasing farm and ranch output, and of course converting the Guaraní. The adventures of French Jesuits in Canada, especially martyrs and others from exotic mission fields including Paraguay and Brazil, written with characteristically superior intellectual quality and flourishing style, became best sellers in seventeenth and eighteenth century Europe. Reports from the Canadian missions promoted the idea of the "noble savage" that reappeared a hundred years later from the pen of Rousseau during the Enlightenment. While these reports from the field served to stimulate recruitment, they also promoted good public relations. They also must have made some other religious orders feel diminished by comparison.

Jesuits and the Jews, the Inquisition and the Index

Since the Jesuits were founded by Spaniards, growing out of Spain's intensely devout Catholicism—Spaniards considered themselves as Catholics without equal in the world—it was only natural that the largest number of Jesuits would come from that country. Their fervor, however, would eventually be perceived as bigotry—even against Jesuits from other countries, but especially against Jews who had converted to Catholicism. Perhaps it was the coincidence of the anti-Semitic practices so prevalent in Renaissance and post-Renaissance Europe and the blossoming of the Jesuits that caused many to believe that the Jesuits of that time played a role in fomenting the Spanish national tragedy of anti-Semitism. Actually the facts, as Henry Kamen describes them in his opus *The Spanish Inquisition*, point in the opposite direction. During the Jesuits' formative years and later, it was the Dominicans who controlled the Inquisition. The popular image of it comes from its heyday in the late fifteenth century when it was first directed by Tomás de Torquemada, a Dominican descended from Jews. His name became synonymous with it and its excruciating, demoniacal, merciless torture.

By the sixteenth century the spirit of the individual and free inquiry was subordinated to the political and religious establishment. Liberalism would vanish from the academic world, but not by the hand of the Jesuits. The first Index of forbidden books was issued in Spain in 1551. It included the *Colloquies* of Erasmus, the renowned Catholic philosopher and the greatest humanist of the century. He became an "unperson." Rome soon followed that lead. In 1559 Pope Paul IV condemned all of Erasmus' writings. Jesuit General, Diego Laínez, Ignatius' successor, objected, saying to Paul that the Index, "restricted many spirits and pleased few." His opposition came to nil. When Francisco Sánchez, professor of philosophy at Toulouse, declared, "Whoever speaks ill of Erasmus is either a friar (meaning a Dominican) or an ass!" he was summoned before the Inquisition, although with no consequence. Such was the temper of the time. Dominican Bishop Melchor de Prega Cano was part of a cabal led by the Inquisition to discredit the Jesuits. He attacked them while denouncing Ignatius' *Spiritual Exercises* as heresy. This led to the Inquisition arresting the Jesuit provincial of Castile and two of his priests. Though Rome revoked the arrest, the whole affair "clinched its [the Inquisition's] victory over the religious orders." As with the Jansenists, the Jesuit-Dominican tensions would continue for two centuries in

Europe and among the Guaraní, ending with the Dominicans getting even, like the Jansenists, in 1773.

For ages, culminating in the fifteenth century, Jews in Spain (and elsewhere in Europe) were persecuted under the rule of *limpieza de sangre* (purity of blood) which became Spanish law in 1449. They were considered "Christ-killers." Later Ferdinand and Isabella gave Jews (and Moors) the option to convert or be exiled. Many became *conversos* or "New Christians," a pejorative term suggesting their hidden retention of Jewish beliefs and practices; therefore they remained suspect. Kamen writes that Ignatius himself, who was suspected of being a *converso*, while having dinner with friends one night, said that he would have considered it a divine favor to be descended from Jews and therefore "to be related to Christ our Lord and to our lady the glorious Virgin Mary." Kamen writes that Ignatius had "become a deep and sincere spiritual Semite." Diego Laínez, Ignatius' second in command and successor general, was a *converso*.

Francisco Villanueva, rector of a Jesuit college, wrote to Ignatius about the anti-*converso* primate of Spain, Cardinal Archbishop Martínez Silíceo of Alcalá, who had demanded examination of prospective priests for Jewish ancestry. Villanueva said, "It is a great pity that there seems to be nobody willing to leave these poor people anywhere to stay on earth, and I would like to have the energy to become their defender, particularly since one encounters among them more virtue than among the Old Christians." Silíceo came to ardently hate the Jesuits. He was joined by other prominent Spanish clergy and by the Inquisition. The election of *converso* Laínez as general of the Jesuits aroused bitter opposition from Philip II and the Spanish Church. The third general, Francisco Borja, had some of his own books put on the Index in retaliation for continuing to accept and defend *conversos*. When asked by the prime minister why his Company's position was that way he replied, "Why should I make an issue about admitting them into the service of that Lord for whom there is no distinction between persons, between Greek or Jew."

In 1593, however, the Jesuits' Fifth General Congregation contradicted Ignatius' fundamental principle regarding the Jews. In the early 1590s, recruitment had been falling off as the Jesuits were whispered as being the party of Jews. The congregation then denied admittance to those of Jewish or Moorish blood on the tortuously rationalized bigotry that Jesuits should be free of those characteristics that give offense. This dark cloud remained over the order for centuries, being removed only gradually until the papacy of Leo XIII who spoke against it in the late nineteenth century. Even then it was not fully and formally removed until the 1946 Jesuit General Congregation XXIX.

Jesuits Own Slaves

By the seventeenth century, Jesuits in South America and the Caribbean owned many thousands of African slaves—7,000 in the Province of Peru alone. Geographically closer to this story, the Jesuits of the province of Paraguay kept considerably more than 1,000 at their nine colleges especially at Córdoba and Asunción. As we shall see in Chapter 15, the pivotal Lavalette Affair involved French Jesuits who kept African slaves on their Martinique plantations. Their *lèse majesté* rational was that the revenues generated were used to beneficial effect in spreading the word of Christ. Jesuit consciences seemed assuaged by the Jesuit Peter Claver "winning a reputation at Cartagena [Colombia], the terminus of the African slave trade, for distributing food, sympathy, and eternal salvation" as he descended into the fetid hell-holds of ships with their human cargo of terrified, tortured, sick, black men and women. Some must have wound up on Jesuit plantations.

Jesuit Order Grows Exponentially

As a result of their reputation, the Jesuits grew exponentially in membership without compromising quality, taking center stage wherever they had meaningful numbers. They came from all over Catholicism and even from important parts of Protestant and Orthodox Europe. In 1556, after 16 years of existence at the time of Ignatius' death, there were 1,000 Jesuits. A century later there were 20,000, roughly three quarters of them priests and one quarter of them brothers.

As for Paraguay, in the early years of the Jesuit missionaries when Spain and Portugal were united under one crown, Spanish xenophobia resulted in relatively few Jesuits coming from other countries beyond Portugal and Italy, especially from the Papal States. Some other Jesuit applicants for the Paraguay missions, eager for adventure and evangelizing, would have their names changed to facilitate phonetic spelling on emigration documents or to deceive emigration officials by providing the required Hispanic ring. For example, the Flemish Nicolas du Toit became del Techo; the Dutch van Suerck was changed to Vansurque; the Irish (or Scot as Cunninghame-Graham and Southey patriotically assert) Thomas Fields became Tomás Fildio; the Englishman John Brown of York metamorphosed into Juan Bruno de Yorca. As the missions' reputation for adventure and success grew and the missions' staffing needs increased in the eighteenth century, Spain had to open the gates. More Jesuits began coming from Belgium, Germany, Scandinavia, and the Netherlands (even though these "heresy-infected northerners" were suspect) as well as from the Austro-Hungarian empire including the Czech and Slovak regions, Croatia, Switzerland, England, Ireland, and even Greece. Few came from France which had its own mission staffing needs in Canada and the vast Louisiana Territory.

Pride sometimes complicated the Jesuits' position. The ultimate example might have been Antonio Vieira, a monumental character among seventeenth-century Portuguese and Brazilian Jesuits for seventy-four years, who once remarked, "The Dominicans lived off the faith while the Jesuits died for it." The Jesuit order did not help its case when Vieira issued a paper (described more in Chapter 4) saying that God wanted to establish a world monarchy under the Portuguese. The paper was condemned even by the Inquisition but not by the Jesuits. An outspoken religious order in an age when faith still predominated but was waning, the Jesuits often wound up in conflicts among kingdoms and between kings and the weakest of their subjects such as the Guaraní, lose-lose situations for the Jesuits.

Jesuits Become Educators

Almost from the beginning, the Jesuits were celebrated for their educational system. In 1545 they started a college for secular students. That year in Gandía, Valencia, the home of General Borja, the Jesuit seminary gave public demonstrations of disputations which so impressed the citizens that they asked that their children be admitted to the college. Other cities in southern Europe quickly followed Gandía's example. Part of their reputation for pedagogical excellence grew out of the high standards set for students as they received instruction in philosophy and rhetoric. Soon thereafter Latin and Greek, the humanities (especially the works of the early Romans, such as Cicero and Virgil), literature, mathematics (Descartes was a Jesuit product), and the natural sciences were added. There was no social promotion; advancing to the next level required a demonstration of mastery of the material already covered. Perhaps most importantly, since Jesuit teachers received little salary, Jesuit schools were usually free. This had a great democratizing effect as access to a superior education became merit-based, remarkable in a time when only nobility enjoyed easy entry to the best colleges and universities. In 1551, after their schools' success had become evident, Ignatius put his position and prestige behind a formal effort to found colleges throughout Europe. He lavished his attention on the structure and methods used by the schools, experimenting with such novel devices as textbooks. (This was a century after Gutenberg.) By the seventeenth century there were *174* hundreds of Jesuit colleges around the world, wherever the order had a substantial presence. In France alone, the Jesuits had as many as 40,000 students.

Jesuits Evangelize

The other great undertaking of the Jesuits was to spread the Gospel to non-Christian people in Asia and the Americas and to a lesser extent in Africa. The missionary endeavors were initiated with the encouragement and funding of Portugal's King John III, devout and high-minded but also a wise strategist when it came to ways of strengthening his far-flung colonial empire. Few do not know that Francis Xavier, the missionary to the East Indies chosen by Ignatius with the support of John, opened routes to India, Japan, and China, countries later evangelized by his followers. Many of his contemporaries soon populated Portuguese Brazil. They, in turn, showed the way for the Jesuits of Spain, under the intensely nationalistic and even more devout King Philip II, to go to Paraguay.

Jesuits Help Launch the Enlightenment

Ironically, Jesuit educators played a role in their own downfall by creating their own Frankenstein's monster. They were teachers of many leaders of the Enlightenment, most notably the prominent *philosophes* Voltaire and Diderot. The Enlightenment was a profoundly influential secular, humanist, anti-religious movement that was a major factor in the destruction of the Society of Jesus. The Jesuits of the eighteenth century had intended to produce leaders of the secular world who would be thoughtful, knowledgeable, and caring, as well as eloquent. Indeed Jesuits even greeted and complimented the Enlightenment's leaders' initial philosophical publications, thus showing the Society's willingness to publicly embrace such radical thinking. After the first edition of Diderot's *Encyclopédie* in July 1751, Guillaume Berthier, editor of the Jesuit *Journal de Trevoux*, wished the new publication well in the *Journal*'s October issue. In November's issue he saluted Diderot's publication as a "noble and mighty work" (more in Chapter

15). The stylishly anti-religious nature of this movement evolved unexpectedly, ultimately ending in the persecution of the Jesuits and the terror of the French Revolution.

Jesuits Take on Jansenism and Nationalism

Jansenism was a powerful religious movement within the Catholic Church, initiated by the book *Augustinus* written by Cornelis Jansen, bishop of Ypres, and published posthumously in 1640. It became the basis of an epic, century-long struggle between the Jesuits and the Jansenists. When Jansenism was grafted onto nationalistic Gallicanism in France and the Jansenists conducted their debates in colloquial French, they won the hearts and minds of powerful government allies who aligned themselves against the Jesuits. Meanwhile the Jesuits continued to conduct too much of their argument in off-putting Latin. According to Wright, the quarrel over Jansenism concerned

> . . . the main conduct of Christian life. . . . It was about journeys toward salvation . . . about how humanity's . . . addiction to sin ought to be accounted for and dealt with by the priest in the confessional. . . . It pitted world views against one another, breathed life into Augustine's corpse . . . and the animosity and importance of the contestants (Jansenists and Jesuits) made it . . . the most considerable matter faced by Catholicism in the entire seventeenth century.

He could have added the first three quarters of the eighteenth century as well. Under Jesuit pressure Pope Clement XI, in the Bull *Unigenitus Dei Filius* in 1713, condemned Jansen's book as too Calvinistic.

The precise theological construct of Jansenism is beyond this book. For this observer, however, Jansenism is a reasonable facsimile of Calvinism. For the contemporary French king, Louis XIV, it was "reheated Calvinism." Both Jansenism and Calvinism emphasize those aspects of the writings of the great Father of the Church, St. Augustine, 354-430 A.D. that support predestination. In fact, Augustine had become the champion of predestinarian Protestants.

Vatican condemnation of Jansenism came too late for much of France. There, the theology had gained a large following that included the influential Abbé de Saint-Cyran, spiritual director of the Cistercian convent at Port Royal "and, fatefully, an opponent of the absolutist governance of Cardinal Richelieu." Jansenists and Calvinists attacked the Jesuits for their "lax moral theology" and for an unduly rosy view of man's nature and prospects for redemption. The Jesuits thought people were worthy of taking communion quite often, while Jansenists felt that man was rarely worthy of such a privilege. The debate raged over the roles of God's grace, free will, and humanity's sinful nature in salvation. An example at the core: Were a person's good deeds a manifestation of a surfeit of God's grace, or did they earn God's grace? Meanwhile, for the French people, because they had friends like the papacy and Richelieu's successor Cardinal Mazarin, the Jesuits did not need enemies. France's power structure turned anti-Jesuit.

The Jesuits' theological battle with the Jansenists boiled over when Jansenist proponent, Frenchman Pasquel Quesnel, launched a "stinging attack" on *Unigenitus Dei Filius* as a "work of iniquity" and on Pope Clement "as a doctor of lies." His timing was disastrous for the Jesuits as it energized a restive Paris Parlement. A series of events—political, philosophical, and religious, in addition to a financial scandal of the Jesuits own making—cascaded down upon their Company, ultimately giving the Jansenists the upper hand over the Jesuits.

By the mid-eighteenth century, the Jesuits were pinioned by an ironic pincer of Jansenism on the right and the Enlightenment on the left. Both considered the Jesuits their most powerful ideological opponent but for different reasons. Lowney writes:

> Enlightenment champions of reason and free will attacked the Jesuits as the most visible and prominent defenders of the Catholic Church. On the other side, the Jansenists [attacked] the Jesuits' ardent adherence to the doctrine of free will.

Meanwhile the Jesuits continued to de-emphasize French nationalism in favor of the transnational papacy. The Jesuits became labeled as *Ultramontane*, literally "over the mountains"—connected to the papacy in Rome over the French-Italian Alps. They were committed to an imperial pope no longer exercising secular hegemony over the nations of Europe as he did during the Holy Roman (and German) Empire of medieval times. The popes of the sixteenth through the eighteenth centuries often acted as though nothing had changed. To make matters worse, during those years the papacy had too often not occupied the moral high ground. Ironically, Europe was becoming more sophisti-cated and judgmental, in good part due to the Jesuit education of the intelligentsia. The papacy's image would pay a high price.

The simple fact was that the civil governments of Catholic monarchies were contending with an increasingly influential body of 22,000 of

Europe's best men who answered only to their general and who functioned with the perfection of a machine. These Jesuits might act at any time in a way that could put them in conflict with their governments, a fear shared by the most ambitious and reformist civil leaders.

In 1761 the Jesuits could have avoided being expelled from all-important France by becoming Gallicanized—answerable to the French clerical hierarchy. It was a step many French Jesuits advocated. Pope Clement XIII, however, imperiously rejected it with "let them be what they are [i.e., answerable to me] or let them not be." His solution to the looming disaster was that they should save themselves through penance and ever more prayer. As the assault on the order peaked, instructions from their general in Rome dutifully came in the form of letters to all members encouraging prayer. In November 1763 the first letter was entitled *On Fervent Perseverance and Prayer, In Greater Fervor in Prayer* in June 1769, and *On a New Incentive to Prayer* in February 1773, just four months before their abolution. Thus the Jesuits' oath of obedience and loyalty to a hard-line yet powerless papacy resulted in their destruction by that same papacy.

Jesuits Have Many Reputations

In the course of their tumultuous history the Jesuits gained (not to say earned) a reputation for righteousness but also for Machiavellian craftiness, for selflessness but also for power-seeking, for material poverty but also for acquisitive greediness, for humility but also for intellectual arrogance. Lowney writes:

> Jesuits inordinately relished . . . high profile polemical battles. . . . Loyola had been prescient in warning . . . to tone down the rhetoric. . . . we have a reputation . . . especially here in Rome, that we would like to rule the world.

Even today many leaders of the western world, Catholics included, harbor suspicions about the Jesuits while maintaining the utmost admiration for them. Very few of those leaders know of the extraordinary work of the Jesuits in Paraguay. The balance sheet of the Paraguayan priests is lopsided. Cunninghame-Graham neatly sums up the recognition that the Jesuit works in Paraguay should have received:

> Buffon, Raynal, and Montesquieu with Voltaire, Robertson, and Southey have written favorably of the internal government of the missions and the effect which it produced. No names of equal authority can be quoted on the other side; yet the fact

remains that the Jesuits in Paraguay were exposed to constant calumny from the first day they went there until the last member of the order left the land.

That great French philosopher Guillaume Thomas François Raynal, after studying with and entering the Jesuit order, left it in 1747 at the age of 34. He became a member of the inner circle of *encyclopédists*, anti-clerical and anti-Jesuit. Nevertheless, his succinct tribute to the work of the Jesuits of Paraguay may be the most eloquent of all: "Maybe never so much good has been done for mankind with so little evil."

CHAPTER 3

Who Were the Guaraní Before the Europeans Invaded?

Weeks and months of a tranquil daily routine punctuated by moments of sheer terror from surprise attacks by neighboring tribes bent on slaughter and butchery, and by man-eating beasts—this was the uncertain life of the jungle Indians.

The Guaraní, a Stone Age People

The Guaraní tribes comprised a cultural group that was part of a huge linguistic group of peoples known as the Tupí-Guaraní. The Tupí-Guaraní lands stretched across the world's largest rain-forest for more than four million square miles—from the Guyanas, north of the Amazon river in Brazil some three thousand miles south to the pampas of Argentina. It included most of South America east of the Andes. The overwhelming majority of these Indians shared common physical characteristics. They were somewhat shorter than the Spanish, sturdily built, and generally with the same olive complexion, but with round flat faces, straight black hair, and little body hair. Their common, widely understood language had many divergent dialects that could complicate but not prevent conversation.

While cannibalism, both ritual and nutritional, was pervasive among many of these tribes, the lives of most of the Guaraní were spent non-violently, as semi-sedentary farmers, hunter-gatherers, and fishermen. Not so for many of their neighbors, especially the Tupí. Unlike the Incas on the other side of the Andes, the Guaraní were truly a stone-age people. Few had any metalworking ability, none had any form of written language, and, most relevant for the missionaries, they had little sense of investing in their future. They lived for the moment. They consumed whatever food they had and would lay little away for tomorrow. There was no need. The jungle, swamps, rivers, and fields were a veritable cornucopia of large and small game, fish, honey, nuts, roots, and fruit. Those Guaraní who farmed cultivated pumpkins, mandioca (cassava) roots, sweet potatoes of various types, and maize. Chickens and ducks were domesticated. Yerba plants, growing wild, were harvested from distant woods. When hot water was added in small quantities to coarsely ground yerba leaves, the result was *yerba maté* or Paraguayan tea, a mild stimulant or medicinal drink. It has a somewhat bitter taste and still is a vehicle for social interaction. A stronger libation was chicha, a liquor (more like a beer) made from the juice of mandioca. Extracted from the root by chewing it up, its juices mixed with saliva in the process, it is then set aside for some weeks to ferment.

Guaraní dwellings—for an extended family of parents and children (usually two or three children per couple) with a dog and the ubiquitous parrot—were typically simple huts made of interlaced bamboo and branches woven tightly enough to exclude insects, especially mosquitoes and blood-sucking flies swarming in their hot, wet summers. Being hunter-gatherers, fishermen, and subsistence farmers, easy relocation to new, less-overworked fields and woodlands was vital, so their possessions included little beyond earthenware, hunting and fishing instruments, and primitive weapons. Those who lived in a large village often lived, cooked, ate, and slept in an extended communal house that was ordinarily an open room, as large as fifty meters on a side.

Water transportation, fishing, and even warfare were abetted by the vast network of rivers that crisscrossed their lands. The rivers were fed by a tropical rainy season of many several months including huge downpours lasting for days. Even the drier regions included never-ending swamps such as the famous Mato Grosso of Brazil. It covers thousands of square miles and during the summer (the North American winter) it is routinely covered with a foot or two of standing water or with swampy grasslands extending far beyond the horizon, a never-ending trackless land in the minds of Europeans entering it. There were few semi-arid and virtually no arid lands.

Guaraní society was organized around a tribal hierarchy with *caciques* (chiefs) and shamans (impoliticly, witch doctors) at the top. *Caciques* were chosen by male consensus based on a combination of oratorical charisma and eloquence, heroic achievements and inheritance, in order of importance. Councils of *caciques* dealt with all great issues, particularly issues of war and peace. Shamans possessed curative powers, attaining high esteem. After elaborate and often lengthy rituals, the shaman extracted whatever evil foreign object had entered the body of the sick or possessed, possibly secreted in the victim's food or drink by the shaman himself. Of course, much good came from psychosomatic suggestion. Shamans controlled natural phenomena and could use their extraordinary powers to the detriment of enemies—including the

Jesuits. In times of relative peace, the shaman reigned supreme. When war threatened the *cacique's* authority quickly became absolute—a reasonable approach. *Caciques* and shamans enjoyed an important perquisite: They could practice polygamy.

Different tribes had different notions of deities, although most had an idea of one overarching being whose mother lived in a land without evil: *La tierra sin mal.* This Garden of Eden was the cause of much wandering by the Guaraní who searched for it north, east, and west, omitting south for unremembered reasons. Was it too cold far to the south? This Garden was happily congruent with Catholic teachings, facilitating conversion.

Ubiquitous Cannibalism

For centuries before Columbus, cannibalism was an accepted part of life for almost all Tupí-Guaraní tribes, some more the predator and some more the prey. For the Tupí it seems to have been an obsession. Cannibalism took many forms and was a source of frequent terror for European missionaries and settlers for almost a hundred years, from the first Brazilian settlements until it was largely eradicated by the Portuguese and Spanish military in the mid-seventeenth century. Since cannibalism pervades this story, it is worth covering its roots and practices.

Cannibalism was an integral part of Tupí-Guaraní warfare. Capturing a warrior from another tribe was a rite of passage for young men. The victim was beaten and tortured and, at the peak of his torment, his skull was cracked open with a stone club. Then he was roasted and devoured as part of the passage ritual. However, sometimes the victor had worrisome second thoughts: He might change his name to hide from the victim's avenging evil spirit. He might even move to a new location to make his escape more complete. For Europeans the lengthy phantasmagorical build-up was as bad as its execution. For Indians it became an unavoidable destiny, to which the captive became virtually inured.

Cannibalistic rituals and practices varied from tribe to tribe. In the vicinity of Asunción, Paraguay's capital today, the Guaraní were "a fierce tribe [who] called all those who did not speak the same language as themselves slaves and waged perpetual war with them, never sparing a [enemy] man in battle." They were well-practiced in ritual executions and consuming captives taken in all-out wars or, more commonly, in surprise raids into enemy territory where a few individuals might be isolated and taken.

In war, torture, and cannibalism, only males were the quarry. The women's participation was solely in feasting. The captors' women might attend to the captives for weeks or even months, providing plentiful rich food for fattening. Upon reaching the desired corpulence, the captives would be taken to the village center to dance amid hooting, howling, and hurled insults, to the amusement of their soon-to-be executioners. Once boredom set in, warriors wielding wooden swords would fell them with blows to the loins. (Metal was unknown to the Tupí-Guaraní except for small amounts of gold and silver traded or stolen in raids on Inca villages far to the northwest in Bolivia.) Then the executioners would take control. These were small boys who would hone their killing skills by attacking the crippled victims and hammering their skulls with small stone hatchets while parents and other tribesmen cheered them on. The first boy to strike the dispatching blow could assume the name of his victim, a signal honor.

A Brazilian version of this ritual was erotically and gruesomely bizarre. The Indian women, acting as captors, provided regular sexual favors to the otherwise resigned, helpless captives while the fattening process was underway. These women tried their best to become pregnant. Their common belief was that a fetus originates solely from the father with the mother providing only a vessel for nutrition. Thus, the captive child would be nurtured and allowed to grow for years only to be slaughtered and consumed at the most nutritionally or ritually advantageous time. Of course, the father would have long ago been devoured.

Savage battles and cannibalism sometimes occurred between clans within a large village. Such a village was often comprised of large communal houses offering little privacy. Everyone could examine everyone else. Teenaged girls reaching puberty customarily made the first move, asking for an appealing boy's hand in marriage. Incest was routine. First cousins regularly married each other. Uncles married nieces they fancied. (Of course, cousins marrying cousins and uncles marrying nieces was well-known in Europe at the time, especially among royalty.) However, if a boy or a man forcibly took a girl from another clan in his own village (an abduction called *saca de moza* in Spanish, or "kidnap the girl"), deadly intra-village fighting might follow, one clan against another. Losers would flee the village and, if they were not immediately caught and devoured, they might set up a new village of their own, not too distant. Internecine feuds lasted for ages.

Tupinamba Capture Others in Raids, Enslave and Consume Them

Cannibalism was a ritual feast of special joy and often religious significance among many Brazilian tribes. Davis describes the Tupinamba as "primitive slaveholding peoples who had no economic need for slave labor" but instead used slaves in important "cultural and symbolic" ways. In productive Brazilian jungles, males had "much time on their hands" after hunting, and were "perpetually at war with their neighbors." This yielded numerous captives for enslavement. The slaves lived with and worked for their captors, often well-treated all the while, until the right time—a time often set by some impending ritual or quasi-"religious" feast day. Their treatment not withstanding, the captives were constantly demeaned so the Tupinamba could feel superior and even god-like. "Before the final acts of "murder and cannibalism, the Tupinamba humiliated their slaves, denouncing and reviling their tribes of origin." The captors also played "cat-and-mouse . . . allowing a frantic slave to escape before being recaptured."

Southey's description of these native people is graphic and, in the parlance of early nineteenth-century England, amusingly droll, similar to Davis' descriptions. The Brazilian tribes considered "human flesh as the most exquisite of all dainties. . . . Delicious as these repasts were . . . they derived their highest flavor from revenge. . . . this sense of honor connected with it [was what] the Jesuits found most difficulty in overcoming." Even the "vermin which molested them [were eaten] professedly for the sake of vengeance." Likewise, a beast of prey (like the man-eating jaguar) captured in a pitfall was killed by myriad little wounds so it would die slowly and suffer much. Southey points out that it was the Tupí race who seem to have brought these practices from the interior jungles, found in all tribes of that particular stock.

But not all native Brazilians were cannibals. The Guaraní were not necessarily so and were more readily converted by the Jesuits. The Tupí remained the most fierce and aggressive of tribes even into the eighteenth century when they were recruited by slavers to invade the Jesuit missions and seize the Guaraní for the plantations of Brazil.

Unlike the Tupí, the Tapuyas ate their own dead as an ultimate demonstration of love, not hatred. This practice included infants who were consumed by their own parents.

Other Fierce and Irascible Tribes

Some tribes of Paraguay were especially ferocious and became a problem for the Spanish settlers and the Jesuits. The Guaycurú, and, to a lesser extent the Agaces, were extreme in their hostility and aggression and, in a way, were among the most primitive. Both tribes became particularly deadly enemies of those Guaraní who would accept the Jesuits and of the missionaries themselves.

The Guaycurú, living north of Asunción, were nomadic hunters and courageous warriors. They were trained as youth to stoically endure pain while suffering torturous piercing and cutting of their flesh and to fight, Spartan-like, in furious mock battles. The Guaycurú had no tolerance for "imperfect" male children not well-suited for war. All deformed and illegitimate babies were killed, as was one in every set of twins, possibly on the suspicion that they were feeble in some way.

The Guaycurú were unusually tall, well-proportioned, rugged, and long-lived. They bore no inhibitions. Jealousy was unknown among men. Their women were the most "promiscuous" of all Indians, perhaps thanks to their being treated as chattel. Their shelter was crude—mats on tall poles for cover. They slept naked on the ground, covering themselves with hides only when seasonal torrential rains leaked through the mats.

Guaycurú women were known for celebrating the battle exploits of their warrior husbands by engaging in savage fistfights with each other. Bloody noses, torn lips, and teeth knocked out were badges of honor, debunking notions of female inferiority. The males would urge their wives on, with cheering and shouted compliments for their courage, all the while marinating themselves with chicha.

For Europeans, the Guaycurú language was difficult to learn and virtually impossible to speak. They articulated indistinctly, barely moving their lips, "speaking" through the nose and throat, with sounds unknown to white men. An even stranger language practice was that married and single people spoke different dialects, partly defined by different terminations for words but also by some different vocabulary. One can imagine the confusion this caused among European negotiators and missionaries.

The Guaycurú remained a center of attention and objects of fascination for the Spanish. For the Portuguese it was different. They suffered several disastrous defeats, including the worst in their South American history, when the Guaycurú teamed up against them with a smaller branch, the Payaguas, of their shared Mbaya nation. The Payaguas wiped out a powerful Spanish punitive expedition in 1536. Mbaya warrior horsemanship was legendary. They rode without saddles, constantly shifting position, sometimes on the horse's back, sometimes on its side, even under its belly to avoid European firearms. Their aquatic fighting skill in the swamps and rivers that laced their northern lands was the stuff of legend.

The Agaces, inhabiting an area on the Paraguay south of Asunción, were practiced river pirates with squads of canoes. Captured Indians were taken back to their own villages and tortured in front of their families until a ransom was paid. Often the Agaces killed them anyway and mounted their heads on stakes on the river shoreline, boasting of their prowess while intimidating passersby.

All of this violence and turmoil would help the Jesuits gather the more peaceable and tractable tribes like the Guaraní, into the missions.

CHAPTER 4

Portuguese Defeat French and Dutch in Brazil, Introduce Slavery

Bantam Portugal—religious, entrepreneurial, energetic, determined, guileful, and lucky, but lacking resources—capitalized on its geographic location to become the world's preeminent seafaring nation in the fifteenth century. It held a prominent position for centuries. Its explorers and adventurers set the standard for trade and the acquisition of land and influence. Portugal was the first to profit from traffic in African slaves. Its global empire was the earliest and longest lasting. Conquering Brazil, a colony more than ninety times its own size and several times the size of the rest of its empire, left a lasting mark in language and culture on the world stage.

French Challenge Portuguese for Brazil

The first to lay claim to Brazil was thirty-three-year-old Pedro Álvares Cabral, a Portuguese fidalgo (a minor nobleman) and navigator sailing under his country's flag (described in Chapter 1). His stay on the east coast, however brief, gave Portugal some claim to that coastal area and a sense of its potential value. It was a head start, though a short one.

Given the scandalous reputations and self-dealing of popes Alexander VI and Julius II along with Alexander's Spanish roots, their brokering the Treaty of Tordesillas between Spain and Portugal carried little weight with other European powers. In 1503 the French, having neglected even to ask for participation in the treaty, became the first of these powers to ignore it and begin trading expeditions along the Brazil coast.

As early as 1516 at Baía de Todos os Santos (the Bay of All Saints), about midpoint on the coast, a Portuguese squadron stumbled upon two interloping French merchant vessels and sank both along with their entire crews. This was the first incident of frequent low-intensity fighting with intermittent major battles between the Portuguese and the French. Some battles involved thousands of combatants with many hundreds killed.

MAP BACKGROUND COURTESY OF NATIONAL GEOGRAPHIC SOCIETY

Maranhão

Recife

Bay of All Saints

Rio de Janeiro

São Paulo
Santa Catarina Is.

SOUTH AMERICA.

Scale of Miles
0 100 200 300 400 500   1000

Sites of Portuguese,
French, & Dutch Fighting
in the 16th and 17th Centuries

The first French settlement—a fort and trading post garrisoned by 120 men—was established early in 1531 near Recife, some 400 miles north of the Bay of All Saints, on Brazil's eastern-most bulge into the Atlantic. The Portuguese quickly besieged it and later that year forced it to surrender. Its men were deported back to France on French ships captured at the site.

France's most important attempt to colonize Brazil took place in 1555 at Rio de Janeiro. Some 600 sailors and colonists under the leadership of a Huguenot, Nicolas Durand de Villegagnon, were in the first wave. Several months later 190 men arrived to reinforce the garrison. Villegagnon quickly established friendly relations with the neighboring tribes. However, his harsh rule over the colonists soon destroyed their morale. It did not help that they were equally divided between Catholics and Huguenots—religions that would soon be in a lengthy, bloody civil war with each other back in France. Within a few years, many colonists returned home, leaving the settlement dangerously undermanned.

Jesuit Helps Portuguese in Battle for Rio, Portuguese Reciprocate

In 1560, Brazil's Portuguese governor, Mem de Sa, accompanied and advised by Jesuit missionary, Manoel de Nóbrega, led an expedition of 120 soldiers and 1,000 Indian allies against the undermanned French garrison at Rio. After two days of savage fighting, they defeated the French forces. The seventy surviving French and 800 Indian allies fled into the jungle. Had it not been for the character of Villegagnon and the Catholic-Huguenot religious strife, there might have been enough French left in Rio to beat back the Portuguese and retain a major presence in Brazil. Southey concludes that it was the partnership of Mem de Sa and Nóbrega that was ultimately responsible for Brazil remaining Portuguese.

Mem de Sa, already a devout Catholic, felt indebted to Nóbrega for his victory at Rio. He recognized a true Portuguese patriot in this stuttering preacher. When the Spaniards of Asunción implored the Portuguese Jesuits of Brazil to come to their settlement to minister to them and their Indian converts, Nóbrega saw an opportunity to extend Portuguese claims to Paraguay even though it was on the western side, the Spanish side, of the Tordesillas line. The governor turned down the idea as leading to a dangerous reduction of his own limited forces, already stretched thin.

Mem de Sa repaid his debt to Nóbrega by championing the Jesuits' missionary work among the Indians along the coast, contributing much to their mission success. He forbade allied tribes from continuing their cannibalism and from making any war that he had not pre-approved. At the same time he worked with the Jesuits to gather the tribes into mission settlements—precursors of the missions of the Guaraní Republic a half century later. For those Indians already converted, he built churches and housing as well as housing for their Jesuit teachers. His instructions regarding cannibalism were at first fiercely resisted. However, capital punishment imposed for breaches of his orders quickly resulted in compliance, or so it was professed. Mem de Sa had much more difficulty with Portuguese settlers who were opposed to treating the Indians as anything other than savages, good for nothing but slavery.

Gómez describes how the Indians reacted to being enslaved by the colonists: In 1553 Nóbrega wrote of Indians fleeing into his church to take sanctuary from the colonists. It was to no avail. He was unable to save them, writing, "We have learned through sad experience not . . . to be pelted with stones . . . not even to dare to preach about it. As a result, through a lack of justice they remain captives, their masters remain in mortal sin, and we lose authority in the entire pagan [Indian] world." His problem continually recurred among all the Portuguese, rich and poor, those in authority and even among the (non-Jesuit) clergy. These depredations resulted in palpable Jesuit frustration over the lack of progress in converting the Indians. In 1555 Nóbrega's deputy, José de Anchieta, was so unhappy with Tibirica, the Christian Indian leader of São Paulo who had taken part in the ritual murder of an adversary, that he wrote to Ignatius himself showing exasperation: "One loses all hope of converting these Indians unless a large number of God-fearing Christians come to these lands and enslave them, obliging them to walk beneath the banner of Christ." An angry Anchieta added, "Nothing convinces so well as the sword and the rod of iron." In 1558 Nóbrega wrote in a similar vein to the king that the Indians were beyond the influence of good and that the king should order their enslavement by colonists capturing them as settlements are built in the back country. Shortly thereafter Nóbrega, now struggling with conflicted feelings, also wrote that the Indians should be informed that "land would be given to them and that Jesuit missionaries would be brought in to [teach] them." This last directive would be the germinal idea that shaped the mission system. An environment would be created leading to "detribalization." Nóbrega's detribalization model, though crude, would be improved and then employed by his spiritual successors in Paraguay fifty years later.

By 1564 Nóbrega and Anchieta managed to establish eleven missions, all of them on or near the coast. Then as a result of a smallpox epidemic and a famine-causing blight on certain crops many mission Indians died. So many others went back into the forest that only a quarter of the original population remained. Six of the missions had to be abandoned. So it was to continue for decades—two steps forward, one step back.

Nóbrega died in 1570 at age fifty-three, worn out by a life of incessant struggle and fatigue. It was four months after the murder, by Huguenot pirates, of seventy-two Jesuits as they were en route to Brazil to work for him. He died before the news reached him. Anchieta, some twelve years his junior, succeeded him as provincial and, despite being crippled, traveled thousands of miles up and down Brazil's coast expanding the earlier mission network and converting thousands of Indians. As Southey sees it, "It was [Nóbrega's] happy fortune to be stationed in a country where none but the good principles of his order were called into action. There is no individual to whose talents Brazil is so greatly and permanently indebted, and he must be regarded as the founder of that system so successfully pursued by the Jesuits in Paraguay." Southey then adds that it was "a system productive of as much good as is compatible with pious fraud." He seldom missed an opportunity to make such a comment about Catholicism, thus making his admiration for the Jesuits in Brazil and Paraguay all the more convincing.

Throughout the next century, the 1600s, the Jesuit presence in Brazil grew sharply with up to 258 priests staffing missions up and down the coast as well as inland along the river banks of the Amazon and its tributaries in the northeastern part of the country. During this time Brazil's missions were dominated by the powerful presence of Jesuit Antonio Vieira, a renowned protector of the Indians. Like the most famous of all the Indian protectors, the Dominican Bartolomé de Las Casas, Vieira did not hesitate to exaggerate in driving home a point. He accused the Portuguese authorities and colonists of causing the death of two million Indians due to mistreatment. The Portuguese slave traders did not take kindly to his charges and repeatedly drove him out of various settlements where he preached. On several occasions he returned to Portugal for lengthy stays. Nevertheless, he founded more than fifty missions before dying in Brazil in 1697 at ninety-one. In spite of the good he did, Vieira's memory is tarnished by some peculiar beliefs and by his impolitic remark about how the "Dominican missionaries lived off the faith while the Jesuits died for it." That was never forgotten or forgiven. Wright muses that Vieira's compassion for the exploited was "somewhat selective." Vieira had once written, "What better way to remove the hideous burden of slavery from the backs of Native Americans than to increase the number of African slaves." That was a common Jesuit failing at the time. Wright also describes a "quirky" Vieira conviction that God wanted to establish a fifth universal monarchy under Portuguese control and that it might be necessary to spill "the blood of heretics in Europe and the blood of Muslims in Africa, the blood of heathens in Asia and America" to achieve it. This theology was not viewed as all that strange in Lisbon where he remained extremely popular and greatly admired by the king.

Vieira's racial bias was shared by other religious leaders in the colonies including famed Jesuit explorer José de Acosta who railed against the idea of mestizos (mixed race Indian-Europeans) being ordained as priests. Acosta's achievements and those of fellow Jesuits in Peru included immense farms, vineyards, and ranches employing African slaves. Although the Indians were referred to as servants, they too worked as *de facto* slaves under Spanish *encomenderos* (see Chapter 8).

Dutch Join the Struggle for Brazil

The Dutch soon joined the fray. Beginning in the late sixteenth century they attacked the Portuguese on both sides of the Atlantic, seriously threatening Portugal's dominance. In 1630 they captured Recife. During the next decade, they seized São Tomé and other Portuguese settlements and forts near Angola on Africa's west coast. Their success at Recife contributed immeasurably to the military and political chaos up and down 3000 miles of the Brazilian coastline, keeping it unstable for decades.

At the height of the most intense Portuguese-Dutch fighting in the first half of the seventeenth century, the Dutch controlled the northern half of Brazil. It could well have become a permanent Dutch colony but for two strategic battles. The first occurred in 1625 at Salvador de Bahia (on the Bay of All Saints) during the union of Portugal and Spain. Their combined forces, mainly Spanish, defeated and expelled the Dutch from that central, critical region. Then in 1654, after Portugal had won its independence from Spain, the Portuguese under Salvador Correia da Sã made a last ditch, do-or-die effort at Recife. It was a stunning success for the Portugese from which the Dutch never recovered.

The fighting became barbaric at times, unlike the more organized, socially acceptable slaughters called "wars" that were occurring in Christian Europe. None of the Portuguese, French, or Dutch was spared. Nor were any of them guiltless. In 1565 near São Paulo, one of the most heinous slaughters occurred as five captured French combatants were gratuitously hanged by the Portuguese. More savagery, especially between the French and the Portuguese, surfaced in their use of their respective Indian allies to kill and eat each other's European captives, while they turned a deaf ear to the tearful appeals for mercy from their terrified fellow Christians. The best illustration of this mutual European hatred combined with cannibalism is Southey's story (excerpted below) of the experience of Hans Stade while he was a captive of Brazilian Indians. Stories like this are so horrific they could become a caricature, causing one to conclude they are fantasies added for shock value. His story uniquely captures the image of the primitive South American environment and helps set the stage for what the Paraguayan Jesuits faced later, in the forbidding interior of the continent, knowing full well what their predecessors experienced on Brazil's coast.

Hans Stade's Saga: Europeans Employ Cannibals Against Other Europeans

In 1549 Hans Stade, a German adventurer, sailed from Spain for Paraguay as a passenger on a three-ship squadron. They were caught in a violent storm off the coast of southern Brazil near the Island of Santa Catarina, several hundred miles short of their Río de La Plata destination. Two ships barely made landfall, badly wrecked, while the third was never heard from again. Expecting the worst, Stade and the crews were surprised to find that the Carios Indians there were friendly, having had some beneficial dealings with visiting Spanish traders earlier. With the Indians' help they soon linked up with a Portuguese settlement. Stade's shipmates were able to reconstruct one seaworthy ship and head for Paraguay via the Río de La Plata and up the Paraná, but he and a few others had to remain behind for a lack of space. One morning many months later, the settlement was attacked by a war party of nearby Tupinamba Indians. Stade and the Portuguese with their firearms, with the help of the Carios, drove off the attackers. Those who were badly wounded and left behind were finished off and devoured by the Carios. Stade, now appreciated as a German who knew about gunnery, was offered regular command of the surrounding small Portuguese outposts, with such generous compensation that he could not refuse.

One day while Stade was hunting in the forest, a band of Tupinamba ambushed him, knocked him down, battered him with war clubs, and shot him with an arrow. Immediately, his captors got into an argument over his fate—some demanding summary execution while others, led by the chief, favored another punishment. The chief's side won. They took Stade, alive, to their fortified village for a great drunken, ceremonial feast at which he would be the star attraction. En route, his captors never missed a chance to taunt him, baring their fangs and biting their forearms to show him what was coming. He kept his spirits up by singing a psalm and praying and commending his spirit to God. As they arrived at their village, some 800 to 900 tribesmen who had assembled to "welcome" him forced him to cry out in Tupí, which he had come to understand earlier, "Here I am, come to be your meat!" Then he was handed over to the old women. They beat him, plucked out his beard, hair by hair, stripped him, and "handled" him until their curiosity was satisfied. The beatings continued for several days with the children joining in. During one drunken revelry, he was forced to dance around while his captors laughed and shouted, "See, our meat is jumping." Then, at another celebration, one captor cried out how happy he was to have caught this hated Portuguese. An opening? Stade shouted that he was not a Portuguese; he was a German and a friend of the French whom the Tupinambas knew were also enemies of the Portuguese. After he traded charges and countercharges with them over who was telling the truth and who was lying, the matter was dropped. His captors decided they did not really care one way or the other. Meat was meat.

Stade was kept tied up for weeks, all the while protesting that he should not be eaten until he had a chance to prove he actually was "French" and thus an ally. In due course, a French interpreter came to the village. The overjoyed Stade figured the man was a Christian and would come to his aid. While surrounded by eager Indians, the two had a brief exchange. Immediately the Frenchman said, "Kill the rascal and eat him. He is Portuguese and as much my enemy as yours." Stade cried out for mercy, but the Frenchman remained unmoved. The Indians' reaction to all this was to shout that Stade was howling from his fear of death, further proving he was Portuguese. Then, as preparations began for the ceremonial feast, three fortuitous events provided a reprieve.

Stade's first bit of luck was a distracting attack on the village by some Tupiniquins, allies of the Carios. This was followed by what the Tupinambas saw as an angry face on the moon. Stade said this was prophetic—God was angry because they meant to eat a man who was not their enemy. Then a pestilence, possibly smallpox, broke out—more ammunition for Stade. The Indians begged for Stade's forgiveness and his aid. After negotiations with the chief, he obtained a promise not to be devoured. The old women who had tortured him so passionately now joined in the supplications. Stade's ministering to the desperately ailing chief was followed by a remarkable recovery. He was not to be killed, but he was not to be freed either; he would become a slave. Soon thereafter, he received some insurance from his beard. As it grew back, the Indians discovered that his was red while Portuguese beards were always black.

At this point, the Frenchman returned and admitted his earlier mistake. He said that he had thought Stade was Portuguese, people who were so cruel that they hung every Frenchman they could get their hands on. He added that their prisoner was a German and thus a friend of the French. While the Tupinambas bought some of this, they insisted that he was their slave and would remain so. With the earlier pestilence fading away, the Indians had yet another change of heart: Whether Stade was French or Portuguese, the meat was still the same. By this time Stade had been their prisoner for five months.

Around the middle of August, a 900-man Tupinamba war party in thirty canoes fell upon a small force of Tupiniquins, including six Christians known to Stade. The slaughtering and feasting started that evening. When Stade went to the chief's hut later that night, he asked what was to happen to the Christians. "Eat them!" was the answer. Stade encouraged him to ransom them, but the chief refused. There was a basket filled with Tupiniquin flesh next to the chief, who took a thigh and put it to Stade's mouth pressing him to eat it. Stade's reply that even beasts do not eat their own kind, had no effect. The chief sunk his teeth into the flesh saying, "I am a jaguar, and I like it." Most of the rest of the Tupiniquins were killed over the next few days, then dismembered and cooked, with the flesh saved for the next feast day. Cooking was a kind of barbecue. Four forked stakes were driven into the ground, sticks were laid across them, and on this the flesh was smoked and dried in the sun. The Indian word for this contraption was "*boucan*," and food thus prepared was "buccaneered," the term that as Southey writes, was applied to that extraordinary race of criminals that were the scourge of the Spaniards in South America for so long.

Stade's run of luck continued. The chief made a gift of him to a benevolent neighboring Tupinamba chief and added an excellent character reference: Stade could predict future events, heal diseases, and procure fine weather. He was received with all the respect such qualifications warranted. But he was still a slave.

Soon a Portuguese ship appeared on the coast, ready for trade. Learning of Stade's plight, the captain invited the chief who now owned Stade along with the chief's wife aboard for a feast of eating flesh—animal flesh—and drinking. Seven days of this entertainment was concluded with a skit performed by ten of the crew who were "Stade's brothers" and who could not possibly leave without him. The now-mellow chief consented to release him.

Apparently the chief and his wife had rehearsed their own skit, for when they openly wept over losing their human possession, they were given a generous "treasure" of combs, knives, and mirrors. They debarked contented. Stade eventually returned to Germany. His memoirs contain almost all the recorded history of the sixteenth-century Brazilian Tupí tribes in their natural environment.

Portuguese Destroy England's Only Settlement

In 1568 the English made a serious attempt to establish a colony at Paraíba do Sul near Rio de Janeiro. It was their only such effort in Brazil. There they married Tupí women. In another generation, writes Southey, "the Anglo-Tupi Mamelucos (ferocious mixed-breed warriors) would have been found to be dangerous neighbors." However, after five years, the Portuguese Governor of São Sebastião (near São Paulo) attacked and decimated the English. Those who survived "fled into the interior where they were either eaten by the [Tupí] savages, as was believed, or lived and died among them, becoming savages themselves."

Portuguese Prevail Over French and Dutch

In 1565, French-Portuguese combat petered out as the French, now weary and preoccupied with religious wars at home, increasingly lost heart. Southey observes that "the French court was too busy burning and massacring Hugonots [sic] to think of Brazil." France was also distracted by its chaotic succession of kings. What passed for French "plans" had been ruined by what Southey wrote was "the villainous treachery of Villegagnon" ten years earlier. But it would take another fifty years to end it all.

In 1614 in Maranhão in northern Brazil a superior French force was badly defeated by the Portuguese. An armistice was signed. France was buying time until it could send reinforcements to its remaining Maranhão toehold. When the expected reinforcements never arrived, the demoralized French surrendered. France was finished in Brazil.

Finally, in the 1650s, after an unbroken string of bloody Portuguese victories over the Dutch, especially Portugal's stunning recapture of Recife, the Dutch capitulated and surrendered their territory. In 1661 a peace treaty was signed between the Netherlands and Portugal, formally ending their long war of attrition in Brazil.

Most of the east coast of South America would eventually become Portuguese Brazil, French Guiana, Dutch Suriname, and British Guyana. With control of the coast, Portugal would gradually move inland—ignoring the Treaty of Tordesillas—and solidify control over its giant colony. Within fifty years, Brazil's Indian and African-populated plantations, especially those producing sugar, would yield huge profits. With the discovery of large amounts of gold and diamonds at the close of the seventeenth century, Portugal's investment in blood and treasure paid off handsomely. Portugal became a big player on the world stage.

CHAPTER 5

Jesuit Missionaries Find Danger at Every Turn

Jesuit casualties began almost from the moment they sailed over the horizon from their Iberian ports of embarkation. Few of those who went to South America ever returned home. Many simply disappeared into the sea or in uncharted lands. Even the most famous and admired of all, Antonio Ruíz de Montoya, lies buried in an unmarked grave somewhere in the jungle ruins of mission Loreto. Those who lived to see their expulsion from the colonies often died on the return voyage to Europe.

Atlantic Ocean Takes Heavy Toll

Crossing the vast, stormy Atlantic was the first threat to the lives of the Jesuits on their way to save souls in the New World. Hardly out of view of their principal harbors for departure, Cádiz, Spain, or Lisbon, Portugal, merchant ships bearing missionaries could be intercepted by lurking pirates. Typically sailing south 750 miles along the African coast to the Canary Islands, they could be fully provisioned for the 5,000 mile southwest crossing of the Atlantic to São Paulo, Rio de Janeiro, or the Río de La Plata and Buenos Aires. The total trip was half again the distance from England to its North American colonies. There are credible estimates that between five and ten percent of such merchant vessels were lost in the crossing, from all causes.

In one of the worst cases of ships lost at sea, in 1643 a ship carrying a prominent Brazilian Jesuit Luís Figueira, returning from Portugal, foundered off the Brazilian coast. Of the fifteen Jesuits on board, three were saved, two drowned, and the ten others including Figueira made it to shore on a raft but were captured and devoured by cannibals. In 1716, the transport ship Sagronis, with twenty-three Jesuits headed for the Orinoco delta in today's Venezuela, went to the bottom in a storm. It was lost barely outside its starting point, Cádiz. There were other less history-making cases in the Caribbean, the Florida coast, and other Spanish and Brazilian colonies too numerous to mention.

Vicissitudes of wind and current often made for extra long crossings, some taking six months while provisions rarely were stocked for more than four or five months. Such merchant transports usually traveled in small groups or even singly. Later, toward the end of the seventeenth century and in the eighteenth century, a sharp rise in privateers required them to travel in armed convoys.

The voyagers' diet was poor often to the point of subsistence, contributing to shipboard disease that commonly took passengers and crew in relatively small numbers. Severe delays in crossing resulted from cyclones that were largely unpredictable even though at the time there was a rudimentary knowledge of the hurricane season. When ships on extended crossings encountered unfavorable trade winds or were stuck in the doldrums for weeks at a time, their food, drink, and other supplies ran out. Then the menu turned to the ship's vermin or nothing at all. It was not rare for a ship to arrive at its destination with all hands on board starving.

Pirates Murder and Plunder

Pirates took a heavy toll. They were a constant menace, and the grisly image they conjured made their threat seem all the more terrible. The most brutal case in Jesuit history occurred on July 15, 1570, just off the Canaries. Three transport ships with seventy-three Jesuits led by Ignacio de Azevedo were sailing from Lisbon to Brazil when they were intercepted by the notorious Huguenot pirate, Jacques Sores. The pirate fleet consisted of five ships from the French Huguenot coastal stronghold of La Rochelle on the Bay of Biscay. Sores was able to seize the lead Portuguese ship, the Santiago, and butcher many of the thirty-nine Jesuits on board. Some were beheaded; some had their limbs hacked off. The rest were thrown overboard, some living, some dying, some dead. (The popular image of "walking the plank" was a myth.) A novice, the fortieth on board, escaped death by virtue of his being in a layman's habit. This removed any doubts about who the targets were. The other two ships narrowly escaped, but only temporarily. After weather forced a stop in Mexico, they headed east out of the Caribbean and south but got caught in the doldrums off South America's coast and drifted some 2,000 miles, all the way to the Azores. There they were attacked by another fleet of English and French corsairs under Jean Capdeville, also a Huguenot pirate. The remaining thirty-two Jesuits on those ships were murdered. Only one of the original group of seventy-three survived, having been left ashore in Mexico.

In one short period, from 1570 to 1571, twelve other Brazil-bound Jesuits were murdered by Huguenot corsairs. In 1587 another party of Jesuits was attacked by an English pirate near Buenos Aires. Their ship was plundered and then towed out to sea with just water on board. Somehow, the boat drifted back against the prevailing winds to Buenos Aires before anyone died. On one occasion off the African coast, Barbary pirates seized a ship with Jesuits and sold them into Arab slavery. The loss of Jesuit fathers and brothers, individually or in small groups, at the hands of pirates occurred too often to recite.

Of course, Protestant merchant ships suffered under the guns of Catholic warships, too. For some, killing Jesuits was justified retribution.

Cannibals Horrify Europeans

Cannibalism was so deeply ingrained in the lives and culture of many tribes that the Jesuits would have found it difficult to abolish the practice even without its encouragement by the colonists and military. Southey quaintly but incisively writes that the banquets of human flesh made the French-Portuguese feud even more deadly, and those Europeans

> . . . conceived it to be good policy to encourage them, and the common shudderings of humanity were as usual, repressed and ridiculed, and the holiest injunctions of religion set at nought. [Indian] priests, warriors, women, and children regarded the practice of cannibalism with equal delight. . . . It was the triumph of the captor; it was an expiatory sacrifice to the spirits of their brethren who had been slain; it was the public feast in which old women displayed their domestic mysteries; and it was the day of merriment for the boys. . . . If the Devil of Romish [disparaging slang for Roman Catholic] mythology had invented a stumbling block in the way of their conversion he could not have devised one more effectual, and accordingly the Jesuits gave him the whole merit of the invention.

In other words, the colonists were doing the work of the devil by promoting cannibalism while the Jesuits were trying to end it. Southey adds the story of a Jesuit who found a Brazilian (Indian) woman in extreme old age, and almost at the point of death. After instructing her in the nature of Christianity and having taken care of her soul, he inquired if he could get any food for her. "Grandam," said he, using the

Tupí word of respect for an old woman, "if could I get you a little sugar or a mouthful of nice things (sweets), do you think you could eat it?" "Ah, my grandson," said she, "my stomach goes against everything. There is one thing I would fancy: The hand of a little Tapuya boy. I think I could pick the little bones, but woe is me, there is no one to go out and shoot one for me!"

Lowney describes how Jesuit provincial Diego de Torres wrote to Rome saying that one of his teams worked in a region menaced by Indians "so cruel that they devour those slain in battle and make flutes of their shinbones and mugs from their skulls." That segues into the story from Southey, with an assist from Caraman, about how Jesuit superior Antonio Ruíz de Montoya was leading a group of Guaraní converts when they were attacked by a stronger force from another tribe. The Indians on both sides

> . . . made no great provision for arrows, counting on picking up those exchanged in the action. Montoya, knowing this, persuaded his people to [hunker down and] receive the enemies' discharge without returning it; the assailants thus disarmed themselves, and then took flight. Among the spoils in the field was a large pot of maize and meat. . . . Montoya's people brought him a portion and he ate it, believing it to be venison, but when they came to the bottom of the vessel a human head and hands were found and recognized for those of a man who used to attend him at the altar and who had fallen in the last battle.

Cannibals could lurk just outside a settlement as in one case in the Río de La Plata estuary when three starving settlers were hanged for stealing a horse to eat. The settlers' skeletal remains were discovered the next morning, having been cut down and devoured by neighboring Indians.

Deadly Lust in the Neighborhood

While cannibals were the main preoccupation of the Europeans, there was always the threat of assault of European women by lustful Indian and European men. Not surprisingly, the rape and abuse of Indian women by colonizers and soldiers was not especially a concern for the Europeans. Southey reports the unusual story of Lucia Miranda, wife of Sebastían Hurtado of Santespiritu. Mangora, a powerful chief of the Timbues, a tribe in the area, fell for Miranda. It was love at first sight. Mangora guilefully took the Santespiritu fort, near Santa Fe, where she resided. Mangora massacred almost all its occupants, but fell in the fighting. His brother Siripus then became enamored of Lucia. Hurtado was away at the time and when he returned to the fort, surmising what happened, he gave himself over to the Timbues in order to be with his wife. Siripus was about to put him to death, but at Lucia's entreaties spared him at the last minute. Siripus then warned them that if he caught them in union both would die. Sure enough, he caught them in *flagrante delicto*. Lucia was burned alive, and Sebastían was tied to a tree and shot full of arrows. This story, worthy of Shakespeare, was one of the most repeated stories in Paraguayan history.

Carnivores of All Kinds Lurk Everywhere

If two-footed enemies were not enough, the ubiquitous jaguars, *"el tigre,"* and occasionally the much smaller pumas were a constant source of dread for the Jesuits and the Indians. The rending and tearing of flesh amid snarls, growls, grunts, and roars in the dark of night added blood-curdling special effects to the horrors of the animals' attacks. The jaguar—from the Tupí "yaguar" or "one who kills with one leap"—of North and South America has coloring somewhat akin to the African leopard with rosettes instead of spots. Half again the size of a leopard, it dwarfs the leopard in strength and ferocity. Rare black jaguars instilled the additional fear of surprise attack since all that could be seen at night were their yellow eyes as they pounced.

Vast numbers of jaguars infested the forests and fields. They normally attacked alone, but on occasion they pounced in groups on cows, oxen, Indians, and sometimes priests. The jaguar's prodigious strength was the stuff of legend. Father Martin Dobrizhoffer, a renowned raconteur, describes two horses tethered together in a remote pasture. One was killed by a jaguar and dragged to its den along with the other still alive, frantically resisting. His gruesome report goes on to describe how they attacked calves, which they preferred, more often than oxen or cows. They would lie on the ground, creep forward softly, then pounce and tear off the head at once, sucking out the blood through the neck. If alone, even a fully grown ox with its huge horns was not safe. The jaguar would leap on its back and with its canines tear open the first joint of its neck, crippling the larger animal and bringing it down. Melodramatic? Maybe so. That is the popular image he left for history.

Jaguars frequently invaded Indian villages and even missions. Night watchmen were set up to sound an alarm. One village near Santo Tomé was reportedly attacked by a pack. The Indians, while holding them at bay, quickly erected a palisade. The jaguars outside besieged it for days, then the priest there ordered a novena—nine days of prayer—and high masses honoring the Virgin Mary. On the ninth day the jaguars left. The prayers had apparently worked—for a while. Soon they returned and, catching the now-complacent Indians by surprise, killed several of them. Luckily for the Jesuits, after the Indians repudiated their sorcerers and confessed their sins to the priest, the jaguars left the scene, apparently having had their fill. While this account also seems embellished, no one knows.

Jaguars were a constant danger to priests on the road travelling between missions or villages, especially at night when they camped. Dobrizhoffer described an experience with one when he and six Indians were en route to Mission San Javier. As they slept by a lake they had a small fire burning for protection. When the fire died out, a "tiger" crept up, waking them. After they shouted at it, the animal drew back, snarling. Soon it returned. Only when the priest's musket was hastily loaded and discharged, missing the beast but creating a terrifying thunder, did it flee.

Jesuit Antonio Sepp spent many days on the road, camping at night with his Indian aides. They always kept a fire burning brightly at night because if it went out "the tiger will be sure to watch his opportunity" and seize the nearest sleeper. He lost two aides this way in his first year at Yapayú. He must have learned his lesson because he never reported the problem again.

The Indians knew that the best defense against a jaguar was to climb a tree and urinate into the eyes of the pursuing beast, burning them and driving him off. No doubt sufficient liquid could be mustered.

In spite of all this, it was the jaguar that lost out in the end. In one province alone during the late seventeenth century, 40,000 jaguar skins were exported annually for the European high fashion industry at enormous profit. Jaguars still inhabit the jungle areas and recently have been reported as far north as Arizona.

The plains of Patagonia were overrun with wild dogs which could threaten a lonesome traveler. Jesuit Thomas Falkner recounted one of his experiences. He had no cooking vessels and used his hat to prepare his meager meals. This caused the hat to grow "so greasy that while he slept it was devoured by wild dogs."

The American crocodile and South American alligator (close cousins) were held in awe by the Guaraní. The animal is also called *caiman* (Spanish for any crocodilian) and *jacare* or *yacare* in the central part of South America that includes Paraguay. The Paraguayan *caiman* is one of the larger of the species, typically ten feet long. They silently lurked everywhere on the banks of jungle rivers and were deadly to those not on guard. The Indians believed it killed with its breath and that even the sight of one could be deadly. It could be killed only by holding a mirror (which they had in a primitive form) in front of its own eye.

At the top of the man-eater food chain was (and is) the anaconda, the largest snake in the world, measuring up to thirty feet long with a girth of forty-five inches and weighing 500 pounds. At the time of the missions, European explorers said they saw some as long as 100 feet—probably a fish tale. Solitary creatures, they lurk in bogs and streams and rivers, seize their prey with their huge fangs, coil around it, drag it under water while crushing or drowning it, and then swallow it whole. No beast is invulnerable. Even jaguars and Indians were victims. Jesuits had some close calls with them.

Special efforts also were made to avoid the numerous poisonous snakes. Southey writes, "The first business of halting for the night or even a meal during the day is to beat the ground and trample the grass for a safe distance to drive away the snakes who are attracted by fire." Electric eels and poisonous stinging rays rounded out the list of aggressive, deadly swamp and river dwellers.

The smallest man-eaters and the most troublesome made up for their lack of size with quantity. Dobritzhoffer said, "If you pass the night [out on the land] you must not dream of sleeping. All the plagues of Egypt seem to have been transferred to the lowlands of South America." Ticks of every size were so numerous to be a curse by themselves. "Swarms of fleas, invisible upon retiring, will cover the body black when arising." Clouds of mosquitoes and blood-sucking flies, battalions of army ants and fire-ants, and other crawling things of every revolting kind imaginable made life outdoors miserable during the rainy season—the Paraguayan summer of December through March—for both man and draught animals. Plagues of ants could devastate mission churches. Burrowing beneath the foundations, they instinctively left as the dry season ended. Then their tunnels would fill with water, softening the foundation and causing the walls and beams to give way. This required major reconstruction or abandoning a building. Dobritzhoffer wrote that at St. Joachín "lurking ants flew in swarms from their flooded [tunnels] . . . and fell upon the priest, the altar, and sacred utensils, defiling everything." Southey describes ants of "two sorts, red and black, both very large, and the bite of either occasioned such intolerable pain for twenty-four hours that the sufferer commonly writhed upon the ground, groaning the whole time; no remedy was known . . . but [when] the force of the venom [was] spent [it left no] ill effect.

Asunción, the capital and the first permanent settlement of the Jesuit Province of Paraguay, was virtually surrounded by water or swampy marshes that "offered little more than mud and mosquitoes." Giant flying bed-bugs entered huts at night to suck blood. Swarms of aggressive wasps could attack with painful, even deadly consequences. Southey describes an awful scene: "The common fly is by far the most serious plague both to man and beast in this country;: it gets into the ears and noses of those who are asleep, deposits its eggs, and unless timely relief is applied, the [eggs hatch and] maggots eat their way into the head and occasion the most excruciating pain and death."

Stealthy vampire bats, which Southey reports as larger than a small pigeon (he seems to confuse the large fruit eater with the smaller blood sucker) favored a sleeping man's big toe and horses' ears, causing the animals to become violently agitated by fear. The bats would bite off the teats of sows so that it became necessary to kill them and their suckling piglets.

Smallpox, Measles Claim Thousands

Epidemics were hardest on the Guaraní, with many thousands, sometimes tens of thousands, dying in a single plague from smallpox and, to a lesser extent, measles. Their immune systems offered little resistance to these European diseases. Outbreaks came in waves over the course of a year or two with an intervening hiatus that might last a decade or more. Even with their European immune systems, many Jesuits died from smallpox. During one plague, ten priests succumbed in a single year. Forty of them died in the worst of the outbreaks, one that lasted for several years. Of course, vaccinations were not available until the early nineteenth century, long after the Jesuits were expelled from the Americas.

The penultimate dangers faced by missionaries came from their fellow European colonists, as we shall see. The worst of all, political perils, arose in the eighteenth century, covered in Part Two.

CHAPTER 6

Spain Begins to Settle Paraguay

Before Francisco Pizarro's conquest of the Inca was completed in 1535, Paraguay seemed promising to the Spanish. However, once the magnitude of Peru's riches were fully appreciated, Paraguay became a backwater strategically. When the added possibilities of wealth from Ecuador and Bolivia were discovered, Paraguay's appeal fell even further. While Spanish explorers and adventurers tentatively probed Paraguay for decades, Madrid's lack of commitment assured a lack of success for serious development.

Cabot Sails up the Paraná

By the second quarter of the sixteenth century, there were regular expeditions from Spain and Portugal to Paraguay and Brazil. Some were driven by rumors of great quantities of gold and silver in Paraguay's interior. In 1526 Sebastian Cabot, having left England and now serving as the chief pilot to the king of Spain, tried to find a passage through South America to the Pacific. Cabot's stormy Atlantic crossing from Cádiz, with three ships and 150 men, had been difficult and his crew was mutinous, so much so that he set loose three of the ringleaders on a deserted island off the coast of Brazil. Sailing south, he encountered friendly Indians who traded badly needed food and supplies for trinkets, knives, baubles, and other piddling things. Cabot returned the favor by kidnapping four of the Indians to take back to Spain. Continued disorder on board ship was such that he had to abandon his original objective. Instead, to be able to show that something had been accomplished, he sailed up the Río de La Plata estuary and then up the great Paraná river, the second largest in South America, and then up its tributary, the Paraguay. He was looking for a water route to the still-rumored riches of the western part of the continent, today's Peru. This was seven years before Pizarro's conquest of the Inca. The Paraguay seemed more promising as it flowed from the north—perhaps it would turn to the northwest—while the Paraná turned to the northeast.

Cabot named the estuary La Plata, Spanish for "the silver" he hoped to find far to the northwest. To his amazement he found one of Díaz de Solís' sailors, having been spared by the Charruas a decade earlier, still living among them. Farther upriver he came upon what were probably Agaces Indian farmers. They took a dim view of his incursion, slaying twenty-five of his party and capturing three, two of whom he later ransomed. Despite his heavy losses, the casualty count was lopsided; he killed 300 Indians. Cabot remained in the area with friendly Guaraní for two years.

Cabot acquired small quantities of gold and silver gotten by the Guaraní by trade or during raids on Inca outposts, probably in southeast Bolivia. This was the first gold and silver brought back to Spain from South America. He might have stayed longer but was prompted to return by the Guaraní, whose hospitality had worn thin. They had enough of Europeans, and Cabot's cause had not been helped by the misbehavior of the members of an earlier Spanish expedition under Diego García.

When Cabot returned to Spain, a Portuguese who had been with him told the king of Portugal about indications of gold and silver far up the Paraguay. The Portuguese, knowing full well that this area was hundreds

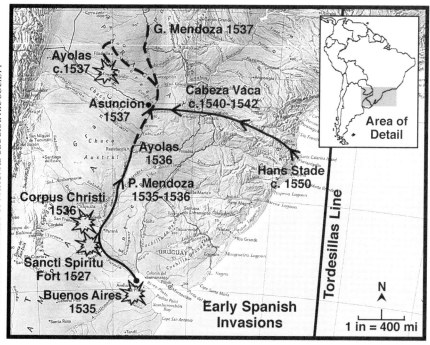

of miles on the Spanish side of the Treaty of Tordesillas boundary line, nevertheless organized a large force of military and settlers, pretending to head for Brazil. When their true intentions were discovered by the Spaniards, the embarrassed Portuguese abandoned the plan.

Pedro de Mendoza Settles Buenos Aires

In 1535 Pedro de Mendoza, a courtier of King Charles I, sailed from Spain with a strong force of 800 soldiers and 1800 settlers and others, headed for Río de La Plata. They landed on the south shore of the estuary to begin a settlement. In thanks to the Virgin Mary and because of its healthy climate, he named it Nuestra Señora Santa María de Buenos Aires. Mendoza soon had a falling out with his trusted lieutenant, the highly respected Juan Osorio. He had other officers kill Osorio, drag his body to the plaza, and denounce him as a traitor. Mendoza's treatment of fierce Quirandi Indians in the area was little better. Testy relations quickly turned to war. The Spaniards attacked with cavalry, usually an effective tactic with Indians who were awestruck by men on huge horses. However, the Quirandi had some exposure to horses from the earlier visits of Díaz de Solís and Cabot. They came prepared, with long thongs weighted with stones at each end. When whipped around and thrown at the horses' legs, they became entangled, bringing the horsemen tumbling down. The Indians were so skilled with this weapon that they even used it to ensnare targets as small as rabbits. Many of the downed cavalry, including their commander, were set upon and killed, but infantry firearms carried the day, and large numbers of Indians were left dead on the battlefield.

With the Quirandi always lurking just outside the settlement's perimeter, Mendoza was unable to forage into the countryside for game and other provisions. His men turned to eating rats, snakes, and anything else they could find. Eventually they turned to their horses and finally to the corpses of dead comrades.

Seeing no alternative but to launch into the interior, Mendoza fled with most of his remaining force up the Paraná. He had lost more than half of the original 2600-man contingent that had sailed from Spain with him a year earlier. At various stops he was able to trade trinkets for food. His health had been waning for some time, but now it worsened rapidly. He probably had syphilis. Returning to Buenos Aires in 1536, he embarked for Spain with so few provisions he had to consume his favorite bitch. He soon went raving mad and died, still en route. The next year hundreds of reinforcements from Spain, including six

Franciscans, arrived at Buenos Aires, but they were too little too late to make the settlement viable.

Ayolas Is Slaughtered

Meanwhile a Mendoza lieutenant, Juan de Ayolas, with 400 men and several Franciscan friars, continued pushing up the Paraná heading for its major tributary, the Paraguay. On the way they found a huge "serpent," an anaconda, resting on the riverbank. It was a monster, larger than anything the Indians had ever seen. It was forty-five feet long, with the girth of a man. The Spaniards shot it and cooked it; the Indians ate it, a delicacy for them. The Spaniards abstained.

Proceeding up the Paraguay, Ayolas came upon a village of hunter and farmer Carios Indians. After unsuccessful negotiations for food and land, the Spaniards attacked. Their guns thundered; several Indians fell, horribly and mortally wounded. Seeing the magic of the loud noise and the destruction it caused, the terrified Carios quickly surrendered. They handed over plenty of their best food as well as two women for each soldier. The Carios remained "friendly" after that. All of this happened at or near the present site of Asunción around August 15, 1536, causing some to argue that this is when Asunción was founded.

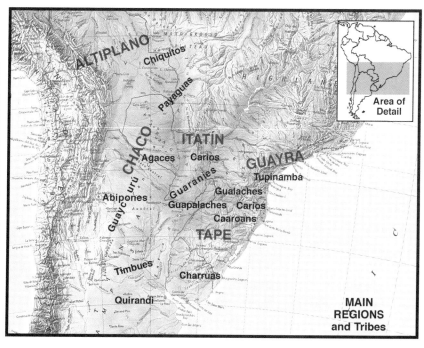

MAP BACKGROUND COURTESY OF NATIONAL GEOGRAPHIC SOCIETY

More likely, the Spaniards' occupation was so brief and superficial as to not constitute a real settlement.

Ayolas, with 200 soldiers and 300 Indians, proceeded farther north up the Paraguay and west into the great, barren, flat country known as the Chaco. He, too, had hopes of reaching the still-legendary gold and silver of Peru—commonly mislabeled "El Dorado." (Pizarro's conquest of the Inca was as much rumor as news.) Domingo Martínez de Irala was left behind with a smaller force. Friars might have been with both of these forces since, by now, those friars were usually present in early Spanish settlements and accompanied any force of this size.

While Ayolas was gone, another Spanish force of 120 soldiers remained in Corpus Christi, a small fort many miles to the south. These men tortured and put to death some local Timbues Indians for reasons unknown. In spite of a warning from a friendly Timbues that big trouble was coming and that they should leave, the Spanish remained. They were tricked into complacency by the Timbues who invited them to a feast. Some fifty of the Spaniards attended. At the most opportune time the Indians poured out of their dwellings, overwhelming the stunned Spaniards and killing almost all of them. Those remaining back at the fort managed to flee down river to Buenos Aires.

As Ayolas' force entered into the wild, desolate, inhospitable Chaco terrain heading for Peru, it found increasing signs of the treasure they sought but also ominous totems from belligerent tribes. After a few months of trekking that was more like wandering in the wilderness, they headed back for the Asunción site. Taking a different route, they passed through the territory of the fierce and wily Payaguas, a tribe that would remain a scourge of Europeans for two centuries. The Payaguas, pretending to welcome them, decoyed them into a marsh where the Spaniards' horses could not maneuver. Every single soldier and all but one of their Indian allies were slaughtered. Since it was the rainy season and the terribly swampy terrain was engulfed in water up to a man's chest, conditions were not practical for Irala to send in a punitive expedition. However, some friendly Carios captured two unlucky Payaguas. Irala tortured these two until they confessed to the slaughter, at which point they were roasted alive.

Gonzalo de Mendoza Founds Asunción

The next year, with Irala apparently disbelieving the sole surviving Indian's story, Pedro de Mendoza's cousin, Gonzalo de Mendoza, launched a new search for Ayolas, some 300 miles along the Paraguay, into the Chaco. Finding not even a trace of Ayolas' expedition, he returned back down the Paraguay, stopping at a site where the Pilcomayo River, a large tributary, flows into the Paraguay. It was ideal for the settlement they then founded. Since it was August 15, 1537, the feast day of the Assumption of the Virgin Mary, they named the settlement Nuestra Señora Santa María de la Asunción. (This practice of naming a settlement after a saint's feast day on which the settlement was founded was common among the Spanish and Portuguese.) It was to become the capital of *Paraquaria*, the Jesuit Province of Paraguay, and of Spanish South America outside of the vice royalties of Peru and Colombia. The small Spanish detachment remaining at Buenos Aires, under continuous attack from the Quirandi, abandoned it and sailed upstream to Asunción. Buenos Aires was eventually re-founded in 1580.

Major battles and celebrated murders obscure the enormous losses on both sides that resulted from constant skirmishes and guerilla warfare lasting throughout the sixteenth and seventeenth centuries. Such fighting was part of the landscape, and only vignettes were ever recorded in the history of the region.

CHAPTER 7

Spain Occupies Paraguay: The Middle Years (1537-1630)

After numerous false starts and military reverses, Spain's tentative colonizing of southern South America gained traction with the settlement of Asunción in 1537.

Spain Focuses on the Treasures of Mexico and Peru

It was disheartening for the Jesuits to observe Spain's lack of commitment to its southern South America colony. The instant riches of Mexico and Peru had obsessed the mother country, making it commercially and industrially flabby, lackadaisical, and self-satisfied. Paraguay had little going for it except "heathen" souls to be converted. It was gold and silver versus the gospel. Even with Spain's devoutly Catholic monarch, God got short shrift.

For most of this era, Spain and Portugal were in a dynastic union (1580-1640) under the Spanish monarchy. In 1580 Portugal's King Henry died, leaving no son. Seeing a power vacuum, Philip II of Spain invaded and quickly overcame what little resistance Portugal could muster. For the next sixty years, the latent rivalry between the two countries and the mutual antipathy of their people were barely contained. During this time the Spanish monarchs repeatedly missed opportunities to permanently unite the two countries. They treated Portugal as a orphan, rarely visiting the country or showing respect by holding court in Lisbon.

Spain was approaching its zenith at the beginning of this era. After the destruction of the Spanish Armada in 1588, Spain began its long, painful downhill slide on the international stage, a slide which accelerated when Portugal broke away in 1640.

Asunción Grows Slowly

The founding of Asunción in 1537 by a few hundred soldiers, adventurers, and settlers was considered a milestone in the Spanish expanding occupation of the Paraguay region, although it took twenty years for the city to grow to any significance, thanks in part to its remoteness. Asunción is deep in the center of the southern part of the continent, more than 800 miles from Río de La Plata and Buenos Aires, up the Paraná and Paraguay rivers. By the late 1550s, however, Asunción had a cathedral and rudimentary ranching and livestock-based industries. It was the *de facto* capital of the immense Jesuit Province of Paraguay—some two million square miles, or thirty percent of the continent. Its ill-defined perimeter surrounded the mostly unexplored regions that today we call Argentina, Chile, Paraguay, Uruguay, southern Bolivia, and the southern Brazilian states of Rio Grande do Sul, Parana, Mato Grosso, and Santa Catarina. Until the mid-sixteeth century, it was virtually void of Europeans.

Spaniards Mix with the Guaraní   women

With few Spanish women present, the settlers and soldiers found the Guaraní women all the more attractive, marrying them or taking them as concubines. Reports of the time agree that they were fine-looking women. In addition, they were submissive, somewhat shy, light-hearted, gentle, and virtuous. They had a strong sense of family, respected their spouses, and doted on their children. Interracial marriages were appreciated, even prized by the Indians as testimony to their worth in the eyes of the Spaniards. Indeed, their mestizo (mixed race) descendents were fully accepted as Spaniards, unlike in Mexico at the time. Mestizos ultimately became the majority in Paraguay. Their long-ruling president-dictator, Alfredo Stroessner, was the son of a Bavarian immigrant and a Guaraní peasant woman.

European–Indian racial mixing in Brazil was less common because so many of the Guaraní died from European diseases, especially smallpox and measles, and from slavery for which they were particularly ill-suited both physically and emotionally. Intermarriages between Indians and Africans were so extensive that, by the nineteenth century, there was little remaining of the original Indian race along the coast and other population centers.

Spain Appoints Progressive Governor, Cabeza de Vaca   1540

In 1540 the king appointed Alvar Núñez Cabeza de Vaca to succeed Irala as governor in Asunción. Cabeza de Vaca set sail from Cádiz late that year with three ships, 400 soldiers, and forty-six horses. Five months later, with scant provisions left, they approached the shoals of Santa Catarina Island off the coast of southern Brazil. With the sailor on the watch napping, the convoy was saved by one soldier's pet cricket. The insect, silent for the entire crossing, apparently sensed land and began its shrill rattle. The watch was awakened, and the ships rushed to drop anchor, not a minute too soon. Half the horses had died in the crossing, but all of the men survived. Cabeza de Vaca then struggled cross country, arriving in Asunción in March 1542, seventeen months after leaving Spain.

Like most such expeditions the overland trip was grueling, some 700 miles as the crow flies, west-northwest, but probably closer to 2,000 miles of trekking through an inhospitable terrain of dense jungle and rolling hills, while crossing innumerable rivers.

The Guaraní they encountered were generally friendly, offering critically needed food for Spanish baubles. The horses terrified the Indians who tried to pacify them with peace offerings of fowl and honey. En route, two Franciscans accompanying the Spaniards began to convert Indians they met, young and old, healthy and sick. Since the converts would then join the train, adding a major burden and slowing their progress, Cabeza de Vaca put a stop to it, while allowing those who were now "Christians" to tag along.

As the expedition prepared to cross the Paraná at a relatively narrow point where its width barely exceeded one-half mile, Cabeza de Vaca purchased canoes from some apparently friendly Indians who thereupon melted into the forest. Within minutes the first group of eighty men, launched from the shore, were swept up in raging currents. Only with a mighty struggle could they return to shore. Any longer on the river and they would have been propelled out of control down stream and swept over the massive Iguazú waterfalls. None could have survived. The Spaniards, now appreciating their situation, portaged the canoes some leagues upstream to a safely fordable point. The rest of their journey, though taxing, was less eventful. Only two soldiers were lost. One drowned in a raging stretch of the Paraná—it had become the rainy season—and one was fatally mauled by a jaguar.

Even then, five years from the founding of Asunción and two years after the start of its diocese, there was still no organized effort in the region to establish anything like a mission church to make religion meaningful in the Indians' lives. Baptisms were haphazardly done with one itinerant friar baptizing many and then leaving them behind with no follow-up. The baptisms became meaningless.

Cabeza de Vaca

Governor Cabeza de Vaca, a physician, ethnologist, and historian, became an enlightened ruler of the Indians, always seeking their material and spiritual welfare. This attitude was to get him into deep trouble.

Cabeza de Vaca, which translates as "head of a cow," had become a prestigious name. Though it was his mother's, unusual for the patriarchal Spanish, he used it consistently. The name originated from a historic victory by Spanish Christians over Muslim Moors in 1212 during the Spanish Reconquest. A distant ancestor had marked a little-known and unguarded but strategic pass in southern Spain's Sierra Morena with the skull of a cow. The Spanish, under King Sancho, launched a surprise attack through the pass and routed the Moors. Sancho awarded the honorific name to the family in perpetuity.

Cabeza de Vaca had a long, stressful, but ultimately illuminating experience with the disastrous 1526 expedition of Pánfilo de Narváez, an expedition launched to conquer Florida. It no doubt shaped his attitude toward Indians. (This was the same Narváez who unsuccessfully tried to arrest Cortés near Veracruz during the Aztec conquest in 1520, losing an eye to a soldier's pike in the ensuing battle and then being imprisoned by Cortés.) Fierce Seminoles fought a guerrilla war to defend their home country, the west central Florida swamps with chest-high water crawling with alligators and poisonous snakes and clouds of mosquitoes. They drove the Spanish back onto the Caribbean beaches.

Things then went from bad to worse for Narváez. Boats that were cobbled together for an escape were caught in a hurricane. Cabeza de Vaca, with three other survivors (one an African Moor named Estevanico), was tossed onto a Louisiana–Texas beach after several harrowing days at sea. For eight years they wandered the American southwest and northern Mexico, generally heading west, hoping to find a Spanish settlement. Early on, they were enslaved by Indians in what was probably west Texas, but eventually they were befriended by these same Indians thanks to the curative treatments Cabeza de Vaca, the physician, administered to their sick tribesmen. Later, he wrote in his memoirs that the successful treatment often consisted of placing the sign of the cross on the invalid, breathing on him and praying over him, thus suggesting psychoneurotic afflictions or placebo power. However, in one case he performed a primitive but major life-saving surgery, removing an arrowhead that was lodged just over an Indian warrior's heart. Two stitches closed the deep wound. The procedure astonished the on-looking

Indians resulting in his safe return to civilization according to *The New England Journal of Medicine*. Its fascinating article, "Sagittectomy—First Recorded Surgical Procedure in the American Southwest, 1535" is rewarding for eager colonial historians. Cabeza de Vaca's care for the Indians of Paraguay was no doubt affected by his experiences with American Indians in their care for him and each other.

In the ninth year, Cabeza de Vaca's little band of naked stalwarts ended their wandering on Mexico's west coast north of San Miguel de Culiacán, now Culiacán, the capital of Sinaloa, a pueblo on the Sea of Cortés. They were the first Europeans to cross the continent on a route north of central Mexico and to report the stunning geological wonders of that region and its peculiar fauna such as the American "buffalo." The four survivors were warmly welcomed and eventually acclaimed by all the luminaries of Mexico.

Cabeza de Vaca's captivating stories inspired the epic but futile expedition of Francisco Vázquez de Coronado from 1540 to 1542 in search of the rumored Seven Cities of Gold. Coronado's failure delayed Spain's colonization of the American southwest by six decades.

In 1537 Cabeza de Vaca returned to Spain and an admiring King Charles I. The king honored him with an appointment as governor and (with the all-powerful title) Captain General of La Plata region (anchored at Buenos Aires). The king added the prestigious title, *adelantado*, awarded to the early conquistadors.

Cabeza de Vaca Subdues Guaycurú, Rebels Overthrow Him

1542 Soon after he arrived in Paraguay in early 1542, Cabeza de Vaca's progressive attitude towards native people alienated many Spanish settlers, especially those who had taken on harems of Guaraní women and those who impressed Guaraní men into a servitude that was thinly veiled slavery. But before he had a chance to introduce any changes, he was forced to deal with invading Guaycurú, Payaguas, and several other warlike tribes to the north and west of Asunción. Late in 1542 he left Asunción with 200 Spaniards and a few thousand Guaraní on a two-year campaign to subdue and punish them. His expedition succeeded. Several thousand were killed in the fighting and hundreds were taken prisoner at a cost of only dozens of Spanish and Guaraní lives.

The fatalities notwithstanding, the expedition proved Cabeza de Vaca's humanity toward the Indians, even the most warlike among them. He was always generous in victory, unlike so many Europeans who slaughtered defeated survivors. As it turned out, his real enemy was not the Guaycurú and their allies but rather his seditious countrymen. About the time of his return to Asunción, he became incapacitated by some sickness and was unable to leave his residence. Domingo Martínez de Irala and his lieutenants, along with many of the soldiers from the expedition, conspired against him. They had become enraged that he had released their one hundred or more female Indian captives they had become "attached to" during the previous two years. They imprisoned him, shackled in irons, and Irala proclaimed himself governor. Large numbers of novice Indian converts, fearing the loss of his protection, fled back into the forest. Fifty of his loyal soldiers fled to Brazil. The Franciscan friars who had been with him took the same path, planning to go on to Spain to testify against him. The friars carried off numerous female Indian pupils.

After eleven months imprisonment, Cabeza de Vaca was shipped off to Spain, accompanied by two of Irala's henchmen to be his accusers at trial. In sixteenth century Madrid lengthy judicial delays were the norm. He wound up being held for eight years before trial. During that time one accuser died and the other went mad. As a result he was acquitted of all charges. There are several versions of what happened next. The most credible one is substantially as follows.

In 1551 Cabeza de Vaca, now nearly sixty, was banished from the Americas for life and exiled to Oran in Spanish North Africa for five years. In 1556 King Charles, now at the end of his reign, awarded him a modest payment of 12,000 maravedis (worth roughly six month's wages for a laborer) and gave him the sinecure, Chief Justice of the Tribunal of Seville. The president of the Council of the Indies had died soon after Cabeza de Vaca had arrived in Spain; he had declared that such sedition as had been perpetrated by Irala warranted summary capital punishment! Cabeza de Vaca's final years and death are unrecorded.

Samuel Eliot Morison, the eminent American historian, wrote the following eulogy:

> Álvar Nuñez Cabeza de Vaca stands out as a truly noble and humane character. Nowhere in the lurid history of the Conquest does one find such integrity and devotion to Christian principles in the face of envy, malice, treachery, cruelty, lechery, and plain greed.

Strong stuff from a renowned American admiral about a kindly Spaniard.

Irala remained in Asunción where he died in 1557. He was succeeded by a series of mostly inept governors. Over the next twenty years the province of Paraguay with Asunción remaining its capital gradually expanded with several substantial new settlements and the permanent resettlement of Buenos Aires.

Inept Governors Follow, Franciscans Begin Conversions

For most of this period there was little meaningful evangelizing of the Indians. However, in 1575, with the arrival of Franciscan Fray Luis Bolaños, there were serious attempts at mission-building. He was the first to establish Indian towns—eighteen of them—to learn Guaraní, to produce a catechism, and to print a Guaraní vocabulary and grammar book. The latter was a truly extraordinary accomplishment as the Guaraní language at the time was made up of various sounds of clicks, stuttering, and coughing that is more like all consonants and no vowels, bearing no resemblance to anything ever heard by Europeans. It also had many dialects with divergent word meanings among the many sub-tribes. Some of the words that would be used in Christian religious services would have rough Guaraní equivalents but with subtle, embedded connotations of witchcraft, superstition, and idolatry, a recipe for disaster if not well handled. Some fathers, never having been able to master the language fully, would have their preaching greeted with gales of derisive laughter from their flock.

The First Jesuits Arrive

While Bolaños and two creole priests assisting him attended to the Guaraní to the east of Asunción, another Fransiscan, Francisco Solano, worked productively with some Chaco Indians northwest of Asunción. Nevertheless, in 1585 Francisco de Victoria, the bishop of Tucumán located seven hundred miles west of Asunción, was the first to invite the Jesuits to his diocese. Given that he was a Dominican, an order often at odds with the Jesuits, the invitation was a remarkable compliment. Having written earlier to Jesuit General Claudio Acquaviva in Rome to ask for help, he did not wait for a time-consuming response but rather approached the Jesuit provincials in both Lima and Bahia (on Brazil's central coast). In early 1587, five Jesuits arrived in the Province of Paraguay—three of them in Asunción and two in Tucumán. The last two then headed on to Córdoba in central Argentina, three hundred miles south of Tucumán, to lay the foundation for a Jesuit provincial headquarters and a college.

The next twelve years of trial-and-error missionary work yielded little. In 1590 the worst smallpox outbreak in South American history [1590] severely reversed their limited progress. In 1593 a flow of Jesuits from Europe began strengthening the college at Córdoba, but their missionary effort was suspended. Much had been learned about what not to do: Do not evangelize, baptize, and leave, and then go on to the next village of prospective converts. Solano's experience had shown this. As an itinerant preacher, he had "converted" thousands of Indians in the Chaco but, since there had been no nurturing follow-up or permanent mission settlements, after a few years there was hardly a sign that he had ever been there.

On the plus side, there were two Jesuits working among the Guaraní— an Irishman or Scot named Thomas Fields and a Portuguese named Manuel Ortega. Their travels extended about seven hundred miles to the east of Córdoba. There they had found large concentrations of Indians with dispositions that made them ripe for the Gospel. Fields and Ortega suffered greatly in the wilds, stretched too thin both figuratively and literally, eating and sleeping little, their clothes in tatters, and no peers for company. In 1599 they were recalled to Asunción, and good intentions notwithstanding, like Solano they left nothing permanent behind.

Jesuit General Gives Up on Guaraní, Angry Paraguay Jesuits Rebel

In 1599, the future looked bleak as Jesuit General Acquaviva issued an order to his men in Paraguay to abandon their work among the Guaraní. But they would have no part of it.

A conference was held in 1602 at Salta in northwest Argentina, among the Jesuits of the province of Peru. At the time that province oversaw Asunción and Tucumán. The Jesuit provincial, Esteban Páez, separately interviewed each of the Paraguay missionaries involved about what should be done. They were of one mind—full speed ahead. To their consternation, he decided the opposite. He would abandon the efforts in Paraguay altogether, not just among the Guaraní! Was he just parroting Acquaviva? Had the outcome been predetermined? One father, a Spaniard named Juan Romero who had been at the college in Córdoba, reflected their feelings in a letter to Acquaviva intemperately asking whether the Guaraní and the interior were to be abandoned in favor of Peru, El Dorado and its gold (more on the real El Dorado in Chapter 9). Such snide disrespect, bordering on contempt, was un-

reduction

heard of in Jesuit circles. Yet it is understandable considering that the clergy in Peru, including the Jesuits, were surrounded by limitless wealth and enjoyed an affluent lifestyle. In fact, twenty years later it was estimated that the clergy controlled more than half the land in Lima.

The rebellion led Páez to quietly shelve his conclusion and instead do nothing. The next year, 1603, the debate resumed at a synod in Asunción. It laid down in detail how instruction was to be given to the Indians, how doctrine would be learned, how Bolaños' catechism was to be used, and that instruction was to be given in the language of the Guaraní. Most importantly, the synod called for the Indians to be gathered into mission settlements.

This gathering was the initiation of the mission or "reduction" approach, central to the success of the Jesuit missionary work in Paraguay. The word "mission" is often used interchangeably with "reduction" which was derived from the seventeenth century Spanish *reducir* (to reduce or gather — into townships in this case). Properly used, reduction means the entire settlement consisting of a mission church, a plaza in front of it, and many buildings including a school surrounding the plaza. We will use the more lay-oriented term "mission" to describe the entire settlement.

Is sources?

Historians, including Southey, Mörner, and Schmidlin, disagree about the source of the Jesuits' ideas regarding the physical, social, and economic organization of the missions. Those ideas included, most prominently, Nóbrega's sixteenth century mission model in Brazil, and Bolaños' settlements south of Asunción at the beginning of the seventeenth century. Other historians have suggested Campanella's *The City of the Sun*, a 1602 version of a utopia; the letters of Bartolomé de Las Casas, a voyager with Columbus, a Dominican historian, and famed protector of the Indians in Central America especially in Chiapas; Plato's *Republic*; More's *Utopia;* and Bacon's *New Atlantis*. The most prolific of Paraguay mission historians, the Argentine Jesuit Guillermo Furlong, argued that the organization was an original creation. It would be presumptuous to dispute him. While Furlong is no doubt right, it is undeniable that the Jesuits of Paraguay *did* draw heavily upon the experience of their fellow Jesuits in Brazil and Peru, adding the humanistic and egalitarian principles of their order along with a dose of common sense and pragmatism.

Jesuit General Relents, Settlers Oppose Jesuits over Slavery

The synod's conclusions meant nothing if more priests were not sent to buttress the few already in the area. Fortunately the bishop of Asunción who had convened the synod, although he was a Franciscan, had extra clout in getting needed reinforcements from the Jesuit general. The power was in his name: Martín Ignacio de Loyola. He was the grand-nephew of Ignatius. That got General Acquaviva's attention. Acquaviva then created a new province, the Chile-Paraguay Province, and ap- *D. de TORRES* pointed Father Diego de Torres to be its provincial. Torres was a high-energy, fifty-six-year-old Castilian. He arrived in Paraguay in 1606 with twenty-three priests in two groups. He immediately built a seminary at Córdoba to produce more native-born priests. He took on the Spanish colonists, letting it be known that his men would be protectors of the Indians under the Laws of the Indies. These laws consisted of thousands of decrees issued by and in the name of the crown, prominently includ-ing a prohibition against the enslavement of the Indians. The good intentions of the Spanish crown on this matter are unquestionable and go back as far as Queen Isabella. They are described further in Chapter 8. However, given the time and distance from Madrid to the colonies, there was a yawning gap between these laws and their enforcement.

The colonists of Córdoba immediately gave their opinion of Torres' *colonists* position on Indian forced labor: They withdrew all of their alms supporting the seminary. The priests were forced to beg to survive. Eventually, a conscientious Spaniard came to their rescue with suffi-cient funds to restore the seminary's activities. The fathers in Santiago del Estero, 250 miles to the north of Córdoba were not so lucky. They were denied food and other essentials by the Spanish colonists and were forced to abandon their facilities.

Then the first of hundreds of charges, continuing all the way to the *cupidity* Jesuits' destruction 165 years later, was leveled against the Paraguay fathers. They were accused of attempting to replace the *encomendero* slaveholder colonists with themselves; the reason given was their "cupidity." The curse of slavery was beginning to show itself publicly for the first time in Paraguay. To prove their strength and the fathers' *colonist's strategy* weakness, colonists in front of a crowd seized and enslaved several Indians who had been in the fathers' care.

The charges apparently reached Madrid for soon after this the Jesuits received support. In 1609 the able governor in Asunción, Hernando de Saavedra received a decree from the king himself, Philip III, ordering him to have the Indians converted by priests, not the military. Philip added that the Indians were the king's subjects and accordingly were to be treated as free men; under no circumstance was an Indian convert ever to be given over to an *encomendero*. For that time, such clear, unmistakable phraseology was unheard of.

Jesuits Begin Their Missions

Early in 1610 two Italian Jesuits, Simón Maceta and José (Guiseppe) Cataldino, were sent by Superior Torres about five hundred miles east-northeast of Asunción into the Guayrá in today's southern Brazil. At the time there had been only two priests in the tens of thousands of square miles comprising that region. One was a vagabond and the other so ignorant that it was doubtful he possessed the knowledge required to validly administer the sacraments. Traveling north on the upper Paraná and then 100 miles east on the Paranapanema, the two Jesuits were welcomed by some Guaraní who had first been approached by Fields and Ortega twenty years earlier. There Maceta and Cataldino established Loreto, the first of the Guayrá missions. Soon they were joined by Antonio Ruíz de Montoya and Francisco de San Martín Xavier, both newly minted Jesuits. Ruíz would eventually lead the push east, deep into the Guayrá, and leave his mark on South American history.

What followed was a huge inflow of Indian refugees seeking to escape from Portuguese slaver hunters less than 300 miles to the east in São Paulo and the Tordesillas line that was supposed to provide safe harbor. While this gave some assurance to these fathers and their flock of Guaraní, it was of no consequence to the slavers setting to attack.

Almost immediately the four began building another mission, San Ignacio, some five miles east of Loreto, upstream on the same river. The four split up the work: Maceta and Ruíz de Montoya took Loreto while Cataldino and San Martín covered San Ignacio. (To the frustration of students of mission history, many missions at different times and places had the same or similar names. In this case a mission, San Ignacio Guazú [the Great], had been founded in 1609 by the Jesuit Marciel de Lorenzana at the confluence of the Paraná and Paranapanema about one hundred miles west of Loreto and San Ignacio. Lorenzana's site was opposite the Franciscan settlement of Itatí [later Itatín] founded soon after his. Both sides agreed it made little sense to have the settlements of two orders so close together. Deciding on a let's-share-the-wealth approach, the Jesuits would evangelize to the east, following the Paraná upstream. In this way the territory surrounding and between the Paraná and Uruguay rivers would become the Jesuits'—the Jesuit Republic of the Guaraní. San Ignacio Guazú was moved in stages towards Asunción, finally winding up north of the Paraná in 1668. Cataldino's San Ignacio ultimately became San Ignacio Miní, an Argentine national historic site).

Jesuits Struggle with Cannibals, Shamans, Smallpox

Much of the initial success in bringing the Indians into the settlements can be attributed to curiosity. When the burden, regimentation, and boredom of mission life became too much, many restless Indians drifted back into the freedom of their ancestral forest home. They would soon be pursued by one of the overworked priests deep into the woods to retrieve them, with mixed success.

More serious setbacks soon struck. Starting in 1618, smallpox plagues came in waves, causing Indian converts to flee to the disease-free forest. There they were met by tribesman who had not joined the mission and who invited them to stay, saying they would celebrate the reunion with an orgiastic party with plenty of home-brewed mandioc beer, drunk from a Jesuit skull! However tantalizing, the offers were usually resisted, and the converts would return to their missions once the plague receded. Those who made it back were fortunate, for the Guaraní could be tough on one another. At Lorenzana's San Ignacio Guazú mission a raiding party of the fiercest among them attacked the mission and carried off many of their converted brethren for fattening, slaughter, and consumption. Lorenzana made ready for the next attack. It came soon enough. Lorenzana had some fifty soldiers with muskets and 200 warriors from Asunción. With those soldiers and with better training for his own mission Indians, the attackers were so utterly destroyed that such large-scale mission invasions by brother Guaraní were never tried again.

Reversion to the old rituals of the jungle was a frequent challenge when shamans—sorcerers and medicine men—infiltrated a mission to do their own proselytizing. One prominent case occurred in 1618. A Brazilian Tupí sorcerer with two companions entered Loreto. He was arrayed in the feathers of a shaman and well practiced in his enticements. Assembling a multitude, he harangued them in Tupí, their *lingua franca*. Shaking a goat-skull rattle, he proclaimed that he was the one true god, the absolute lord of death, seed, and harvest. He could destroy all things and recreate them all by his breath. He was a trinity; with his companions he was three persons in one god like the one the Jesuits preached about. As he raved on, Father Cataldino came upon the scene, and the sorcerer repeated the performance, flaunting it in the priest's face, threatening him and his converts with annihilation. Cataldino had his converts seize the man and, based on a decision by the mission Indian officers, he was given 100 lashes. Since he was a trinity, this was repeated on each of the next two days. All the while he cried out, confessing his blasphemies to the great delight and amusement of his Indian captors and especially their children. Punishment completed, he was banished from Loreto, but he soon returned to become a model convert.

Guayrá Missions Grow Rapidly

The area of southern Brazil that came to be called the Guayrá was the epicenter of the political, military and religious intrigues between Spain and Portugal, eventually leading to the 1750 Treaty of Madrid and the Guaraní War of 1753-1755. Events there also contributed to the liquidation of the Society of Jesus in 1773. Guayrá was the Guaraní name of a *cacique* (chief) who had been helpful to Irala during his time there. Irala named the area for him, and it stuck through all the years of its historic importance.

The Guayrá's ill-defined borders consisted of the upper Paraná on the west, the Iguazú on the south, the Treaty of Tordesillas line on the east, and the wild, unexplored, trackless woods and marshes to the north— in all tens of thousands of miles of virgin land.

The missions there expanded rapidly in size and number in response to the refugees pouring in. A dozen years after Loreto and San Ignacio Guazú came San Francisco Xavier (1622), Encarnación (1625), San José (1625), San Miguel (1626), San Pablo (1627), San Antonio (1627), Concepción (1619 or 1627), San Pedro (1627), Los Siete Arcángeles (1628), Santo Tomás (1628), and Jesús María (1628), serving more than forty thousand Guaraní neophytes (newly converted Christians) and curious others. All these missions were concentrated within a 150 mile diameter circle.

Maintaining the momentum of growth was a struggle. Even though the missions were beginning to become self-sufficient, many supplies had to be acquired from Asunción or other distant Spanish settlements. The long supply lines were subject to bureaucratic delays, negligence in handling products, accidents, and natural and human hazards, sometimes with fatal results. In 1614, Cataldino journeyed a great distance from San Ignacio south to the Spanish outpost of Santa Fe in search of medicine for his grievously sick partner, Martín Xavier. Upon his return he discovered that Martín Xavier had expired. He was twenty-six.

Torrential rains, typical for such a subtropical region, often flooded those missions that were low lying, in flat areas next to this region laced with rivers. The floods provided their own little dramas. On one of the worst occasions Father Ortega and several Guaraní neophytes were caught between two rivers during a summer downpour. (Normal peak days have 3.5 inches of rain.) Unconcerned initially, they continued their journey as the water became waist-high—nothing they could not handle, yet. Then it became a deluge, compelling them to climb trees or drown. Even the animals and reptiles were dislocated. A huge anaconda ascended a tree were Ortega and a few of his neophytes had taken refuge. With no way to escape and no weapons handy, their prospects seemed dreadful until the branch on which the beast had anchored itself broke off, plunging it back into the water. Strangely, it swam away. Two days passed without let-up. Then one neophyte swam from his own tree to Ortega's tree imploring him to save the souls of six others who were near the point of death. Swimming to them, he baptized several and gave absolution to those who already were Christians. Minutes later, five slipped off their perches and submerged. Soon after that the rains abated, and the rest survived.

González Takes Center Stage

Roque González de Santa Cruz, the son of Spanish *hidalgos* (minor nobility), was born in Asunción in 1576. He was tall, slender, charismatic, an inspiring preacher, and fluent in Guaraní from childhood. His brother, who was acting governor in Asunción at the time (1615), granted him permission to establish a number of missions on or near the Paraná. That same year, González began mission Nuesta Señora de la Encarnación (there is confusion over the date of its completion) at or near the present Argentine city of Posadas on the Paraná. Visiting Posadas today one finds not a trace left. A year later, a new governor encouraged him to direct his efforts southwards towards the Uruguay to protect navigation for the missions to export their products. Just north of that river he founded Concepción.

González had been a diocesan priest before joining the Jesuits. An architect, engineer, mason, carpenter, and teacher of Indians, he was assigned to San Ignacio in 1613 after his failed attempt to convert the fiercely independent Guaycurú west of Asunción. His organizing and design abilities made that mission a model for many that followed. The layout of a great plaza with the church on one side as its anchor, a school, dwellings for the two priests and the Indians, and common buildings for civil meetings and manufacturing was a prototype for missions built in the future. He understood that a stable economic foundation was essential for mission success. He gave each mission Indian family iron tools, previously unknown to them, and trained them to be fully self-sufficient in light manufacturing, tanning, weaving, and similar trades, as well as in farming and ranching. A leather export industry gradually emerged. Cattle and sheep multiplied geometrically in the region's lush pastures. He made mission life richly rewarding both religiously and emotionally for the Indians as they took to his music, hymns, fiestas, and entertaining liturgy. No man had a more beneficial effect on the Republic of the Guaraní.

González Has Rapid-Fire Successes

Late in 1619 González was approached by a powerful *cacique* convert, Nicholás Neenguirú, with an invitation to found a "town" for his people. After some initial death threats from Indians who apparently had not gotten the word from Neenguirú, he made his way a few miles south and founded the settlement of Concepción on December 8, the date of the Immaculate Conception. Soon, with his advocate Neenguirú present this time, he founded the mission of Nuestra Señora de la Candelaria. This first Candelaria was destroyed by raiding Indians soon after its founding. It was rebuilt across the Paraná in Argentina on February 2, 1622, becoming the Jesuit headquarters of the Guaraní Republic and the operating headquarters for the whole Jesuit Province of Paraguay.

The use of Neenguirú to convert others in the Tape was a sort of jungle version of *cuius regio eius religio* (the ruler of a territory chooses its religion), a principle that has applied everywhere there has been an absolutist government. The Jesuits had cleverly introduced it to great advantage in Paraguay as they also tried to, for a while, in China, India, Japan, and other lands.

González' rapid-fire successes earned him the position of superior, thus putting him in charge of the missions in a large area. More journeys led to more missions.

Caaroans Slay González

The last of six missions that Roque González founded was in 1628 at Asunción del Iyúi, about twenty miles northwest of Candelaria. Later that year he pushed a good distance southeast, deeper into an unexplored area of the Tape to start a mission. It was around November 1 and thus it was to be called Todos Santos, for All Saints' Day. The site was a daring location, too daring. The Caaroan Indians there were numerous and warlike, dominating much of the region. They were led by Ñezú, an unpredictable and fierce *cacique* and shaman, an unusual combination. He was considered a god. His word was law. He was greatly feared by his own people and neighboring tribes. When he ordered his warriors to kill the fathers and any Indians who supported them, they obeyed, unquestioning. When he said he would send jaguars to devour any who resisted his commands and great deluges to drown them, they believed.

One day when the Todos Santos wooden church building was nearly finished, González stooped over to attach the clapper for the church bell used to announce and enliven the Sunday evening services. Suddenly and surreptitiously Ñezú's subordinate *cacique*, Caarupé, arrived with a slave, Marangue, who struck the unaware González on the head with a stone hatchet. Down he went, unconscious. A second blow spilled his brains. A companion priest, Alonso Rodríguez, came running to see what the commotion was about and was immediately struck and killed in a like manner. Their bodies were mutilated, dragged about in celebration, and burned along with the church, its ornaments, and offending images. One aged Christian *cacique* who protested was choked to death, one of the hundreds of anonymous Indian martyrs in the jungle. González, fifty-two years old, was the first of twenty-three Paraguay Jesuit martyrs.

A day or two later a third priest, Jesuit Juan de Castillo, assigned to González but remaining at the previous mission, Asunción de Iyúi, was seized from behind by another of Ñezú's *caciques*, Araguirá, and with the same Caaroans, bound and beat him. Then he was dragged with a rope along the ground half dead and with an arm dislocated. A slave of Ñezú threw a heavy rock, crushing his belly. Then they dragged his lacerated and bloody body over stones and logs into a quagmire where they smashed his head with another large stone. After burning his remains they shouted, "Let the jaguars devour him." Later, when asked why they killed the fathers, they replied that they had orders from Ñezú's to do so "to preserve our way of life and ancient songs."

Ñezú celebrated his triumph by "unbaptizing" the Asunción de Iyúi children. His curious ceremony consisted of washing the head with hot water, rubbing sand on the tongue and scraping it away with a shell to clean off any baptismal salt which had been placed on it. He smashed the church vessels, burned down the church and told the Indian converts that they should no longer fear anything. They could take as many wives as they liked, just as their fathers had done before. As for he himself, his divinity was no longer questioned. No one dared.

Spanish and Christian Indians Defeat Caaroans

In response to Ñezú's assaults, Jesuits at other missions rallied their Indians, mainly Guaraní, and Spanish settlers. *Cacique* Neenguirú, accompanied by Jesuit Diego de Alfaro, led an army of 800 Guaraní to Todos Santos. A surprise attack on Ñezú's forces decimated them, with Ñezú fleeing for his life at the outset of the fighting. He crossed the Uruguay. The mission Indians on that side of the river lived in constant dread of his reappearance for years until they learned he had been slain by some wandering bands.

Meanwhile, Jesuit Pedro Romero, on horseback, commanded Indian converts in defeating another Caaroan force threatening Calendaria. Soon thereafter yet another force of Caaroans, this time a huge one, descended on Candelaria. Just when a disaster seemed inevitable, a wealthy Portuguese from Corrientes named Manoel Cabral Alpoino quickly assembled a troop of Spanish horsemen and made a forced march of over 100 miles to join the fray. As he arrived at Candelaria he linked up with Father Diego Boroa, the rector at Asunción, who had also recruited more men. These two forces mounted a counterattack on the Caaroans. Many were killed and captured. Twelve of the most aggressive leaders, participants in the earlier murders of the three Jesuits, were summarily executed. Ñezú's deputy Potivera escaped but was soon handed over by some frightened Caaroans with whom he had sought refuge. He too was executed. The Jesuits put an end to the executions after that. We know all this from Indians who testified years later, especially from the two Guaraní altar boys who were witnesses to the Jesuits' murders at Todos Santos but were allowed by the Caaroans to flee.

All of these events had an unintended consequence: They added to the Jesuits' rapidly growing reputation. All these tribes had been accustomed to premature death, even treating it as routine—such was the violent fabric of their societies—but they were not prepared for what followed upon the death of the missionaries. Public rejoicing by other Jesuits over the fate of those who had been exalted by martyrdom affected the Indians as much by its sincerity as by its peculiarity. They readily believed that whatever "miracles" were reported (there were several) resulted from the intercession of the three dead priests. They also could not, as Southey writes,

> . . . contemplate without astonishment the conduct of the Jesuits, their disinterested enthusiasm, their indefatigable perseverance, and the privations and dangers which they endured for no earthly reward. They who had heard of these wonderful men became curious of seeing them; but they who once came within the influence of such superior minds and felt the contagion of example, were not long before they submitted.

The paperwork surrounding the three priests' cause for sainthood was huge. In González' case, the devil's advocate, Salvator Natucci, argued for years that González and his aides were murdered for being part of the hated Spanish colonial forces, not for their faith. Despite that, all three priests were canonized when Pope John Paul II visited Paraguay in 1988.

Ruíz de Montoya Promoted to Superior

Antonio Ruíz de Montoya would become a giant of the times. Born a creole (full-blooded Spaniard born in the colonies) in Peru in 1585, he was orphaned at age nine. A few years later, around the turn of the century, suffering from the ennui of his schooling he quit and joined the Spanish conquistadors in Chile. He was wounded four times in combat and returned to Lima in 1606. Quickly becoming a man of the world, he planned to set sail to Spain for more adventure. However, while awaiting transportation he took up the writings of Ignatius of Loyola. In a Pauline conversion later that year, he suddenly changed his plans and entered the Jesuit seminary at Córdoba. He was ordained around 1610 and was placed among the Guaraní a year or two later, following Diego de Torres into the Guayrá and Brazil's Paraná state just to the north.

From the beginning, Ruíz demonstrated extraordinary powers of persuasion not only among the Indians but also more importantly among the Spanish provincial authorities and, most importantly, before the king of Spain himself. Perhaps his rich and varied background helped develop his boundless self-confidence and persuasive charisma.

In 1620, the Jesuit provincial of Paraguay in Asunción appointed him to be a superior and thus one of his direct reports. He would do great things for the Guaraní.

CHAPTER 8

What the Jesuit Missions Were Like

Over a span of two centuries, from Nóbrega's mid-sixteenth-century missions in Brazil until the Jesuit expulsion from the Spanish empire in 1767 and 1768, the Jesuits of Paraguay learned how to perfect all aspects of mission life. At their triennial meetings in the capital Asunción or at their operating headquarters in Candelaria, the fathers from all of the Paraguay missions shared experiences in a continuous improvement process covering all aspects of mission governance, and operation. The resulting mission society, often called "theocratic communism," evolved to become the paragon of how to move a primitive people into the modern world.

Government of the Missions

The Jesuit Republic of Paraguay was a loose confederation of semi-independent missions. There was no republic in the legal sense of the term. The term was invented by an unlikely combination of idealistic and romantic historians, philosophers, and authors, as well as Jesuit adversaries who claimed the Jesuits were trying to set up an independent state.

The executive branch of government at each mission consisted of a subtle power-sharing relationship between two Jesuit fathers assigned to the mission and an Indian administration elected annually. At the top of the Indian hierarchy was the *corregidor* (mayor). Under him there were typically: a deputy (the *teniente*) and then three *alcaldes* (supervisors). Next came several *regidores* or councilors and then the chief of police and several lesser officials. All of these comprised the town council or *cabildo*. Other more junior officials included the clerk or procurator with some administrative and fiscal powers, the treasurer, the military captains, jailers, block wardens, livestock counters, and various church sacristans (leaders of music and lectors)—all chosen by an adult male vote.

The *caciques* (chiefs) played a prominent role in the process especially in the selection of candidates, and often wound up holding the most exalted positions themselves. But even the *caciques*, usually the most

1) persuasion
2) heroism in battle
inheritance

intellectually gifted, eloquent, and persuasive men of the community, had great difficulty with abstract thought and analysis asked of them by the Jesuits. When a village chose a *cacique*, his powers of persuasion were the most heavily valued, while heroism in battle and inheritance played secondary and tertiary roles.

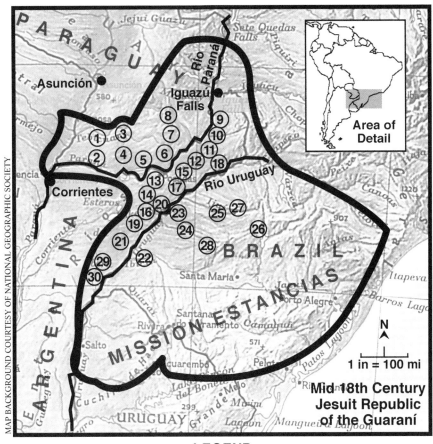

Mid-18th Century Jesuit Republic of the Guaraní

MAP BACKGROUND COURTESY OF NATIONAL GEOGRAPHIC SOCIETY

LEGEND

1. Santa María de Fe
2. San Ignacio Guazú
3. Santa Rosa
4. Santaigo
5. Santos Cosme y Damien
6. Itapúa
7. Trinidad
8. Jesús
9. Corpus
10. San Ignacio Miní

11. Loreto
12. Santa Ana
13. Candelaria
14. San Carlos
15. Mártires
16. San José
17. Santa María la Mayor
18. San Javier
19. Apóstoles
20. Concepción

21. Santo Tomé
22. San Borja
23. San Nicolás
24. San Luis
25. San Lorenzo
26. San Juan
27. Santo Ángel
28. San Miguel
29. La Cruz
30. Yapeyú

The fathers always had a strong voice in candidate selection, but only by persuasion. Such persuasion was effective, however, since the unwritten understanding was that if the fathers did not approve of any elections or administrative actions, they might leave. That, of course, would place the community at the mercy of Spanish opportunists and Portuguese slavers, a Hobson's choice for the mission Guaraní.

Lists of elected officials were sent to the governor in Asunción for approval and, although it was routine, the return back to the mission of the official endorsement documents was treated as a singular honor warranting great jubilation and celebration. The subsequent investiture of officials played to the Indians' love of theater, with parades, special uniforms of crimson, yellow, and blue velvet, and gold and silver lace, along with music, singing, and dancing. The plaza became ablaze with brilliant swirling colors set against the brown, flat faces, and bare feet—always the more familiar and comfortable bare feet—of the celebrants. On gala days Indian leaders might dress in a formal Spanish suit, with shoes and stockings, especially if they were to assist at the altar. As soon as the church service was over, however, off came the shoes and stockings. The elaborate insignias of office adding to the festivities included badges, banners, scarves, keys, staffs, and decorative swords. A hundred richly festooned horses would lead the parade. Music poured from bugles, guitars, violins and drums from the missions' musicians and those of neighboring missions who were honored to be invited to join in. The instruments were locally made, and they equaled those made in Europe in quality. After the plaza festivities were complete, the entire community filed into the church for more celebration at a passionately, yet reverentially celebrated solemn High Mass. The only day rivaling these for such merrymaking was the feast day of the mission's patron saint, a kind of national holiday.

All of this process—of voter selection, investiture and celebration achieved what must have been the Jesuits' intention: The average Guaraní felt he was a part of an egalitarian collective in which all of his needs—spiritual, emotional, and material—were well-satisfied.

As for the two fathers at each mission, one was senior and responsible for overall administration. The junior father typically ran the school and day-to-day operations. A Jesuit brother was frequently added in start-up or large missions to assist the fathers. The mission fathers reported to a mission superior who was in charge of a number of missions in a large region. He in turn answered to the Provincial of

Paraguay, who was located initially in Asunción, the capital, and later in Candelaria, the operating headquarters. At their peak in 1756, the Jesuits in the Province of Paraguay numbered about 400 (those in the Republic about 75).

In 1710 the total was 269; in 1735 it was 352; and in 1749, due to epidemics, it dropped to 303. The average over their century and a half was perhaps 200. *reasons for*

The relationship of the Jesuits and their missions with the secular bishops (that is, not members of a religious order) was at times wary, even testy. As long as the missions were just that—missions—there was no problem. However, as the missions matured and their role evolved from converting the Indians to maintaining a well-established Christian community with regular, perpetual parishes, the question arose as to whether the missions should remain independent. This would be permitted only if the secular bishop in Asunción or the pope himself explicitly agreed.

In 1617 Jesuit General Muzio Vitelleschi wrote to his provincial in Paraguay that his fathers should hand the missions over to the secular bishop when he was ready and willing to take the Jesuits' place. Decades passed without change. However in 1652, in a typically Jesuitical cat's-paw maneuver, the Jesuit provincial formally offered to surrender the missions to the bishop, knowing the offer would be declined. It was. The civil authorities in both Paraguay and Madrid believed that handing the missions over to regular diocesan priests would mean their falling into ruin. As part of the subsequent negotiations the authorities and the provincial won a concession from the king: Although the missions might be regarded technically as parishes, only the provincial would have the right to choose the father to run each mission. Stipends for the fathers and other civil support would continue. How prescient were the authorities' predictions about the missions "falling into ruin." In 1768 when the Jesuits were expelled from Paraguay—in spite of the missions having matured and in spite of the presence of many other priests recruited to continue their work—the missions fell into ruin.

With a strong executive branch of government, the *cabildo*, while nominally a legislative body, played a distinctly secondary and largely advisory and honorific role.

The judicial system for resolving criminal cases was nothing more than the senior father at each mission serving as judge and jury. Killing and eating a community steer without permission was a typical crime that would result in the police bringing the offender before the father for judgment and punishment. Other common crimes were drunkenness, adultery, and neglect of work duties. An Indian's guilty conscience usually led to a public confession, immediately followed by punishment of ten to twenty lashes applied by a policeman or administrator, never by a Jesuit. Women applied the lash to convicted females. The disgrace of the affair more than the beating would lead to a promise, usually kept, of better behavior in the future. In the early years the Guaraní had a complete ignorance of "morality." They would always err on the side of a scrupulous conscience, spending as much time in private, sacramental confession as would ten Spaniards, often telling the same "sins" over and over again just to make sure.

A serious criminal offense that might result in capital punishment elsewhere was dealt with in any of several ways that varied over the years. By mid-seventeenth century, there had been twelve murders in the missions. Until then punishment had been limited to the lash, possibly followed by imprisonment of a year or so, and then permanent banishment from all of the missions. Given the environment into which a criminal was released, the punishment was greater than it might appear at first blush. Later in the seventeenth century, a "life" prisoner was always released after ten years although in the minds of the Indians, used to living free, when the sentence was passed it seemed to be for the rest of his life. A common, primitive prison was shared among the missions. The Jesuits' outlawing of capital punishment might well have been unique at the time with the exception of Scandinavia. Another type of punishment was to hand the villain over to the Spanish civil authorities where anything could happen since these authorities had not renounced capital punishment.

Excessive punishment was studiously avoided. In one case, when a father allowed a *corregidor* to apply disproportionate punishment, he was imprisoned in a Jesuit house. This incident was apparently behind Jesuit General Frantisek Retz's order that "any missionary who was excessive in punishing Indians should be removed instantly from the reductions [missions]."

Civil cases—usually disputes between Indians over such things as their personal plots' boundaries—were resolved by a tribunal of three neutral Indian judges chosen from other missions.

A night watchman on duty from dark-to-dawn provided protection against prowling jaguars, criminals climbing over the mission walls, fires, and other disturbances. He also had an unintended effect of reducing adultery, since a man (or woman) leaving or entering his dwelling for another's might be observed.

Cunninghame-Graham contrasts "the Paraguayan state of things" with the "savagery of English law" with "twelve years for stealing a teapot . . . a life sentence for the theft of some wearing apparel."

Council of the Indies

In spite of the self-government accorded the Guaraní, they still had to live under certain Spanish laws and rules. Colonial affairs were managed first and foremost by *El Consejo Real y Supremo de las Indias* (The Royal and Supreme Council of the Indies) in Madrid. Its genesis was the 1506 Portuguese government regulatory body called the *Casa*. It imposed a state monopoly on trade in certain valuable commodities such as precious metals, especially gold, and spices. Some time around 1520 in Seville, Charles I copied the *Casa* arrangement with his own *Casa de la Contratación* (House of Trade), formalizing the operations of what would become Spain's monopolies. A few years later in 1524, he created the Council of the Indies to supervise his House of Trade and make its functioning more detailed, forceful, and effective.

The council, comprised of up to ten crown-appointed members, was the final authority on American affairs—fortunately so, given the general lack of ability of the Spanish monarchs throughout the seventeenth century. An essential role of the council was to oversee the issuance and implementation of royal *cédulas* (decrees) in the Americas and to ensure the Indians were fairly treated.

The council's main impact on the Jesuit missions was indirect. Royal laws, or Laws of the Indies, were handed down through the council. While they applied directly only to Spanish civil settlements in the Americas, most missionaries used at least some of them as models. The council codified all its decisions for the Americas thereby specifying all aspects of imperial policy and trade. Its legislation covered law and order, town planning including specifications for buildings and open spaces such as the central plaza, the labor force, and many other matters affecting the daily life of Spanish colonists.

As for the House of Trade, it controlled shipping and all other aspects of colonial commerce, levied fees due to the crown from such commerce, and ensured that only Spaniards could travel to the Americas, especially those immigrating to the colonies.

While such a detailed approach to colonial management from across
the Atlantic might seem reasonable and achievable today, in the sixteenth, seventeenth, and eighteenth centuries it was delusional. A
round trip voyage between Spain and its South American colonies
routinely took a year, assuming it was completed at all, given all the
hazards ships and travelers faced. Messages and couriers would be lost
in the vast expanse of stormy oceans, soaring mountains, and impenetrable jungles. Insect-borne diseases, brigands, and pirates were a
constant menace. Adding to the council's ineffectiveness was the fact
that its Laws of the Indies were primarily a collection of *ad hoc* pre-
scriptions and decrees issued over many decades and sometimes
self-contradictory. The practical effect of all this was that the council's
dictates were honored more in the breach than in the observance. It
also meant that the survival of the empire depended on a practical
decentralization that gave the viceroys, the crown's most senior representatives in the Americas—initially in Mexico and Peru—much
freedom of action, bordering on independence. Yet their power was, in
a way, limited by a three-year term in office. The decrees of the viceroys, like those of the *audencias* (the Supreme Courts of Justice) which
exercised an inefficient checks-and-balances type of control, became
the law of the land. The relative authority and jurisdiction of the
audencias varied over the centuries. A district encompassed by an
audencia was divided into *gobiernos* (provinces) headed by governors
who exercised the highest political and judicial power under the
supervision of the viceroy and *audencia*.

[handwritten margin note: 1573 building code]

In 1573 specifications—a sort of building code—were added to the
Laws of the Indies for the construction of Spanish settlements in the
New World. Jesuit missions generally followed those specifications that
applied to Spanish towns, even though they were not required to do so.
For example, the Jesuit's own informal building code recommended
that the mission should be built on high ground for sanitation purposes
(rains would carry pollution away from the settlement and toward the
nearby river); there should be a large plaza at the center of the settlement, up to four hundred feet on a side (Jesuit plazas would be square)
with the finest grass, kept short by sheep; many buildings would
surround the plaza with the church occupying the most prominent site,
so that it would be the first and most inspiring image one would have
upon entering through the main portal; an open space, typically a few
hundred yards wide, was to surround the mission for gardens and
protection against surprise attacks; and the perimeter should contain a
high wall and often a trench surrounding the wall for defense.

Economics, Agriculture, and Industry

Jesuit mission economic activity became complex and vigorous compared to that of the rest of Spanish South America. It began with harvesting crops with which the Guaraní were familiar such as manioc, maize, and sweet potatoes for consumption within the mission. Gradually it expanded to other crops for export, especially yerba for maté. It evolved to ranching and organized fishing. Skilled trades and light manufacturing became profitable when their products, such as musical instruments, were exported to markets elsewhere in South America.

Yerba was the key to mission prosperity. In his trip to Madrid, Ruíz de Montoya had obtained a government agreement for the mission Indians to collect and sell yerba. Yet it took five years, until 1645, for the required decree to be issued, typical of the bureaucratic delay under the Laws of the Indies and Spain's micro-management of colonial affairs.

Cunninghame-Graham wrote of the halcyon years of the Jesuit missions as being the period from 1650 to 1720. This was the time after the slave raiders had been driven back to São Paulo, after the internal upheaval conflicts of the Cárdenas years (Chapter 11), and before the betrayal of the missions by the Treaty of 1750. There was burgeoning economic prosperity, growth, and satisfaction for the Indians and the mission Jesuits. Virtually all of the arts, crafts, and trades of Europe were taught to the Guaraní by the Jesuits. The missions, taken all together, had tanners, potters, coopers, masons, blacksmiths, silversmiths, tailors, boat-builders, firearm and gunpowder makers, and almost every other industry that contemporary European countries had except shoemakers. The Guaraní loved their feet to be bare. Huge quantities of cloth were woven from mission-grown cotton. At the top of the trade hierarchy were musicians, craftsmen of many types of musical instruments, sculptors, painters and even printers. Children older than pre-schoolers had assigned tasks, suitable to their age and gender, when not in class or engaged in games and sports. A kick-ball game, remotely resembling soccer was popular among boys. The Jesuits managed an Indian printing press, the first in southern South America. Surprisingly, one item never well made was wine. The grapes were always under assault by blight and insects, and the wine was reported to taste horrible, like medicine. So even sacramental wine was imported.

Guaraní artists learned to copy European styles and methods, resulting in a Guaraní version of European baroque that included obvious Indian facial features as well as indigenous animal and plant scenes.

Tailors made cotton cloaks, shirts, breeches, and ponchos like those seen even today. The love of elaborate dress, especially ceremonial dress, was a universal passion. Silversmiths made jewelry out of silver, copper, brass, and other metals, mostly imported from Europe via Buenos Aires. They added decorative, locally-mined quartz crystal and small amounts of semi-precious stones, glass beads, and even some rare gold or gold-thread for liturgical vestments and ceremonial clothing for *caciques* and other prominent functionaries. A few gold wedding rings that a mission might craft were the property of the community and were loaned to each new couple only for the ceremony. Use of the rings was a high honor made especially so by its short life.

The era of the yerba, what we call today a "cash crop," began late in the seventeenth century. No other single economic force was as powerful as this plant. It provided profitable employment for thousands and was the principal source of the mission equivalent of foreign exchange. There was also a side benefit for the Jesuits as it gave them a way to wean the Indians away from chronic drunkenness. Caraman gives this amusing example: The *caciques* would start their war conferences with many rounds of chicha—in this case the maize-based liquor or beer. Once they were drunk they would begin discussing battle plans. Then they would declare war while assuring themselves of a glorious outcome. The discussion, however, would often descend into a violent fight among the drunks, leaving the enemy little to fear.

For many years yerba maté had been considered by Europeans to be harmful. It was even prohibited, by excommunication no less, for Spaniards except for medicinal purposes. Its reputation as a miracle drug grew to snake-oil absurdity: If you had insomnia it put you to sleep; if you were sleepy it would perk you up; if your stomach was upset it would give you an appetite; and if you were hungry it would satiate. It was also an antidote for melancholia and any number of other emotional and mental disorders. Eventually the bishops stopped opposing the plant's use, becoming resigned to its inevitability.

Before the fathers figured out how to cultivate yerba—it was with some difficulty and took several decades—the cost of gathering it in quantity in the wild was almost prohibitive. Most yerba forests were several hundred miles from the nearest significant settlement, Asunción. In a typical mid-seventeenth century yerba-gathering party of 200 Spaniards and Indians who were sent out to the distant harvest up to one-third would die from poisonous snakes, jaguars, and sickness. Hundreds of oxen and mules were needed to carry the yerba or drag carts loaded with it through overgrown forest paths. Flat-bottomed barges were used when navigable rivers were nearby—the exception. The end product was from a yerba tree cut down just for its leaves, decimating the forests' supply. It took twenty-five years for new trees to reach their mature, fifty-foot height. End-to-end, it was a terribly costly and inefficient process. Yerba leaves were ground to powder with pounding logs and sticks or under horses' hooves. The stems and fibers were ground up with the leaves and left in the end product, resulting in miserable taste and texture.

The mission response to the problems of harvesting wild yerba was to cultivate yerba on plantations. That took time and patience given the slow growth of the trees. But it paid off handsomely in the end as Guaraní yerba production reached its zenith in quality and quantity by the 1740s. Almost every mission had its own nearby yerba fields. High quality yerba processing was (and still is) time-consuming. First the stems and fibers were removed leaving only the tender, more succulent leaves. These were chopped to pieces rather than ground to powder thereby retaining more flavor. Sometimes the Jesuits spiked the yerba with bits of fruit to add interesting aroma and flavorful accents. The end result was a yerba product that brought twice the price of the Spanish wild version. As long as the former was available, the latter could not be sold at any price. It was a stunning revelation for merchants to learn that workers took more care in manufacturing a product if they themselves benefited from any improved quality. Here was yet another Jesuit offense against the settlers who went so far as to complain to Madrid of a Jesuit yerba monopoly and other anti-competitive Jesuit practices. This situation contributed later to the widely believed charge of Jesuit profiteering.

Jesuits normally accompanied yerba shipments some 500 miles down river from the missions to Buenos Aires. Their presence was needed to ensure fair dealing in the market, something the Indians were incapable of doing for themselves. The stakes were huge. Cunninghame-Graham estimates that the republic's annual cultivated yerba harvest was roughly two million pounds, fetching some $2.5 million. Putting this in context, since one dollar then has no meaning today, a diocesan priest then was paid about $600 per year, a Jesuit about half that. To adjust for inflation these numbers could be multiplied by perhaps thirty or forty, yielding total revenues in the range of

$75 million to $100 million in today's dollars. Like so many other things, the estimates of yerba production, while coming from otherwise credible sources, are all over the lot. Caraman believes the quantity to be about 300,000 pounds annually. It is likely that the differences can be explained by estimates being made for wildly differing years. Either way, it was a lot of money for the people and the times.

Besides agriculture, the missions' enormous cattle herds—at their peak exceeding two million animals—gave unsupervised employment to thousands of Indians. These cowboys or *vaqueros* earned popular admiration like today's Argentine *gauchos.* The cattle herds as well as hundreds of thousands of horses, mules, and oxen, and huge flocks of sheep were common property of the missions. Tens of thousands of cattle and mules were exported annually to Peru during the period of peak prosperity in the late-seventeenth and mid-eighteenth centuries.

Several other products, especially animal products, added greatly to the missions' income. Steer, oxen, and other hides were exported to Europe at the rate of 50,000 to100,000 annually at $3 each. Some 10,000 pounds of horsehair was also exported at an unreported price. One year 50,000 jaguar skins were shipped to Europe's high fashion market at a price that must have dwarfed that of the hides. Hundreds of barrels of honey, 100,000 pounds of tobacco, and hundreds of tons of fine Paraguayan forest hardwoods, when taken altogether, added several million dollars in a bumper year. This is in addition to the many agricultural and light manufacturing products exported to other regions of South America.

Profits were plowed back into the community. The size of a Guaraní family dwelling increased several-fold during the century ending in 1750, reaching a few hundred square feet. Increasingly, they became made of stone rather than adobe. Public works such as paved streets were underway everywhere. With more money, ceremonial costumes became more elaborate. But most of all, the profits were directed into new missions to be built to the north and west, coincident with the arrival of more Jesuits from German-speaking countries in Europe— among the best Jesuits anywhere.

Transporting the yerba and other exports to Buenos Aires was a major undertaking. The trip was plagued by river pirates and natural disasters en route. Once there, the fathers' negotiations in the marketplace apparently gave the impression that they were pocketing the profits, even though the overwhelming majority of trade was barter for items a *yerba for metal tools, oil, salt, linen.*

mission society would need, such as metal tools, oil, salt, linen, silk, gold thread, and sacramental wine. Later events proved that impression of Jesuit theft was wrong. When the Jesuits were expelled they had zero accumulated wealth.

3 Spanish taxes

The Spanish crown got a share of the colonial economy in the form of three chief types of taxes: sales taxes, customs duties, and miscellaneous fees; taxes from the Church accruing to a patron; and royalties, particularly from mining, where a fifth of the production of certain items, especially precious metals and gems, was apportioned to the government. A capitation tax was added, but for the mission Guaraní it was set at an artificially low rate, justified by their defending the province. They had become a brave, dependable, and extremely effective military force once they had been armed in 1640. The king's approval of arming them, not only with harquebuses and muskets but even with some cannons, instilled a special loyalty borne out of pride. As a result, the Portuguese paid an increasingly unacceptable price for their forays into Spanish lands and for their stealthy encroachment into Spanish defensive gaps. The low capitation tax rate did its job.

Adult Guaraní males, eighteen to forty-nine years old, paid taxes of one dollar annually, about one day's pay for a Jesuit. *Caciques* and certain other personages were exempt. Here too, taxable population estimates vary wildly, ranging from 19,000 to 50,000. With a total population in thirty missions, averaging 150,000, or 5,000 per mission, one might split the difference, yielding 35,000 taxpayers. One dollar each was an infinitesimal part of total mission income. In addition, each mission paid one hundred dollars to the crown, adding another $3,000 in total for the republic, hardly worth mentioning. If the Guaraní had paid taxes at the rate paid by Spaniards, they would have paid a high multiple of the Guaraní capitation tax. However, a direct comparison is not possible as the Spanish paid fees and a monopoly tax to the crown and, in wartime when extra revenues were needed, the Spanish paid variable and irregular taxes.

All of this economic vitality had the unintended effect of hitting the Spanish labor market hard. The missions removed untold thousands of Indians from exploitation by Spaniards who would have preferred to pay them slave wages or worse. Jesuit good deeds would not go unpunished.

The net economic effect of the missions was an industrious, productive, prosperous, and virtually self-sufficient society, the likes of which have not been seen again in rural areas of Latin America to this day.

Site Selection for New Missions

When the Jesuits planned a mission for a new area, a precondition was that there would be a large concentration of Indians receptive to proselytizing. A mission in a newly developed area typically comprised several thousand Indians. When the population grew beyond what the mission could support, the fathers were often forced to "hive" the excess population to a new nearby site—usually about five miles or so away. The exact location chosen would have to be promising for productive agriculture, yielding the best harvests for staples, fruit, and for fishing. A nearby river was a clear advantage, and there were plenty from which to choose. Inland water transportation allowed heavy loads, such as the yerba harvest, to be shipped on shallow-draft barges, barks, or brigantines. This was far superior to overland cartage on the area's few rough, rock-strewn roads. Homemade barges consisted of two large tree trunks lashed five to ten feet apart with the gap filled with cane to provide flooring, similar to a catamaran. Priests employed such barges to visit satellite ranches, villages, and chapels at least semi-annually.

Mission Building Construction

Individual missions generally evolved in stages, over many decades. When a site was first chosen and construction began, the buildings would be made largely of wood or of wattle and daub for the church and other large structures. (Wattle is a series of vertical rods or poles interlaced with twigs and vines to comprise a wall. The daub is a coating of soft adhesive plaster or, more often, a mixture of straw, mud and cow dung, often tinted.) Such churches had thatched roofs, simplifying their construction. Later in their development, the missions' architecture advanced and more durable building materials including adobe and eventually sandstone and volcanic or other rock provided a solid foundation. Sandstone, being soft, was particularly suitable for the Indians' beautiful, elaborate and intricately detailed sculptures which adorned the friezes at the tops of the columns and walls, both interior and exterior.

The first reference to the Spanish mission-style tile roof was in the 1630s, about the same time adobe walls were reported. Tile was a deterrent to occasional mission fires. The enormous weight of such roofs, especially by the mid-eighteenth century when a church roof could exceed 2,000 square yards in area and weigh 200 tons or more, required the use of massive fifteen square foot (cross section) stone and adobe support columns. These were placed in a row on each side of the church, well inside the perimeter walls, in order to minimize the thrust of the roof pushing the walls outward. There was over-engineered truss construction with strong beams anchored near the top of the pilasters (columns in the outside walls) supporting the roofs. Since few fathers had formal training in architecture, most of the design was by amateurs. Austrian Tyrol Father Anton (Antonio) Sepp, the builder of San Juan Bautista, said he traveled throughout Europe observing and learning from the design of great churches and cathedrals there. He was considered the most skilled of missionary architects. Among the professional contributors was José Brasanelli, a famed painter and sculptor who worked on four of the greatest missions. The renowned architect Juan Bautista Prímoli, who designed many historic buildings in Buenos Aires, was behind three mid-eighteenth century churches now in ruins: San Ignacio Miní, San Miguel, and Trinidad. The last of these was done in collaboration with another noted architect, José Grimau, a Jesuit brother.

The immense size, weight, and strength of the churches, especially their three-foot thick walls, made them impregnable to most destructive human efforts. In their heyday São Paulo slavers and Portuguese troops often tried to blow down mission church walls with their cannons. These were not even remotely up to the task. Not to be thwarted, they figured out the churches' Achilles heel: Blow off the tile roofs and let the tropical rains wash away the adobe portion of the buildings. It worked. Most often all that remained was the stone foundation, and even this was often scavenged by local people seeking stone to build their own homes. The few remaining hulking skeletal ruins show the effects.

With their indefatigable optimism right up until the end, the Jesuits had major church projects still underway in the 1760s. The most notable of these was Paraguay mission Jesús de Tavaranque, the ruins of which are worth visiting.

Indian communities vied with each other to make their churches the most profusely endowed with the best sculpture, tile mosaics, paintings, and gilding. The church of an eighteenth century mission was built to contain the entire population of the community—up to 8,000 Indians, though usually not much more than 5,000. This way no one would be excluded from participating in the elaborate weddings, baptisms, and other rituals that bound the community together. Such celebrations were filled with music, singing, and sometimes dancing by male children. Pomp and circumstance were exhilarating for the Indians. Ceremonies could last for hours with 5,000 bodies participating. There was a pressing need, therefore, for ventilation in the church. During festivals the church was adorned with flowers, sprinkled with orange-flower and rose water, augmented by incense. The air became so heavy that numerous spacious windows (usually just rectangular openings) were always part of the church walls. Of course, the windows were also needed for brightening the otherwise dark cavernous building.

The largest churches such as Trinidad, San Ignacio Miní, and São Miguel were paced off to be about a hundred yards long (including the sacristy) and thirty yards wide, approaching the footprint of an American cathedral today. The church towered over all the other buildings in the mission. By the eighteenth century, new mission churches exceeded thirty feet in height with a much higher, majestic façade and a stone or adobe bell tower on one corner of the back, often higher than fifty feet. An upper level choir loft in the rear was common.

This multi-stage approach of starting with simple buildings allowed for the rapid initiation of many missions in the first half of the seventeenth century. An example of the iterative process of multiple stage improvements is San Juan Bautista, first established in 1697 by Antonio Sepp. A year later it was still a temporary wooden structure, but gradually a more permanent church was built and completed in 1708. In 1714 work began on the permanent stone church. It took several additional years to complete. The bell tower was added in 1724.

The largest and most impressive churches, a few still standing as ruins and serving as tourist attractions, were built in the first half of the eighteenth century. The three most awesome of these are São Miguel in Brazil which was built between 1735 and 1744 or possibly as late as 1747. It was a stone church with three great naves. Such churches consumed 2000 man-years of Indian labor to complete, all of it done with exquisite craftsmanship and immense pride. Also inspiring is Argentina's San Ignacio Miní, a national historic monument. Trinidad in Paraguay is remote but also imposing.

The Jesuits took care to separate their living quarters from those of the Indians to avoid scandals that had hit other orders. Fathers never entered an Indian woman's room, nor would the female Indians be allowed to enter theirs. The Indians' earliest housing was in groups not exceeding ten contiguous units, with spacing between groups to contain fires. Each unit was a small room, often less than one hundred square feet for each family including parents and two or three children as well as a dog and a parrot. As missions blossomed in the late seventeenth century, a family's dwelling approached 400 square feet in large part due to increased wealth. The two fathers had rooms that were relatively spacious but spartan. All of the rooms had projecting roofs supported by wood columns, forming a continuous veranda that provided cover during rainy season downpours.

Cemeteries were adjacent to or near the church and had gardens with flowers and trees. Bodies were folded in the fetal position and allowed to dry to conserve burial space. *Caciques* and some other dignitaries might be accorded the singular honor of interment in subterranean vaults at the front of the church just below the altar.

Common buildings inside the perimeter walls included a spacious meeting room for the *cabildo*, a small library with seldom more than a few hundred books, workshops, and a huge common outhouse with separated pits connected to sluiceways leading down toward the river. There were also buildings for manufacturing and the trades, usually at one side of the mission's perimeter.

Outside of the mission walls was a hostel for visiting Spaniards, such as traders. This maintained the all-important literal wall between the exploiters and those who might otherwise be exploited which the Jesuits had always maintained was so necessary. Dominican friar, Bartolomé de las Casas, was the original developer of Indian segregation to protect them from colonists' aggression in mid-sixteenth century Guatemala. The rules allowed whites and blacks to stay in the missions for only a few hours at a time, at most a day. For merchants it could be for as long as three days, but at the hostel. The isolation of the Indians was also beneficial in protecting them to some extent from European-borne diseases. This separation would be used during the expulsion as even more "proof" that the Jesuits were clandestinely amassing huge fortunes at the expense of the Indians and the government.

No matter how well building foundations were planned, dilapidation was always a threat due to environmental hazards from the surrounding jungle. Ants tunneled under the main load-bearing walls, causing them to shift and buckle, and causing roofs to collapse. Other jungle creatures invading mission buildings included frogs and toads squirting their blinding urine, blood-sucking insects, scorpions, tarantulas, snakes, and other vermin.

farmed land

The farmed land was divided into a huge parcel common to the community, with smaller parcels allocated to, but not owned by, individual families. Unlike the experience of similar Western socially engineered farms, the Guaraní took more care of the common parcels than of their own individual pieces due to their sense that shared prosperity should take precedence over individual gain.

The Daily Regimen

The daily activities were initially insufferable for Indians raised in the wilds with unfettered liberty and few duties. They would flee back into the forest at the slightest provocation but would almost always return. Workplace entertainment made the drudgery of manual labor bearable, even enjoyable when it included music and singing.

A typical day began with the church bell pealing at about 4:00 a.m. calling the inhabitants from their animal-skin beds spread on the dirt floor or from their hammocks suspended in their dwellings. Each family's room included a central fireplace which burned continuously and some cookware. A bench or perhaps a few stools and a small chest comprised the furniture. No more storage was needed, because they had few possessions.

The first assembly, also announced by bells, came at 6:00 a.m. when Mass was celebrated. Breakfast followed. They ate with their hands directly from the pot or pan. Liquids like yerba maté were taken from gourds or home-made pottery. The *corregidor* and his assistants would then decide on the day's activities, followed by work for adults and school for the children. Reading and writing lessons were in Guaraní, but Spanish and even Latin also were taught. Since the Jesuits encouraged the boys to marry by sixteen and girls by fourteen to channel their teenage appetites, some school children were already married. The mission youngsters often maintained their pre-Columbian tradition under which the girl initiated the marriage proposal.

Lunch was at noon. In-home food service was provided for the sick and infirm. After extended rest, another two to three hours of work was done. This was followed by more late afternoon rest, leisure, recreation, sports, and games. The workday rarely exceeded six hours, six days a week. (Many laborers in Europe put in a work week almost double that.)

Supper was typically in the early evening, followed by early-to-bed. The high protein diet was rich in meat, especially after the arrival of great herds of mission steers. Domestic poultry, wild fowl, and much fish provided variety. Produce, especially plantains and cassava bread from both the communal and individual land parcels, added carbohydrates. In the early years and the rare hard times that occurred later, hunger was assuaged by roots, nuts, ants, and other less appetizing fare.

Labor and Slavery

To understand the use of labor in the Spanish colonies and the missions' impact on the labor supply, one must first consider the various forms of Indian serfdom that the settlers practiced. This serfdom, both controversial and often misunderstood, was intended to circumvent the many unambiguous prohibitions against enslaving the Indians—both Christian and unconverted—that had been decreed by the Spanish crowns. As early as 1499 under the direction of Columbus, the administrators in practice had imposed an *encomienda*-like system of serfdom on Caribbean Indians, provoking the natives' constant protector, Queen Isabella, to ask her famous question, "By what authority does the Admiral [Columbus] give my vassals away?"

Buffeted by passionate court advocates on all sides of the slavery issue, Ferdinand and Charles, his son and successor, agonized over the issue for decades. No other European colonizer, before or after the Spanish conquest of America, engaged in such a struggle for justice as did the Spanish crown. The Protestant Scottish historian William Robertson wrote, "Nothing similar [to this struggle] occurs in the history of human affairs." Further as to the sincerity of the crown, Hanke writes that we can "ponder the will of . . . Isabella whose last thought was for her cherished subjects beyond the seas." Cunninghame-Graham adds that under Philip II's law "offenses committed against the Indians should be punished with greater severity than those committed against Spaniards."

Dominican friar Antonio de Montesinos became the first to cry out for justice. In a 1511 sermon in Puerto Rico he admitted to being a "voice crying in the wilderness" against the spreading enslavement of the Indians, while arguing that they had "rational souls" just like Europe's Catholics. His message was not welcomed by the settlers.

In 1512 Ferdinand signed the Laws of Burgos (the city where the laws were written), which were precise and humane but unenforceable and largely ignored in the colonies by the adventurers, convicts, settlers, and corrupt administrators. In 1526 Charles ordered Cortés not to enslave the conquered tribes of Mexico "because God created the

Indians free." The order had little effect. That same year the king capitulated and legalized a compromise *encomienda* system that he believed was enforceable. It too was not.

The crown's prohibitions were augmented by even more ineffective papal Bulls beginning in 1537 that condemned slavery as a "grave crime." (It is worth noting that it took three centuries for the Anglo-Saxon nations to abolish slavery.)

The attitude of the Spaniards in the Caribbean might have been summarized best by Cortés when he refused a land grant, "I came to get gold, not to till the soil like a peasant." This attitude would dominate the invaders for 250 years, causing Spain to lose ready-made economic opportunities. Instead of enjoying a flourishing commerce, Spain earned little, even less than France gained trading with its island of Martinique alone. In its pursuit of conquest Spain neglected the biggest resource at its disposal—the Indians who could have been drawn into productive schemes instead of being oppressed and exploited. This was the struggle for justice into which the Jesuits of Paraguay were inserted a century later.

Notwithstanding the royal condemnations and prohibitions, some form of *de facto* slavery was inevitable given the time and distance from Madrid and the rich rewards for non-compliance with the law. There were three main types of enslavement, sometimes barely distinct from one another: First, the most well-known and widely used was the *encomienda* system, also called *servicio personal*, loosely modeled on fifteenth century feudalism in Spain. It required Indians in a given jurisdiction to provide mandatory day labor or tribute (in the form of goods such as food stuffs they had gathered or hunted, human labor on plantations and in mines, or military service). The *encomienda* was a grant made by a governor to a colonist, an *encomendero,* or a company of e*ncomenderos* who "held" the grant. The Spaniards who took possession of land were given ("commended") Indians—*encomiendas*—who lived nearby. The grant was for one to two years and not for life, although that's how it sometimes happened. The *encomenderos* were not to mistreat the Indians in any way but rather to protect them and educate them in Christianity. These constraints could not be enforced from Madrid. Appeals to the king, in person, by Dominican friar Bartolomé de Las Casas, "the famous Apostle to the Indians" and one of the most remarkable figures of sixteenth century America, were of little effect. *Las Leyes Nuevas* (The New Laws) of 1542, inspired by Las Casas, failed to suppress the *encomienda* system.

In practice, in some times and places, the *encomendero* had the right to possess the Indian for the Spaniard's lifetime and that of his first heir. In the viceroyalty of Peru it was extended to his grandson for a fee paid to the government. It should be noted, however, that *encomenderos* comprised only a small proportion of the white population.

The system was condemned graphically by Jesuit Francisco Angulo when he compared *encomenderos* to the dreaded Turks: "From birth to death fathers and sons, men and women labor . . . for the . . . enrichment of their masters [not] receiving a garment in return or even a handful of maize."

The second system was made up of *yanaconas* or *originarios* who were descendents of Indians captured in war. They were perpetual slaves, typically living in the house of an *encomendero* who was expected only to feed them and instruct them in Christianity. They could be bought and sold like chattel.

Third were the *mitayos*, Indians who had submitted to the Spaniards without fighting. Men between eighteen and fifty could be called to this *"mita"* service, as it was named. They worked for two months a year and were supposedly fully free for the remaining ten months.

Many *mitayos* worked in the dark, massive, stifling Potosí* silver mines in the cold thin air of the high *altiplano* of upper Peru, now Bolivia. Given the circumstances of the Indians—they hardly understood the Spanish language, they had no concept of human rights and laws, they had no practical route of appeal about Spaniard abuse of the

---

*Potosí is a city in what is now southwest Bolivia, near the headwaters of the Pilcomayo river, a tributary of the Paraguay river—an efficient route to Buenos Aires. It is near Sucre, the country's co-capital and seat of its supreme court. Potosí is on a mountain, 2000 feet above a plain that is at 13,000 feet. At its peak in the mid-seventeenth century it had over 150,000 inhabitants, comprised of 40,000 to 50,000 Spaniards, 10,000 Africans and mulattos and 100,000 Indians and mestizos. Given the harsh daily regimen, few of the hundreds of thousands who labored there over the years ever lived to see fifty, the age limit. At the time it was the largest city in the western hemisphere. The mountain it sat on was high grade silver ore. When large quantities of mercury, used to refine silver, were fortuitously discovered nearby, the sterling silver output of Potosí's mines exploded so that it dwarfed in value all of the gold taken from the Inca—seventy million pounds of silver (Kamen, p286) worth about fifteen billion dollars today. The silver shipments en route to Spain were a pirate's dream. In one raid in 1577, Francis Drake seized twenty-six tons of pure silver (silverinvestor.com). Early in the nineteenth century, when the silver ran out, its population imploded to less than 10,000. Today it is about 160,000.

---

encomendero system—who could say whether an Indian claim was valid. Had he been captured in war? Or worse, had his grandfather been captured in war? What if his other grandfather had been a *mitayo*?

How could an Indian know his rights? Only the settlers knew how to use and abuse these obscure local rules. The net of it all is that the Indians had no way to fight back, except through the Jesuits.

 These were the motivations for the Jesuits to isolate the mission Guaraní, both Christians and potential converts, from the Spaniards. It was complete isolation—geographic and social—no exceptions.

In a major milestone in the history of slavery, in 1610 King Philip III, under pressure from the Jesuits, decreed a royal commission to investigate enslavement in Paraguay. It was headed by Francisco de Alfaro, a member of the supreme court for the Río de La Plata province. Alfaro openly chose Jesuit Provincial Diego de Torres del Bollo as his right hand man for all to see; Alfaro was sending a message. Two years later the commission reported that every Indian without exception was a free man under the laws of Spain. He could give his labor, but only in return for a fair wage and decent treatment. The report also endorsed Torres' plan to immediately have the Jesuit missions answerable directly to the king himself. Spanish historian Jesuit Antonio Astraín wrote afterwards, "If Torres had done nothing else in his life he would have a just title to be regarded throughout the world as one of mankind's principal benefactors."

CHAPTER 9

Slave Hunters Invade the Guayrá, Desperate Guaraní Escape (1630)

The wealth, size, and serenity of the Guayrá missions made them an enticing target for slave-hunters seeking to re-supply the sugar and other plantation owners' increasing need for cheap labor—slave labor. Out-gunned, the mission Guaraní pursued their only option—a desperate gamble to escape.

Guayrá Missions Thrive

As the 1620s came to a close, the Jesuits were making headway in many directions. To the east of Asunción in the regions of Guayrá, Paraná, and Tape, the Jesuits had achieved success that exceeded their hopes when they first arrived in 1587. The missions there had thriving agriculture and sprawling satellite ranches (which the Spaniards called *estancias* or *vaquerias*) surrounding them. All together they covered much of today's southern Paraguay, northern Argentina, and Brazil's lush Rio Grande do Sul state, parts of its states of Santa Catarina and Parana just to the north—the lion's share of southern Brazil. Expansion was so rapid that some of the fathers imagined a Jesuit-led Guaraní society stretching from Río de La Plata at Buenos Aires to the upper reaches of the Amazon River basin 2,000 miles to the north. That would mean the great bulk of South America east of the Andes with millions of Guaraní souls to be saved together with those of pygmies and strapping goddess-warrior women rumored to live on the Amazon.

The only area where progress was slow-to-none was the wild Chaco region west and north of Asunción, the domain of the Guaycurú Indians who were among the most ferocious and intractable, as Cabeza de Vaca had learned eighty years earlier. Their conversion, first tried in the sixteenth century, would have to wait until the eighteenth century when more missionaries were available.

Meanwhile, the Jesuit generals in Rome, first Acquaviva and then Vitelleschi, gave moral support, men, and money, drawing on the order's burgeoning resources and influence in Europe. All felt upbeat.

Then suddenly and without warning, their exciting, satisfying, and harmonious world was torn apart when their Guayrá missions came under attack by hordes of heavily armed, rapacious Portuguese mercenaries from Brazil's southern Atlantic coast city of São Paulo. Since the mission Indians had virtually no firearms, the fight would be one-sided and defense would be bloody for them.

São Paulo Harbors Slave Hunters

São Paulo, situated on the Tropic of Capricorn, was 200 miles east of the nearest Guayrá mission, San Miguel. São Paulo barely made it onto the Portuguese side of the Treaty of Tordesillas line. The line and the 200 miles did little to discourage the Portuguese from invading the Guayrá to capture Guaraní slaves.

São Paulo was a rough and tumble city of 15,000, surrounded by mountains and thick forests. It was so lawless and violent that the Portuguese governors had washed their hands of ever controlling it. (Portugal and Spain were united under the Spanish crown from 1580 to 1640, but administration of São Paulo was run from Lisbon.) Starting peacefully enough in 1554, Jesuit Manoel de Nóbrega celebrated the first Mass there on January 25, the feast of St. Paul's conversion on the road to Damascus, thus the city's name. It became populated by the dregs of Europe, wild and stateless adventurers and cutthroat criminals from Portugal, Spain, France, England, Holland, and Italy. These men, along with disenfranchised and disaffected mixed-race whites, blacks, and Tupí Indians fed the slave needs of the area's Portuguese plantation lords. Contemporary reports say that two million Indian slaves were sold to them over the years. That was purposeful exaggeration by religious activists to alarm anti-slaveholder monarchs. Nevertheless, the number was no doubt far in excess of one hundred thousand. The Indians did not last long in captivity so a new supply was constantly being sought. The only land still rich with Indians and near enough was to the southwest—the Guayrá with its thirteen missions. It was also far more convenient and safer than transporting African slaves from Portuguese colonies in distant West Africa. The Dutch, with Recife as their stronghold on the central Brazilian coast, were positioned to interdict Portuguese ocean commerce as late as the 1650s. In fact, the capable Dutch navy had greatly reduced Portugal's importation of Africans, keeping them for their own Dutch sugar plantations. This made the Guaraní all the more valuable to São Paulo's planters, dramatically increasing the price they fetched.

As the slave hunters' fearsome reputation grew—they excelled at all the martial arts and were unencumbered by conscience—they earned the name "mamelucos" after the ninth century mamelukes, warrior-slaves of the emirs in Baghdad, Syria, and Egypt. In later centuries they rose from slaves to nobility there. The mamelukes were renowned for their courage, pride, cruelty, and invincibility until Napoleon slaughtered many thousands of them in a 1798 battle outside Cairo. A less ominous expletive used for the mamelucos of Brazil was *bandeirantes* from the bandeiras or flags they carried to uniquely identify each of their many groups and bands. The most common name, "Paulistas" or being from São Paulo, belies their war-like behavior and makes them sound less evil. Since these men earned the name mamelucos, we will refer to them that way. They were macho, energetic, and enterprising, and had no inhibitions about invading Spanish lands, while the Spaniards were complacent and phlegmatic. The deluge of gold and silver from Peru and Mexico contributed to the Spanish indifference toward their poor cousins in Paraguay. Thus, a huge land west of the Tordesillas line was becoming Portuguese by "right" of possession, land that would have radically changed the map of South America had the Spanish asserted their interests. And the window of opportunity for Spain was still open since it would be another decade before Portugal would break away from the Spanish crown.

The mamelucos first appeared on the Guayrá mission scene in 1611, coming on and off the stage for eighteen years with relatively little harm done. During those years these ruffians often pursued wealth in less evil ways than slave hunting. Traces of gold and diamonds were discovered earlier in what are now the Brazilian states of Mato Grosso, some 500 miles west, and Minas Gerais, a hundred miles north of São Paulo. It was not until 1699 that a gold stampede resulted from the discovery of large quantities of the metal and in 1730 considerable quantities of gems. Yet the *bandeirantes*, as the mamelucos were called in those states, captured tens of thousands of Guaraní to work the mines and plantations.

Mamelucos Invade the Guayrá 1629

Then in 1629, with the price of slaves surging as the Brazilian Indians suffered a peaking mortality from disease and maltreatment, the mamelucos attacked the Guayrá missions in force. Several hundred heavily armed mamelucos had with them 2000 Tupí Indian allies—the fiercest of warriors, feared especially for their poison arrows. The San

Antonio and San Miguel missions in eastern Guayrá were easily overrun, and then Jesús María, seventy-five miles to the west, was captured after a spirited defense. All three were torched and totally destroyed. Fifty miles south of San Antonio, Concepción, having been alerted, also put up a determined defense under Father Diego de Salazar. The mamelucos, unable to break through the walls, began a lengthy siege. With the defenders' food running out, their fare became dogs, snakes, and vermin. The siege was lifted by a relief column of other mission Indians led by Father José Cataldino. At Jesús María, Father Simón Maceta had gone out with several *caciques* and the mission's council bearing peace wands—their equivalent of white flags—to meet the mamelucos. The latter set upon them anyway and bound all but Maceta who, thinking he might move them by appealing to their assumed Catholicism, put on his surplice and stole and went into the church as a show of Christian piety. The attackers, unimpressed, looted all things of value and enraged at not finding any of the alleged hidden Jesuit riches, smashed everything else to pieces.

Maceta's entreaties were not totally wasted. He managed the release of a dozen or so Indians including the grand *cacique* Guiravera, a recent convert, together with his wife and six others. Guiravera had once told his concubines, pre-conversion, that he would "titillate their palates with a roast Jesuit." Some fifteen thousand captives, fettered or with hands bound, started the grueling four hundred mile trek to São Paulo. Then the cruelest thing happened along the way: Many who were deemed too old or feeble to continue, were tied together in threes and fours and flung into a huge fire, writhing and screaming until they burned to death.

Maceta and fellow Jesuit, the Dutchman Joost van Suerck from San Miguel, joined what was turning into a death march. The route was littered with thousands of bodies of the dead and dying, some from sickness, some from malnourishment-caused exhaustion and disease, and some from outright starvation. Jaguars and vultures had a feast. One can only imagine a picture of the strong in a chain gang, many with infants, children separated from parents, men struggling to support failing wives, elderly mothers and fathers and the increasingly infirm, all propelled along by the merciless scourge. At one point van Suerck tried to move the chain gang leaders to compassion by chaining himself to an Indian whose partner had died along the way. The priest was then roughed up and driven away.

When the shrunken column arrived in São Paulo, the survivors were divided among the mamalucos and quickly sold to nearby Portuguese planters. There was no concern for keeping families together. They were split up as often as not.

The mamelucos' invasion and return had taken nine months and netted 1,500 Guaraní slaves. Several times that number had started the trip from the Guayrá.

It might have been about this time that Superior Ruíz de Montoya told a story: A Jesuit put his arms around a Guaraní to protect him, but he was instantly covered with the man's blood as a mameluco plunged a lance into the Guaraní. The Jesuit condemned the attacker who then reposted with a version of Jansenist dogma, "I shall be saved . . . for to be saved a man has only to believe." While many were hammering the Jesuits in Europe with this peculiar theology, one would not have expected to find it so neatly presented in such stark terms in the wilds of a South American jungle 6000 miles away. Groh suggests that Ruíz's reminiscence of the event was colored by an anti-Lutheran bias since Lutheran dogma places heavier weight on salvation through faith. In a phone call to Reverend Groh he assured me that Lutheran doctrine does not give a blank check to such a killer. He said some theologians use the term "cheap grace" to characterize the mistaken view that a penitent need not be worthy of God's grace and the forgiveness that accompanies it. Such cheap grace is not Lutheran teaching. This dogma, based on St. Paul's epistles and St. Augustine's writings, is basic to a number of Christian sects (Chapter 2).

The modi operandi of the mamelucos, as described by Cunninghame-Graham, were as follows. First, they attacked the missions on Sunday when the sheep were gathered at Mass, murdered or incapacitated the priest, and carried off the congregation. Second, they disguised themselves as Jesuits, thereby calming the congregants, then their henchmen in the woods rushed in to overwhelm the actual Jesuits and congregation. This latter approach, when reenacted as theatre in São Paulo, was the source of much amusement—in Montoya's mind even more damnable than the actual crime.

The appeals for justice made by Maceta and van Suerck were referred to the Portuguese central criminal courts in Rio de Janeiro, 200 miles to the north. Getting no help there, they went back to Santos, just outside São Paulo, to appeal to the governor of the colony who was located there. There is disagreement over the facts here: Caraman tells the story as above, but O'Neill writes that they went to see the governor general in Salvador (Bahia) 700 miles north of Rio where they were kept cooling their heels for four months before he deigned to see them. This was the period when Portugal and Spain were still united under Philip IV in Madrid and were strongly antislavery. His predecessor Philip III had issued a royal decree authorizing the Jesuits to convert the Indians of the Guayrá in the first place. The governor's procrastination would become understandable. There seems to be agreement that he finally gave them a mandate to take back to São Paulo requiring the Portuguese authorities there to free the Jesuits' captured slaves.

The governor's mandate was poorly received in São Paulo. Although the fathers had gotten some support from an honorable, governor-appointed commissioner, a well-positioned lawyer named Barrios and a few other Portuguese personages, the fathers were menaced by the townspeople and imprisoned. A shot was fired at the commissioner, scaring him and Barrios enough to flee the scene. The effort to free the Guaraní collapsed. Realistically there was no way to enforce the mandate with such strong opposition from the planters, from numerous citizens beholden to them, and from the hundreds of mamelucos still hungry for more human plunder.

Rumors circulated that a new mameluco expedition was planned to finish off the Guayrá missions. This caused the fathers to make a hasty retreat from São Paulo, speeding down the Aniembi river to the Paraná and home to their ruined settlements. (São Paulo is on a high ridge with nearby rivers flowing westward, away from the Atlantic coast and then south to Río de La Plata and Buenos Aires.) To their gut-wrenching grief they found that some Portuguese Jesuits had sanctioned a mameluco expedition, leading Maceta to write:

> What can be expected from a people among whom are found [our own] priests that encourage and direct such criminal raids? Not among Turks or Moors are done such things as are done or approved in Brazil.

The effort to free the Indians had taken the three Jesuits a whole year, and they had nothing to show for it.

Indians Suspect Jesuit Betrayal

Meanwhile back in Paraguay the Guaraní in the remaining missions became suspicious that the Jesuits might be co-conspirators with the mamelucos—just what the few remaining non-Christian sorcerers wanted. Some Jesuits were menaced and threatened with death. These sorcerers built two large temples filled with primitive idolatry to which the Indians now flocked on Sundays and Catholic feast days for witch-craft rituals. One involved a sorcerer's mummy in a hammock with fresh flowers. Large baskets hung on the walls for offerings; native perfumes were sprinkled around; a perpetual fire burned, honoring Satan. The mummified sorcerer would rise from the dead to issue oracles heard only by the officiating sorcerer who then consumed part of the offerings and distributed the rest to the congregation. Then the sorcerer, with his caricature of the Catholic Mass, took the pulpit to preach that the Jesuits were in league with the slavers, that their hands were the source of smallpox and measles epidemics, and that the salt placed on the tongue in Baptism was poisonous gunpowder. On and on it went. Unless the Indians left the missions, the mamelucos would seize them and burn down all their mission buildings, and the rivers would flood and drown everyone. Many Indians bought into these rantings and relapsed into old ways, wanting nothing more to do with the Jesuits. For a time they were intractable and even threatening.

Ruíz de Montoya writes that he then took over the chaotic scene. He burned the sorcerers' temples and, with the grateful grand *cacique* Guiravera, whom Maceta had recently rescued from the mameluco death march, reinvigorated those Indians who were still loyal. Immediately he started building a new Jesús María some distance to the west and led a celebration of burning and trampling the relic-bones used by the sorcerers. One of the sorcerers, hideously deformed, who had been an object of worship, was handed over by the Jesuits to the mission boys to be ridiculed. His followers, seeing his utter despair and humili-ation, were cured of their awe and reverence for him. He requested instruction in Catholicism, converted, and thereafter enjoyed all the benefits that came with his acceptance into the mission.

Sure enough, within weeks, the earlier rumors of another mameluco invasion proved true, but this time it turned out to be with an even greater force of 900 mamelucos, accompanied as before by 2000 Tupís led by Manoel Preto, a respected plantation owner.

The first mission to fall and be destroyed was San Pablo, seventy-five miles west of the cluster destroyed in the prior raids. Then Encarnación, fifty miles to the southeast, was abandoned in favor of San Javier, forty miles east of San Pablo. San Javier became the Jesuits' easternmost outpost in the Guayrá.

If the mamelucos were not enough, the Spanish settlers of the prosperous town of Villarica joined in a pincer movement. They waylaid the Guaraní fugitives and sold them to Spanish planters who were clandestinely using slaves in Paraguay, or they kept them for themselves.

Spanish Governor Refuses Help

At Ruíz de Montoya's direction, Father Francisco Díaz Taño appealed for relief from other local Spanish authorities but to no avail since the Jesuits had become even more hated by the Spanish settlers for their recent pro-Indian efforts. Next, Taño went to Asunción to approach Governor Luís de Céspedes Jeria. Upon his appointment two years earlier in 1628, Céspedes had sailed to São Paulo and then crossed overland to Asunción. This had been in direct violation of his instructions to go to Asunción via Buenos Aires. While in São Paulo he married the daughter of a high Portuguese official and, according to the Jesuits, acquired a large sugar plantation. He quickly became an apologist for the Portuguese and a Jesuit adversary. He made no bones about it. Taño made it clear to Céspedes that without his military help the remaining missions in the Guayrá were facing total ruin. In response Céspedes said, "Leave these poor Portuguese to help themselves as best they can in their poverty." When Taño persisted Céspedes replied, "May the devil take all the Indians! Write that to your missioners!" This was a far cry from the intentions of the king, neutralized by being 6,000 miles and a year away. But justice was around the corner.

In 1631 Jesuit accusations against Céspedes reached the *audencia* in Charcas, the district which included the province of Paraguay. He was charged with having received a share of the slaves for his Brazilian plantation. In 1636 he was tried and found guilty. The punishment was a fine and suspension from governmental authority, consistent with the mild treatment of such officials at the time.

Meanwhile one mission after another was overrun. In the worst case, San Javier fell with fourteen of its fifteen hundred families enslaved. How even a hundred escaped is unknown. The situation was desperate, and the Jesuits had nowhere to turn for help. It was now 1631, and tens of thousands of mission Indians had been captured over the last three years.

Jesuit Provincial Vásquez Trujillo convoked his men in the Guayrá to the new Jesús María mission to strategize. The meeting turned into a heated debate. The choice was simple: Stay and fight, or flee west hundreds of miles across the Paraná to a presumably safer region. There was general agreement that the military option was a mismatch. All the mamelucos were well armed with small-bore, long-barrel harquebuses and plenty of ammunition. They wore coats densely stuffed with cotton to resist Guaraní arrows. The Guaraní had no guns to speak of, the Spaniards having been sure to keep them from becoming an offensive force; Céspedes had prohibited the sale or gifts of firearms to priests or Indians. Was that to aid the mamelucos? The simple choice turned out to be no choice at all.

Jesuits Vote to Flee the Guayrá, Great Exodus Down the Paraná

Nevertheless, the fathers put it to a democratic vote. With Trujillo in the majority, the vote was to abandon the Guayrá, its two beautiful and stately missions still standing—San Ignacio Guazú and Loreto, the first and now the last—and to cast aside over a decade of a massive commitment by over 120 Jesuits struggling in the region. However, abandonment did not mean deserting the Indians.

Most of the Indians accepted the fathers' decision to flee, understanding its cruel necessity. Some disagreed and returned to their old ways in the jungle. Some decided to stay behind and met the inevitable fate.

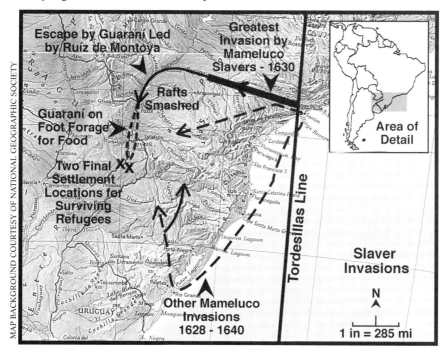

Ruíz de Montoya had the Indians who agreed to flee build a motley fleet of 700 long rafts made from 50-foot canes, thicker than a man's leg, that grew in profusion in the nearby forest. Hundreds of canoes were added. All together they would carry some 12,000 Indians on a phantasmagoric journey. It would be 400 to 500 miles and take many weeks sailing down the wildest part of the Paraná from just below Loreto on the Paranapanema. The Spanish settlers of Villarica, just months before having sold many Guaraní into the hands of Spanish planters, now had the astonishing gall to come to protest the evacuation. They had the prescience to fear the mamelucos would sack their town. They were not welcomed by Ruíz.

The Indians abandoned their huge herds of cattle and extensive plantings at San Ignacio and Loreto and trooped down to the riverbank, men and women, young and old, mothers nursing infants and the feeble. None would be left behind for expediency. They hauled their meager possessions onto the rafts: bows and arrows, tools, sacks of food, maize and mandioc flour, chickens and ducks, statues and sacred vessels—the remnants of the original thirteen missions. Other vestiges to be loaded were the disinterred remains of their fellow priests who died in the Guayrá, so that as Ruíz said, "They who shared our labors and life . . . might . . . not be left by us abandoned in these deserts."

The rag-tag flotilla launched only days ahead of the attacking mamelucos. Upon arrival, the frustrated invaders torched San Ignacio and Loreto.

The pitiful refugees sailed down the Paraná for some 100 miles to a broad lake above the Guayrá Falls. The river in this wintry, dry season—June, July, and August—was relatively smooth. Spirits were kept up with reassuring hymns that had become so familiar through repetition back in their churches. Other times the silence of the river was broken by a cacophony of chilling animal cries and crashes, monkeys nattering, hawks and eagles shrieking from high above, and the chatter of parrots, parakeets, and macaws, the calls of honey-suckers, toucans, herons, hummingbirds, kingfishers, wrens, and drumming woodpeckers, and others—a veritable symphony of jungle tree-dwellers.

The Guayrá Lake was two to three miles wide, depending on the season. It exited into the Guayrá Falls, eighteen discrete cataracts, the greatest of them with a 130-foot drop, pouring through a boulder-strewn channel, as narrow as 200 feet and as wide as 1,250 feet. The first serious cataract they encountered dropped fifty-five feet at an angle of fifty degrees. It created a roar heard ten miles away and a mist rising so high it could be seen from almost as far. The cloud of vapor creates a "perpetual shower with such drenching force . . . that they who visit the place strip themselves naked to approach it." This channel was followed by a succession of falls, rapids, and whirlpools for another 100 miles. Then the Paraná flowed over the immense Iguazú cataracts, the world's largest waterfall when measured by volume, a third higher than the height of America's Niagara Falls. It was centered by a monstrous U-shaped precipice, splendidly named *La Garganta del Diablo* (The Throat of the Devil). But the rafts never got past even the first serious Guayrá cataract. To portage these rafts through the dense riverbank jungle was not practical. They were much too heavy. Ruíz took a chance sending the rafts down the cataract empty, but in minutes they were all smashed to bits on the rocks at the bottom.

Now the journey became more painful than before. The descent along the banks of the Paraná continued for another 200 miles. The first part was through a truly primeval forest with its frequent rapids and dense mists. Under this strain, more and more of these wretched refugees fell by the wayside. The helplessness of the situation attracted more human vultures—this time Spaniards in their path, hoping to carry them off as captives. Ruíz got wind of this treachery, ran ahead and confronted them in a wooden fortress they had built to corral the Indians. What happened next is subject to disagreement among historians: Either he frightened the Spanish into thinking that the Indians were ready and able to defeat them or he diverted his people onto a forest track that circled around the ambush. Possibly he did both, although the latter would not seem to jibe with the fact that so much noise would have accompanied the roundabout as to prevent its being done in secrecy.

A relief party coming upstream with provisions from Paraná missions was largely destroyed by the river which was now raging in the rainy season. With food running out, Ruíz had to divide his column into four parts so they could forage better as they progressed. Two of the columns found temporary refuge at two small mission settlements on rivers entering the Paraná: Natividad on the Acaray and Santa María la Mayor on the Iguazú. One column led by Maceta lived three months on wild fruit and berries. Another column rested while its leader Father Pedro de Espinoza, with several Indians, went to collect sheep from the nearby settlement of Santa Fe for his starving followers. As he returned with a flock, he and his men were waylaid and murdered by a band of

Guapalaches, the fiercest of the Guaraníes' enemies. They cut up his body and left it out for beasts to eat.

Another leader, Father Cristóbal de Mendoza, with two Indian escorts also fell into a Guapalache ambush. He would have escaped had his horse not sunk in a swampy stream. He defended himself as best he could but was quickly overcome, stretched out on the ground and left for dead. During the night he came to and dragged himself away. In the morning the Indians followed his trail, recaptured him, taunted him for following some god that did not come to his aid or was at best a powerless god, tortured him, murdered him, and tore out his heart. His last words were to recommend his soul to God, according to Indian witnesses. Then the Guapalaches made a hearty meal out of his two Guaraní escorts. In telling this story Cunninghame-Graham mused whether Christians of his time—the end of the nineteenth century—knew what they owed to men like Mendoza. He wondered

> . . . if the Christians of today, their creed so firmly fixed by the martyrdoms of simple folk, who held their faith without perhaps much reasoning on it, know what they owe to men like Father Christopher Mendoza, slain by the Indians in the Paraguayan woods. Your ancient martyr, fallen out of fashion and forgotten by the Christians of today, should have his homage done to him.

At this same time, 300 recently baptized Guaraní were slaughtered and devoured by another group of Guapalaches back at mission Jesús María.

Eventually, the remnants of all four columns reunited at Natividad and Santa María la Mayor. From there they were dispersed among the other missions on the Paraguay and Uruguay rivers and two new missions that Ruíz started in 1632, San Ignacio Miní and Loreto. He named them for those sacked by the mamelucos at the beginning of the exodus. (A team of Italian volunteers "reclaimed" the successor to Loreto from the jungle, meaning it is purposefully left in the badly ruined condition in which it was found but with all of the jungle's overgrowth cleared away. Both sites are in far northern Argentina having been relocated from the original 1632 sites.)

As Ruíz and his Indians were about to settle in, they were hit with another round of smallpox, sweeping them away by the hundreds. Jaguars and pumas, having gorged themselves on the dead and having acquired a taste for human flesh, continually terrorized the living. The tribulations would continue for years.

Some Sense of Normalcy Returns

Gradually, some sense of normalcy returned to the lives of the refugees, not only through the generosity of nearby missions which contributed thousands of cattle and oxen, but also through Ruíz spending all of what the crown had allotted for priests' salaries. The two new missions grew toward self-sufficiency in 1633, a remarkable recovery testifying to the resilience of the fathers and the Guaraní. Both had learned to carry on despite being constantly surrounded by violence and death.

Looking back over the preceding four years, the surviving Guaraní, while thankful to be alive and not enslaved, must have shed the briny tears of endless sorrow when remembering lost family and friends. Early estimates of Christianized Indians in the Guayrá before the mamelucos invaded ranged from 50,000 to 100,000. The smaller number seems more plausible, given that there were only thirteen missions. In any event, at the end of it all, not quite 4,000 had survived. The greatest numbers lost, perhaps half, had become mameluco captives. Others melted back into the forests. Disease, fatigue, malnourishment, rafting accidents and predators took the rest. The numbers are almost beyond comprehension. If it had happened in Europe it would have been considered a monumental massacre. Instead it happened to little, swarthy, faceless, nameless people in the care of troublesome priests in a dark and mysterious, faraway land. Thus it is barely a footnote in history, known to few.

These horrific events had a postscript that should appeal to any *schadenfreude* or any desire for retribution lurking within us. The mamelucos, frustrated by barely missing the booty due to the great escape, turned their attention to the Spanish residents of Villarica and of Ciudad Real, 100 miles to its west. Those people had connived and profited at the Indians' distress. Their fears that the mamelucos would plunder their communities were realized and worse: Both Spanish towns were totally destroyed. The inhabitants had to flee to Paraguay. The Guayrá would go the way of the Mato Grosso, Paraná, Rio Grande do Sul, and Santa Catarina states, all hugely valuable but lost to Spain when Portugal broke away from it in 1640.

Spaniards Discover Amazon Women

The earlier-mentioned musing of some Jesuits about extending their work all the way to the Amazon River included an extravagant story of an isolated tribe of spectacular, dominant women living in almost constant warfare, who took time out only to order men in nearby tribes to get them pregnant. The truth of the matter is less fantastic but still is one of the most interesting true stories of mid-sixteenth century interior Brazil. It left a mark on history. The story that follows involves a Spaniard who, while exploring an immense river which was by far the most voluminous and almost equal to the Nile as the longest on earth, came upon a race of fierce female Indian warriors. Today we call that river, the "Amazon," in their memory. The story goes on to show just how fragile life was and how fleeting fame and fortune were in those times, even for the rich and powerful.

In February 1541 a heavily armed force of 300 eager Spaniards and several thousand Indian servants, banners flying, set out from Quito, Ecuador, formerly an Inca stronghold, heading eastward in search of two fabled Indian cities. According to two prominent and very aged chiefs, one was La Canela (Spanish for cinnamon), supposed to possess huge stocks of that prized spice, and the other was El Dorado, their term for a golden city. Soon this force was nearly doubled by more than 250 reinforcements. They took thousands of hogs for food and hundreds of attack dogs for protection. Huge quantities of grain, salt, and wine were borne by mules and llamas. They had some 500 horses.

En route, the Spaniards experienced every evil nature could muster: a powerful earthquake, violent, torrential thunderstorms and rains for weeks without let-up, extreme cold in the high altitudes of snow-capped mountains (they had not progressed fifteen miles before some 100 Indians died in the cold) and intense heat and humidity in the jungle valleys. The terrain comprising the converging of Ecuador, Peru, Colombia, and Brazil was the worst in all the Americas for the European: Hundreds of miles of tangled masses of dense underbrush created a virtually impenetrable wall, and the forest canopy let little light down to its floor. Often one could not see twenty feet ahead. Slippery rocks along streams led to precipitous cliffs; deep swamps pockmarked the lowlands. Deadly insects, fire ants, poisonous spiders, scorpions, snakes, and blood-sucking bats were as ubiquitous as man-eating jaguars and lurking alligators. Packs of wild, pig-like peccaries could turn on an isolated man, tear him apart, and consume him in minutes. Howler monkeys added bloodcurdling sound effects. Fierce cannibalistic tribes could be encountered at any time to contest their way. Some days, hacking through the vines and brush with axes and machetes, they would make headway of less than a mile. Even today, it is the most remote, wild, and dangerous place on the planet. The lands the Jesuit missionaries traversed were often horrendous, but never quite like this.

The Spaniards were led by the treacherous Gonzalo Pizarro, half brother of Francisco the conquistador of the Inca. Along the way Pizarro tortured many Indians whom he encountered and believed were being uncooperative when they denied knowledge of such cities. Some were burned alive. Others were fed to his attack dogs. Indians further downstream got the message and, fearing to disappoint, deluded the Spaniards into continuing their search.

At a major river junction late in 1541, Pizarro split his forces, sending one large force under his cousin, Francisco de Orellana. He was also from Trujillo in western Spain, the one-eyed captain and lieutenant governor of two Peruvian cities. They traveled down a stream in the area where Ecuador borders on Brazil. They were to search for food and return. Orellana and his men, some sixty of them, were accompanied by a Dominican, Fray Gaspar de Carvajal, who tended to their spiritual needs including saying Mass for the soldiers and the Indians as they prepared to depart and again en route. He continued on to the end of the journey and became its main chronicler, later on.

By the end of 1541, nearly defeated by the watery terrain which was worsened by the rainy season—the rain was incessant—and virtually starving, Orellana built the San Pedro, a flat-bottomed bark, a two-masted sailboat. It was twenty-six feet long with an eight foot beam and a two foot draft, designed to ease and speed their trek. After weeks of sailing with the currents and under frequent harassment by Indians with poison-tipped arrows, their prospects for making it back to Pizarro's camp became increasingly dim. Rarely, Indians offered food. More often the Spaniards seized it from villages along the river banks.

On March 1, 1542, Orellana concluded that he had only two options: continuing and eventually facing a court martial or turning back and facing almost certain death along the way. At this point Orellana formally relinquished his command, thereby avoiding responsibility for the obvious next step. It was a clever move, as he must have known that his troops would have none of it. He was popular, and they had no other potential leader. Swearing on a Mass-book before two friars and a scrivener, they unanimously requested that he resume command and signed a written petition that he do so. He agreed, and they sailed on. Some do not buy into his maneuver, arguing that he simply betrayed Pizarro.

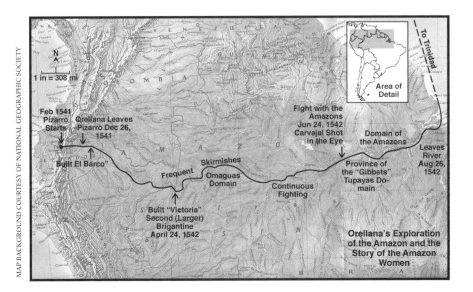

Feb 1541
Pizarro Orellana Leaves
Starts Pizarro Dec 26,
1541

Fight with the
Amazons
Jun 24, 1542
Carvajal Shot Domain of
in the Eye the Amazons

Leaves
River
Aug 26,
1542

"Built El Barco"

Skirmishes
Frequent Omaguas
Domain

Province of
the "Gibbets"
Tupayas Do-
main

Continuous
Fighting

Built "Victoria"
Second (Larger)
Brigantine
April 24, 1542

Orellana's Exploration
of the Amazon and the
Story of the Amazon
Women

Area of
Detail

To Trinidad

1 in = 308 mi

At about this time, Orellana built a second larger bark, the Victoria, and sharply increased his headway. A few friendly Indians greeting the barks along their route told him of a rich land downstream inhabited by Amazons. (This name might have been a romanticized corruption of the Indian name for an upstream tribe called the Omaguas.) Continuing on and now under almost constant attack by Indians, he passed riverbanks lined with gibbets displaying human heads like trophies. In June they came to a large, well-ordered Indian village. Orellana's peace overtures rejected, a fierce fight ensued. Ten or twelve tall women fought in front of all the Indian men. The women fought courageously. It was said that their men would not dare flee, or the women would kill them with clubs right in front of the enemy. These women were very white and tall, and they had long braided hair. They were "very robust and go about naked but with their privy parts covered." The Spaniards shot and killed at least seven or eight of them, and the rest withdrew with their men. This number of ten or twelve was reported in the news of the times as a large army of strapping women. Fray Carvajal had an eye taken out by an arrow, the only Spanish loss in the encounter.

That Indian women there took up arms to fight is no novelty. It was widely accepted that among the Indians the Spaniards fought along the river, they had seen a "number of women marching in front of their fighting squadrons." An Indian captive related that "by use of force they brought Indian men to their own country, particularly those belonging to a great overlord who was called the White King [he was fair], for the purpose of taking pleasure with them in [satisfying] their carnal desires in the multiplying of their race." The infant males were killed and sent back to their fathers while the women raised the girls with great solemnity, instructing them in the arts of war. Carvajal solemnly warned those machos among the Spaniards who fancied themselves as satisfying the conjugal needs of these voluptuous women, "Anyone who should take it into his head [to suit them] was destined to go a boy and return an old man."

The Tapuyas might have been the tribe; they were known for the women fighting alongside the men. Orellana was told by a captive that this entire region was ruled by such women and that they possessed much gold and silver. However, no more of them were seen, and no precious metal was found during the entire voyage.

Nevertheless, thanks to the chronicles of Fray Carvajal and the testimony of Orellana's men when they returned to Spain, the account became the stuff of legend, alluding to ancient Greek mythology. Thus, mythology might have been the second source of their name when these women were immortalized, many decades later, and their great river was renamed from the (Rio) Orellana to Rio Amazonas (River of the Amazons).

While much skepticism surrounds Carvajal's chronicle especially because of the Amazons story, Heaton augmented it with the testimony of fellow travelers. Mann writes, "As anthropologists have learned more about the vagaries of fieldwork, they have treated Carvajal more kindly." He quotes Tulane anthropologist, William Balée, "He may not have been making up the Amazons out of whole cloth." The twentieth-century discovery of Chichén Itzá and the sophisticated Mayan societies camouflaged in a Meso-American jungle gives pause to those who are quick to dismiss eyewitness reports of sixteenth century adventurers.

Orellana's journey was relatively uneventful thereafter, although starvation remained a constant companion. He had covered about 4,000 miles down this incomparable river, taking almost a year. In August 1542, after arriving at its 200 mile wide mouth, he passed the last of its superlatives—the island of Majaró, the size of Switzerland, sitting like a stopper in the neck of a bottle. He then turned north, hugging the coast headed for the Spanish settlements at Trinidad. There he re-outfitted and sailed for Spain to report personally to King Charles I. Penitently offering convincing reasons for his betrayal of

Gonzalo Pizarro, he was pardoned by the king and was granted a huge swath of the lands he explored. In 1544, he returned with a strong military force to what was now *his* great river. He navigated upstream but had not gone far when he was struck down, probably with malaria, and died. Orellana was held in high esteem thereafter and was honored for not behaving cruelly towards the Indians as had the Pizarros and so many others of the time.

As for Gonzalo Pizarro, he and the tattered remnants from his decimated band managed to stagger back over the Andes, reaching Spanish settlements in June 1542. Pizarro never had a chance to exact revenge on Orellana. Being the reckless miscreant that he was, in 1544 he invaded Peru, starting a civil war there. He was defeated and executed for treason in 1548.

Adding to the fleeting pleasures and treasures of the time, right after Orellana's death a Portuguese by the name of Luiz de Mello da Sylva sought a grant from the king of Portugal for a settlement on the lower Amazon. The king agreed and provided Mello da Sylva with five ships. After four of them were wrecked on shoals off the Brazilian coast, he returned to Lisbon, broke. He went on to Portuguese India, became wealthy there and set sail again for his Amazon grant. His ship, the San Francisco, was seen departing Indian waters and was never heard from again. *Sic transit. . . .*

CHAPTER 10

Guaraní and Jesuits Fight Back, Savage Battle at Mbororé

For more than a decade, the mamelucos had held the field, virtually unchallenged, while enslaving tens of thousands of Guaraní and killing thousands more. Finally Spain awakened to the simple fact that arming its Indian vassals was in its own strategic interest. Soon the tables would be turned.

Slavers Attack the Tape

In 1632 the Guaraní of the Guayrá were relatively secure in their new lands several hundred miles southwest of their starting point. They were in the heart of the Paraná mission country which was safe for now. The same cannot be said for the mission Indians of the Tape, which was south of the Guayrá in the center of today's Rio Grande do Sul. In late 1636, a band of 1600 mamelucos attacked mission Jesús María in the Tape and other missions nearby. While the mission Indians were learning how to fight back, their lack of firearms meant that even if they drove off the attackers they were doomed to suffer unacceptably heavy losses. Besides such losses in combat, 1637 had been a disaster for the mission population of the Tape and for the Guayrá remnants. The mamelucos brought 25,000 Indian captives back to São Paulo when they returned in 1638. In a new twist, many of these had been captured by non-Christian, non-Guaraní Indians living along the rivers of the Tape, who sold their captives to slave traders sailing along the coast in small ships.

For the first time, Madrid was beginning to understand the strategic issue—the mamelucos and their Portuguese sponsors had to be prevented from encircling the entire Spanish mission region including Asunción, the capital of Paraguay. By pushing due west from the Guayrá in the north, and concurrently making a big looping maneuver around the Tape in the south then heading northwest, a pincer could cut off Asunción from its river route to Buenos Aires. After that, Asunción and most of the Paraná missions could be easily picked off by the Portuguese. The Portuguese would have an open road, northwest to the *altiplano* of Bolivia, which could lead to its capture. That would leave the Portuguese with an unobstructed route to the mountain of silver at Potosí and on to the treasures of Peru.

One might ask, why did it matter? Portugal had been under the Spanish monarchy since 1580. What Spain's King Philip IV failed to see was that his own cavalier attitude and indifference towards the sensibilities of the Portuguese (e.g., Spanish monarchs would not hold court in Lisbon) would lead to a rupture between them in 1640. In a revolution in December of that year Portugal regained its independence. The relationship between Spain and Portugal became increasingly testy. Soon Portugal again became allied with Spain's archenemy, England. After all, the Spanish Armada's attempted invasion of England had only been fifty-two years earlier. A formula for serious hostilities was brewing.

Spain Needs the Guaraní

With the Guayrá now partly lost to the mamelucos and Brazil, Jesuit Superior Antonio Ruíz de Montoya and the Spanish governors in Buenos Aires and Asunción understood that the remaining Guaraní missions needed to be able to defend themselves and to resume expanding. Such expansion was constrained for a want of Jesuits and firearms for the Guaraní. Although the Jesuits had been in the field for only a quarter century, their reputation among the Indians had spread far and wide. By the 1630s they were receiving invitations from the Indians themselves as far away as the Chiquitos tribes, 500 miles northwest of Asunción, near Sucre, Bolivia. More Jesuits would soon be coming from Europe, but the lack of weapons was a major problem.

For the first time, the civil authorities understood that they and the Jesuits had a common interest: arming the mission Indians. If they were to serve as a serious military force and defend Spanish strategic interests, they had to be given firearms in quantity. In 1637 Father Diego de Boroa, the provincial in Asunción, with the support of the governor and the bishop there, chose Ruíz to sail for Madrid to plead the case for arming the Indians. Superior Díaz Taño, would accompany him on the four-month crossing from Rio de Janeiro to Madrid. Taño would then continue on alone to Rome to tell the story of the mamelucos to Jesuit General Vitelleschi and hopefully to Pope Urban VIII. The two fathers spent five months in Rio awaiting passage, profitably using the time to preach on the evils of slavery. Some plantation slaveholders got the message and released Indians taken by the mamelucos in the most recent raids. Most of them were just alienated by the priests' lectures.

Ruíz de Montoya Gets King's Qualified Permission to Arm the Guaraní

In Europe, both fathers eventually achieved everything for which they had hoped. In Rome, Taño so impressed Vitelleschi with his tale of the Indians' misery at the hands of the mamelucos that the general got him an audience so he could repeat the story to Pope Urban. The pontiff became so indignant that he issued a papal brief, *Commissum Nobis* (To Us It Is an Offense), a severe censure of the Church against all persons who enslaved the Indians under any label or disguise whatsoever.

Taño returned to Madrid to find Ruíz's progress to be agonizingly slow. While Ruíz had been well received in several audiences with Philip IV, it took him a year and a half to obtain the sought-after royal decrees to more clearly protect the Indians. These should not have been necessary given the history of the crown's opposition to slavery. But the extra time spent was worth it, because in May 1640 he got the king's decree satisfying his most important need—permission, though qualified, to equip the Indians with firearms. The qualification was that the permission was subject to the discretion of the viceroy of Peru, the king's most senior representative in South America.

The approval to arm the Guaraní stirred up emotional opposition from those who feared that the weapons someday would be used against the Spanish. The decree was so unpopular in Brazil and Paraguay that it dredged up an extraordinary number of anti-Jesuit calumnies. The main charges were as follow: The Jesuits owned secret mines and treasures; they bought and sold goods contrary to their own rules of poverty and against trading; they fostered bad feeling between Spaniards and Indians; they did not allow Indians to serve the Spaniards as they should; they kept their missions off-limits to the governors and bishops; they held the Indians by force rather than by persuasion; they moved the Indians from location to location without civil approval; they hid the missions from royal, fiscal, and other authorities; they had already armed the Indians without permission. The pro-slavery and anti-Jesuit voices were so effective that Ruíz had to refute them during his enforced delay. He did so with his *Conquista Espiritual del Paraguay*, a focused, typically erudite Jesuit monograph that became widely circulated and read in Europe. It gave a full appreciation of the missions and the fathers' work in Paraguay, although in partisan, adulatory language. Nevertheless, the calumnies listed above would simmer for a century and a quarter, ultimately to be used against the Society of Jesus during its 1767 trial in Madrid.

Taño left Madrid for Lisbon in late 1639 to embark for Buenos Aires. Ruíz, with his work unfinished, remained in Madrid until May 1640 when Philip signed the decree. In Lisbon, the pro-slavery party was influential. Only with the support of women in the royal family who intervened in the struggle among senior members of the government, was Taño permitted to continue. Storms at sea diverted his ship to Rio de Janeiro. There, after consulting with the local clergy and obtaining their approval, Taño read the pope's brief in public. But they had given him bad advice. Might it have been intentional? That is not known. In any event, many of the inhabitants were profitably connected to the mamelucos and, with the street rabble on their side, they attacked Taño and some Paraguay fathers who had joined him. They were saved from being murdered only by the last minute intervention of Governor Salvador Correa. A similar riot occurred in Santos, near São Paulo, 250 miles to the south. In both cities the mobs were calmed only by sundry written assurances given by the Jesuits, under duress, to the effect that the papal brief could not be enforced since there was a universal objection to it. Other non-Jesuit priests argued that this objection was a "lawful impediment" to its implementation and that such an interpretation was implicit within every brief. In São Paolo, a city of much human refuse, the inhabitants rose up against the brief and drove out all the Jesuits, both Brazilian and Paraguayan.

Portugal Breaks with Spain

After the fiasco in São Paulo, Díaz Taño hastened his departure for Buenos Aires at the beginning of November 1640. He left just in the nick of time. The Portuguese revolution, bitterly breaking ties to Spain, began the next month. Most importantly though, the king's decree arming the Indians had arrived in both Paraguay and Peru. Ruíz's return to South America led him straight to Lima to represent the Jesuits at the court of Viceroy Mancera mainly with regard to the decree on arming the Guaraní. The viceroy was completely sympathetic. A new day had dawned.

The Portuguese revolution had two major effects on the Jesuits of Paraguay. First, Spain became even more xenophobic towards Jesuits who were not already subjects of the king. A large reinforcement of non-Spanish missionaries about to embark from the river port of Seville was turned back. This severely reduced the pool of available

European missionaries, forced the abandonment of new missions in the Chaco west of Asunción, and halted other expansion in areas such as the Chiquitos. Second, the mameluco invasions of Paraguay became tactics of "lawful warfare"; these atrocities became rationalized in Brazil as being legal.

Slave Hunters Plan Huge Invasion of Tape

Early in 1641 Guaraní spies roaming the northern Tape, far to the east of their missions along the Paraná, heard rumors of a new, large-scale mameluco invasion of the missions. It involved an attack, mainly on the central and southern Tape. Yet it was so large that it might not end in the Tape but might continue on to those missions far to the west, in the Guaraní Republic's heartland between the Paraná and the Uruguay. Those latter missions were concentrated in today's Misiones province of far northeastern Argentina.

This bad news followed several catastrophes in the late 1630s. Father Diego de Alfaro had taken charge of Ruíz's missions while he was in Madrid. Now Alfaro was forced to abandon the smaller San Joaquín, with its Indians fleeing into the forest or escaping to other southwestern missions. In December 1637 the larger mission, Santa Teresa, with its 4,000 Guaraní was invaded by the mamelucos. They captured most of the Indians and sacked the mission. The new Visitación, not yet completed, was also abandoned. The Guaraní at Santa Ana scattered for a second time as the invasion rolled on. Alfaro's attempt to defend San Pedro y Pablo collapsed as panic seized the Indians and they fled. That mission and San Carlos were destroyed. Of the 10,000 Indians in those two missions, only one-third escaped capture.

A small group of Spanish soldiers from Buenos Aires were forced to marshal 4,500 Guaraní to resist further incursions. In 1639 at Caazapá Guazú, they managed to effectively surround newly invading mamelucos who then pleaded for an armistice. Alfaro, in his naivete, made the mamelucos swear they would never return and let them go on their own recognizance. Not surprisingly, they lurked in the forest and returned. Soon after, Alfaro, musket in hand, was punished for his naiveté by being shot dead by the same mamelucos.

Slavers Try Surprise

In 1641 more news from the Guaraní spies included efforts by the mamelucos to build a large fleet to attack down the Uruguay for the first time, thereby surprising their unprepared quarry. The fleet, led by

Manoel Pires, was comprised of 300 barges transporting more than 400 mamelucos and 2,700 Tupí allies. The mission's force comprised 4,100 Indians, but only 300 of them had firearms. It had taken too long to carry the king's decree to arm the Indians to the viceroy of Peru. Even then, after the viceroy's approval, his factories had barely begun manufacturing and distributing the harquebuses and muskets to the Jesuits for their army. Worse still, many of these weapons had to be shipped from Spain. Additional time was consumed training the Guaraní to use the weapons effectively. More time would have allowed for a well-armed Guaraní army.

The Jesuits devised a clever plan to ambush the invaders as they approached the San Javier mission near the confluence of the Uruguay and Mbororé (now Acaragua) rivers. The Jesuits assembled many rafts and canoes to be hidden amid jungle overgrowth on the south shore of the Uruguay; they built camouflaged fortifications on the north shore,

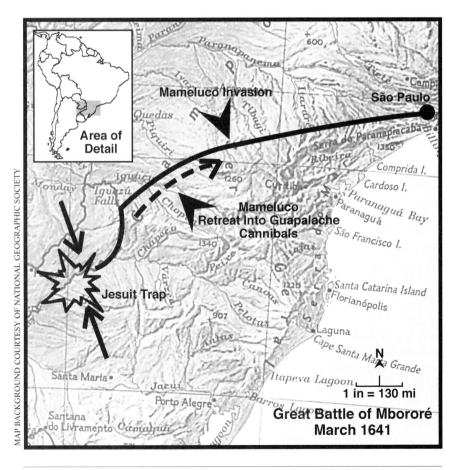

just opposite the rafts and canoes. The mamelucos would have to sail between these forces to get to the mission. This was a strategy worthy of the Jesuits present who had served in Europe's military. Mbororé would be the most important military battle in the history of the Jesuits in the Republic.

Jesuits Lead Guaraní in Savage Battle

The struggle started on March 8, 1641, with an advance of some 100 craft coming down the Uruguay, manned by the mamelucos and Tupís coveting the many thousands of Guaraní and the huge profit they would bring. The Jesuits countered with thirty boats manned by 250 Indians and a grand surprise—a cannon that was mounted on the bridge of the "flagship" of *cacique* Abiarú, the leader of the Guaraní. A forward contingent of the unsuspecting invaders sailed blithely into the trap. Abiarú's first cannon shot sank three of their boats instantly, and their astonishment led to a hasty, disorderly retreat. But it was only temporary.

The next day a violent storm suspended hostilities. The Guaraní were heartened. Their training in firearms under Jesuit Brother Domingo Torres, an ex-soldier, was obviously paying off. Three days later, under the overall direction of Father Juan Romero, the Guaraní were hidden and ready to pounce as the mamelucos returned in full force. Brother Claude Ruyer, a Flemish Jesuit, managed the battlefield tactics. In trying to encircle the Guaraní navy, the mamelucos unwittingly put themselves between the Guaraní boats on the south side and the Guaraní palisade on the north riverbank. The battle degenerated into a crossfire slaughter, with the victor and vanquished roles reversed from past mameluco-Guaraní battles. The mamelucos abandoned their boats that had become sitting ducks and tried their luck on land. A three-day guerilla war ensued. The Uruguay shoreline was densely wooded, typical for rivers in that heavily-forested region. The fighting became "hide-and-seek, with the jungle silence broken only by murderous interludes" of screamed commands, war cries, shooting, and the moans from hundreds of mamelucos and Tupí in their death throes.

Then the mamelucos decided to steal away upstream during the night, possibly to regroup. Brother Ruyer would have none of that. He remembered Alfaro's experience three years earlier when the mamelucos murdered him. No mercy this time! Ruyer's pursuit resulted in a final score of one third of the mamelucos killed—many outright. Some died the next day as they tried to retreat further up the

Uruguay and fell into the hands of ferocious Gualache cannibals. The Tupís suffered even greater losses with the vast majority of them dying in the battle or captured and devoured by the Gualaches. The contemporary Jesuit historian Nicolás del Techo described with unpriestly relish how the Gualaches first "tore off their beards and hair and flesh from their arms and thighs before eating them . . . and fixed their heads to poles on the roof of their huts." Those who were captured had a battlefield conversion and joined the victors. The final casualty count for the victors was about fifty killed and wounded; for the vanquished, between 1,500 and 2,000. Jesuits led the Guaraní in following up their advantage, managing to rescue more than 2,000 of their countrymen being taken to São Paulo by other mamelucos.

The mamelucos never again presented the same threat to the missions. While they had been crushed, they were not totally wiped out. New raids would follow, but never again on a large scale with such deadly consequences. *Cacique* Abiarú's gunboat with the cannon on the bridge became the archetype for a new, river-version of a man-o-war and the theatrical center of celebrations, annual festivals, and welcoming parties for visiting dignitaries. The Guaraní never got tired of flaunting it.

Guaraní Become Spain's Army, Golden Age of the Republic Begins

News of the victory at Mbororé spread throughout greater Paraguay. Indians from hundreds of miles in all directions gravitated back into the fold or joined for the first time. The new governor of Paraguay rejoiced in this gift of a loyal, proven, and growing military force that would keep his enemies at bay—not only the mamelucos but also the Portuguese soldiers in Brazil who encroached into every Spanish soft spot they could find. The armed Guaraní would become Spain's frontline troops in Paraguay for a century and a quarter. The golden age of the Jesuit Republic of the Guaraní had begun.

Great Celebrations Held Throughout Paraguay

Southey describes a delayed centennial celebration throughout the province of Paraguay, held in 1642, for the Jesuits founding 102 years earlier. Coming on the heels of Mbororé, the Indians had much to celebrate. Córdoba held an eight-day carnival including a pageant in which Ignatius darted through a fire which consumed his pursuers, "a hydra Heresy and a giant Pagan." There were festivals and a nighttime boat race on the Paraná by torchlight. The missions had many pagan-like celebrations. In one at Encarnación, an old, costumed giant representing the Company of Jesus was followed by 100 boys dressed in variously colored costumes singing his praises, followed by 100 oxen. The procession passed under 100 festooned arches into the church where 100 loaves of bread were offered and 100 candles burned upon the altar. Beyond these were laid 100 compositions honoring the Company. Then an immense triumphal chariot passed by, filled with images of saints and martyrs. Southey is uncharacteristically forgiving of all this "Romish superstition," for the "noble efforts which [the Jesuits] made in behalf of the oppressed Indians, and for the good which they effected: The centenary of their institution could not be celebrated by these tribes with more gratitude and joy than were justly due."

Ruíz de Montoya Never Returns Home

Ruíz de Montoya, the Guaraníes' greatest protector, never returned to the missions on the Paraná. He would not see the results of all his efforts. Having embarked at Seville for Peru, he was detained at Lima trying to obtain assurance that the viceroy remained committed to the Guaraní being armed. In Lima, too, there was much opposition to that policy. After some time, with that work finished, he set out for his "home," his missions on the Paraná. He had gotten as far as Salta in far northwestern Argentina, about two-thirds the way home, when he received a new order delivered by Jesuit Father Juan Pastor, rector of the Jesuit College of Esteco in Salta, to return to Lima to lobby for other needs of the missions. There he stayed for a protracted period dealing with the lunacy of Bishop Bernardino de Cárdenas, (see Chapter 11), making the case against him before the viceroy on behalf of the Jesuits' Province of Paraguay.

In early 1652 Ruíz's health deteriorated rapidly and he died in Lima in April of that year. He was 67. The viceroy and the senior members of the government there accompanied his body to the grave as pallbearers. The Archbishop of Cuzco eulogized him as "no ordinary saint; he is a giant in holiness, a great saint of the highest order."

When the news of their hero's death reached the Paraná mission, forty Indians from the Loreto mission made the journey of well over 2,000 miles northwest, diagonally across the continent, to Lima to beg for his body. The request was in the name of the Jesuit Province of Paraguay. It was granted. The simple funeral cortege wended its way back to Loreto, stopping at a number of missions along the way. At Loreto he was laid to rest in the sacristy of the church. Today, the sacristy and his remains are unidentifiable within the reclaimed rubble of that mission deep in the forest. Local Guaraní legend had it that several miracles showed the glory he enjoyed in heaven.

Reverend Groh's epitaph on Ruíz reads:

> Like most men and missionaries, Montoya was subject to two kingdoms . . . the ecclesiastical and the political. . . . As a missionary committed . . . to Holy Church and his Majesty . . . [he] was under constant pressure to display publicly his ultimate commitments. In the course of his life he was neither more nor less than he claimed to be: a man, but a man of God.

Photographs

These photographs were taken during the tour of the thirty mission ruins of the Jesuit Republic of the Guaraní.

Trinidad (Paraguay) with church front and back towards the right.

Inset: Trinidad with dentil detail and frieze.

PHOTO BY ED VERNON

Trinidad (Paraguay) interior of church facing the front.

Santos Cosme and Damian (Paraguay) portico with numerous classrooms.

San Ignacio Guazú (Paraguay) with St. Michael slaying the dragon.

San Borja (Brazil) altar.

Black Robes in Paraguay

Corpus (Argentina) has just a few mounds of collapsed mission stones deep in the forest.

Candelaria (Argentina) has a few remaining sections of the church's wall with vegetation growing from the limestone.

San José (Argentina) has a few limestone pieces left deep in the forest.

Loreto (Argentina) was reclaimed from the jungle but was purposefully left unrestored. Ruíz de Montoya's unmarked grave is here.

Santa María la Mayor (Argentina) with a few wall sections left.

Santa Ana (Argentina) with what little is left of the right wall of the church.

Inset: Santa Ana (Argentina) with vegetation growing from limestone corner and graves in front.

PHOTO BY ED VERNON

San Ignacio Miní (Argentina) facade and church portal. Argentine National Historic Site.

Inset: Close-up of left portion of facade with fine carving.

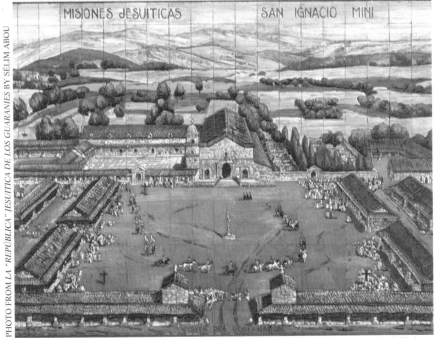

"Kechuita," a ceramic mural by Léonie Matthis (1883-1952) of San Ignacio Miní.

San Miguel, also São Miguel (Brazil) facade.
National Historic Site.

Inset: San Miguel with column capital
carving.

Jesús (Paraguay) interior of church facing the rear. Note remaining stone bases
of limestone support columns washed away long ago.

The Iguazú Falls from the shoreline.

The Iguazú Falls from 1500 feet. Note orange roof of multi-story hotel in background near top, for a sense of scale.

The Iguazú Falls dramatic *La Garganta del Diablo*— the center of the action. Also from 1500 feet.

Guairá Falls on the Upper Parana River. These falls were on the route of the exodus lead by Ruíz de Montoya in 1631.

Black Robes in Paraguay

CHAPTER 11

A Rapscallion Bishop Harasses the Jesuits for 125 Years

With the 1641 rout of the mamelucos at Mbororé and an ineffectual last gasp attack by them in 1642, the way was clear for the missions to thrive and multiply, free from outside interference. Yet it was not free from the antics of others inside the Catholic Church. In the 1640s, one of the most weird, larger-than-life characters in the history of South American Catholicism strode onto the Paraguay stage. He was a bishop no less.

Cárdenas Arrives on the Scene

Don Bernardino de Cárdenas was revered and despised, pitied and admired, saintly and a brigand, a truly farcical rapscallion. The Jesuits considered him a "gifted and pernicious spiritual clown." The Franciscans "held him up as one who fought through his life for the honor of [their] founder." The Indians "loved and revered him . . . and considered him a saint." Southey calls him "half crazy." His story must be told partly because his accusations against the Jesuits figured prominently in the prosecutor's case of Jesuit crimes at their expulsion trial in Madrid 125 years later, and partly because his escapades illustrate the tenor of the times.

Cristóbal de Cárdenas was born in La Plata, now Sucre, in the high *altiplano* of Bolivia in 1579. At nineteen he joined the Franciscans and took the name Bernardino. (Franciscans took the name of a Franciscan saint upon entering the order.) A complete extrovert, he was not an academic but was a brilliant and captivating orator in a society where charisma was paramount. A master showman, he performed spectacular public penance of fleshly mortification, sometimes too theatrical for his superiors who often reprimanded him.

Often garbed as a poverty-stricken pilgrim and bearing a wooden cross, he would lead multitudes of the devout in ritual processions. His performances were so ideally suited to the impressionable Indians that in 1614, notwithstanding the earlier reprimands, the Franciscans appointed him to be chief missionary over many tribes. His repeated claims of knowledge of Indian gold and silver mines earned him a large following among adventurers as well as the creole and mestizo poor.

Cárdenas Nominated to Be Bishop

Thanks to the advocacy of a prominent Asunción lawyer who was mesmerized by Cárdenas, in 1640 several well-connected personages in Lima nominated him to be a bishop. The humble friar was suddenly gone. He was succeeded by a blow-hard, who was full of himself and the trappings, emoluments, and veneration attached to his office. Yet he was uneasy, since the papal Bull authorizing his formal consecration failed to appear. As unease turned to fear, he decided to make an end run around the Bull.

Cárdenas Seeks Jesuit Support

At the Jesuit College in Salta, in northwest Argentina, Cárdenas showed the highly- regarded Jesuit teachers there a forged letter dated 1638 from a papal secretary, Antonio Barberini, appointing him bishop of Asunción. He asked them to authorize his consecration saying that should be no problem for them since the official Bull was sure to arrive soon, providing the formal approval. The Jesuits of Salta honored his request and endorsed his proposed consecration. He should have declared victory and gone back to Asunción, but he blundered by over-reaching. To cement the Salta fathers' approval, he carried his case all the way to a higher authority, Jesuit Diego de Boroa, rector of the leading college of South America, the College of Córdoba, 500 miles to the south. Boroa consulted his associates and concluded the opinion from Salta was not justified. Enraged at this turn of events, yet keeping it secret, Cárdenas doubled back some 400 miles north to Tucumán, stopping for a while in Santiago del Estero to plead his case to Bishop Melchior Maldonado, a highly-respected Augustinian. Cárdenas presented the opinion from Salta while keeping secret the overrule by Boroa.

Cárdenas Becomes Bishop

The easygoing Bishop Maldonado was persuaded, and he formally consecrated Cárdenas. It was 1642. Fifteen years later a congregation (a sort of tribunal) in Rome ruled that both Cárdenas and Maldonado had gravely violated Church law in the procedures they followed. In spite of that, the consecration was still valid. However, Rome would not confer on him the diocese of Asunción. Various shenanigans followed as he usurped that diocese anyway. Events soon spun out of his control, and even a written rebuke in 1644 from King Philip IV himself did not rein him in. He waved it aside as the secular intruding into Church affairs. Philip failed to follow up. He was more focused on matters in Spain including a life of philandering (his various mistresses reportedly issued thirty children) and the progression of the Thirty Years' War. Meanwhile Rector Boroa never ceased questioning Cárdenas' authority, earning the bishop's everlasting enmity not only for the rector but also for all Jesuits.

Cárdenas Attacks Jesuits

Cárdenas' first attack against the Jesuits took the form of a letter to the Council of the Indies arguing that the Jesuits were undercounting their mission population to reduce the per capita taxes owed to the crown and that only bishops could be trusted to represent the crown's interests.

Using his position as a bishop, Cárdenas became a nuisance and soon even a threat to the Jesuits. His pre-consecration histrionics—flagellation and mortification, wooden cross-bearing, performing the duties of a simple parish priest that were normally considered beneath a bishop such as preaching in the streets—metamorphosed into something new: He put on the most ostentatious regalia of a plenipotentiary. En route up the Paraguay to his cathedral in Asunción, he was flanked by elaborately arrayed boats forming an escort. Indian canoes and Spanish launches added to the melodramatic naval column. Each midnight while at anchor, his disciples were treated to the sound of his scourging himself. Rumors circulated that he was St. Thomas Aquinas reincarnated, this being based on a Guaraní legend that the saint had preached in the region and had retired to a cave south of Asunción on the line of Cárdenas' approach to the city. He entered Asunción to operatic pomp.

The new, two-faced bishop Cárdenas pandered to the Spanish settlers, taking their side against the Jesuits' protection of the Guaraní from enslavement, while at the same time preaching of his friendship to the beleaguered Indians. Next he ordained as priests, a cadre of trustworthy followers—trustworthy to himself—including criminals and others lacking even a semblance of a priestly education.

Cárdenas Quarrels with Governor

Then Cárdenas entered onto a collision course with Governor Gregorio de Hinestrosa, a Chilean creole. The governor's dealings with the intractable Guaycurú Indians near Asunción had been inconclusive.

Cárdenas took charge, declaring that such dealings were reserved to him alone. After a widely heralded meeting with some Guaycurú *caciques*, he baptized them and claimed he had Christianized the most fearsome of Indians, thereby removing a long-standing threat to Asunción. He even wrote of his triumph to King Philip. Days later the same Guaycurú were back on the warpath and burned down a nearby Spanish town.

New quarrels erupted between Hinestrosa and Cárdenas. When Hinestrosa blasted Cárdenas' nephew, Fray Pedro de Cárdenas, over Pedro's consorting with a prostitute, the bishop excommunicated the governor. A second excommunication followed days later after the governor arrested Pedro for grossly insulting him in public. (Why a second one? For emphasis?) Needing influential allies, Cárdenas suddenly turned to the Jesuits and began wooing them. After he paid some public compliments to the Jesuits, other priests, now jealous, roundly objected. Perhaps it was Cárdenas' purpose all along to use the Jesuits as pawns and to ultimately put them on the defensive.

Meanwhile, Hinestrosa shipped Pedro down river in a canoe that soon proved to be too lightly guarded. The bishop countered with a fusillade of excommunications against the governor and his officers. It had become theater. He then took to the streets, scourging himself in penance for Pedro's misdeeds. This was highly effective in rallying support among the easily impressed. En route down the river Pedro escaped, predictably enough, from his guards.

From 1642 to 1644 the excommunicated civilian and military leadership of Asunción drifted, disorganized and uncertain of what to do. One day during this period several hundred Guaycurú prepared to assault the city. So that an effective defense could be organized, Cárdenas lifted his excommunications against the leadership. After the Guaycurú were beaten back, the excommunications were promptly re-imposed.

For their part, the Jesuits tried to contain the Hinestrosa-Cárdenas power struggle. Around 1644 Cárdenas made plans to seize a Jesuit ranch to use as a villa for himself. The ranch generated enough income to provide free tuition for the students at the Jesuit College of Asunción. Closing the ranch would be tantamount to closing the college. Hinestrosa sent troops to protect the ranch as well as the fathers and Guaraní running it. Open hostilities broke out with Cárdenas pitted against both the governor and the Jesuits.

Cárdenas Issues His Manifesto Against the Jesuits

Later that year, Cárdenas let loose an earthshaking salvo against the Jesuits in an infamous, history-making sermon at Yaguarón. That sermon, containing compelling "proof" of Jesuit crimes, would be a prosecutor's centerpiece more than a century later at their 1767 expulsion trial.

About thirty miles southeast of Asunción, Yaguarón was a Franciscan mission that served as a quasi-headquarters for Cárdenas and his disciples. Cárdenas' sermon played out against a backdrop of excuses for his fellow Franciscans that their pueblos were poor through no fault of their own but rather because of the evil deeds of their competitors, the Jesuits. It was also these evil deeds that were the cause of the Jesuit missions' prosperity.

In his sermon, this spellbinding demogogue spun a convincing web of seven fabrications, which Cunninghame-Graham wrote were "so ingeniously contrived that royal, national, and domestic indignation were all aroused by them." The sermon's accusations, repeated over and over for many generations, became by 1767 "known facts" to all in Paraguay and Madrid, even to the Vatican.

Cárdenas' seven accusations, not all of his own invention, were:

- The Jesuits prevented the Guaraní from paying taxes to the crown.

- They withheld tithes due to the bishops (like Cárdenas).

- They had rich mines worked by their Indians for the benefit of their order's headquarters in Rome.

- They violated the secrecy of the confessional.

- They used these secrets to their own enrichment.

- The mission lands rightfully belonged to the Spaniards because of their conquests.

- They had created a great republic over which they alone ruled.

According to Caraman, Cárdenas went on to say that the bishops of Paraguay were under secret orders to expel the Jesuits from their dioceses, but only he had the courage to actually do it. (Later he did do it.) He ended with an impassioned appeal: When the Jesuits were gone the king would enjoy his rights; the settlers could restore the *encomendero* form of Indian quasi-enslavement with a plentiful supply of Indians "freed" from the Jesuit missions; and every community would share in the Jesuit riches. Just as the Portuguese had driven the Jesuits from São Paulo in 1640, he would expel them from Paraguay, and those Franciscans still loyal to him would take over from the Jesuit "heretics."

Most of the rebuttals to these charges have already been noted. Some rebuttals came during the 1767 trial. In short, where the accusations were true, each was for a good and sufficient reason. For example, the crown had fully understood the special dispensations given the Jesuits and the Guaraní. The absurdity of Jesuit hidden mines and riches was proven time and again; they were pure fabrications. The rest of the assertions were based purely on Spanish greed. To the credit of the benevolent though feckless King Philip, this was understood in Madrid if not in South America.

Cárdenas Forms an Army

Cárdenas then formed his own army, comprised in large part of scoundrels and vagabonds, to seize the government in Asunción and capture his adversary, Governor Hinestrosa. With the support of the Jesuits, Hinestrosa obtained critical military forces in the form of some 600 mission Guaraní to supplement his Spanish troops, since many of them were of uncertain loyalty. This was soon after the great battle at Mbororé. The 600 were a force to be reckoned with.

Cárdenas' opening gambit was to excommunicate Hinestrosa (yet again) and this time the Jesuits too, for good measure. He forced his subservient clergy and camp followers to affirm in writing the Jesuits' crimes, listing them in a document for Madrid. Many settlers, anticipating a windfall of Indian slaves and Jesuit treasure, rallied to Cárdenas' side. Hinestrosa, with support from Dominicans, Jesuits, and other non-Franciscan clergy, expelled Cárdenas on the grounds that Cárdenas' appointment as bishop of the Asunción diocese was fraudulent. To drive home his determination, the governor erected a prominent gallows in a plaza in Asunción, an action sobering to all pro-Cárdenas Spaniards who had hungered to be rid of the Jesuits.

Cárdenas Is Defeated

Then Cárdenas crossed his Rubicon. He returned from his stronghold in Yaguarón to a Franciscan monastery in Asunción. While pretending to accept the governor's order of banishment, he converted the building into a fortress, strengthening defenses and opening holes in the walls for harquebuses and light cannons. Hinestrosa's troops encircled the monastery, forced its capitulation, and expelled the bishop. Ever the showman even in defeat, Cárdenas made a climactic departure down the Paraguay, sitting in the poop of his ship surrounded by his still-adoring counterfeit clergy. Some 250 miles later he arrived at Corrientes and was interned there. He fulminated a new series of excommunications and interdicts, now wholly ignored. For a while there was peace.

Guaraní Are Scandalized, Flee into the Jungle

The two-year struggle was a disaster for the missions. The spectacle of the Catholic bishop being deposed by a Catholic governor representing a Catholic king, aided by Jesuits and their Guaraní, was shockingly scandalizing to the Indians. Cunninghame-Graham wrote of the absurdity of "the supremacy of the royal government [having to be] supported by men just emerging from a semi-nomad life, who owed the tincture of civilization they possessed to the calumniated Jesuits." Many returned to the forest, lost to the missions; some forever.

In 1647, with Cárdenas still at Corrientes, his last act began to play out. That year Hinestrosa was replaced by a more vacillating governor, the fat, good-natured Diego Escobar y Osorio. A year later, seeing an opening, with a small force and under a compliant Escobar who was now willing to hand the mission Guaraní over to Spanish slavers, Cárdenas invaded the area east and north of Asunción. It was an undisguised maneuver to encircle the city. Escobar removed the Jesuits in two outlying missions in the far northern Itatín region, Santiago and Nuestra Señora de Fe. The Guaraní, realizing they had lost their protectors, fled into the forest just ahead of the approaching slavers.

However, the governing tribunal (in Spanish, *audencia*) of Charcas, while observing events from a distance of some 700 miles to the northwest, became increasingly fearful of creating a power vacuum. Such a vacuum would embolden the Portuguese to seize the Itatín region just a few hundred miles to the north and west of Portuguese Brazilian strongholds. The tribunal eventually reversed Escobar's moves, but it was too late for many of the Indians. Only half of them could be lured back. Dutch Father Joost van Suerck, an Itatín pioneer, died during the attempt. These events illustrate the difficulty Spanish colonial authorities had in administering their territories even when the authorities were present in adjacent regions. The distances were huge, the roads poor or non-existent, hazards from hostile tribes and nature itself, along with the economic interests of the slavers all combined to give rebels like Cárdenas much freedom of action and little accountability for their illegal activities.

Cárdenas Alleges Jesuit Mines

Cárdenas' next attack was to play up rumors of Jesuit mines near the Uruguay river missions. The rumors originated with a previously disregarded Indian named Bienaventura, who had been whipped for running off with another man's wife. Bienaventura's elaborately detailed description of working Uruguay mines was so convincing that after an initial inept false start, Buenos Aires governor Jacinto de Láriz, along with Peruvian mining magnate Martín de Vera, led a forty-soldier search party up the Uruguay. During the search, Bienaventura wisely disappeared. Despite promised rich rewards for any soldier finding the prize, the search turned up nothing. Láriz did not appreciate being made a fool, and after some Jesuits captured Bienaventura Láriz ordered him given 200 lashes and condemned him to death. The same Jesuits secured his release on the grounds of insanity. It took two more searches over twenty years before the case of the Uruguay mines was closed.

Early in 1649 the wily Cárdenas used the occasion of the sudden death of Governor Escobar to his advantage. With the help of an accommodating lawyer, he found an old royal decree which seemed to give certain colonial cities the right to elect an interim governor and interim government should the colony suddenly be left without them. The city council, with a strong majority of pro-slavery, anti-Jesuit members overwhelmingly elected him Governor of Paraguay. He quickly took possession of Asunción's cathedral using his bishop's chair and a counterfeited order from King Philip to expel the Jesuits, referring to them again as "excommunicated." The action was applauded by settlers to whom he promised a gift of 20,000 mission Guaraní *encomiendas*.

Cárdenas Expels the Jesuits from Asunción

The expelled Jesuits, hands tied like felons, were loaded into poorly provisioned canoes bound for Corrientes. The tables had been turned. Don Bernardino—the subject of years of longing and scheming—had gained the upper hand. He sacked the vacated Jesuit college, again finding nothing of value. He seized the ranch with its large cattle herds, the one that was denied to him earlier by governor Hinestrosa.

Yet Cárdenas was not satisfied. O'Neill says that he continued his fabrications against the Jesuits while procuring libelous documents endorsed by his minions and forging others. His chief operative in this duplicity was his personal secretary, Gabriel Cuéllar de Mosquera. Two years later Cuéllar made a public and documented deathbed confession that Cárdenas had forced him to promote lies against the Jesuits that included placing his own signature and the signatures of thirty-six other conspirators on many false documents. These documents accused the fathers as:

> . . . disloyal traitors to his Majesty, as gatherers of gold, and senders of money to foreign parts, as heretics, schismatics, and pernicious to the state. . . . These accusations are all utterly false and I [Mosquera] should like to have the voice of a trumpet to proclaim this all to the world and to undo the calumnies contained in said papers.

At Corrientes in the diocese of Buenos Aires, as opposed to Asunción, the Jesuit exiles were enthusiastically greeted and implored to start a school. That was done. Cárdenas' power base was proven to be only local.

Governor Captures Cárdenas

The tribunal of Charcas, still worried about the Portuguese capturing the strategic Itatín missions and the sprawling lands they occupied, called for Cárdenas to present himself at Charcas and to bring with him the king's decree authorizing him to govern Paraguay. Cárdenas ignored the tribunal's summons. Governor Don Sebastián de León y Zárate, newly appointed by Viceroy Conde de Salvatierra in Lima, would not tolerate Cárdenas' insolence. With a mixed army of a few hundred Spanish soldiers and 700 Guaraní, he marched on Cárdenas. León's army collided with Cárdenas' force of misfits on the sandy plain of Campo Grande, fifteen miles east of Asunción. It was a rout. Cárdenas and his band fled in wild confusion back to his cathedral. There the pursuing León found him, absurdly arrayed in pontifical vestments, seated on his bishop's throne, and crowned by his miter. Some months later in 1650, abandoned by his once-devoted disciples, Cárdenas was sent packing to Charcas. He lived there for fifteen years on a pension, revered by the populace and greeted with flowers wherever he appeared in public. In 1665 the dying King Philip, in pity, appointed the eighty-eight-year-old bishop to the diocese of Santa Cruz in Charcas, putting a face-saving end to this strange and embarrassing episode in Spanish Catholicism. Cárdenas died there three years later at ninety-one.

Cárdenas Leaves Lasting Shadow over Paraguay's Jesuits

After Governor León expelled Cárdenas from Asunción to Charcas, he justified his reputation as a serious and fair administrator. He restored the Jesuit properties seized by Cárdenas and his disciples and recalled the fathers from their exile in Corrientes. He also set the stage with the council of Charcas for Cárdenas' confinement there.

The legal entanglements Cárdenas caused were unraveled in Rome and Madrid over many years and at great expense. In 1650 and 1651 alone—years for which Caraman gave data—some 38,000 pesos or well over one million dollars (U.S.) in today's buying power, were paid by the Jesuit Province of Paraguay to European lawyers "who were the only persons to derive unquestioned benefit" from the Cárdenas affair. *Plus ça change, plus c'est la même chose.*

Notwithstanding the *exposé* of Cárdenas' fabrications and distortions, one of them continued to prove intractable: the vast Jesuit hidden treasure, especially gold. The possibility, no matter how remote, that this might be true would remain a burr under the saddles of King Philip and later King Charles right up until the order's expulsion. As for the Jesuits, they could not prove a negative.

Additional lasting damage to the missions came from Cárdenas' charge that non-Spanish fathers were remitting huge shiploads of gold back to their native countries. Only the most vigorous entreaties from the viceroy convinced Philip to rescind his 1647 decree expelling all foreign Jesuits from Paraguay. However, the viceroy was too late to prevent the embargo of seventy Jesuits who were ready to sail for Paraguay. As a result, the Jesuit missions in Paraguay were not expanded for some forty years. Only by the end of the seventeenth century would reinforcements from the huge Austrian empire be allowed in. These new men were among the most talented of all the Jesuits to arrive. But they and those from German kingdoms and principalities and today's Czech Republic, Switzerland, and other German-speaking countries were never given enough time to establish missions in the outlying regions like the Chaco, Pampas, and Mato Grosso before their expulsion in 1767.

Cárdenas' mischief cast a long shadow.

Jesuit Republic's Golden Years of Prosperity and Growth (1651-1721), Then Civil War and a Communist Revolt (1721-1736)

After the chaotic episode of Bishop Don Bernardino de Cárdenas ended in 1651, the thirty missions of the Jesuit Republic had an open road to growth, prosperity, relative peace, and harmony.

Missions Radiate Outward from the Republic's Core

During the next seven decades, lasting until 1721, the Jesuit mission frontiers expanded outward in all directions. To the northeast in the Guayrá and the east in the Tape, missions were greatly improved spiritually, socially, and materially. Several were relocated from risky or temporary locations to what became permanent sites.

Far to the north-northwest of Asunción (the Chiquitos region in what is now southeastern Bolivia) ten missions eventually would cover much of its 25,000 square miles. In a semi-circle west of Asunción, the vast, wild Chaco region of many thousands of square miles would be evangelized and thirteen missions established. But these came only after decades of spasmodic fighting continuing as late as the 1730s, involving many war-like tribes—Abipones, Mocobíes, Guaycurú, Tobas, and others living there. Even after conversion many of these people harkened back to their old ways as they admitted that beef, jaguar, emu and other animal flesh tasted insipid compared to human flesh. Cannibalism died slowly. Beyond the Tobas, on the Pilcomayo river some 300 miles west-northwest of Asunción in today's extreme northern Argentina, dwelt the largest of the Chaco tribes—the Chiriguanos—reportedly fifty thousand of them, although estimates of the period were often greatly exaggerated. Their cunning and belligerent nature made them the most feared by the Spanish and neighboring tribes. They were especially known for capturing so many enemies in raids and in battle that they formed whole villages of slaves.

Jesuit work among the Chaco peoples began in 1696, meeting with little success for thirty years. Those who kept to their ancient traditions—especially Chiriguanos—remained in the great majority and regularly preyed on the converted. In 1726 a general uprising destroyed every sign of Christianity among the Chiriguanos' nearby tribes. From 1733 to 1735 the Jesuits tried again. Led by Juliàn Lizardi, they built two noteworthy missions—Concepción and La Virgen del Rosario. On May 16, 1735, Lizardi met his end when a marauding band invaded his church at Concepción while he was saying Mass, dragged him out, stripped him, and shot him with thirty-two arrows. His congregation was enslaved, and his mission destroyed.

Shallow Christian roots and regular reverses notwithstanding, conversions in the Chaco continued right up until the expulsion in 1767 when every tribe, even in the remotest regions, had at least one mission.

Much of the late seventeenth and early eighteenth century progress resulted from an influx of German-speaking Jesuits from central European states. The Germans brought with them special musical talents. Their missions excelled in choral and orchestral performances with fine home-made instruments (as many as thirty pieces)—strings, brass, woodwinds, percussion instruments, and an organ or two. O'Neill called these seven decades their "golden years."

Perhaps the most satisfying experience of the Jesuits of Paraguay took place in the Brazilian state of Rio Grande do Sul, east of the Uruguay river. There, seven of the grandest missions of the Republic developed into showcases for the fathers' efforts. These were also among the most commercially successful, in large part due to the fertile grasslands supporting vast herds of cattle, horses, mules, and oxen. There also was much game and rivers of fish. Later, after Roque González was murdered in the Tape, they were relatively safe as Indians hostile to them withdrew further south. In 1687 the greatest of these missions, San Miguel which would become so visible in the 1754 Guaraní War, was founded at its present location.

Portuguese Raiders Cause Mission Growth in the Far North

As with the earlier missions near the Paranà and Uruguay rivers in the Republic, the Jesuits got an assist from Portuguese invaders. Even the warlike Guaycurú and Payagua to the far north and west of Asunción were frightened by mameluco rampages. These tribes came to see the slavers as a relentless, irresistible force. Although they exacted a high price on the invaders, they realized like so many others earlier that the Jesuits were their only hope for the long-term future.

The early eighteenth century history of the region is replete with savage battles. One of the most bloody occurred in 1725, when a strong Portuguese force of 300 men in twenty large canoes invaded the northern Itatín region on the upper Paraguay where it is fed by the Cuyuba. That part of the famous Mato Grosso near the Bolivian border, some 800 miles west of São Paolo, even today is remote and wild. Hundreds of warriors—Guaycurú, Payagua, and possibly their allies— ambushed them, killing all but two whites and three African slaves who somehow managed to escape amid the slaughter and confusion. This was the largest loss ever suffered by the Portuguese at the hands of Indians. Six years later another large Portuguese force of uncertain size but certainly in the hundreds was annihilated on the Paraguay, 600 miles north of Asunción in the same part of the Mato Grosso. They were eating a meal as they glided carelessly in their fleet of thirty canoes, on the Paraguay, there just a stream. Indians, probably the same tribes, sprang on them from the shorelines. Only seventeen Portuguese escaped by leaping to the shore and hiding in the woods. But the Indians paid dearly, losing an estimated 400 warriors. This battle was a triple windfall for the Spanish of Asunción. While they were at peace with the Payagua, it did not hurt to have such losses among a tribe which could become hostile in the future or to have their arch-enemy Portuguese suffer so. There was also a financial windfall for the Spaniards. The Portuguese had been carrying gold back to São Paolo from mines in the Mato Grosso. Now the victorious Indians were ready to trade it in Asunción. There one Indian bought a pewter plate for six pounds of the precious metal. The Portuguese-Indian bloodletting would continue for years, see-sawing back and forth, adding much appeal to the Jesuit missions.

In the early 1690s Father José de Arce became famous for his leadership, teaching skills, and successes in converting the Chiquitos Indians. His party consisted of seven other Jesuits: two Spaniards, a Sardinian, a Neapolitan, a Belgian, an Austrian, and a Czech. The Chiquitos were friendly and open to the message. Two crude missions were built. The Catholic liturgy and rituals fascinated them. But the Chiquitos' response to the fathers was driven more by the belief that conversion would protect them from the mamelucos, who were encircling from the west, north, and south in a big arc, coming from São Paolo and passing through the Mato Grosso. Arce, getting wind of the invasion now underway, raced hundreds of miles northwest to Santa Cruz de la Sierra deep in Bolivia. There he enlisted the aid of the supportive governor of the area. The governor loaned 150 soldiers to join the Chiquitos, now armed and ready. When the mamelucos arrived, they sent a reassuring letter to the fathers thus trying to draw them out. The letter was seen for the ploy it was. A short intense battle ensued on August 19, 1694, with the utter destruction of the slavers. Taking a page from Ruíz de Montoya's book sixty years earlier, the fathers and their charges fled even further north, deep into the Amazon watershed, way beyond the reaches of slavers, Spanish or Portuguese. There they prospered and multiplied for seven decades until the Jesuits were expelled.

In 1715 Arce, now sixty-four and quite aged for the tasks at hand, and an assistant, Father Bartolomé Blende, a Fleming, along with a party of Guaraní took one of the longest journeys in Jesuit mission history. They traveled north 600 miles up the Paraguay from Asunción to Lake Mandioré on the Mato Grosso do Sul-Bolivian border, and another 210 miles northwest through virgin rainforest deep into Bolivia to the remotest of missions, San Raphael. Just before arriving there Arce had to leave behind the ailing Blende in the care of the Guaraní. At San Raphael Arce met an old companion, Father Miguel de Zea, obtained medicine and supplies, and returned to the place where he had left Blende with the Guaraní. He found them all killed; soon thereafter he himself disappeared in the wilderness. He is believed to have been slain by Payaguas, like the others.

Several additional attempts were made to start missions west and north of Asunción between 1720 and 1740. All were failures, mainly due to Indian resistance. Only in 1760 did successful, permanent missions begin sprouting among the northern Mbaya nation living there so that, by the time of the expulsion seven years later, ten missions had been established among the Chiquitos, these under the direction of Father José Sánchez Labrador.

Had they been allowed more years the Jesuits would likely have had great success among the tribes in eastern Bolivia and western and central Brazil. The interior of Brazil all the way up to the Amazon was Spain's for the taking.

Guaraní Serve as Spain's Military

From the mid-seventeenth to the mid-eighteenth century, the mission Guaraní were regularly used as Spain's first line of defense. Seven times in the second half of the seventeenth century they came to the rescue of Buenos Aires. In 1697 some 2,000 Guaraní drove off an invading French force. In the early eighteenth century, about 4,000 Guaraní repelled repeated Portuguese assaults on the Spanish settlements of Colonia and Montevideo across the Río de La Plata from Buenos Aires. In all of the battles taken together, beginning in 1637 and lasting until 1745, the Guaraní lost many hundreds of warriors killed and thousands seriously wounded. They were tough men who did not consider any wound serious unless it was disabling or cost an eye or a limb. There was never any gratitude shown by the Spanish cities so well defended.

Toward the mid-eighteenth century, as the threat of Portuguese infiltration increased, provincials Bernardo Nusdorffer and then Manuel Querini ordered a draft of all able-bodied Guaraní men. Training in firearms became intense. Mission armories—eight of them at the peak—were well stocked, and Jesuit brothers with military experience were appointed to supervise them. The Jesuits anticipated the coming storms.

Civil War Breaks Out in Paraguay

In 1721 the missions' momentum and promise of the "golden years" were interrupted for a decade and a half starting with a rebellion under a charismatic lawyer, Don José de Antequera y Castro. A creole from a respected Lima family, he was educated in a Jesuit college and at the University of Lima. He was able, strong-willed, and had a fantastic imagination unencumbered by any scruples whatsoever. He had a great sense of timing, seizing opportunities as they arose. He eventually came to make big trouble. In these ways he had an eerie resemblance to Don Bernardino de Cárdenas eighty years earlier.

Pro-Slavery Cabal Rebels in Asunción, Jesuits Expelled

In 1720 a cabal of lawyers in Asunción launched an attack on Governor Don Diego de Los Reyes de Balmaseda, a decent man, charging him with a litany of offenses. The charges had an anti-Indian, anti-Jesuit, anti-mission theme. The cabal was driven by a pro-*encomienda*, Indian servitude agenda.

The royal council (*audencia*) at Charcas (roughly today's Bolivia) under the viceroyalty of Peru, appointed Antequera to inquire into the charges, a choice that seemed reasonable at the time. Governor Reyes was absent when Antequera arrived at the cathedral in Asunción and proceeded to exhibit a grand sense of self-importance. With his wig elegantly braided he alighted from his coach and, upon being led to a place where he was to make a brief show of respect in prayer, he refused to do so, complaining that there was no red carpet and cushion to kneel on.

Antequera promptly took complete charge of Asunción and ordered Reyes not to return to the city. Then, Càrdenas-like, he used *audencia* documents, out-of-context, to appoint himself governor. With the aid of the lawyerly cabal he seized Reyes and placed him under house arrest.

Things went from bad to worse. Reyes escaped and fled to Buenos Aires. Antequera blamed the Jesuits, concocted a list of accusations about them and the mission Indians, and sent it to the viceroy of Peru. It just so happened that the viceroy was also the archbishop of Chuquisaca (in southeast Bolivia), a common combination of church and state in Spanish America. In addition to Antequera's missives, the viceroy received contrary reports from others. He wound up agonizing over the confusing state of affairs for some months. Concluding a grave mistake had been made, he ordered Reyes reinstalled in Asunción and commanded Antequera to return to Lima. The strong-willed Antequera ignored the viceroy's order and immediately assumed dictatorial power under the ruse of an impending Jesuit—Indian military threat against Asunción. He threw Reyes into prison in chains and expelled the Jesuits from the city.

In 1724 Antequera led an army against four nearby missions intending to put the Guaraní there into "public service." However, when the Indians got wind of his attack, they fled into the forest. He had to settle for plundering the missions' churches. The Indians would hide in the forest for four years until the Jesuits returned and coaxed many back into their missions. Many others never did return, having been too scandal-ized by the sight of Spanish Christians fighting Spanish Christians.

Soon there was reason to suspect that Antequera, with his fantastic imagination, planned to declare himself "King of Paraguay." He was sane enough not to publicly show his hand, at least not yet. In response to Antequera's actions, the viceroy dispatched General Garcia Ros to restore law and order in Asunción. Garcia Ros' 2,000 man force, comprised mainly of Indians, was ambushed by Antequera allies, including his *encomienda* sympathizers. Some 300 Indians were killed and many taken prisoner, as were two Jesuits. Soon after this fiasco, the viceroy was succeeded by the tough, combative, no-nonsense Marqués del Castellfuerte.

Back in Asunción, a long-awaited, kindly Franciscan named José de Palos arrived as the new bishop. Palos unsuccessfully tried persuasion to bring Antequera around. As for the Jesuits, Palos showed his feelings, writing to King Philip V that he had been

> . . . profoundly impressed by the care and zeal with which those Fathers attend to their Indians, by the good education and spiritual nourishment they provide, their attention to temporal needs, and their training in devoted loyalty to your Majesty. These things are a matter of common knowledge; still I find the reality better than I could have imagined and so desire to bring it as fully as possible before the enlightened understanding of your Majesty.

The words came cheap. Action was needed.

Rebel Leader Is Executed

By 1725 Viceroy Castellfuerte had enough. He angrily directed Governor Bruno Zabala of Buenos Aires to march on Antequera. Zabala assembled a huge army of 6,000 mission Indians and 200 Spanish soldiers, an army that was too awesome for Antequera to resist. When Bishop Palos added the threat of excommunication for any Antequeristas resisting Zabala, Antequera became fearful and fled in secrecy, never to be seen in Paraguay again. Eventually he was seen in southern Bolivia where he somehow imagined that the authorities would support him. Instead he was put in irons and transported to Lima for imprisonment. A five year trial resulted in a sentence of beheading. On July 5, 1731, as an apparently repentant Antequera was led to a scaffold in the central public square in Lima accompanied by his Jesuit confessor, a vast throng of sympathizers threatened to free him. After one of them, a Franciscan friar, cried out, "A pardon, a pardon," the crowd became unruly. Soldiers fired into it, killing many. Two soldiers shot Antequera dead. His corpse was lifted onto the block and decapitated. The angry partisans melted away as the sun set on the grisly scene.

During the five years of Antequera's trial, his fellow conspirators back in Asunción were hatching more intrigues and plots. The *encomienda* advocates were led by a new governor, Martin de Barua, a man who was "commonplace, of a vulgarity of views and aims rare among even the bad specimens of . . . Spanish administrators." Barua and his followers resisted the return of the Jesuits expelled earlier by Antequera. However, thanks to the steady support for the Jesuits from Bishop Palos who managed to overcome Barua's clandestine maneuvers (such as stealing the king's mail addressed to Palos), a royal decree was issued in 1726 and implemented in 1728 returning the Jesuits to Asunción. Also, importantly, the decree transferred control of the thirty missions of the Guaraní Republic from Asunción to the governor in Buenos Aires.

Jesuits Return to Asunción

The Jesuits' entrance into Asunción was greeted by vast crowds, thundering cannon salutes, and religious celebrations. Many letters of appreciation were dispatched to the king. One respected magistrate, Matias Angles, wrote to him saying:

> The Fathers of the Society of Jesus are the only competent persons of the province of Paraguay, and consequently are opposed and antagonized by all the inhabitants of it who have done their best through the governors of the province to keep it in its primitive condition.

That thought would be repeated for almost half a century as the Jesuits' trials and tribulations expanded, not only in Paraguay but also throughout much of Catholic Europe.

Governor Barua had no option but to resign. In 1730 he was succeeded by Governor Ignacio Soroeta, a friend of the Jesuits and their Indians and of public order. But the *encomenderos* and the rabble supporting them were not yet totally defeated. They launched a movement called the *comuneros* (communists), setting up a *común* based on it.

Communists Seize Power in Asunción

The *común's* chief propagandist was a demagogue named Fernando de Mompó y Zayas, a convicted criminal and escaped prisoner. Late in 1730 he marched at the head of a revolutionary horde of 500 armed Spanish would-be *encomenderos* and sympathizers and seized the government buildings in Asunción. Governor Soroeta became their captive. After four days Soroeta was expelled; only by taking an unexpected route out of the city did he escape a murderous *comunero* ambush.

The Jesuits of Asunción, anticipating their expulsion by Mompó, appealed for help from the governor of Buenos Aires who had oversight of their missions since 1728. He responded by quickly raising a 10,000 man Indian army, the largest in South American history outside of the Incas, and positioned it at key points between Asunción and the thirty missions.

To the consternation of Bishop Palos, three prominent religious superiors came to the support of the *comuneros*. He complained to the king, writing:

> There appeared in our episcopal hall three religious superiors, the prior of the convent of St. Dominic, Friar Juan Vallejo; the guardian of that of St. Francis, Friar Alonso Meléndez; and the father commander of Our Lady of Ransom, Friar Tomás de Villasante; who said they came on behalf of the *Común* to beg us . . . not to prevent the expulsion of the Jesuit fathers . . . as the general peace of the province was of more importance than the continuation . . . of those fathers in it. . . . We answered that we were astonished that such a proposal should come from religious persons . . . of learning . . . who ought to cooperate in the defense of ecclesiastical immunities and of the government of the king, our lord.

On February 18, 1731, a mob of *comuneros* and would-be slaveholders battered down the doors of the Jesuit college in Asunción, looted the building, and carted the fathers off to a *comunero* farm outside the city. Soon thereafter they deported the fathers to a distant mission.

In April 1731 the aging, well-intentioned but naïve Franciscan, Juan Arregui, was appointed bishop of Buenos Aires. He fancied himself as a populist and soon was defending the *comuneros* in Asunción from his Buenos Aires pulpit. The idea of Arregui heading the communist movement took hold, and, with the acquiescence of his brother Franciscan bishop Palos who earlier had been opposed to the Communists, he headed off to Asunción. He arrived there in December 1732 for his consecration as a bishop by Palos.

At this time a new governor arrived in Asunción—a professional soldier of long experience, Manuel Agustin de Ruiloba. With the capricious Arregui unexpectedly deciding to provide political cover, Ruiloba began to assert himself, declaring his intention to crush the movement. Of course, the *comuneros* would have none of this.

On September 13, 1733, an army of 800 *comuneros* appeared outside Asunción, intending to remove Ruiloba. The old Bishop Arregui rode out to join them. Governor Ruiloba's force was comprised of 350 well-armed local soldiers of unproven loyalty. When the opposing forces confronted each other, Arregui stepped forward, begging to make the case for the rebels. Riuloba refused to negotiate. At a signal from the rebel leaders, almost all of the governor's troops deserted to the other side. Ruiloba the soldier stoically faced the increased horde and cried out, *"Viva el Rey, caballeros!"* The rebels replied, *"Viva el Rey, e muera el mal gobierno!"* (Long live the king, and death to the evil government!) Ruiloba's horse was shot out from under him, and as they swarmed over him their blows cracked his skull open. His few loyal soldiers quickly obtained protection from Arregui. As the victorious rebels marched into Asunción they proclaimed Arregui to be the governor of Paraguay.

From that point on anarchy reigned as Arregui, the rebel leader, became frightened and submissive to his own mob. Pressured, he consented to the *comuneros* taking possession of the Jesuits' thirty republic missions, even though they belonged to the province of Buenos Aires and its governor. By now his fellow bishop, Palos, had had enough. Somehow he managed to reassert some measure of authority and convinced Arregui to return to Buenos Aires.

Spanish Restore Law and Order, Jesuits Reinstated

With all the political and military confusion swirling about, it took a year and a half for the Spanish authorities to respond. In January 1735 Governor Zabala left Buenos Aires at the head of a large army of Spaniards and Indians. His well-planned expedition arrived at Asunción to a demoralized, chaotic rebel "government" which promptly fled. Those who were captured were exiled or shot.

Bruno de Zabala appointed a new, honorable governor for Paraguay, Martín Echauri. Echauri restored civil government and returned the Jesuits to Asunción and its environs. The rebels' expulsion of the Jesuits from their thirty missions had never been attempted, thanks to the protection accorded by the army of the prior governor, Soroeta.

The Jesuits, wishing to correct the official records for the sake of history, asked for Echauri's formal nullification of all of the *comuneros'* defamatory government documents aimed at the fathers. They also requested restitution for one half of the value of their missions' losses. Both were granted. Eventually Echauri burned all of the *comuneros'* documents but only after pressure by Jesuit General Frantisek Retz in Rome. Retz had sent a message that leaves the impression of a cover-up. History and the Society's reputation were the losers. As for the Jesuits on the ground, O'Neill writes: "Exonerated and . . . vindicated, the fathers returned to their posts and, amid . . . sincere and widespread rejoicing, resumed after four and a half years of interruption their course of apostolic activities."

The bad example set by the Spanish civilians and clergy during the *communero* period once again demoralized many mission Indians who deserted. When their number was added to losses in death from plagues, the mission population declined from 141,000 to 107,000.

In 1738 Bishop Palos died. As he faced his death, he wrote to the king:

> The accusations brought against the [Jesuit] fathers are founded in blind passion or in a covetous design to tyrannize over the Indians and make unjust gain from their labors. If this province were deprived of the fathers I am certain it would sink deep into ignorance and vice. These men, Sire, warn men frankly concerning their duties and sins, and this frankness is thought intolerable. They are the seed God blessed.

Palos saw what would result in a few decades.

Five years later in Buenos Aires, Bishop Arregui's successor, another Franciscan, José de Peralta, after visiting the thirty missions in his province, wrote to the king:

> It was with difficulty that I could tear myself away from those [missions] . . . so full of devotion that I repeat every day thanks to our Lord for the blessings he diffuses among those peoples by the hand and guidance of holy and apostolic religious men. To see the churches, the performance of divine service, the piety . . . skill in sacred music . . . splendor of the altars, the respect and magnificence with which our Lord in the Blessed Sacrament is honored, caused me inexpressible emotion, and at the same time *shame and confusion at seeing such a difference between these people just drawn from their barbarism and the ancient Christians in our land who would do well to go amongst these Indians to learn from them* [emphasis added].

CHAPTER 13

Spain and Portugal Try to Resolve Their Paraguay Dispute,
Treaty of Madrid and the Guaraní War,
The Beginning of the End

In 1750 Spain and Portugal signed the Treaty of Madrid, setting in motion a series of events that would doom the Republic of the Guaraní and contribute to the liquidation of the Jesuit order. The treaty also led to a great battle. Second only to Pizarro's 1535 conquest of the Inca, it was the most horrific, one-sided slaughter of an indigenous army at the hands of Europeans in a single battle in all of western hemisphere history.

Treaty of Madrid Sells Out Seven Guayrá Missions

The Treaty of Madrid is also known as the Treaty of Limits, the Boundary Treaty, and the Treaty of 1750. Under the treaty, the land on the east side of the Uruguay river, with seven of the most flourishing missions in the Americas, was ceded by Spain to Portugal. In return, Spain received the fortified town of Colonia del Sacramento on Río de La Plata. The purpose of the treaty was to bring to a conclusion more than two centuries of political tension and skirmishing between the two countries over the area that is now Uruguay as well as Brazil's states of Rio Grande do Sul, Santa Catarina, Paraná, and Mato Grosso do Sul. Altogether, they comprise hundreds of thousands of square miles in southeastern South America. Ironically, the treaty's terms were so imprecise that it failed in its purpose and became an additional source of friction between the two countries for a decade.

All of this land, and most of the rest of Brazil were originally designated as Spain's under the 1494 Treaty of Tordesillas between the two countries. However, Portugal's territorial aggressiveness and Spain's focus on the wealth of Mexico and Peru—and its decline in power over the preceding century—had resulted in most of the region effectively being acquired by Portugal. This acquisition was based on the legal principle of *uti possidetis* (literally, as you now possess). Under international "law," Portugal had taken possession and control, however superficial, and therefore it was Portugal's. This principle was guaranteed to hold only as long as it favored a strong nation, which Portugal was solely by dint of its alliance with England. That would be enough. Further to Spain's disadvantage was England's ability to menace Spain's far-flung empire—from the Philippines to the Americas to northern Africa and to the Low Countries. These widely scattered colonies were difficult to defend and thus were ripe pickings for England's mighty navy, as Madrid was to fully realize ten years later.

Spain's objective for the Treaty of Madrid was to secure the Río de La Plata estuary, dangerously exposed to invasion, by permanently controlling both of its shores, the Colonia side on the north and the Buenos Aires side on the south. Portugal had used Colonia for offensive military operations, harassing Spain's river commerce that went west and then north from Buenos Aires a thousand miles, all the way up the Paraná, Paraguay, and Uruguay rivers into the heart of Spain's Paraguay province and the Jesuit missions.

Over the years, Colonia and its surroundings had been captured by Portugal three times and re-taken each time by Spanish troops with the help of the Guaraní. In 1704 and 1718 thousands of armed Guaraní decided the outcome. (After the 1718 recapture of Colonia by Spain, it was ceded back to Portugal as part of complex territorial negotiations.) In 1724 a large Guaraní force routed the Portuguese at Montevideo (in today's Uruguay) and then built defensive fortifications around it. The Guaraní-Spanish victories did not come free; the 1704 battle lasted for eight months with 130 Guaraní killed and 200 wounded. Needless to say, the Guaraní, given their sad experience with Spanish settlers and colonial administration, would not have made the sacrifice they did had it not been for Jesuit persuasion.

Spain had two other objectives: It hoped the treaty would halt the westward encroachment of the Portuguese into settled Spanish lands and into huge virgin jungles west of the upper Paraná. It also seems to have naively harbored hopes that, by reducing friction with Portugal, the halcyon years of their union (1580-1640) might return, removing England as Portugal's ally.

Portugal's immediate objectives were to consolidate and legitimize its hold on the interior lands east of the Uruguay and to capture "Jesuit riches," especially gold "known" to be hidden among the seven sprawling missions. Not having to continue costly fights that had recently occurred with the armed, tough Guaraní in Colonia, would be a bonus. Portugal had other reasons for compromise: Large gold and diamond mines lay in the states—especially Minas Gerais—northwest of São Paulo that were to be formally ceded by Spain. Securing the Amazon basin and three large rivers feeding it from the southwest would establish Brazil's expansive western boundary once and for all. The three rivers were the Tapajos, Tocantines, and Madeira, the last having many Portuguese Jesuit missions near its banks.

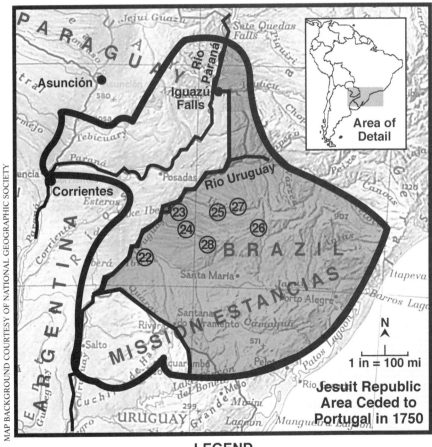

MAP BACKGROUND COURTESY OF NATIONAL GEOGRAPHIC SOCIETY

LEGEND
Missions Ceded to Portugal

22. San Borja	25. San Lorenzo	28. San Miguel
23. San Nicolás	26. San Juan	
24. San Luis	27. Santo Ángel	

The treaty was a good trade for Portugal and a bad one for Spain which only managed to secure the Río de La Plata and its Paraguay territory. Negotiations led to bitter infighting among Spain's ministers. By formally ceding all of those areas to Portugal, Spain's government knew that it could be setting the stage for a Portuguese behemoth that could eventually dominate the continent. However, Spain's peace-loving, submissive, and mentally unstable King Ferdinand VI, ruling under his domineering Portuguese wife Queen Barbara, was in no condition to rally his negotiators to drive a harder bargain. Besides, England's support for Portugal would make any further demands problematic.

The seven missions in the land east of the Uruguay to be ceded to Portugal included the great mission of San Miguel, now the restored Brazilian historic site of São Miguel in Rio Grande do Sul, a few hours' drive from Santo Tomé, Argentina, across the Uruguay river. San Miguel was the most monumental of all mission churches. Its architect was Juan Prímoli, a professor of architecture from Milan, whose works in Buenos Aires include the magnificent church of El Pilar. All to-gether, the seven missions and their satellite ranches, with some 30,000 Indians, covered most of the state. Its lush grasslands supported hundreds of thousands of cattle roaming free. Hidden gold or not, this region was a prize for its agricultural and ranching assets alone. The other missions were San Angel, San Borja, San Nicolás, San Lorenzo, San Juan, and San Luis.

After three years of secret negotiations, the treaty was signed in Madrid on January 13, 1750. Portugal's chief negotiator, Gomes Freire de Andrade, had been a wily, strategic thinker, greatly overmatching his Spanish counterparts. Once its terms became public there was an uproar. The Spanish public saw it as surrender. Portugal's merchants were also dissatisfied, expecting even more. They wanted everything Portugal got, but argued that it was unnecessary to cede their highly profitable contraband smuggling in Colonia.

Spain's future King Charles III, still in Naples, complained that he was not involved with the treaty negotiations. Even the highly respected English ambassador to Spain, Sir Benjamin Keene, though nominally Portugal's ally, realized the unfair treatment of the Jesuits of Paraguay and encouraged Ferdinand to resist the treaty. There were reports that the king's Jesuit confessors influenced him against it, but the secrecy of the confessional kept their advice private.

O'Neill comments movingly:

> Among the most affecting tragedies of history have been the forcible extractions of whole peoples. The two dispersions of the Jews, the driving of the Irish "to hell or Connaught," the desolation of Arcadie and its French colonists—these have moved the pity and indignation of generations ever since they were perpetrated. They have had one feature in common—that they were the work of hostile powers, the expression of hostile mind and intent. But what are we to say of a power that expels its own subjects, men, women and children, without a crime on their part, with barely a hint of compensation and without attempt to make any provision of the new homes to replace those abandoned? This is what Spain proposed to do and proceeded to do. . . . And for the execution of this infamous plan she asked the help and cooperation of the apostles and pastors of the people she was expatriating.

Jesuits Oppose Treaty

Most importantly to this narrative, the Jesuits of Paraguay saw the treaty as a betrayal of the Guaraní who had been so loyal and valuable to Spain. Making matters worse was the condition that Colonia would be surrendered only after the seven missions were fully occupied by the Portuguese. This turned out to be a critically important point for the missions, making their evacuation a priority for both Spain and Portugal.

The Indians were initially uncomprehending, then incredulous. After months of rumors and calumnies against the Jesuits spread by Spanish colonists—including a charge that bribes were paid by the Portuguese to the Jesuits for the "sale" of the missions—incredulity turned to rage. Several Jesuits barely escaped being murdered.

Jesuit General Frantisek Retz in Rome, was operating largely in the blind. The already poor communications between Asunción and Rome worsened in mid-1750 when two Jesuits carrying a report on the Uruguay missions from Asunción to Rome were intercepted en route by Portuguese in Rio de Janeiro. They were forced back to Asunción. Retz was faced with an unsolvable dilemma. For him the issue was the "very existence" of the Jesuit order. Paraphrasing the cardinal-visitor in the movie, *The Mission*, the jungle that Retz saw vicariously in Paraguay looked like a well-tended garden compared to the political jungle he faced in the Catholic courts of Europe.

In January 1751 the fathers in Paraguay received an uninformed, unrealistic and disastrous letter from Retz in which he demanded not only unquestioning obedience from them in matters relating to the treaty but also that they induce the Guaraní to accept it. The letter's timing was ruinous to the fathers' morale. A few months later Retz died and was succeeded by Ignacio Visconti. Only seventeen days after his election, Visconti wrote to the fathers that they must obey all instructions of the Spanish authorities in executing the treaty provisions. Visconti, like Retz, was unencumbered by any real knowledge of what was going on in Paraguay. Yet he sought no advice. He feared that the rumors of Jesuit mission riches, circulating among the upper classes of Europe and especially in the Bourbon courts, were gaining credibility. (They were.) Those rumors were only the most recent of many verbal assaults being heaped upon the order in Europe.

O'Neill writes that Visconti was "in a panic" as he wrote that anyone impeding or resisting, directly or indirectly, the transfer of the missions would do so "under the pain of mortal sin." Visconti was playing to the man in Europe most friendly to the Jesuits, Spain's Ferdinand VI. Retz earlier and now Visconti desperately wanted to please him. He might become the salvation of the order. Visconti also wrote:

> Endeavors have been made to have a clause inserted in the treaty manifesting the fear that the two sovereigns [Spain's and Portugal's] have of the evil designs of the Jesuits. [The clause would declare that Jesuits must obey the treaty and force will be used if necessary.] His Catholic Majesty [Ferdinand VI] whose goodness and kindness to us can be fittingly rewarded only by the King of kings has been entirely unwilling to adopt such a measure. Rather does he stand guarantee for the good faith and obedience of [our] Society.

To Visconti's credit, he must have had a good appreciation for how isolated the Jesuits were becoming in the early 1750s, surrounded by their enemies. The *philosophes* of the Enlightenment such as Voltaire; the emerging nation-states and their powerful anti-clerical and especially anti-Jesuit enlightened prime ministers; Louis XV's royal mistress Madame Pompadour; the Jansenists and their strongly held doctrine of predestination; and, most dispiritingly for the Jesuits, other Catholic orders including the Franciscans, Dominicans, Benedictines, Capuchins, Augustinians, and minor orders—all opposed the Jesuits or were angry at them for a variety of reasons.

Visconti's reasoning bore little traction with his priests at the front in Paraguay. Protecting the Jesuit order at the expense of the God-given, king-confirmed rights of the Guaraní was too high a price to pay. As they debated alternative actions among themselves, they came to realize that if they publicly resisted the treaty, the Guaraní would take it as a cue and there would be a general uprising among them in all the missions. All those in powerful positions would blame the Jesuits, saying this proved that they had been trying to set up an independent Jesuit Republic of the Guaraní all along. Also, an uprising could not succeed for any length of time given the forces arrayed against them. The fathers concluded that the answer was simple: They had to publicly comply with the treaty or the outcome would be inevitable—the military destruction of everything they had achieved over 150 years. This would be done by the combined armies of Spain and Portugal in concert with their allies, the mamelucos and their supporters among the Spanish settlers. Adding insult to injury, the outcome would be blamed on them.

Manuel Querini, the provincial of Paraguay, convened a strategy meeting of his priests in April 1751 at San Miguel. Seventy came. Alternatives were debated. Retz sugggested that the Indians remain in their missions as Portuguese subjects; that idea was ridiculed. The Indians would die first or most certainly soon thereafter. The *caciques* were already leading an outcry of lamentations and invective hurled at the Portuguese; they were one and the same as the mamelucos in their eyes. The fathers concluded that moving the seven missions—some 100 years old—and their 30,000 Indians hundreds of miles to the west was not realistic. Unlike the conditions during Montoya's successful exodus 120 years earlier, the arable land west of the Uruguay was now fully occupied. There was little extra water or timber for construction and fuel. Most of all, it was clear that the real problem was that the Indians simply would not go. The missions were theirs. They had worked for generations to create masterpieces of which they were immensely proud. Moreover, they had inherited these lands from their distant ancestors, cultivated them with care, created profitable ranches and yerba and cotton plantations, built small but comfortable homes and productive workshops, and established cemeteries for their honored dead. So there was only one avenue open: They would try to get the treaty modified.

The Jesuits took a two-pronged approach: One was aimed at Spain's strategic interests, the other was a moral and theological one. Father

José Quiroga, held in esteem by Ferdinand VI for his earlier explorations on behalf of the king, became the nominal author of a letter to José de Carvajal, the king's first minister, arguing Spain's interests. He pointed out that the Portuguese would become a more dangerous military threat, with the east bank of the Uruguay serving as a new advanced base for attacking the rest of Paraguay. In the north, the Portuguese would have a promontory aimed at the Potosí silver mines in the high *altiplano* of upper Peru (now Bolivia) and further—with the help of the Inca Pretender who was suspected of collaborating with the Portuguese—all of Peru.

The moral and theological argument against the treaty was inspired and written by the theological faculty of the renowned Jesuit University of Córdoba in northern Argentina. Addressed to the king's Jesuit confessor Francisco de Rábago, it was simple and direct, pulling no punches: The forced relocation of the Guaraní violated their rights as free persons, their rights to property, and even their very right to live. The treaty condemned them to permanent exile, to the loss of their farms and fields, and to the lack of life's necessities while they began to replace what had taken them 130 years of extreme effort to create. It broke the contract of conscience between the king and his Guaraní subjects who had proven themselves so faithful, a fidelity to which the king and his predecessors had so often testified. Now this treaty promised not only their death and destruction here on earth, but even the ruin of their souls! The theologians then left the door open a crack: If it were necessary for the general good that a sovereign dispossess such innocent parties, then the sovereign had an obligation to compensate them for their loss (their version of eminent domain). Madrid's reaction was absurd. It proposed 4,000 pesos for each of the seven missions even though the estimated worth of each was over one million. Another reasonable estimate was double that. Then the letter concluded with an ominous argument that could be viewed as insubordinate:

> We [the Jesuits in Córdoba] do not feel safe in obeying the civil law [the treaty] which is so plainly in contradiction with laws natural, divine, ecclesiastical, and civil.

The letter to Rábago achieved little. Of course, since he was the king's confessor, whatever effect it had on the king's thinking we will never know. Apparently Rábago rallied some modest support among others for the fathers' views, but it was at the price of their being accused of encouraging a rebellion in Paraguay. He sent his brethren in Paraguay his sympathy and consolation. Nothing more.

By 1752 the Guaraní anger at the fathers evolved to respect, as the fathers' angst became obvious to them and as the letters of the prior year became known. They redirected their anger and hatred against the Portuguese. Even so, it was hard to get their uncomprehending minds to adopt any practical measures in the face of such a grave emergency, assuming that anything *could* be done. For example, some Guaraní would begin an unplanned exodus from their mission only to turn back after a day or two for the most trivial reasons. This happened several times until a need for a plan was understood. It had become tragicomedy. Even after five generations they still depended on the fathers for strategic and even tactical planning—a dependency that does not reflect well on the Jesuits' efforts over the years.

Then a new Jesuit provincial of Paraguay was appointed, an aging and feeble outsider, Father José Barreda, who had no knowledge of the country. Wisely, he delegated all responsibility to Father Bernardo Nusdorffer, a mission veteran and former provincial of Paraguay. Nusdorffer had lived in the missions for thirty-five years, knew the Indians well, and was respected by them as their own father. Knowing the task, he seemed at first to have shrunk from it. His first act was to survey possible relocation sites west of the Uruguay. Complicating the relocation problem would be the farming and ranching lands that were east of the Uruguay but owned by the missions on the west side. Presumably these missions would get first priority for scarce land should there be a relocation. In any event, the survey found little space except for that occupied by non-Christian Indians—a land infested with army ants, either swampy or arid, or otherwise uninhabitable.

Jesuit Visitor Plenipotentiary Altamirano Arrives on the Scene, Disaster Follows

In early 1752 General Visconti blundered by appointing Jesuit Father Luis Altamirano as visitor plenipotentiary to Paraguay and as his personal representative. Altamirano would have full authority to make decisions for the order with respect to the Guaraní and the treaty. Caraman seems not to care for him much, writing that he was "the worst type of court priest." He had "no knowledge of the situation," was "too proud to acquaint himself with it," and "too imperious to seek advice from his brethren in the field." Worst of all, Altimirano was convinced that the Paraguay Jesuits were actively opposing the treaty.

O'Neill is not an Altamirano admirer either, writing that "he was woodenly impervious" to "suggestions of the most experienced" Paraguay fathers. He goes on archly, "Though he (Altamirano) showed little personal courage in facing dangers, he was tenacious in imposing the most painful, difficult, and dangerous tasks on his temporary subjects." The Jesuits of Paraguay had not been given a fair deal by their own general in Rome.

Arriving with Altamirano in 1752 were ten boundary commissioners co-headed by the Spaniard Don Gaspar de Munive, Marquis de Valdelirios, or simply Valdelirios, and the Portuguese political luminary, Gomes Freire de Andrade, governor of Rio de Janeiro, who had been the main architect of the treaty. He proudly called it *mi gran negocio* (my grand negotiation). Valdelirios seems to have been both intelligent and fair-minded. After listening to wise old Barreda and learning from him of the impossibility of any wholesale resettlement, Valdelirios bought into the argument that, as the treaty had been made without any understanding of how it could be carried out, it was reasonable to appeal to Ferdinand for a delay in its execution. Then Valdelirios, on his own dubious authority, granted a three-year delay to the Jesuits for the impossible resettlement. They were overjoyed. As for Altamirano, he suspected a hidden Jesuit hand behind the rebelliousness of the Guaraní.

Yet, in a 1753 letter to Valdelirios, he had to admit that he had used "exquisite diligence" to find such a hand so that he could "cut it off" but he had failed to find "any trace of it."

Paraguay Jesuits in Open Revolt Against Rome, They'll Follow Their Conscience

Visitor Altamirano then wrote to General Vitelleschi, duplicitously, that the inaction and opposition of the Jesuits were delaying the migration in two ways: First, because of their "excessive and blind confidence" the treaty will come to nothing. Second, that the fathers' "firm and erroneous conviction . . . which I have confirmed with our theologians in Córdoba [is] that your precepts do not oblige them in conscience. . . . Consequently, my precepts do not oblige them either." Altamirano was right about one thing: the gauntlet had been thrown down. The Jesuits of Paraguay were going to follow their conscience, not the orders of their general in Rome!

Altamirano then threatened the fathers with excommunication and expulsion from the Society. While the Indians did not react immediately, eventually they learned of his machinations and became enraged. Rumors spread that he was a Portuguese in disguise (he wore lay garb) and should be thrown into the Uruguay. Conspiracies for his murder were exposed. Characteristically, he had visited only one of the seven missions, San Borja. Right after that, while he was residing at Santo Tomé, west of the Uruguay, an angry band of 600 Indians led by *cacique* Sepé Tiarayo, *corregidor* of San Miguel, marched on Altamirano's residence to confront him as a fraud. Learning of their approach, he lost his nerve and fled 400 miles south to Santa Fe, a remote region of the Paraguay mission territory that was safely out of danger. Then Altamirano's attitude became even more petulant. He was sure the Jesuits were behind his problems, but he had no more proof than he did the year before.

Spain and Portugal Join to Attack Guayrá Missions

Notwithstanding Valdelirios' three-year extension for the resettlement, which seems to have been ignored by Altamirano, and after nine months of muddling, matters reached a crisis. It came in the form of a confrontation on February 27, 1753, between the Guaraní and a joint Spanish-Portuguese survey team. It happened at a ranch called Santa Tecla that belonged to San Miguel, about seventy-five miles south of that grand mission. Sixty-eight armed mission Indians led by Sepé barred the Europeans from surveying any farther. A Jesuit, possibly Tadeo Ennis, offered to mediate. He had been involved in earlier disputes and had a reputation (although never proven) as a troublemaker for inciting the Guaraní. Sepé rejected the offer, suspecting a trap, and made a counter-offer that they meet in the ranch's chapel, a building of which he was particularly proud. When the Europeans agreed and arrived at the chapel, Sepé barred the door to the Portuguese members of the team. The Spanish, maintaining solidarity with their Portuguese allies, withdrew from the site. By the time the story went public it had become grossly exaggerated. The sixty-eight man Indian force had swollen to 80,000! They were armed with artillery and led by Jesuits! Andrade wrote to Valdelirios describing what really happened, but European pride had been wounded. Within a year events would spin out of control.

Andrade and Valdelirios had to avenge their honor. This was a special need for the Portuguese since the anti-Jesuit, anti-clerical Marquês de

Pombal had become the first minister in Lisbon. They appealed to Buenos Aires' Governor Don José Andonaegui to initiate military operations. That was another mistake. The governor had a love of repose, befitting any seventy-five year old. He was also wise enough not to enter into a guerrilla war amid an impenetrable jungle with thousands of armed Guaraní, possibly led by Jesuits. Besides, he did not really believe these anti-Jesuit stories. After a meeting with the two commissioners, he agreed only to rely on the more pacific measures of dialogue and persuasion. These could be backed up with force if ultimately necessary. It was a recipe for inaction.

Then Provincial Father Barreda initiated a major change in the chain of command. Taking the unanimous advice of the fathers he consulted and with Altamirano's apparent concurrence, he handed over all responsibility for the missions to Governor Andonaegui. But the conniving Altamirano then double-crossed Barreda and discharged a salvo of excommunications against his own Jesuits. It was "the most terrific set of fulminations ever issued in the Society of Jesus."

He followed with something truly unprecedented and bizarre; He threatened the expulsion of all of Paraguay's Jesuits from the order unless they acted on twenty-four commands he imposed. These commands directed the fathers to surrender the seven missions and lead the Guaraní in retreating west across the Uruguay. One command called for their taking only their breviaries (books containing psalms, hymns, lessons, and prayers needed to be said daily by priests) and not even one other possession to Buenos Aires and submitting to the governor there. This the fathers unanimously agreed to, but with a twist. Craftily, they gave him their resignations, too. Altamirano's bluff, if it had been one, was called. He reversed himself and requested that they remain on duty until replacements could be found. They agreed. Then he removed his excommunications of the fathers, and they returned to their seven missions.

For eighteen months the Europeans had done nothing. The Guaraní would make good use of this time by preparing for war. They accumulated extra provisions. They practiced target shooting; even the women joined in. They made extra arrows, but these had steel tips to penetrate the Portuguese' padded cotton, arrow-resistant, full-length coats. They built new chapels and offered prayers to the Virgin Mary and the angels, patrons of the Guaraní army. They wove elaborate battle flags and mounted them on new staffs. They were ready for the worst, or so they thought.

Europeans Lose the First Round

In February 1754 the Guaraní fired the first shot, and the Guaraní War (also called the War of the Seven Reductions) was underway. They attacked a small Portuguese stockade on a bank of the Rio Pardo, capturing it after a month's siege. An attack on another fort failed. By July, two European armies were on the move. The Spanish with 2,000 soldiers under Andonaegui followed the Uruguay upriver from Buenos Aires, while 1,000 Portuguese soldiers under Andrade attacked from the east. Following the Yacuí River inland, the Portuguese planned to loop up and around, descending upon the seven-mission region from the north.

The Portuguese expedition was poorly planned. They quickly ran out of provisions; the weather turned bad—the rainy season had commenced in full force; and many deserted. As the flood waters rose, the soldiers built huts up in trees, encamping that way for a wearying two months. As supplies and morale ran down, they retreated. The Spaniards fared little better and retreated back down the Uruguay, harassed as they went by Indian guerrillas. The Guaraní of the seven missions had been reinforced by their brethren from missions west of the Uruguay and by an extraordinary alliance with the fierce Charruas coming up from the south. This was the same tribe that spoiled Díaz de Solís' 1515 expedition. Valdelirios was mortified. This previous Jesuit ally rationalized the fiasco by blaming it on Jesuit leadership. Altimirano, acting on that, wrote to the king accusing his Jesuit brethren of instigating the rebellion.

Spain and Portugal Attack Again, Slaughter Ensues

Now the Europeans had to make up for past incompetence and save face. In late 1755 a single combined army of 1,600 Spanish and 1,200 Portuguese, under the same leadership as in the 1754 disaster, advanced north, upriver from Río de La Plata towards the seven missions. On February 10, 1756, they engaged the Guaraní at a promontory called Caaibaté, a ranch belonging to the San Juan mission, roughly one hundred miles to its south.

What followed was a slaughter. The 1,700 massed Guaraní, again led by *cacique* Sepé, the only Indian with any aptitude for leadership, seemed inexplicably disorganized. Their heavy weapons were made of bamboo rods lashed together to form a cannon barrel. They had seven such cannons that could fire neither a far distance nor for a long period, disintegrating after the first few shots. Sepé was killed almost immediately after the shooting started, adding to what would soon be chaos. In his place Nicolás Neenguirú took over. Finding his force surrounded, he sent an agent to surrender. Valdelirios demanded that they immediately scatter back to their respective missions. Furthermore, as his army approached each of the seven missions, all the officials including *caciques*, *corregidors*, and justices as well as minor officials were to come out and submit to him. There apparently was some misunderstanding about how much time Neenguirú had to agree. Valdelirios had supposedly said one hour. After an hour and a half, with the Indians allegedly reorganizing for more fighting, the Europeans attacked, first with artillery, then with their cavalry leading a charge ahead of their infantry. In little more than an hour 1,500 Guaraní lay dead and 150 were taken prisoner. Three Spaniards and two Portuguese were killed. Andonaegui and twenty-nine others were wounded, but all recovered. Surviving Indians said that they had been waiting in vain for 200 of the Charruas and other pagans to come to their aid. This would have been meaningless, for the outcome was certain with or without the Charruas. Most of the Guaraní were buried

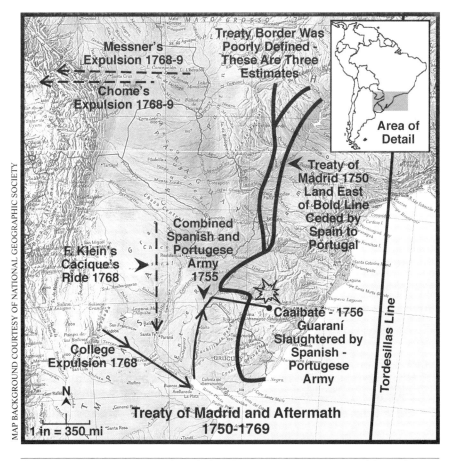

in the trenches they had dug as fortifications. Jaguars, peccaries, ravens, vultures, and vermin feasted on the rest.

The mopping-up operation was militarily uneventful. Each of the seven missions was surrendered as ordered or was abandoned. Yet the Indians retained a thread of hope. It was based on their confusion from seeing the anguish of their Jesuits on the one hand, yet seeing Altamirano, himself a Jesuit, demanding that they submit on the other.

As they marched into San Miguel's grand plaza, the conquerors were astonished to see its size and grandeur. The Spanish captain of the dragoons wrote in his diary that they were awed by the splendor of the June 16-17 Corpus Christi procession—the marching band, the dances, and the liturgy. His army joined in a parade while saluting the Blessed Sacrament with artillery salvos.

Guaraní Plead to Governor to Spare Them

Eighteen days after the Caaibaté slaughter, the Indian *corregidor* of San Miguel, Primo Ibarrenda, wrote the following pathetic letter to Governor Andonaegui:

> This is our writing that I send to you, that you may tell us finally what is to be our lot, and that you take a resolution what it is that you shall do. You see how that last year the father commissary [Visitor Altamirano] came to this our land to bother us to leave it, to leave our towns and all our territories, saying it was the will of our lord the king; besides this you yourself sent us a rigorous letter telling us to burn our towns [missions], destroy the fields, even pull down our church which is so beautiful, and saying also that you would kill us. You also say, and therefore we ask you if it is the truth, for if it is, we will all die before the Holy Sacrament; but spare the church, for it is God's, and even infidels would not do it any harm.

Ibarrenda went on to say that they had always been obedient subjects of the king, and it is impossible that his wish could be to injure them.

Cunninghame-Graham added:

> It was the letter of innocent men, half civilized, and thinking [that] justice, mercy, and right-doing were to be found with governors and kings. . . . Then when the fields were desolate, the villages deserted, and the Indian population half dispersed,

statesmen in Spain and Portugal saw fit to change their minds, to annul the treaty, and to pass a diplomatic sponge over the ruin and the misery they had caused.

Spain and Portugal Have Falling Out

As is so often the case the victors, intensely detesting each other as the Spanish and Portuguese did when not facing a common enemy, fell to quarreling. The Portuguese' sense of urgency in taking over the missions evaporated when they found there were no Jesuit gold mines or hidden treasure after all. Andrade was disillusioned and disgusted. His "great affair" of the Jesuit gold mines and hidden stashes of the metal had proven to be a pipe dream. Nevertheless, at Andrade's insistence, a new, open, and fair-minded governor of Buenos Aires—a marques by the name of Don Pedro Antonio de Cevallos y Cortés—felt honor-bound to enforce the treaty. Cevallos was forty-two and had a distinguished military career, especially in Italy where he attained the rank of field marshal, the equivalent of major general, at only thirty-two. He began enforcing the treaty by compelling the Indians to move from their seven missions west across the Uruguay, an exodus that took many months, not ending until August 1758.

Then Portuguese trickery escalated. Andrade claimed the Indians were still too near their former homes for his security. Cevallos showed him that there was nothing in the treaty limiting new locations for the missions, and he added a demand that Andrade hand over the Indians that the Portuguese had captured. The bickering continued over which of the two branches of the Ibicuí River was the boundary specified in the treaty. Meanwhile, the Portuguese refused to surrender Colonia, the main issue in the treaty as far as Spain was concerned. In fact they were fortifying it even further. It was fortunate for the Paraguay Jesuits that General Visconti died at this time. His death ended Altimirano's insidious role. He retired to permanent obscurity, the best he could have hoped for.

Cevallos took it upon himself to conduct an inquiry into the Jesuits and their role in the treaty's implementation. Many dozens of witnesses— military officers, civilian officials, and seventy Indians—testified as to the innocence of the Jesuits. Based on this he declared them to have been loyal throughout and sent his conclusion to Madrid. In it he described the accusations against the Jesuits as a "mere tissue of lies." He charged Altimirano and his accomplices to be "gross liars"—strong language, especially considering the people and the time.

In rapid-fire succession, many changes then took place in Madrid. First Minister Carvajal died in 1756. He was succeeded by Ricardo Wall, a surprisingly pro-English, anti-religious, anti-Jesuit Irishman at a time when England's oppressive occupation of Ireland was raw. Spain's Queen Barbara died two years later. The unstable Ferdinand, who had barely been held together by his wife, was overcome by profound melancholy and physical collapse, dying in 1759.

Enter Ferdinand's half-brother, King Charles III, and a whole new day for Paraguay.

Charles III Annuls the Treaty of Madrid

One of Charles' early actions was to annul the Treaty of Madrid. He recognized the treaty was to Spain's disadvantage, and the continuing subterfuge and treachery of the Portuguese in retaining Colonia was the perfect pretext for the annulment. The court in Lisbon gave its consent reluctantly. No doubt it had been embarrassed by the lack of Andrade's predicted Jesuit gold and by his double-cross in refusing to surrender Colonia. More importantly, Portugal's new First Minister Pombal believed that, while it was advantageous to have the treaty legalize Portugal's possession of the four huge Brazilian states it already occupied, *legalizing* that possession was at too high a cost. The cost was Colonia. And might it not keep Colonia eventually anyway?

Charles then instructed Cevallos to obtain support from the now compliant Andrade for a public pronouncement to settlers, traders, miners, Jesuits, Indians, and all government officials that the treaty was null and void. Everything was to be returned to the *status quo ante*—to its pre-1750 condition.

So it was. Three years of negotiation were followed by ten years of human misery and the mass murder of Guaraní, thousands scattered to the forest like leaves in the wind, broken families and hopes, and an incalculable economic loss for the Indians of the seven missions. By 1762 the seven missions were re-inhabited by 14,000 Indians, less than half the number that were there before the war started. Even the 14,000 were there thanks only to the fathers' scouring the forests and distant refuges. These Guaraní returned to pick up the pieces of their prior lives, and to eventually restore, for a while, the prosperity, harmony, and happiness they once had in their now-ruined missions.

Cevallos earned the everlasting gratitude of the Jesuits not only in Paraguay but around the world. His verdict of Jesuit innocence was affirmed even by Spain's First Minister Ricardo Wall.

Spain Battles Portugal in La Plata

In August 1762, after the Portuguese refused to surrender Colonia, the newly promoted Lieutenant General Cevallos blockaded Colonia. He assembled a fleet of several warships, five barges, and twenty-six launches, making plans to attack the city. In early September his flotilla carried 650 veterans, 1,500 inexperienced militia, and 1,200 armed Guaraní brought hundreds of miles down from the missions by Jesuit Father Segismundo Bauer, across Río de La Plata from Buenos Aires, disembarking them three miles outside Colonia. Drawing on his extensive military experience, Cevallos used thirty-seven artillery pieces to provide cover as his troops approached the fortified walls. With two huge breaches blown in the walls, the Guaraní poured in under covering fire from the Spanish troops. Southey writes that the Guaraní behaved with great fervor; the presence of the Spanish and especially the charismatic Cevallos inspired them with courage; and they were fighting an enemy whom they hated.

The city was taken almost in its entirety, and two months later, on October 30, the Portuguese Governor Vicente Silva de Fonseca surrendered. Once again the loyal Guaraní had borne the burden of combat and carried the day for Spain.

Two months later, on January 6, 1763, Cevallos repulsed an attack by a joint Anglo-Portuguese eleven-ship naval force, launched from Rio de Janeiro, intending to re-capture Colonia. They also had designs on Montevideo and even Buenos Aires. Southey says that the English ships were privateers of an uncertain provenance and its officers had been commissioned by the Portuguese in Lisbon. Was this a ruse to remove any British fingerprints and responsibility for the assault? That's uncertain. Nevertheless, before the battle an English lieutenant Primrose wrote to his future wife that their ultimate objective was to "seize the treasures of Potosí's mines."

It was a rare occasion for the Spanish to defeat the English, as we'll name them for convenience. It even included the sinking of the English flagship, the sixty-four gun Lord Clive, with its Irish-born admiral John MacNamara. He went down soon after his ship did with 400 of its 480 crew. The eighty survivors were taken prisoner. A sailor who was a good swimmer took MacNamara on his back and made for shore. When the sailor's strength ebbed and the admiral perceived this, he gave the sailor his sword, then "bade him to look to his own preservation, let go of his hold, and sunk."

The Portuguese frigate, Gloria, and the other English ship, the Ambuscade, were driven off with the latter losing eighty of its 350 crew. Cevallos' victory was all the more impressive given the cowardice of Carlos José de Sarria, the commander of the Spanish fleet who fled in his own frigate, the Victoria, to avoid having to engage the English. Cevallos lost only four men killed, a 120 to one casualty ratio. The survivors from the Lord Clive were taken prisoner and sent to Córdoba where most or perhaps all of them settled. They thrived and introduced improvements to agriculture and the manual arts unknown to the Spanish there.

Anglophiles might be relieved to hear Southey's description of the fleet's origin confirmed. The English ships were not from the Royal Navy. A Royal Navy website states that the ships had been sold to a group of merchant adventurers and entrepreneurial noblemen. It also refers to MacNamara as "Mr." and not "Admiral."

Had the Anglo-Portuguese attack succeeded in taking Colonia and then Buenos Aires, La Plata and everything upstream from it including Potosí and all of the Guaraní Republic would have been strangled. Then, if the politicians in Paris had not interfered, the political map of South America would have been vastly altered. As it turned out, a month later, on February 10, 1763, the Treaty of Paris reconfigured colonial possessions around the world, including the return of Colonia to Portugal, while leaving Buenos Aires safely Spanish.

The Treaty of Paris was still unknown (round-trip trans-Atlantic communications took most of a year) before Cevallos, energized by his victory, and with an unprecedented army of some 2,000 Spaniards and 6,000 Guaraní, went on the march. He had an open field over which he advanced, virtually unopposed, into today's Uruguay and Brazil's Rio Grande do Sul (largely the Guayrá) state. Almost all of that huge region was recaptured from the Portuguese who panicked and fled in front of his attack. For Cevallos it was all for naught. The treaty would return the Spanish-Portuguese border to the *status quo ante* (although the border had been in such a state of flux that no one was quite sure which *ante* was appropriate).

Treaty of Paris Ends Fighting

The Treaty of Paris had brought to a close the Seven Years' War, also known in North America as The French and Indian War. It was a war that could be fairly argued to be the first world war, as it was waged throughout Europe, the Americas, India, and the Philippines.

Only many years later would the original intent of the Treaty of Madrid be codified in a new Treaty of 1777, also known as the Treaty of San Ildefonso. This redrew the border, giving Rio Grande do Sul to Portugal and giving Colonia along with some additional disputed Paraguayan territory to Spain. By then however, the Jesuits were long gone, having been expelled by Charles III a decade earlier.

It is supreme irony that under Cevallos' leadership Spain with its Guaraní soldiers defeated the Portuguese army on a South American battlefield for the first time and were on the verge of taking back huge portions of Brazil, only to lose it all at the negotiating table in Paris. If Spain had not been sucked by France into the Seven Years' War at a time when the war was virtually lost, the political and cultural makeup of South America and its Guaraní people would have been dramatically different.

Jesuits of Paraguay Lose in the End

The long-term losers in Charles' rescission of the Treaty of Madrid were the Jesuits of Paraguay and the Guaraní. Cunninghame-Graham writes that what appeared to be a triumph contributed towards their ruin, "for the jealousy which they evoked by their persistent fight raised up much animosity toward themselves in Spain." Yet the only demonstrable "fight" they put up was to send petitions to the king, an action certainly within their rights. As for the Portuguese and the slavers of São Paulo, they lost the battle but won the war when the Society of Jesus was expelled from Portugal, France, Spain, and their possessions, and ultimately suppressed by the pope.

Luckily for the Guaraní, by the time the Jesuits were expelled from Paraguay the mamelucos had lost much of their interest in capturing more Indian slaves. Their attention had turned to easier pickings—the burgeoning gold and diamond mines in the state of Minas Gerais, north of São Paulo.

Black Robes in Paraguay

PART TWO

Jesuits Are Expelled from Europe and South America

CHAPTER 14

Portugal's Jesuits—The First to Fall

By the late 1750s France was in such political and religious turmoil that some leading Jesuits began to fear their order's days were numbered. The *philosophes* of the Enlightenment and Gallican nationalists had spread their doctrine of populism, nationalism, and deism throughout the political and religious scene. Before the crises of France had reached a climax, the same forces had crossed the Pyrenees into Iberia. There these forces would intersect with the career of the Marquês de Pombal, a tall, imposing, self-assured, experienced, energetic, audacious, determined, anti-noble, anti-papist, popular nationalist. He was a Machiavellian schemer and a patriot in the eyes of his admirers, but a diabolical tyrant in the eyes of his detractors. He burst onto the Portuguese scene as the result of a catastrophic earthquake at a most inopportune time for the Jesuits. Pombal the activist would beat the French to the punch by expelling the Jesuits first.

Portugal in the Mid-Eighteenth Century

Portugal was a small country both in size (a sixth of Spain's) and population (a tenth of Spain's), and poorly endowed in natural resources. Feeling they had to live by their wits as a trading and colonial nation, the Portuguese became courageous explorers and astute merchants while subjugating native peoples in their far-flung colonies from Macao to Angola to Brazil. This mindset and its huge success helped the Portuguese convince themselves that their opportunistic and self-serving behavior in Brazil and Paraguay was justified. This was especially true of their disregard for the rights of their subjugated Indians and for the Treaty of Tordesillas setting the line between Spanish and Portuguese colonial control.

By the 1750s the relationship between the Portuguese government and the Roman Catholic Church was at a low ebb, even more so than it was in France, and for mostly similar reasons. One large difference was that while France's Jesuits in North America had no such problems with the French government, Portugal's Brazilian Jesuits had increasingly become a nuisance to its civilian leadership. While France's anti-clerical, anti-Jesuit attitudes had been brewing for two centuries, during that period Portugal's kings and Jesuits had a mutually supportive relationship. Indeed, the missionaries had often been agents of the crown. Nevertheless, coincident with Pombal's ascent to power, pressure was building to secularize Portugal's society and reduce the control that the country's nobles exercised over the government.

In the first half of the 1700s, the Guaraní Republic grew and expanded to the north and east just as Portugal's Brazilian settlements were expanding to the south and to the west. These two societies, built on fundamentally different human values, were on a collision course that would result in war and the inevitable destruction of the Guaraní. In a world that was increasingly governed by great-power greed and nationalism, the outcome should have been predictable. What the Paraguay Jesuits of the time did not seem to anticipate or appreciate was the capacity of Europe's leaders to collaborate in scheming, even with their adversaries in Europe. At the start of the second half of the century, who would enter Europe's center stage but Pombal, the quintessential manipulator.

Pombal, the Man and the Politician

Sebastião José de Carvalho e Melo arrived on the Portuguese scene for the first time as a senior official in 1750, at the beginning of the crises in the Guaraní Republic. He is better known to history as the Marquês de Pombal, or simply Pombal. (Pombal was a region where he maintained his estate.) The honorific title was awarded by the king in 1770 in recognition of his numerous accomplishments both domestically and in foreign affairs. He was the right man for the job, assuming the job was to strengthen Portugal and eliminate the Jesuits and their missions in the Republic and in central Brazil. Jesuit enemies would say that he was able to accomplish much of the former by doing the latter.

Pombal arrived at his job on the heels of stagnation in Portugal, largely due to the long reign of João V (John V) "the Magnificent." This lethargic and complacent king reigned from 1706 to 1750. As is often the case, Portugal was able to postpone the effects of inept leadership thanks to wealth accumulated earlier and to the discovery of substantial quantities of alluvial gold in 1699 and diamonds in 1730 in eastern Brazil. The gold added about $30 billion (in today's U.S. dollars) to the Portuguese treasury during the eighteenth century; the diamonds, several billion more.

When John V died in 1750, he was succeeded by his thirty-year-old son, José I (Joseph I), self-indulgent and ineffective like his father but even worse as he was "lazy, sickly, eternally bored [whose] favorite occupation was to go for walks along the Tagus [the river adjacent to Lisbon] surrounded by beautiful women and musicians." Perhaps the best thing that Joseph did was to immediately name Pombal, whom he had come to know and of whom he was fond, to be minister of foreign affairs. Then the king stayed out of the way. With Pombal's superior intelligence, domineering personality, and extraordinary experience, his competitors in the government were soon so diminished that the king gradually transferred all power to him. This enabled Joseph to fully devote himself to a life of pleasure-seeking, especially music and hunting—the latter being a passion of his Spanish wife, Queen Marianna Victoria.

It is important to understand Pombal's philosophical underpinnings, both as a man and a politician, because he as much as any other single person caused the downfall of the Jesuits and their missions.

Pombal was born to a country squire (upper middle class) in 1699. After studying law at a Portuguese university and serving briefly in the army, he married a woman ten years his senior and of higher social standing (the niece of a count) after she agreed to his "kidnapping" her. The marriage had been opposed by her family who proceeded to make their life together difficult, a possible reason for his later intense dislike of nobility. She died young, in 1737.

It was rumored that at some point the youthful Pombal had taken a fancy to one of the daughters of the Távora family who figure prominently later. The young woman's mother, the Marchioness Távora, had responded by forbidding Pombal to enter her house, rejecting him as an adventurer. His later actions might have been guided by bitter personal hatred for the Távoras that spilled over to the Jesuits.

In 1738 his cousin, Azevedo Coutinho, now a minister of state and former ambassador to Paris and London, sent Pombal to replace him in London. Pombal's six years in England were in the middle of a period of revolutionary political and philosophical thinking among such luminaries as the two William Pitts (father and son), Alexander Pope, Adam Smith, and the *philosophes* across the English Channel. It was well after John Locke and Isaac Newton, but only nine years after Voltaire's exile there. The Enlightenment leaders of both England and France, in spite of those countries' epic struggles for colonial dominance, had entered into a sort of informal alliance of ideas, drawing philosophical and political strength from one another. Pombal's own intellectual development evolved during those years, especially his admiration for British merchants and the benefits of their commerce and capitalism; the country's relative religious tolerance; its support for the natural sciences; and, most importantly, the Anglican Church's subordination to the English crown. Pombal developed what is today called a "political theology," the political captivity of the Church in the service of the modern nation-state. He would bring this re-ordering of human society to Portugal and set an example that took hold for the French in five years (they really needed no example) and for Spain in a decade.

By the time Pombal left England he had become an Anglophile. The English would reciprocate. Some years later the English ambassador to Lisbon said of Pombal, "With all his faults, he is the sole man in this kingdom capable of being at the head of affairs." Of course, it did not hurt that they had a common adversary in Spain.

In 1745 he was transferred to Vienna to help repair strained relations between the Archduchess, later Empress Maria Theresa, and the pope. He succeeded. John V's Austrian wife, the Archduchess Maria Anna, a Pombal fan, encouraged Pombal's marriage to his second wife, the daughter of Austria's revered Field Marshal Count von Daun. During his exposure to the Austrian monarchy he came to appreciate "enlightened" autocrats. This was due to Maria Theresa's high moral principles, her administrative and social reforms, her popularity among her subjects, and her support for music and the arts that made Vienna a world leader in culture.

Earthquake of 1755 Destroys Lisbon

After Pombal returned to Portugal in 1749, he quickly became Joseph I's most prominent minister, starting as minister of foreign affairs. He was well positioned to demonstrate his leadership abilities when a national calamity struck. At 9:30 on the morning of November 1, 1755, two monumental earthquakes—each lasted several minutes, separated by five minutes, the worst ever in European history—rocked Portugal. Lisbon was at its epicenter and was almost totally destroyed. Many thousands of worshippers attending All Saints' Day ceremonies were crushed as churches collapsed. Tens of thousands more were buried by other buildings as they disintegrated. Within minutes a twenty-foot high tsunami inundated the port, swamping numerous ships anchored there or tossing them up on land, drowning uncounted thousands in the low lying neighborhoods along the Tagus River mouth. National monuments, art treasures, and archives were consumed in an after-fire that lasted three days. Criminals escaped from prisons to plunder the ruins and "rob corpses in the street." Many other cities and towns were heavily damaged. Estimates were that from fifty to seventy thousand people died in the quake and the immediate aftermath.

One of the few houses spared was Pombal's. The king was told that this was considered a sign of divine approval. He was deeply moved. But a discontented noble, the Count of São Lourenço, pointed out that the Almighty had also spared the Rua Suja, the city's street of brothels. Another reason for Pombal to hate nobles.

Upon meeting with Pombal, the panicked king exclaimed, "What can be done?" Pombal calmly responded with his most famous quote, "Sire, we must bury the dead and feed the living." And that he did. Nevertheless, disease and famine stalked the land for many months.

Pombal took charge of maintaining public order and bringing relief to survivors. Under the direction of architects whom he appointed, Pombal used Lisbon's rebuilding to completely redesign the city. Ostentatious displays of individual wealth were prohibited and a progressive approach to the design of commercial and government buildings was adopted. Remembering their happy relationship with Pombal when he was ambassador to London a decade before, England's Parliament helped with 100,000 pounds in aid, a handsome sum in those days, as well as with a huge amount of food and construction equipment. Spain sent "four wagon loads of money." His leadership in restoring the country was widely acclaimed as an historic accomplishment. This helped convince the king to appoint him to be first minister and *de facto* head of state in 1760, then Marquês de Pombal in 1770. All the while that Pombal's political star was rising, his relationship with the Jesuits was falling.

Why Pombal Broke with the Jesuits

There were three major reasons for the hostility that Pombal showed toward the Jesuits. This hostility came from a man who once respected and admired them. Underlying it all was a deep fear and resentment of Jesuit influence in the Portuguese court and their power throughout its empire. As an example of their influence with the court, it was reported that the devout King John V groveled before the famed saintly and revered Italian-born Jesuit, Gabriel de Malagrida, imploring his blessing. The priest responded with, "Bless the King, thy servant." To which the kneeling royal penitent mumbled, "Do not call me *king*, call me *sinner*." The king later died in the Jesuit's arms. As for the queen, she extracted a promise from Malagrida that he would return from his missionary work in Brazil to minister to her when the time of her death approached. This he did. He became both a major irritant and a major disgrace for Pombal.

The English author, Marcus Cheke, writes that Malagrida's adventures in Brazil could fill a volume. He preached repentance to the people in the streets of Pará in northern Brazil. His eloquence inflamed his listeners as crowds assembled wherever he went. People became hysterical! He avowedly sought martyrdom as he preached for twelve years in the jungle, converting and baptizing Indians. Many times he almost got his wish. Once he barely escaped from cannibals by swimming between two soldiers across a lake filled with crocodiles. In an ambush his hat was pierced by an arrow. His miracles grew with his fame. He built convents and churches, seminaries and retreats, working as a laborer himself and trundling a wheelbarrow and lifting heavy stones. His appearance added to his reputation: He was fair-haired with a flowing white beard even in his early years.

Malagrida's devotion to the Virgin Mary was legendary, as illustrated by his carrying her image with him wherever he went. It was the "cause" of his miraculous preservation from harm. As he returned to Lisbon in 1754 at age sixty-five, after twenty years in Brazil, his reputation preceded him. The dying, pious King John learned "with rapture" that not only would Malagrida give him the Blessed Sacrament but also this "prophet" was bringing the miraculous image of the Virgin. The king gifted a costly robe and a set of jewels to festoon her image which the king kept in his royal chamber.

Malagrida returned to Brazil on the same ship as Francisco Xavier de Mendoça Furtado, Pombal's half-brother and now the captain general and governor of Maranhão, a large strategically important part of northern Brazil. Mendoça was warned to be on his guard against Malagrida—an ominous sign. The pious Queen Mother had insisted that the Brazilian Jesuits relate to her everything that went on in the missions, including any misdeeds of officials like Mendoça. When Pombal secretly intercepted her mail from Brazil he learned everything he needed to know about her Jesuit "spies." They were soon exiled by Mendoça.

Two years later Malagrida returned to Lisbon for the dying Queen Mother as promised, a return Pombal viewed with a "grim eye." This suspected instrument of Pombal's enemies was enjoying immense popularity while "whispering sedition in the corridors of the palace, in the royal chapel and the confessional box." Malagrida was said to have "given him open offense by urging the recall of Mendoça from [Brazil]." Pombal was beginning to "get Jesuits on the brain." He would not forget.

Cheke lists the Jesuits' refusal to carry out the evacuation of the seven missions of the Republic of the Guaraní as the first reason for Pombal's hostility. Second was their opposition to his trade "reforms". Third was their "continual intrigues" against him in Lisbon. Additional irritants for Pombal were the Jesuits' influence at the court as illustrated above and their control over the educational system of the entire country. In Lisbon alone they had four substantial colleges.

The Treaty of Madrid (of 1750), which transferred a large area of southern Brazil, including its seven great Guaraní missions, from Spain to Portugal, turned out to be a fiasco for Pombal even though the treaty was not of his doing. It was unpopular among both Portuguese and Spanish colonial interests, each thinking that the other had been advantaged. As we saw in Chapter 13 on the Guaraní War, although the rebellious Guaraní were eventually defeated, it was only after embarrassing initial setbacks of the combined Portuguese and Spanish military forces at the hands of the disorganized and poorly armed Indians during Pombal's rule. The Jesuits in the Guaraní Republic, especially their superiors and provincial, did everything possible to avoid war knowing the inevitable outcome would be disastrous for the Indians. Nevertheless, it was widely believed among the Spanish and especially the Portuguese, both in Europe and America, that the rebellion had been instigated by those Jesuits in the field.

Pombal was able to use the insurgency in Paraguay to paint an alarming picture of the empire for King Joseph. The economy was in bad shape. Its bleak outlook resulted from the costly suppression of the Guaraní, and the far more costly rebuilding of Lisbon and other cities after the earthquake. The latter turned out to be worse than ever imagined. The increasing flow of gold and diamonds from Brazil that began in 1699 had helped the financial situation, but not nearly enough. By September 19, 1757, Pombal had convinced the king that a principal cause of the problem, the Jesuits, had to be dealt with. On that date the king ordered the Jesuit confessors to his court and royal family, including his own confessor, to leave the court, retire to their colleges, and never to return. They were replaced by the principal of the Franciscans for the king and the superiors of the Augustinians and the Carmelites for the others.

As first minister, Pombal thought that his economic problems could be solved if he could seize the alleged enormous assets of Portugal's Jesuits and of its two richest families, the Aveiros and the Távoras. He would work on that next.

Pombal went after the low-hanging fruit first—the Jesuit missions of central Brazil. In 1758 he dispatched three magistrates to seize all their mission assets and return them to Portugal. The dates are revealing. Arriving there on August 28, the magistrates immediately set to work. They confiscated everything of value—as it turned out there was relatively little—that would be helpful in meeting the government's huge needs. Then, on September 3, there was an attempt on King Joseph's life. The attempt was six days after the magistrates had arrived in Brazil and about three months after they had left Lisbon. Yet, as various official documents prove, Pombal rewrote history. The Jesuits' "complicity" in the attempted assassination was used by Pombal as the justification for confiscating all their assets, including those that were seized by his magistrates in Brazil before the attempt even took place! The attack on the king would soon turn out to be a political bonanza for Pombal.

Pombal's Business Deals Cause Conflicts with Jesuits

Pombal's business practices—he called them "trade reforms"—during these years were questionable. In 1755 he formed the Grão Pará Trading Company, loosely modeled on England's immensely successful East India Company. It was intended to revive Portugal's commercial activities and to counter a large British presence in Lisbon and Oporto. The company was given a monopoly on trading with Brazil in African slaves and the sale of colonial products at prices fixed by Pombal himself. He arranged special naval protection for its merchant fleets and had unique and preferential legal privileges. All this gave rise to strong opposition from other parties who were financially disadvantaged, including the Jesuits who were excluded from trading with their own Brazilian missions. Jesuit Manuel Bellester spoke from his pulpit in the Patriarchal Church in Lisbon opposing the company. Pombal immediately sent him into exile. He brooked no opposition.

More sinister was Pombal's General Company (also known as the Company of Wines of the Upper Douro), a *de facto* monopoly of the immensely profitable, world-famous wine exports of Oporto, the center of Portugal's port wine business. It was formed in 1756, and in short order the British whom Pombal accused of exploitation and Portuguese merchants lost business to it. Surging prices for his wine—caused mainly by unfavorable weather for nearby vineyards—and aggrieved tavern-keepers led to the 1757 "Tipplers' Revolt." The General Company was blamed by residents for both the prices and the revolt.

The resistance climaxed when some 6,000 residents of Oporto rioted in the streets and surrounded the house of the city's magistrate. They forced him to promise to abolish the company. No major damage was done nor was anyone seriously harmed, but being the man he was Pombal went on the offensive. He surrounded Oporto with thousands of troops and set up a special tribunal to arrest, try, and punish the ringleaders. Thirteen men and four women were hanged; twenty-five were condemned to the galleys, some for life; eighty-six were banished; fifty-eight were fined and imprisoned. Oporto was required to pay for the quartering of 3,000 soldiers. Portugal had gotten its first taste of Pombal the tyrant. Rumors in Oporto and Lisbon implicated the Jesuits for inciting the mobs. Yet there was no evidence that they played any role whatsoever, not withstanding their large share of the port wine market. Their only "crime" was that they had complained that their own wines were not capable of being used in their masses. But they were not to be punished, yet.

Pombal Sees Jesuit Intrigues

Beginning with his frustration over the Paraguay missions, Pombal developed an adversarial relationship with all Jesuits, seeing Jesuit "intrigues" against him everywhere. He had good reason. One of these intrigues became an intensely personal reason for his falling out with the Jesuit order. It was a tendentious spiritual paper published by the same Jesuit Gabriel Malagrida with the required permission of his superiors. It was endorsed by a number of other Jesuits and clergy. Entitled *Judgment of the Real Cause of the Earthquake . . . of 1755*, it blamed the catastrophe as divine retribution for the immorality of the people of Lisbon and, implicitly, their government. This Pombal took personally. He was especially angered when Malagrida distributed complimentary copies to the king and many nobles. Some other Jesuits did not help their order's image when, from their pulpits, they indicted Pombal for the earthquake and appealed to the public for acts of faith to prevent a repeat. Then they insensitively requested contributions for founding new Jesuit colleges. Pombal had all copies of the paper confiscated and had Malagrida exiled from Lisbon to Sétubal, twenty-five miles to the south. Subsequently, Pombal had him imprisoned there. Five years later, Malagrida would pay with his life.

Another Jesuit intrigue might have been over a proposed royal marriage. Pombal, the strategically thinking diplomat, Anglophile, and Hispanophobe, tried to arrange the marriage of King Joseph's eldest daughter, Maria Francisca, to the Protestant Prince William Henry, son of the King of England. Apparently Joseph's Jesuit confessor, José Moreira, was able to turn him against the marriage on the grounds that the prince was a heretic. Maria might not have been enamored of the idea, for she would become Pombal's nemesis in his later years after she ascended the throne.

The Jesuits also appear to have thwarted Pombal's desire to grant certain privileges to the Jews in return for their financial aid in rebuilding Lisbon after the earthquake.

Meanwhile, Pombal kept his presses busy printing scurrilous pamphlets entitled *Nouvelles intéresantes* (the French version published in Amsterdam), mainly about the Jesuits of South America and Portugal written under Pombal's direction by a defrocked Capuchin monk. The pamphlets condemned the Jesuits for their rapacity and exploitation of the Indians and their efforts to build an independent empire. Well after the Guaraní War, he published a sixty-eight-page *Abridged Relation of the Republic Which the Jesuit Priests Have Established in the Overseas Dominions of the Two Monarchies, and of the War They Have Provoked Against the Spanish and Portuguese Armies.* Paraguay had become an obsession. This one backfired in Madrid when the Spanish took umbrage with the idea that the Guaraní had at first humiliated the combined armies of Portugal and Spain. The work was burned by Castile's executioner. The pamphlets kept coming, a regular drumbeat of derogatory and libelous attacks on the Jesuits. Pombal's cause got help from a former Jesuit who had been expelled from the order in 1757, with his publication, *The Jesuit Kingdom in Paraguay.*

Pombal's scheming continued when he appointed his cousin, Francisco Almada e Mendoça, to be ambassador to the Vatican. Almada's importance cannot be overstated. He was a force behind the anti-Jesuits close to Pope Benedict XIV. He bribed shamelessly and organized a network to spy on the Jesuits. Three weeks after the king expelled the Jesuit confessors from his court, Almada pressed Benedict to sanction a reform of the order because the Jesuits had

> . . . sacrificed all Christian, religious, natural, and political obligations to a blind wish, insolent and unbounded, to make themselves masters of government . . . an insatiable desire to heap up foreign riches . . . to usurp the dominions of sovereigns.

Four months later, in February 1758, Almada treated Benedict to a laundry-list of complaints about the Jesuits, including discontent fomented by the Jesuits in Paraguay, intrigues in court against the king, opposition to commercial companies that would interfere with the extensive commerce they themselves monopolized in South America, attempts to increase the general confusion during the earthquake, instigators of the riots that took place in Oporto who said that the General Company's wines were not fit for the Holy Sacrament. Soon after this, the terminally ill pope, apparently unconvinced, was bombarded with every mentionable crime that could be mustered against the Paraguay fathers including their living opulently while impoverishing the Indians and enslaving them, ignoring the laws of the king and Church—a litany of accusations that Pombal had published in several languages and circulated throughout Europe while reviving and recruiting animosity against them.

Pombal's Pawn, Cardinal Saldanha, Appointed Primate

Early in 1758 Pombal began a maneuver to get Cardinal Don Francisco de Saldanha appointed by the pope to be primate of Portugal. Bangert says he was a "good-natured man of no exceptional competence or endowments," the subservient kind of man on whom Pombal could rely. Pombal had gotten him his cardinal's red hat and his title: "Patriarch of Lisbon, Visitor and Reformer of the Society of Jesus in the Kingdoms of Portugal and the Algarves." The title told it all.

Pombal had ambassador Almada approach the dying Benedict XIV and two of his key advisors in the Curia, Cardinals Achinto and Passionei, with the above-mentioned litany of accusations aimed at the Paraguay Jesuits. Later this list would show up in public condemnations of the Jesuits fulminating from Saldanha. Almada rushed his accusations and his demand for Saldanha's appointment to the Vatican, fearing that if the pope died before acting a huge delay and much uncertainty would result. While hoping to mollify Pombal and head off a possible schism in the Church, Benedict relied on the advice of the two Curia cardinals. Almada then bribed the two with cases of Brazilian sugar supplied by Pombal. The appointment was subject only to the king's approval. It was a colossal mistake on the part of Benedict, a normally worldly-wise statesman. He had handed Pombal control over religion in Portugal.

At this point the eighty-three-year-old Pope Benedict died and was succeeded by a well-meaning Venetian, the bishop of Padua, Carlo della Torre Rezzonico, who took the name Clement XIII. He would reign for eleven years—emotionally battering for him—during the height of the Bourbon and Bragança (Portuguese) kings' persecution of the Jesuits. Immediately Almada, still Pombal's ambassador in Rome, presented to the new pope the list of formal charges against the Jesuits. As Southey writes:

> The list contained . . . charges . . . which the king had long abstained from preferring because of his incomparable clemency and his pious devotion to the Saints Loyola, Xavier, and Borja. But such . . . was the extreme corruption into which the Jesuits in his dominions had fallen that they now seemed to be merchants, or soldiers, or royalets, rather than religioners. Many . . . were ruined by their insidious artifices; they had formed establishments from the [Amazon] to the Uruguay, binding the two Americas, Spanish and Portuguese, with so strong a chord that in ten years more it would be impossible to untie the knot. And now they had unmasked themselves: They had waged war in Paraguay against the two allied sovereigns; they had promoted disorders and mutiny in Pará [a huge state in northern Brazil straddling the Amazon—the ambassador had to be referring to the missions along that great river and its tributaries and not to the missions of the Guaraní Republic far to the south]; . . . and they had opposed the Royal Laws and Papal Bulls more openly than even the Knights Templars, who for their offenses had been punished with such severity and extinguished as an order.

Southey finishes by saying that these charges were as "silly as they were false."

Then, fortuitously, there was a most historic event, this time a truly malevolent one that played the ultimate role in Pombal's drive to expel the Jesuits. It was known as the Távora Affair. This bizarre and horrific "affair" involved an attempt on the life of King Joseph. If the pro-Pombal historians are correct, he was the unintended beneficiary of his opponents' ineptly attempted regicide, followed by their subsequent exposure and punishment. If the anti-Pombal historians have it right, he was a murderous tyrant.

Attempted Assassination of Joseph I, the Távora Affair

The Távora Affair began toward midnight on September 3, 1758. King Joseph was returning from an evening tryst with one of his mistresses, the young Teresa Leonor, wife (and aunt!) of the eldest scion of the Távora family—Luis Bernardo. This was despite the king's reportedly happy domestic life that included four daughters whom he loved dearly. Nor was he constrained by being "in strict mourning" from the death of his sister, the Queen of Spain, a few days before. Habitual infidelity was not uncommon for royals of that era.

Teresa Leonor's father-in-law, the Marquês de Távora, and her mother-in-law, the Marchioness, headed a powerful noble family that had close connections to other important families including the most prominent and wealthy of all, that of José de Mascarenhas. He was the Duke of Aveiro, Count of Santa Cruz, Marquês de Gouveia, and Grand Marshal of the Royal Household. Known as Aveiro, he was married to the Marquês de Távora's sister. British Ambassador Benjamin Keene praised Távora as "the best bred and most agreeable man among them [Portugal's nobility]." The marchioness was a star of King John V's (Joseph's father) court, known for her beauty and wit. Her fame was sung by poets. All were bitter enemies of Pombal, understandably so, given his first marriage and his resulting anti-noble tendencies.

As the king proceeded home from his liaison with Teresa Leonor, his coachman found a gate on the main road to be jammed. This was a first. So they took a dark and lonely side road. Suddenly three masked men on horseback appeared, surrounded the coach (an open-sided chaise), and opened-fire. The blunderbuss, a pistol-like short musket, aimed at the coachman misfired, so the coachman pressed his mules to a gallop and sped away. Moments later there was a second ambush. This time the king was allegedly wounded in the right shoulder and arm. The coachman was also wounded, but not seriously. Pedro Teixeira, the king's confidant, seated next to him was not hit. One report alleged a third ambush was thwarted when the coachman took a detour for the house of the king's doctor who dressed the wounds. The king returned to the palace without delay. He recovered with miraculous rapidity with no outwardly visible signs of having been wounded. What happened in the next few days is "shrouded in mystery and obscurity."

What is certain however, is that within days, under Pombal's direction, two suspects were arrested, secretly interrogated, and possibly tortured. They allegedly confessed and implicated the Távora family as co-conspirators. They said that the Távoras, at the instigation of Jesuits, were planning to place the Duke of Aveiro on the throne. Both men were immediately hanged, also in secret.

Pombal knew that Aveiro and the Távoras were in close contact with people in Brazil, and he suspected that they would write to them about the assassination attempt. At that time, ships could not leave Lisbon without government approval. Pombal arranged with the captain of a brig, Nossa Senhora (Our Lady) to announce a sailing to Brazil in early November. Immediately, "innumerable letter-bags" were put on board by unnamed persons. Then, the captain was given orders to stop in the Portuguese Azores en route to Brazil and surrender the letter-bags to the governor there. The governor examined the letters and found incriminating material that was placed on a warship directed to Lisbon. Soon, Pombal had a treasure trove of damning documents from the conspirators' own hands—twenty-four letters from Aveiro, the Marquês and Marchioness Távora, Gabriel Malagrida their confessor (now seventy years old), the young Távoras, and others. All the letters contained news of the attempt along with threats and denunciations against the government. Meanwhile, Pombal was also gathering testimony from witnesses.

Then Pombal had a proclamation, over his signature, posted in Lisbon announcing that "certain infamous persons unknown" had prophesied the king's death and had conspired to cause it. It then described the attack and offered large rewards for aid in bringing the would-be killers to justice. The phraseology was clearly aimed at Malagrida who had preached and written a letter about "divine punishment" being brought down on the king whom he called "the anti-Christ," unless he ceased persecuting the Jesuits. A search located such a letter that was found, conveniently, in Malagrida's papers after he was arrested. Just what Pombal needed.

Conspirators Tried

On January 4, 1759, Pombal appointed the investigating judge and the members of a tribunal to serve as a jury, together comprising the "court." The tribunal "humbly" suggested that the king "should suspend his innate royal mercy so far as to allow the employment of torture" and that the trial be conducted in secret so "the accused might give their evidence without fear." The king obliged with a decree reinstating torture as the permitted method of interrogation — in this case, having one's limbs stretched and torn on the infamous "rack."

While the king's mistress Teresa Leonor and her husband were spared, the Marchioness and Marquês de Távora were arrested. They quickly confessed in private to a Jesuit-instigated plot to place Aveiro on the throne. Aveiro confessed that four Jesuits were involved. Later in public they claimed to have been tortured into their confessions and retracted them. Nevertheless, mass arrests of the Távora and Aveiro family members were followed by those of other nobles. Gabriel Malagrida was also arrested with nine other Jesuits but, after his years of exile and imprisonment by Pombal, he had descended into his dotage. This bought him time. His Italian origins were cited as evidence that Jesuit General Lorenzo Ricci was involved. Pombal was gradually getting even for the priest's 1756 spiritual paper on the great earthquake's causes.

Conveniently, witnesses came forward with useful, though hearsay, testimony. One, a spy, said that he overheard in a tavern a French teacher saying that he had a friend named Antonio Ferreira who had borrowed a pistol from him a few days before the attempt and returned it a few days after. This testimony corroborated that of a certain glove-maker in Lisbon who had come to Pombal's house and revealed that the same Antonio Ferreira had borrowed a musket from him on August 3 and returned it on August 8, saying, "Thanks. With this gun I did a better piece of work than I've ever done in my life." In response to the glove-maker's inquiry, Ferreira told him that he was in the service of the Duke of Aviero.

A youth, hiding next to Aveiro's home awaiting his girl friend who was a servant in the home, testified that he heard the duke cursing at his gun for misfiring and that he recognized Aveiro's companion as a Távora son. He even described the son's clothing. His testimony survived for eighteen years until a new investigation into the whole affair totally discredited it, as described later.

No effective defense could be mounted. Counsel for the accused was appointed by the king two days before sentencing and was given twenty-four hours to prepare. No witnesses were allowed to be cross-examined, nor could defense witnesses be called even though there were compelling alibis from unimpeachable sources.

Finally, the tribunal concluded that the Jesuits played a "nefarious" part in the plot because of their waning power and their "colonies" in Paraguay being destroyed.

The tribunal found all of the accused "guilty" and recommended that these "monsters vomited from hell" should be punished "with a severity that would leave an indelible impression on the minds of his Majesty's faithful vassals."

Death sentences were then generously passed out for treason and attempted assassination.

Horrifying Executions Follow

The findings of the court were published on January 12, 1759. On the next day at dawn a cold drizzle was falling on the Plaza de Belén near Lisbon as the horrific and gruesome spectacle of the executions was about to begin. They were held in front of the king, other nobles (who presumably needed a lesson), relatives of the condemned, and an immense crowd of on-lookers which had gathered. Pombal observed from a window in a building on the square. The Marchioness—the same woman who had banned Pombal from her home many years before—was the first to be executed. But before that, she was allowed a fifty minute confession and absolution from a priest, not Malagrida. Then she mounted the scaffold. The executioners insisted that she look at the hammers, rolling wheel, and pyre that would be used next to torture and execute her husband and sons. Then she was beheaded.

Next, her youngest son, the one who had refused to confess under torture and give up his family, had "his limbs . . . tied to two diagonal pieces of timber; the eight bones of his arms and legs were broken with hammers while his executioners strangled him with a cord." Two of her other sons immediately followed him. Five others were dispatched in a like manner.

For the head conspirators—Aveiro, 50, and the Marquês de Távora, 63—there was special treatment. Their arms, legs, and *ribs* were smashed while they were rolled on a wheel. Under this Middle Ages form of torture, the wheel was placed on an axle perpendicularly driven into the ground, the person was tied to the wheel which was spun close to the ground, and executioners beat the victim with iron hammers. But this was not cruel enough for Aveiro and the Marquês. They were not strangled, so they had as much time in agony as possible while one more was executed. Then they were burned alive. Only the direct intervention of the queen and her daughter Maria, heiress to the throne, prevented many more executions than the twelve already carried out.

The executions had taken the whole day; at the end the entire stage with its corpses and its scaffold was set on fire. The ashes were thrown into the Tagus River. The title, Duke of Aveiro, was extinguished forever. The king's mistress, Teresa Leonor, was consigned to a nunnery (where royal visits were, of course, permitted).

Within days, another royal decree placed all of the 850 Jesuits in Portugal under house arrest or imprisoned for "their part" in the attack on the king. Soon, hundreds of Jesuits in the colonies received the same sentence. Their property and land were seized by the government. Added to the list of Jesuit crimes were their missions' "profiteering" and their "support" for the rebellion of the seven Guaraní missions.

Of course, Pombal's *Novelles intéressantes* would promptly comment on the affair:

> The King of Portugal [despoiled] the Jesuits of that sovereignty which they usurped in Paraguay. . . . The Jesuits give lessons not only in revolt and sedition but also in murder and bloodshed. . . . It is not even a venial sin to kill the King . . . only the Jesuits would have been capable of such enormity. . . . They are the only ones who teach it, in an unbroken tradition of more than 250 years . . . the only ones who have ever adopted it as a code of conduct and have applied it to their own interests."

Here Pombal was, no doubt trying to encourage the French to follow his lead; they had been attacking the Jesuits over the issue of regicide for almost 250 years. It must have played well in the salons of Paris.

Two years later, Gabriel Malagrida, now into his seventies, was added to the list of victims. Imprisoned in a dungeon two-and-a-half years before for his 1756 paper on the earthquake, he developed symptoms of derangement. He talked to angelic hosts in his cell; he wrote that St.

Anne had taken vows of religion in her mother's womb, that she had used angels as bricklayers to build a girl's sanctuary in Jerusalem. Pombal's brother presided at his trial. A Dominican on the tribunal, objecting to the cruel questioning, was removed and transferred overseas. Malagrida was found guilty of heresy, deceit, and other crimes. However, the state did not have the authority to execute a priest. Only the Inquisition did. Pombal replaced uncooperative inquisitors with his own men who decreed a death sentence. On July 1, 1761, he was strangled and then, barely alive, he was burned to death in a wok-shaped device. At a dinner that night in the Palace of the Inquisition, Pombal celebrated the triumph of "the Catholic faith" over "Jesuit wickedness."

All these events happened in a country that had abandoned both torture and capital punishment.

The salons of Paris and their anti-Jesuit *philosophes* were appalled by the brutality of the executions, especially Malagrida's. Voltaire called it "infamy" and "a supreme combination of the ridiculous and the horrible." Pombal had used instruments and methods of a bygone era; the rack and stake were from the loathsome Middle Ages and their Catholic persecutions. Worst of all he had used the hated Inquisition to execute a senile old priest. Pombal's pamphlets proclaiming the executions were judged in the salons as repellent to good taste. Pombal's personal hatred for the Jesuits was considered "grotesque" by European society.

Pombal Expels the Jesuits

Saldanha, now the patriarch, then collaborated with Pombal to issue a pastoral letter to all Portuguese bishops accusing the Jesuits of corrupting the consciences of the executed would-be regicides. Saldanha virulently attacked the Jesuits in all manner of ways that were tragic at the time; for the observer centuries later they are almost amusing in their absurdity. In his attack he singled out the Brazilian missionaries for special opprobrium. He said they were

> . . . profiteering [interfering with the profiteering of the Portuguese colonists being the *real* crime] against the teachings of our Redeemer himself who had forbidden priests from engaging in worldly concerns. . . . He [our Redeemer] had cast the money-changers out of the temple and . . . Church laws, from the earliest times, had forbidden priests from engaging in trade . . . [adding] "Ye cannot serve God and mammon." . . . Jesuits

ignored previous popes' wishes and profited accordingly. . . . Jesuits had no fear of God and had hardened their disobedience, especially in the colonies—such was the corruption into which they had sunk.

Then Saldanha declared that, according to the laws of Portugal and the Church's own sacred canons, all goods belonging to such persons should be confiscated. Pombal was well pleased with his puppet. He had stuck to the script.

The new pope, Clement XIII, was presented with a *fait accompli* and he, like Benedict before him, was fearful of Portugal's splitting from the Church. He acceded to Pombal's wishes. The Society of Jesus was finished in Portugal and its dominions.

Pombal's law of expulsion was signed by King Joseph on September 3, 1759, the first anniversary of the alleged assassination attempt. The law read in part:

After having heard the opinions of many wise and pious ministers, full of zeal for the honor of God, I decided the above-mentioned religious [the Jesuits] to be corrupted, deplorably alienated from their saintly institute, and manifestly indisposed by so many, so abominable, so inveterate, and so incorrigible [in] vices, etc.

Then he expelled them and threatened death to any Jesuit who remained within Portugal and death to any person who might harbor a single Jesuit or even deal with one.

Two weeks later over 800 Portuguese Jesuits were shipped off to the Papal States. More than 300 Jesuits returning from the missions were also exiled there. Some 180 others returning from the missions were stuffed into dank, underground dungeons, barely surviving in barbaric conditions. Seventy-nine died there; many went mad. After fifteen years and Pombal's political demise, about sixty survivors emerged gaunt and confused.

Clement's concessions in attempting to mollify Pombal kept the pope from making any public protest over the treatment of Portugal's Jesuits. Clement's only objection was to refuse to greet the expelled fathers as they landed on his shores; that way he would not to seem to endorse their expulsion. The concessions had no effect. Pombal made the Portuguese bishops report to him as he took on roles normally belonging to the pontiff. They reported to the pope only nominally. Pombal, through his king, became *de facto* head of the Portuguese Church. He justified and formalized it in a book, *A Theological Demonstration of the Right of the Metropolitan of Portugal to Confirm and Consecrate the Suffragan Bishops Named by the King*, published by a subordinate named Antonio Pereira. "Metropolitan" was another term for "primate," in this case Pombal's subservient Cardinal Saldanha. The book declared that Portugal's bishops could be named without the approval of the pope and without compromising the authority of their office. In 1770 Pombal broke diplomatic relations with the Vatican. Henry VIII redux!

After the Jesuits' expulsion from Portugal there was another attempt, little remembered, on the life of King Joseph at Villa Viçosa. Cheke describes the culprit as "half-crazy" and largely incoherent. Pombal had him put on the rack which "sent the wretch totally mad." No one could establish even the slightest connection with the Jesuits, yet Pombal publicly announced that the Jesuits were proven responsible and had ambassador Mendoça so inform Clement. The accusation was soon recognized as a "palpable falsehood," but the damage had been done.

Cheke describes the book, *Chronological Deduction*, comprised of three enormous volumes, circulated throughout Europe in 1769 when the dispute between the monarchs and Clement XIII over the Jesuits was at its peak.. Pombal directed the tome and rewarded the author, José Seábra de Silva, with the position of secretary of state soon after its publication. Seábra was aided by the Abbé Platel, a "notorious" monk in Pombal's pay "and by a hack staff of professional pamphleteers of various nationalities and more or less shady antecedents." The book described in immense detail how Portugal was flourishing until the Jesuits arrived, after which it rapidly declined. The work was a "masterpiece of vindictive indictment" and a sulphurous contribution to anti-Jesuit propaganda. Cheke finishes with, "If there still [in 1938] clings to the Society of Jesus a certain sinister reputation, the fact must be largely attributed to Pombal."

Downfall of Pombal

The Távora Affair precipitated Pombal's own downfall. Queen Maria I, daughter of King Joseph, ascended to the throne upon the king's death in 1777. With the image of the mass executions still burning in her memory after eighteen years, she officially outlawed the death penalty except in war, dismissed Pombal, exiled him to his estate 110 miles north of Lisbon, and put him on trial. As he left the capital, demonstrators clamored for his death and pelted his coach with stones. Mobs freed 800 prisoners and razed the main prison-fort.

When examined as to why he had proceeded with such barbaric cruelty, Pombal claimed it was at the order of the king. Pressed to admit that the attack against the king had been staged, he gave nebulous responses. He denied that he used his position to defraud the government and competitors—charges that were made by several prominent witnesses. All that was clearly evil—like the hangings in Oporto—he blamed on the king. He took responsibility only for actions that were beneficial to Portugal and good government. He admitted to having destroyed all relevant documents for fear of their "falling into the hands of the Jesuits."

His trial was suspended due to his advancing illness that included excruciating pain and other physical suffering too unsettling to be described here. The findings exonerated the Távoras from any role in the "supposed attempt" on Joseph's life. They concluded that, if there had been an attempt, it was probably aimed at Joseph's confidant Pedro Teixeira, who regularly rode alongside the king, over an issue of personal honor involving the Aveiros. Teixeira had taunted Aveiro about the king's known dalliances with both the duke's wife and his eldest daughter Mariana—in addition to Teresa Leonor. Further, one of the principal "witnesses" to the attempt had to have lied about his presence with testimony, obviously fabricated. This youth had claimed that, as he lay hidden that night of September 3 by Aveiro's home waiting to speak to his girl friend on the household staff, he recognized Aveiro's voice as he cursed at his pistol for not firing, saying, "Go to the devil. When I have need of you, you fail me!" Yet he had never met Aveiro or heard him speak before. He also claimed that Aveiro's companion, a son of Távora, wore white breeches (knee length pants). But seen on a moonless night? And under a black cloak?

Sebastião José de Carvalho e Melo, the Marquês de Pombal, long afflicted with leprosy and in continuing fear of punishment from Queen Maria, died from the ravages of the disease at his home in 1782. He was eighty-three. Many admiring clergy attended his funeral, including the Bishop of Coimbra who presided. A well-known Benedictine, Joachim de Santa Clara, gave the eulogy.

Pombal had no children. With his encouragement, his brother married a niece of the Marquês de Távora; their descendents carry the blood of that ill-fated family as well as its executioner.

There is no denying that Pombal did much good. He used his authority to outlaw slavery in the colonies and to eliminate all remaining discrimination against the "New Christians" (Jewish converts) and Jews generally. An often repeated apocryphal story about Pombal, told in variations, goes something like this: When the king wanted all New Christians to wear white caps (or were they yellow? or green?) to easily identify them, Pombal arrived at the palace the next day with two white hats. When the king asked what they were for, Pombal replied, "Your Majesty, one hat is for you and one is for me." He also terminated all discriminatory laws and applied the law equally to all classes. He transformed the Inquisition from a powerful, independent religious body into a mere department of the state. He installed badly needed (and successful) commercial and financial reforms and other improvements in the military, in public education, and in the press. He left a full treasury upon the death of King Joseph in 1777.

Nevertheless, his rule was also regarded as a reign of terror by many. The horrific executions of so many members of prestigious families and an old senile priest, whether they were guilty or not, left a cloud over an otherwise historic legacy. Today he is regarded by the Portuguese as one of their greatest leaders.

CHAPTER 15

The Enlightenment Overwhelms France's Jesuits, They Fall

"Après moi le déluge!" So said King Louis XV. Fifteen years after Louis, it came in the Paris of 1789. With all constraints swept away, France became violently anti-clerical. The Bastille fell, heads rolled, and the streets ran red in blood. By then the Jesuit order in France was long gone. The Enlightenment had won.

For a thousand years, ever since Clovis was crowned the first French king in the sixth century, *une foi, une loi, une roi* (one faith, one law, one king) had been the unquestioned belief for Frenchmen. For Roman Catholics, France was "the first daughter of the Church" and its king was "the most Christian king." All that would change when France became a secular state—multiple faiths, capricious law, no king, and, after 1764, no Jesuits.

Wars of Religion and Sectarian Assassinations Set the Stage for the Enlightenment and the Jesuits' Downfall

The expulsions of the Jesuits by the Portuguese, French, and Spanish monarchs was precipitated by many forces. "By far the most crushing was the Enlightenment" personified by the mid-eighteenth century *philosophes* (philosophers). These men comprised a loose grouping of mainly Parisian revolutionary thinkers who had peers across the English Channel and elsewhere in Europe. Their metaphysical movement was modestly called the Enlightenment. Its objective was to remake society by overthrowing established religions and beliefs, creating a new orthodoxy of *"secular* humanist" principles. These principles emphasized non-religious values and rights based on human reason, *not* divine revelation, as the best way to achieve a just, orderly and peaceful society. After all, had not the Christian establishment, especially the Church, failed miserably to do this ever since Europe emerged from the oppressive Middle Ages and entered the Renaissance three centuries before?

The Enlightenment's main target was the Catholic Church, starting with its elite—the Jesuits. Eliminate the Church as a force opposed to change, and the other religions would be easy to dispose of.

Ironically many Enlightenment leaders were educated in Jesuit schools—the best in France—getting their values, beliefs, and ability to reason, write, and debate from the Jesuits. Thus the *philosophes'* humanism, *sans* secular, was close to the Jesuits' humanism. Indeed, some contemporary Jesuit leaders were complimentary of much *philosophe* thinking, until it turned anti-religious. By then it was too late for anyone to change its direction; the genie was out of the bottle. The main problem for the Jesuits was their loyalty and obedience to the pope. That would do them in.

It is a supreme paradox that the *philosophes* and their Enlightenment eventually played such a prominent role, however indirectly, in the destruction of the Jesuits of the Republic of the Guaraní. The *philosophes'* quarrel was not with *those* Jesuits—they often expressed profound admiration for *them*—but the *philosophes* would not focus their attack on the Jesuit order narrowly enough to exclude the missionaries in the Republic.

To appreciate the Enlightenment one must understand that its roots took hold as a result of two centuries of almost continuous, chaotic, and barbarous sectarian carnage—including a civil war in France that was sparked by often trivial doctrinal differences. The internal conflict known as the Wars of Religion lasted thirty-six years (1562-1598), tearing France apart as Catholics and Protestants mindlessly slaughtered each other over who had the *one true* faith. Foreign wars, with crushing losses of ordinary soldiers, between (mainly) Catholic France and Catholic Austria were fought over minor territorial disputes and royal paranoia over European hegemony. The Thirty Years' War (1618-1648) was at the outset a religious conflict, engaging all the major European powers with France at the center of it all. The French middle class paid with their blood and taxes during these years far more than those of any other country. Sectarian-based assassinations of two French monarchs and political and religious leaders also inspired the *philosophes'* revulsion for all religion. Most *philosophes* adopted deism—a belief in some kind of all-powerful God but not in any particular religion and usually not in life after death.

The events of these 200 years leading up to the expulsion of the Jesuits and the downfall of the old order in France began in the mid-sixteenth century. To understand these events is to understand the inevitability of the *philosophes* and their Enlightenment; why the philosophical and political defeat of the Jesuits occurred in France; and how that created the climate for the Jesuits' expulsion from Portugal, France, and Spain.

Kings Have Brief Reigns, Persecution and Religious Massacres Ensue

As early as 1545 a minor but ancient French heretic religion, a sort of fundamentalist Calvinism known as Vaudois, was brutally suppressed by Francis I, an otherwise relatively peaceable and progressive monarch. Upon Francis' death in 1547, his son Henry II was crowned king and began persecuting France's Huguenots, followers of the Protestant reformer Jean (John) Calvin. Henry's reign would be cut short. In 1559 he was wounded in a joust and suffered for an excruciating eleven days before expiring at age forty.*

Crises Lead France to Withdraw from Brazil

It was soon after this that France ceased to be a player in the drama that was unfolding along the Brazilian coast. Domestic crises resulting from religious struggle and its economic consequences as well as European political conflicts would draw France's attention away from South America. Southey writes that by 1567 the "French Court was too busy burning and massacring Hugonots to think of Brazil. . . . The day for emigration [from France] was over." Brazil would be conceded to Portugal. Given France's humane and often brotherly treatment of Native Americans compared to Portugal's, the withdrawal of France from Brazil was unfortunate for the Guaraní.

---

*Henry's "cruel death" had been forewarned a year earlier in a famous quatrain by the astrologer and occultist Michel de Nostradamus. Henry was celebrating the wedding of his daughter Elizabeth to King Philip II of Spain, the most powerful monarch of Europe. As part of the festivities the macho Henry, disregarding Nostradamus' warning, insisted on a joust for himself with Count de Montgomery, captain of the Scottish Guard, a younger man in his prime. They would use non-lethal wooden lances. However the captain's lance shattered on the king's protective headgear, sending splinters through the slit into his right eye and temple. The best European surgeons were rushed to his side. There was little they could do. The wound was mortal. After Henry's death his queen, the scheming and ruthless Catherine de Mèdici, showing her stripes publicly for the first time, had the captain executed. She made Nostradamus, though Jewish, a court favorite. The *Journal of Neurosurgery* (on the internet under Henry II) gives a more complete, medically rigorous, fascinating account of the event.

Succeeding Henry II were three of his sons from his marriage to Catherine de Mèdici when they were both fourteen. She was from the famous and infamous Mèdici family of Florence, a niece of Pope Clement VII. Their first two sons were Francis II and Charles IX, both of whose reigns were cut short by illness.

Charles IX's brief reign—much of it under his mother Catherine as regent—is remembered as the time when eight wars between the Protestant Huguenot party and its rival Catholic party began. The first of these wars was initiated on March 1, 1562, when Catholics under the leadership of François, the prominent Duke of Guise, attacked a group of Huguenots attending a religious service at Vassy in far western, heavily Protestant Normandy. An unknown number of Protestants were killed, and many were wounded. During the ensuing twelve-month war, the duke was assassinated by Protestants. Meanwhile, Catherine vacillated between the Huguenots and the Catholics. Sometimes inadvertently, sometimes not, she cunningly fanned the flames of civil war. All tactics were for short-term advantage, and she had no long-term strategy. Eventually it all blew up in her face as her elaborate dissembling led to self-contradictions that caused her credibility to collapse.

Saint Bartholomew's Day Massacre in Paris

The worst of these eight wars, but not the last, was marked by the slaughter of Huguenots during the massacre on August 24, 1572 (Saint Bartholomew's Day), in which several thousand were killed in Paris. Several tens of thousands were killed elsewhere across the country. When the news reached Rome, Pope Gregory XIII and the cardinals celebrated the victory over Protestantism with a papal Te Deum sung in the Church of St. Mark.

Catherine seems to have had a hand in starting it, as this time she hoped to dispose of the Huguenots "once and for all." In a way she did, as the massacre led to the first of several large emigrations by many Huguenots, among France's most enterprising citizens. It was at a huge cost for France.

The frequent murders and persecutions became so convoluted that even leaders one would think would be natural allies became implacable enemies, murdering each other over theological minutiae. A fine case in point was that of Michael Servetus (the Anglicized name of the Spanish physician Miguel Serveto), born in 1511 to a noble, devoutly

Catholic family. Servetus became an anti-Catholic, Reformed theologian. His story shows that there was plenty of blame to go around when it came to Christians persecuting and murdering each other.

John Calvin Encourages the Execution of Protestant Michael Servetus

Roland Bainton begins his story of Servetus, with:

> [He] had the singular distinction of having been burned by the Catholics in effigy and by the Protestants in actuality. His clash with John Calvin [at the peak of the Reformation in 1553] was more than personal. It was the conflict of the Reformation with the Renaissance, and of the right wing of the Reformation with the left. . . . [in Servetus' story] one meets the most significant currents of the sixteenth century."

Early in Servetus' philosophical development he seems to have been influenced by Erasmus and his opposition to debating Biblical passages and traditional teachings when there was no way to bring them to a certain conclusion. In that regard he especially focused on the Trinity. In mid-1530 he went to study in Basel, a bastion of religious upheaval and reform. A month later a prominent theologian was put to death for questioning certain traditional doctrine dealing with Christ's nature. Servetus took a cue and fled to Strasbourg, the first of several cities where he was to study and write. After returning to Basel around 1532, he sent one of his books on the Trinity to the bishop of Saragossa, a man he highly respected, who passed it on to the Supreme Council of the Inquisition in Spain. The council tried to induce him to return for an examination, but he wisely declined and moved to the Paris of King Francis I, "a prince of the Renaissance whose religion sat lightly." Meanwhile he changed his name to Michel de Villenueve. In 1533 Servetus failed to attend a planned meeting with Calvin in Paris for unknown reasons. They would not meet for twenty years. Soon both of them would flee Paris, fearing its own prejudices, Calvin to Basel and Servetus to Lyon. Meanwhile Servetus took up medicine—he referred to himself as Docteur en Medecine—to support himself. He also began corresponding with Calvin. Soon Calvin would refer to him "as a satan."

While Servetus was living in Vienne (near Lyon), someone exposed him to the Inquisition. Under questioning, he admitted to having placed certain contemptuous annotations on a theological book written by Calvin. Servetus returned it to him, and it promptly fell into the prosecutor's hands. Their bad relations came into full bloom.

While in the Inquisition's custody, he assumed a disguise and with the assistance of a complicit jailor he fled Vienne for northern Italy where he had friends. His route took him northeast through Geneva, a Reform bastion. He thought he would be safe there, the home of fellow-Reformist and erstwhile ally Calvin. He had not fully appreciated how much Calvin's feelings for him had changed. He was unaware that seven years earlier Calvin had written to a mutual friend:

"Should he [Servetus] come [to Geneva] if my authority is of any avail I will not suffer him to get out alive."

Calvin had been angered over differences they had concerning three subtle articles of doctrine dealing with the Trinity, the exact nature of Christ's divinity, and child baptism.

In Geneva, Servetus was again "exposed by certain brothers from Lyon," arrested by Protestant authorities, and put on trial with the encouragement of Calvin. Calvin wrote:

"Because the Papists persecute the truth, should we on that account refrain from repressing error?"

During the trial, Calvin testified:

"[Servetus] at first growled that he had not written [a heretical passage] but this cold cavil was at once refuted, for this he was shown to be a clear impostor" and that Servetus soiled every page of the Bible with "futile trifles and impious ravings."

He was found guilty and sentenced to be burned at the stake; Calvin would have preferred the sword to the stake on humanitarian grounds. Servetus' death at forty-two was slow, as the pyre wood was still green. A crown of straw sprinkled with sulfur was placed on his head. As he was consumed he cried out in a fearful wail, "O Jesus, Son of the Eternal God, have pity on me." He took half an hour to die. It was October 27, 1553.

When critics argued that heretics should not have been put to death, Calvin responded with his *Defense of Orthodox Faith against the Prodigious Errors of the Spaniard Michael Servetus,* arguing that "to spare Servetus would have been to endanger the souls of many."

Sebastian Castellion, formerly a prominent member of a French Catholic centrist, humanist group and now a disciple of Calvin, who was forced by the government to declare for Protestant or Catholic, was appalled at Servetus' execution. He loathed Christians persecuting Christians. He accused Calvin of being opposed to persecution by Catholics but being for it when Catholics were persecuted. Castellion became famous by arguing for tolerance across-the-board, a pioneering position at the time. His attempts to become a Reformed minister were blocked by Calvin over another narrow theological dispute dealing with grace and predestination—not the worst that could have happened to him. Unwittingly, both Catholics and Protestants were collaborating to help create the Enlightenment with its anti-religious humanism and to give it ammunition to use against them later.

Religious Civil War Rages as Monk Assassinates Henry III

Back in France in 1574, Catherine de Mèdici's third son became King Henry III. Religious strife continued unabated. The leaders of the Calvinist Huguenot Party had hoped to find refuge in this Henry; but like his mother he was unsure which way to lean, vacillating between them and the Catholic party. Fearing that the resurging political power of the Catholic party would threaten his reign, the king had the remaining scions of the Guise family—Henri and his brother Louis, a cardinal—murdered by his royal guards. Their bodies were torched and thrown into the Loire.

Soon a full-fledged civil war raged with Henry III now allied with his brother-in-law Henry of Navarre against the Catholics. As these two mounted a siege of Paris in mid-1589, a Dominican friar, Jacques Clément, assassinated Henry III at St. Cloud, a western suburb of Paris. The siege was then abandoned, and the troops scattered in wild disarray. Henry of Navarre was, arguably, next in line for the throne. After religious and political maneuvers too tortuous to describe here, a consensus developed that if Henry of Navarre converted to Catholicism he could become king. He did so. Meanwhile, the hard-line Pope Clement VIII initially insisted on Henry's publicly humiliating "rehabilitation" before lifting his excommunication of this "ex-heretic." French Jesuit Alexandre Georges came to Henry's defense and plied the pope to the point that he lifted the excommunication, but absurdly it was eighteen months after Henry had been crowned. For a while there would be reconciliation and peace, law and order in France.

Henry IV Issues Edict of Nantes

On February 27, 1594, the coronation of Henry of Navarre as King Henry IV took place in Chartres Cathedral. He soon went to war. After initial battlefield victories against the Hapsburgs of Austria and Spain, Henry's reign became marked by peace and prosperity. But most of all, Henry's place in history was assured by his Edict of Nantes in 1598, a compendium of prior edicts that was bold mainly in its enforcement. This watershed of French tolerance ended the Wars of Religion by guaranteeing security to all Protestants and bringing a peace for which all of France longed. The edict coincided with Henry's evolving conciliatory and cordial relationship with the papacy.

Parlement Expels Jesuits from Paris over Regicide

Meanwhile, as 1594 ended, the Parlement of Paris expelled the Jesuits from that city for two incidents which would help form the pattern of evidence that the Jesuits endorsed regicide, allegations that would haunt the Jesuits for a century and a half, until their expulsion. In 1592 Pierre Barrière, allegedly once a Jesuit student, attempted to assassinate Henry IV, blaming a Jesuit Father Varade for instructing him to do so. In late 1594 another attempt was made by twenty-year-old Jean Châtel, a former Jesuit student. Henry was paying a visit to his mistress Gabrielle d'Estrées at a hotel near the Louvre. Châtel was also there, intending to kill the king. Knife in hand he lunged, but he only cut Henry's lip and broke a tooth before he was seized. As soon as the public heard of the attempted assassination, enemies of the Jesuits blamed them for putting the idea in his head. Some wanted to slaughter the Jesuits wholesale while others wanted to roast them alive and burn down their house. Parlement ordered the arrest of the Jesuits from the Collège de Clermont. Father Jean Guéret, a Châtel instructor, was interrogated under torture but denied any foreknowledge of the attempt, nor did he take any responsibility for it. Châtel affirmed the priest's statements. His execution consisted of being pulled limb from limb by four horses. Guéret was exiled from France for life.

Parlement then took possession of the personal papers of Jesuit Jean Guignard. They included several incriminating statements including one that hailed Clément's murder of Henry III five years earlier as a gift of the Holy Spirit. Although there was no evidence of any connection between Châtel and Guignard, this priest was hanged. Parlement expelled the Jesuits from Paris and all towns and places where they had colleges, ordering them to leave the country within two weeks for high treason. It also forbade all the king's subjects from sending their children to any Jesuit college outside France on pain of high treason. The parliaments of Bordeaux and Toulouse refused to follow Paris' lead. (The Paris Parlement was spelled with the "e"; the others, with the "ia.")

Mousnier writes that Parlement's proceedings against the Jesuits were highly irregular. No formal accusation had been made, nor had they been brought before a judge or allowed to put forward a defense. It was obvious that they were not complicit in Châtel's plans or actions. The Paris Jesuits' views on tyrannicide were no different than those of any other theologians of the day. The issue was really the politics of Church versus state. The Jesuits gave the impression of being an army fighting for Jesus Christ and his vicar, the pope. It became a convenient symbol for the Company's enemies to surround it "with a myth of duplicity, tortuous intrigue, double-dealing, and cruelty."

Notwithstanding these charges, the Jesuits became Henry's beneficiary as he readmitted them to Paris in 1603. The Jesuit College at Flèche, resurrected by Henry, was an institution in which he took particular pride, calling it "my Flèche."

Religious Zealot Ravaillac Assassinates Henry IV

Tragically for all of Europe, on May 14, 1610, Henry IV came to a bloody end at the hands of a deranged religious fanatic. In the middle of a congested Paris street with traffic stopped, François Ravaillac broke past the king's guards and lunged into the royal coach, stabbing him twice in the upper chest with a long knife. He died minutes later. He was fifty-six.

Ravaillac, thirty-one and unmarried, was destitute and at one time was jailed for debt. He was raised a pious Catholic and joined the Feuillants as a lay brother. This order was connected with the wider Benedictine family. The Feuillants took away his habit after six weeks because he had visions during worship. He applied to be a Jesuit but was rejected because they never took in a former member of another order. Mousnier says he looked like a half-educated neurotic who lived predominantly in his imagination. A Jesuit confessor told him he had hallucinations rather than visions, instructing him to go to his home village and lead a quiet life, which Mousnier says was the essence of good sense. Instead, after several failed attempts to have an audience with the king, Ravaillac began to stalk him. The stalled royal coach provided the opportunity.

Ravaillac's reasons for the assassination were driven by hatred for Huguenots and the belief that the king was their ally, bent on making war on the pope. Under torture ordered by Parlement and intended to expose accomplices, he swore repeatedly that he acted alone. Despite the boot with screws crushing his joints, his story remained unchanged. The arm "which committed the murder was plunged into burning sulphur." Mousnier continues, "The flesh on his chest, arms, thighs, and legs was torn by red hot pincers, then molten lead, boiling oil, boiling resin, [and] a mixture of molten wax and sulphur was poured into the wounds." Finally, his body was burned and his ashes were scattered. Some in later years tried to pin the assassination on the Jesuits, a futile effort unencumbered by any evidence. No one at the time tried to make such a case.

Upon Henry's assassination, his eldest son Louis ascended to the throne at age nine. His mother acted as regent until 1617 when the sixteen year old was crowned King Louis XIII. At age fourteen, Louis married the Hapsburg Spanish Princess Anne. The young couple were distant and unhappy, often living apart. His dalliances, including a special regard for a certain nun, the Mademoiselle de La Fayette, became court gossip. So did his vanity; he introduced the wearing of wigs, in his case to cover his baldness. In 1637 the king's Jesuit confessor, Nicolas Caussin, intervened over the state of his twenty-two year marriage, apparently successfully. A year later, Anne gave birth to their first child. He would become Louis XIV, Louis the Great.

During Louis XIII's reign, France continued to prosper. Under policies initiated by his father and through additional clever alliances, the country came to dominate Europe. However, the religious tolerance established by his father's Edict of Nantes began to erode under Louis, resulting in the Huguenots chafing at first but then in 1627 aligning themselves with England in a rebellion. In the resulting 1628 siege of their stronghold, La Rochelle on the French west coast on the Bay of Biscay, Louis' forces crushed the Huguenots and routed an English fleet.

To try to win back the Huguenots and restore the earlier harmony established by his father, Louis issued the Edict of Nîmes in 1629, giving a general amnesty to the Huguenots and returning to them their earlier possessions and property. However, in the process they were annihilated as a political party, causing them to lose popular support and never regain their ten percent share of the French population.

Cardinals Richelieu and Mazarin Run France

During Louis XIII's reign, the *de facto* head of state was the towering Armand-Jean du Plessis, Duq de Richelieu, one of the most famous (many say infamous) characters in European history. France's successes during the first half of the seventeenth century can be attributed to this brilliant, opinionated, charismatic, cunning, and energetic statesman known simply as Richelieu. He excelled academically and was consecrated a bishop at twenty-two. At thirty-one, he was made secretary of state, a cardinal at thirty-seven, and president of the council of ministers at thirty-nine.

Richelieu's two strategic objectives were to strengthen and safeguard the crown after a century of domestic chaos, and to position France against the imperial designs of the Hapsburgs of Austria and Spain. When The Thirty Years' War (1618-1648) broke out in northern and central Europe, nominally over religion (Catholics versus Lutherans and Calvinists) but really over Hapsburg hegemony, Richelieu the cardinal sided with European Protestants against the Catholic Hapsburgs, thus proving that his French nationalism came ahead of his Catholic religion. He succeeded masterfully at achieving both his strategic objectives while never hesitating to use capital punishment to rid France of his opponents. Beheading was a useful tool as was learned by Minister of Justice Michel de Marillac, found guilty of treason by Richelieu's hand-picked judges for opposing him over a war with Austria. A noble, François de Montmorency-Bouteville suffered the same fate for provoking a number of deadly duels with other nobles—a waste of nobles in Richelieu's opinion. Richelieu never softened. In 1642, while on his deathbed, he ordered the executions of two other nobles, François August de Thou and Henri Coiffier-Ruze d'Effiat, a handsome twenty-two year old favorite of King Louis no less, for conspiring against him.

The Santarelli Treatise Fiasco

More than any other single person, Richelieu set the stage for strengthening the French state at the expense of the papacy. He adroitly alternated between threat and compromise to bring the Catholic Church to heel and to make it answerable and submissive to the crown. Richelieu received some unintended help from outside the country in the form of an explosive incident called the Santarelli Affair. In 1625 Italian Jesuit Antonio Santarelli issued his *Treatise on Heresy, Schism, Apostasy, Solicitation in Confession and the Power of the Roman Pontiff to Punish These Delicts* (civil wrongs). It repeated a contentious doctrine that the pope had indirect power over the princes in civil matters whenever he chose to declare that the interests of religion were in any way concerned. He could revise their laws and policies, and if they did not comply he could release their subjects from allegiance and head a crusade against them. The "enemies of the [Jesuits] sounded a call to arms. In a violent speech before the Paris Parlement, Louis Servin dropped dead of apoplexy." Richelieu's response was, "Maxims of this kind can ruin the entire Church of God." Even Pope Urban VIII was annoyed. The uproar continued into the next year when Parlement placed demands on the Jesuits under which they had to concede the sovereignty of the state in temporal matters—a milestone in Church-state, and Jesuit-Parlement relations. Richelieu's objectives were well served by Santarelli.

From his deathbed Richelieu hand picked his successor, Cardinal Jules Mazarin, recommending him to Louis XIII. He had mentored Mazarin for many years. Five months later in 1643 Louis died of tuberculosis. He was forty-one. With Louis' wife Anne now acting as regent for the four-year old Louis XIV, Mazarin was appointed *de facto* head of state. Although not as well known to history as Richelieu, Mazarin came to outshine him in important ways.

Mazarin, seventeen years Richelieu's junior, handled his mentor's diplomatic assignments so well that his appointment as papal nuncio to France was forced on Pope Urban VIII. After being fired by Urban for anti-Spanish, pro-French bias, the bitter Mazarin ingratiated himself with Richelieu who then forced the pope to make him a cardinal. For the next twenty years Mazarin was highly influential in developing the governing principles and practices of Louis XIV, actually overshadowing the king until the cardinal died at fifty-eight in 1661 when the king was twenty-two.

Even more so than Richelieu, Mazarin prepared the way for Louis' omnipotence. Mazarin was a strategic thinker. Well after France under Richelieu had joined the Protestant side in the Thirty Years' War, he convinced pivotal Catholic and Protestant German princes to form the League of the Rhine in order to counter-balance Austria. Those princes, legions of them, joined in the Peace of Westphalia (1648) with Mazarin as architect, thereby closing that war and placing France in the forefront of Europe *nonpareil*. That peace treaty solemnly recognized Calvinists internationally to the discomfort of the Vatican. For Mazarin, revenge was a dish best served cold.

In 1648 Mazarin faced a rebellion by two *frondes* or groups opposed to the accretion of royal power. (*Fronde* means sling. Slings were used by street mobs to pelt the windows of Mazarin supporters.) As is often the case, the precipitating event was sharply increased taxes. Two groups, one comprised of Paris Parlement officers and the other made up of disaffected nobles, worked together to bring Mazarin down. They almost succeeded. At the last minute the loyal French army, fresh from its final victory in the Thirty Years' War, marched into Paris just in time to save him. Typically, the interests of ordinary Frenchmen were never considered by either *fronde*.

Meanwhile, the Catholic Jansenists, in their century-long bitter theological dispute with the Jesuits over predestination, were suspected by Mazarin of being *fronde* supporters. In addition, the influential Abbé de Saint-Cyran of the Cistercian convent at Port-Royal helped Jansenism gain a larger following in France. His opposition to absolutism contributed to the cardinal's disgust for Jansenism. On his deathbed in 1661 he urged Louis "not to tolerate the Jansenist sect, not even their name." As Mazarin handed the reins over to Louis, France was at its zenith, never to be equaled again.

The law of unintended consequences soon operated in its typically perverse way. After so many years of war, assassinations, quarrels, and anarchy had exhausted the whole country, additional rebellions in the 1640s made France ready, even eager, for the absolutism of Louis XIV. Mazarin would make it happen.

Mazarin had lived well, even ostentatiously. As the leading cardinal he made sure he had income from many abbacies (revenue-producing monasteries) to the point that his estate would be measured in tens of millions of today's U.S. dollars, more fodder for the Enlightenment, creeping ever closer.

Louis XIV Persecutes Huguenots, Builds Versailles, Drains the Treasury

The first recorded words of Louis XIV, Louis the Great, baptized Louis Dieudonne (gift of God), may be from the following exchange: King Louis XIII, as he lay dying, asked his four year-old son, "What is your name?" "Louis XIV," the precocious little boy answered. "Not yet, not yet," said the father. Unlike his predecessors who kept dying early, the boy was to reign for seventy-two years, longer than any other French monarch. His reign was dissolute, leading to a rupture in the Bourbon tradition of a strong central authority, further facilitating the rise of the Enlightenment and the fall of the Jesuits.

Starting as a teenager, Louis XIV showed remarkable vitality in exploits with the opposite sex. His liaisons included Mazarin's nieces, his own brother's wife, her maid-of-honor, a friend of the maid's with whom he had two children, and a governess of the children whom he secretly married after his Spanish wife Maria Theresa died in 1683. Nevertheless, he always appeared devoted and attentive to his queen.

After Mazarin's death, Louis engaged France in four wars, shattering the country's alliances and squandering its wealth. Additional economic burdens resulted from the construction of an enormous and lavish palace northwest of Paris at Versailles. The palace had huge on-going costs from both the upkeep of its sumptuous buildings and from support for thousands of court lotus-eaters. Onerous tax increases needed to pay for all the extravagance fell exclusively on France's peasants and bourgeoisie, since its nobles and clergy were exempt from taxes. Thus began a collapse of even the pretense of a social contract between the rulers and the ruled, a collapse that would culminate in the French Revolution a century later.

Louis obsessed over the *fronde's* attacks on Mazarin and the cardinal's close call, having had them burned into his psyche when he was a child. Never would Louis let anyone diminish his absolutism, one that was reflected in his famous quote: *"L'etat c'est moi"* (I am the state.) He also identified himself with Apollo, the god of the sun, becoming known as the Sun King.

Huguenots could not be trusted to sign on, so he issued the Edict of Fontainebleu in 1685, stripping the Huguenots of all civil rights and giving their Reformed ministers two weeks to leave the country. And that they did, in wave after wave, taking hundreds of thousands of their followers with them—disproportionately among the most accomplished and energetic of France's citizens. One of them was Alexander Hamilton's maternal grandfather, a physician named Jean Faucette. They took their talents and assets—including millions of livres easily worth nine figures in today's dollars—to the Low Countries, England, Germany, the Cape of Good Hope, and in Faucette's case the French West Indies, Hamilton's birthplace. Louis' growing numbers of adversaries were enriched immeasurably.

Next, Louis neutralized France's parliaments in its various provinces, especially the Paris Parlement, making them docile judicial bodies. The nobles now became mere ornaments of the court, out-pandering one another in seeking Louis' favor. As waves of obsequious adulation blanketed France and when the "divine right" of kings (Louis' more than all the others in Europe) had taken hold, even the remaining

Huguenots were swept up in it. They gave their uncritical support to the divine right principle. Their leaders' sermons were filled with panegyrics for Louis' absolutism. They had made a pact with the devil that lasted right up until their fatal year of 1685.

Cleverly led by Jesuit Pierre Meynier in his *Execution de l'Edit de Nantes*, the Catholic clergy began chipping away at the rights given the Huguenots in that edict. Where the edict was silent, the clergy could fill in the gaps to their liking. For example, since the edict made no explicit mention of daytime funerals, all Huguenot funerals would have to take place at night. Louis would routinely approve such seemingly minor interpretations. More and more such barely visible erosions of liberties followed. Individually they were not much; cumulatively they became intolerable. Stankiewicz writes that the clergy were best at gaining their objectives from him "when, during a bout of piety, he felt he must expiate his amorous liaisons." He would show his devotion by bending to their wishes, but actually they had co-opted him.

The Edict of Fontainebleau banishing the Huguenots provoked the formation of the League of Augsburg which comprised most of Europe, including William of Orange who would become king of England and France's nemesis. The Edict launched a nine-year war against France. The war ended in 1697 with the Peace of Ryswick, halting French expansion and leaving the country economically drained. France's maritime ambitions were destroyed, her competitiveness in trade was vitiated, and her overseas colonies were crippled or lost. It took half a century before economic reconstruction would begin at home.

In his waning years, personal grief would be piled onto Louis' financial catastrophes and international political and military reverses. In rapid succession he suffered the deaths of his son the Dauphin who was first in line for the throne, then his grandson who was second in line, then his wife and their eldest son, then another grandson. He left the French throne to a five-year-old great-grandson, Louis XV. Yet another grandson ascended the Spanish throne as Philip II. These were his only happy legacies. Thus did all the earlier glories and promise come to a pathetic end. He died at age seventy-six.

By now it had become *inevitable* that the Enlightenment would emerge from the loins of these two murderous and ruinously profligate centuries.

Louis XV Reigns During the Enlightenment

Little good can be said of the reign of great-grandson Louis XV. Unfortunately, it, too, was a long one. At age two, his father, mother, and older brother all died within a week of an undisclosed disease. In 1715, at the age of five, he was crowned king. His uncle Phillippe acted as regent until Louis reached his majority at age thirteen after which he reigned alone. He died of smallpox at Versailles, age sixty-four.

Louis XV was weak and vainglorious. His interests were mainly in women, especially the notorious, beautiful, intelligent, and adroit Jeanne Antoinette Poisson Le Normant d'Étoiles, Marquise de Pompadour, his long-time paramour and political confidant. She wielded great influence over him. Eventually she would, in a pout, join the anti-Jesuit forces at a critical juncture. As he advanced in age, he became obsessed with girls, keeping several at a time in his royal chambers. The idle dissipation at Versailles initiated by his great-grandfather marked the rest of his reign. The Seven Years' War with England and others ended in the Treaty of Paris in 1763, a historic and monumental humiliation that stripped France of Canada, its possessions in India, the Mississippi River region, and Louisiana in North America, thus ending once-and-for-all her global imperial illusions.

The king's famous evaluation of his own reign was also a prophecy: "*Après moi le deluge*" (after me, the deluge).

Louis XV had started off promisingly. He had become known as the "well-beloved" when the whole country prayed for him during a critical illness in 1744. He died thirty years later, well-hated.

Philosophes' Predecessors and Christian Humanism, Erasmus and the Philosophy of Christ

By the middle of the eighteenth century, the wind (the Enlightment) that was blowing in Europe, especially in France, had become irresistible. The 200 years of horror, debauchery, and shame that came before the *philosophes* were practically scripted to ensure the achievement of two of their goals: the Jesuits' destruction and the decapitation of the French monarchy.

But the *philosophes* did not simply spring from the brow of Zeus. Their philosophical forebears can be traced all the way back to Aristotle and his teacher Plato in fourth century B.C. Greece. Indeed, conventional wisdom is that western philosophy started with Aristotle.

After many centuries lost in the Dark Ages, Thomas Aquinas recovered Aristotelian logic in the thirteenth century and applied it to Christianity. Aquinas and his disciples, known as the Scholastics, laid the groundwork for humanism—*without* the prefix "secular"—during the fourteenth and fifteenth century Renaissance. The humanists, almost all of them practicing Catholics, argued that by celebrating the human race they were paying tribute to God who made humans in God's likeness and image. Almost all humanist thinking at that time was God-centered.

Indisputably the greatest and most profoundly influential Christian humanist was Desiderius Erasmus (c. 1466–1536) the Latinized name of the illegitimate son of a Dutchman, born in Rotterdam. Orphaned in his early teen years, he was sent to a monastery at Emmaus, a joyless experience that he called the greatest misfortune of his life. Nevertheless he excelled academically, became a priest, and as luck would have it caught the eye of a bishop who mentored him and sent him to the University of Paris. His writings grew so noteworthy that in his early forties he began traveling throughout Europe to universal acclaim. His message—an overdue exposé of the Catholic Church's abuses and follies—was eagerly received. His many critical works, replete with bitter sarcasm, inadvertently helped set the stage for the Protestant Reformation. He treated the Bible just as he did ancient classical myths, as a collection of allegorical narratives. His humanism was based on the *"philosophy* of Christ" as embodying the ethical ideal—the moral life. He argued that the Church had lost its original evangelical mission, that its theologians' discourse had degenerated into interminable, "hair-splitting" philosophical debates, "metaphysical speculations," and "over-curious discussion of unsolvable mysteries" unrelated to Christ's message. All taken together these were to become the fundamental viewpoint of the *philosophes* and the Enlightenment two centuries later. Erasmus' joy in the scholarly pursuit of theology, philosophy, and the classics contributed to his rejecting offers to be elevated to bishop and later to cardinal at the invitation of Pope Paul III.

Erasmus' humanism might well have fit in at Jesuit colleges founded twenty years after he died or in Guaraní missions seventy-five years later.

Erasmus and his contemporary, Martin Luther, became opponents over Christian teaching that man in his fallen state was incompetent to perform moral acts without God's enabling grace. Their squabbles, sometimes bitter, were not over the enabling grace itself, but rather what role humans had in earning or rejecting it—the degree to which human desires held sway over free will. Luther placed emphasis on the amount of unmerited grace in determining salvation. His was the antithesis of Erasmus' humanism which emphasized the role of free will—a subtle distinction that led to so much blood-letting among Christians. Paradoxically, his humanist *Colloquies* found enemies at opposite poles: both the Inquisition with its Index and Luther who wrote of the *Colloquies*, "See what poison he scatters . . . and goes craftily at our youth to poison them."

Erasmus' death from dysentery at about seventy, was twelve months after one of his friends, Thomas More, lost his head to another friend, Henry VIII. Erasmus was buried at the Basel Cathedral with pomp and esteem. He is accorded admiration far exceeding any scholar since his day. He remains today a hero of Christian humanism.

By the mid-sixteenth century, Christian humanism was being called into question by Michel de Montaigne (1533-1592) and his movement called "cultural relativism." It thrives today in many influential quarters. It held no truths to be self-evident. Montaigne reasoned that if our values do not come from God, then who are we Europeans to criticize, for example, Brazilian Indians for eating dead human flesh if that is valued in their society. Unfortunately, he was burdened by little knowledge of their practice of capturing, torturing, and murdering other human beings for the express purpose of creating the dead human flesh. Cultural relativism would become a dominating theme of the Enlightenment.

The stage had been set for the *philosophes* and the Enlightenment.

Philosophes of the Enlightenment Rise, Disparage Jesuits; Voltaire Dominates the Scene

Standing head and shoulders above the other *philosophes*, at least in today's popular mind, was Voltaire. François Marie Arouet was born in Paris in 1694 to a middle class family. At age ten, he was admitted to the Jesuit College of Louis-le-Grand, reputed to be the best school in France. It had among its 2,000 students as many nobles' sons as could meet the school's rigorous standards. He maintained advantageously friendly relations with those well-connected classmates for the rest of his life. As was typical of the curriculum, he received training in the classics, literature, and drama. He excelled especially in the last two of these, where his interests and abilities lay. One of his teachers, alarmed at his anti-religious comments and quips, predicted that he would become the standard bearer for French deism. A good prophecy. Yet he looked back with warm respect and gratitude on his years with the Jesuits who the Durants say "had disciplined his intellect to clarity and order." When he was fifty-two, Voltaire wrote:

> I was educated for seven years by men who took unrewarded and indefatigable pains to form the minds and morals of youth. They inspired in me a taste for literature and sentiments which will be a consolation to me to the end of my life. Nothing will ever efface from my heart the memory of Father Porée, who is equally dear to all who have studied under him. . . . What did I see during [that time], , , , The most industrious, frugal, regulated life; all their hours divided between the care they took of us and the exercises of their austere [life]. [Of] the thousands educated by them . . . there is not one who would belie my words.

After Voltaire's graduation, his father insisted he study the law, since the literary career he planned to pursue "was an open sesame to destitution." Obediently, he studied the "practice of Paris" for three years. The Durants write that Voltaire at age twenty-one described himself as "thin, long, and fleshless, without buttocks." And that "he pranced from one host or hostess to another, welcomed . . . for his sparkling verse and ready wit, imbibing and effusing heresy." Playing with fire, he frequently satirized the Regent Phillippe, quipping that when the regent "reduced by a half the horses in the royal stables . . . he would have done better to dismiss half the asses that crowded his Highness's court," bitingly true at this time of Versailles' lavishness and lasciviousness. These lampoons got him exiled from Paris. After he begged for forgiveness, he was allowed to return. Seven months later he was back "fluttering and rhyming, sometimes obscenely, often superficially, always cleverly." Resuming his provocations, he landed in the Bastille in 1717, yet he managed to get himself placed in what today we would call the white-collar crime section where he often dined with the warden and socialized with the guards and staff. Eleven months later he was freed by the king, due mostly to his protesting his innocence while begging for release. It was at about this time in 1718 that he adopted the pen name, Voltaire, possibly from the name Veautaire, a small farm he had just inherited. He briefly referred to himself as Arouet de Voltaire, but with his blossoming notoriety he soon needed only one name to identify himself everywhere in Europe.

When he was twenty-four, Voltaire wrote his seminal drama *Oedipe*, a tale about royal incest, much like Sophocles' fifth century B.C. original, but this time a thinly disguised attack on the regent and his daughter. It was a smashing success, setting a box office record. The Durants say the Jesuits were "gratified to see how well their pupil had profited from the dramas they had staged at the College of Louis-le-Grand." However the Jesuits were not so effusive over two lines, hailed by freethinkers, that were to become Voltaire's life-long theme song:

> Our priests are not what a silly populace supposes; all their learning consists in [depends on] our credulity.

Never a true democrat, Voltaire distrusted the masses while he cultivated the wealthy and high born. Using his influence and legal talents, he helped one friend secure large military contracts; he was not above war profiteering. He was also a clever investor and soon became rich, a multi-millionaire by today's standards. Voltaire was a revolutionary only when it came to religion. He relished the good life and delighted in the acclaim of the nobility and the trendy.

In 1722 Voltaire wrote his famous *Épître à Uranie* (Letter to Uranie) to a friend, the Countesse Marie de Rupelmonde, a thirty-eight-year-old beautiful, intellectual widow. The Durants suggest that it bares his soul perhaps better than anything else he ever wrote:

> I wish to love God . . . [but what kind of God do these theologians offer?]. . . . A tyrant whom we should hate. . . . He made us love pleasure, so that he might torment us with frightful pains . . . eternal. . . . [The Durants then paraphrase him: He sent his Son to atone for our sins; Christ died but apparently in vain . . . and the Son of God, so acclaimed for mercy, is represented as waiting vengefully to plunge most of us into hell, including all those countless people who never heard of him]. . . . I do not recognize in this disgraceful picture the God whom I must adore; I should dishonor him by [following such a religion].

Yet he admires the Christian *concept* with:

> His [Christ's] example is holy, his morality is divine. He consoles in secret the hearts that he illumines; in the greatest misfortunes he gives them support; and if he bases his doctrine on an illusion, it is still a blessing to be deceived with him . . . believe that . . . the soul of the just man is precious; believe that the modest Buddhist monk, the kindly Moslem dervish,

find more grace in his eyes than a pitiless Jansenist [who believes in predestination] or an ambitious pope.

In 1726, after insulting one too many noblemen, he was exiled, yet given his choice of location. He chose England as his sanctuary. There for more than three years he studied John Locke, Isaac Newton, and other great thinkers of the time. He became a disciple of England's rationalism, a supporter of its sciences and its relative tolerance of all religions and economic freedom.

From 1750 to 1753 Voltaire was hosted by Frederick the Great at his palace in Potsdam near Berlin. He enlivened Frederick's often-dour court until an angry rupture between these two monumental egoists caused his abrupt departure under threat of imprisonment. Voltaire had written a satire with Frederick as its target and began dissembling to the king about whether it had been distributed to others. (It had.) Only Voltaire's renown and Frederick's uncertainty as to its distribution saved him from serious consequences. After returning to France, he wrote prolifically—plays, books, monographs, and letters—to his large circle of friends and benefactors while never ceasing his criticism of French Catholicism and its intolerance.

In 1758 Voltaire wrote his most celebrated work, *Candide*—a novelette full of philosophical fantasy and humor—that in one scene pokes fun at the Jesuits of Paraguay. *Candide* tells a story of a global wanderer who in one vignette meets Jesuits there, living high, taking their lunch on "golden plates in a verdant room adorned with parrots, hummingbirds and flycatchers," while the Indians live in poverty eating "maize in wooden gourds in their fields by the heat of the sun." Yet his serious side showed through in his most sober, penetrating observation about the Paraguayan Jesuits:

> When in 1768 the missions of Paraguay left the hands of the Jesuits, they had arrived at perhaps the highest degree of civilization to which it is possible to conduct a young people, and certainly at a far superior state than that which existed in the rest of the new hemisphere. The laws were respectful there, morals were pure, a happy brotherhood united every heart, all the useful arts were in a flourishing state, and even some of the more agreeable sciences; plenty was universal.

In Voltaire's waning years during his self-imposed exile at Ferney, his estate in eastern France, a Jesuit often said Mass for him privately, and several of them enjoyed his hospitality. He died at eighty-three after returning to a hero's welcome in Paris. Some say that the excitement from his reception was just too much.

Diderot Publishes *L'Encyclopédie*

Denis Diderot (1713-1784), nineteen years Voltaire's junior and arguably second only to Voltaire among the *philosophes,* was born of a middle class family. He too was Jesuit-educated, but was a more consistent hardliner on Jesuit matters than Voltaire who had love-hate feelings toward them. Diderot was the editor and publisher of *L'Encyclopédie,* a monumental, sophisticated collection of anti-clerical and especially anti-Catholic polemics from many Enlightenment writers including Voltaire himself. Its theme was the self-sufficiency of humanism as well as the irrelevance and deception of religion. It contained much radical, revolutionary political opinion, but also many apolitical mathematical, scientific, and economic articles and other commentary. Published between 1751 and 1772, it comprised seventeen volumes of text and eleven of engravings, 18,000 pages in all, containing 72,000 articles and twenty million words, a true *magnum opus.* Diderot spent six years working on it before even the first volume was printed.

Bangert writes that the Jesuit reaction to *L'Encyclopédie* showed their openness to such an effort. Its first issue was welcomed by Jesuit Guillaume Berthier, editor of the *Journal de Trévoux.* But soon the first clouds began forming when "he suggested that the editors . . . indicate their sources and use quotation marks when citing other works." Six months later he exposed "over a hundred articles which had been extracted, word for word without acknowledgements" and he "revealed that some parts had been lifted directly from the writings of Jesuit Claude Buffier who had died fifteen years earlier." The subsequent issues of *L'Encyclopédie* assumed an increasingly open hostility to Catholicism in a style of "verve, smartness, and wit" that overwhelmed its dry Jesuit competition. Under Voltaire's "withering scorn the prestige of the [Jesuit] journal shrank."

Bangert writes further, "In a way more fundamental than style the Society did not rise to the full measure of the serious challenge of the age. The theological questions raised by the deists called for . . . new approaches and new ideas, but . . . the Jesuits relied on older ways [of] earlier generations." Even their language had been passé, because over many years and venues they had made their case in Latin, barely understood by "ten out of a thousand." Was this seen as intellectual snobbery similar to the criticisms hurled at them by other Catholic orders? After all, their opponents argued in the popular language, meeting the audience on its own terms. A necessity for them; a mistake for the Jesuits. As mentioned in Chapter 2, even Ignatius had warned about toning down the rhetoric.

Thus, it was not by accident that *L'Encyclopédie* coincided with the climax of anti-Jesuit, anti-Catholic, and anti-religious passion in Bourbon Europe. It was a major contributor. The fervor soared to a pinnacle of erudition when the *philosophes* entertained the intellectually narcissistic, idle rich in their fashionable Paris salons "tinkling with fresh opinions formulated in vivacious, witty, and refined language" with scintillating ridicule of the Jesuits and the papacy. A round of laughter rippled through Paris at Voltaire's mischievous lines about one of his Jesuit teachers, René-Joseph Tournemine:

> It is our Father Tournemine
> Who believes everything he makes up.

Diderot's writing spared no one. Even sisters in convents were not exempt from his poison pen. In his *La Religieuse* (The Nun), a young novice pressed into the convent becomes harassed by a sado-masochistic, lesbian mother superior, finally also assuming that lifestyle. This was beyond the pale for those times. Other works, including the first two volumes of *L'Encylopédie,* were so militantly anti-Christian that they landed him briefly in the Bastille.

Rousseau Influences Revolutionaries, Declaration of Independence

Jean-Jacques Rousseau (1712-1778), although not as witty and famous as Voltaire or as prolific a writer as Diderot, was perhaps the most influential Enlightenment *philosophe.* The penetrating clarity of his discourses on the human condition, especially the relationship between the governed and their governors, profoundly affected his generation and generations to come. Born in Calvinist Geneva, his mother died soon after his birth. He was raised by a violent, dysfunctional father, possibly the reason for the bitter, paranoid, and friendless isolation of his later years.

Rousseau moved to Paris at age thirty and found his way into Diderot's inner circle with perfect timing, at the launch of *L'Encyclopédie.* There he produced some of the most influential works of revolutionary, abstract political thought in all of history. He wrote in 1762 that what we call government is not derived from divine inspiration nor the "divine right" of kings; it is a "social contract" between the rulers and the ruled. The only reason why men are willing to delegate their freedom to their rulers is because they see that their rights and their "pursuit of happiness" are best served through the medium of a just government. When the rulers are unjust, a new form of government should be introduced. These profundities were found in the Declaration of Independence fourteen years later.

Charles de Secondat, Baron de Montesquieu (1689-1755), contributed some of the clearest political thinking of the time to *L'Encyclopédie* by building on Locke and advocating the separation of powers—legislative, executive, and judicial—to provide checks and balances, a concept that profoundly influenced the American Constitution. Notably, these three "estates" as he called them excluded the clergy.

These years encompassed the expulsions of the Jesuits from the three Catholic kingdoms and their order's liquidation by the pope. The Jesuits' nemeses—France's Choiseul, Pombal of Portugal and Aranda of Spain—made no secret of the fact that their inspiration came from the polemics of the *philosophes* in *L'Encyclopédie.*

Attempted Assassination of Louis XV Blamed on Jesuits

In 1757 Robert François Damien attempted to assassinate Louis XV. He almost succeeded. Damien had been a servant at a Jesuit college twenty years before, but later became close to Jesuit antagonists for reasons lost in the murk of passing years. Some believed that he had Jansenist tendencies, but that would have put him, inconveniently, diametrically opposed to the Jesuits. So Jesuit adversaries focused on that youthful involvement. The old canard, repeated over and over since the assassinations of Henry III and Henry IV that Jesuits condoned regicide, was now promoted again in speeches and political pamphlets published by anti-Jesuit forces. The lie told often enough for long enough turns to fact. These arguments helped drive a wedge between the Jesuit order and the intimidated king.

The incessant drumbeat of invective hurled at the Jesuits during much of this period and their unwavering support for a discredited papacy were taking their toll, creating an incendiary situation that needed only a spark to embolden the opposition. The Jesuits themselves would provide that spark in the form of a crippling financial scandal. It arrived as if on cue like other wonderfully useful justifications did in Portugal and Spain. This one was real, however, no doubt about it.

Jesuit Financial Scandal Enrages Paris Parlement

At the time of Damien's attack on the king, a second event occurred that was more effective—the ultimate gift from the Jesuits to their enemies. It was a decade-long financial scandal triggered by Jesuit Father Antoine de Lavalette's failed investments in the French West Indies. More than any other event, this fiasco brought down the French Jesuits.

Lavalette was an engaging, enterprising man from a prominent merchant family, members of the Catholic Church's prestigious Knights of Malta. He was the Jesuit agent and the superior of the missions in Martinique during the 1740s. No doubt he had learned how to succeed in business from his family. At that time and place, enormous profits could be made in the infamous "triangular trade" of sugar and other staples for rum, and then rum for African slaves. More money could be made from plantations operated with that same slave labor. After a decade of success that benefited the Jesuit treasury, he was accused of violating the order's rule of poverty. Back in Paris he defended himself, justifying his profits as enabling good works in the Indies. His collaboration in the enslaving of Africans did not seem to be of concern.

Lavalette was given a second chance, but back in Martinique two catastrophes resulted in devastating financial losses that proved his undoing. First, one of the frequent epidemics there killed many of his slaves. Second, English buccaneers captured all but one of his fifteen or more ships loaded with sugar and coffee valued at a handsome 600,000 livres. Soon things went from bad luck to outright fraud. In covering up his losses, he defrauded his French investors while borrowing more from a merchant bank. Now he was in debt for one and a half million livres. The investors detected the fraud and brought suit against him.

As the legal proceedings ground on, regularly making the headlines, Jesuit General Luigi Aloysius Centurioni in Rome as well as French superiors in Paris including Lorenzo Ricci felt it necessary to take charge. Centurioni dispatched a visitor (Jesuit for "inspector") to Martinique to stop Lavalette's dealings, but it was already too late to affect the scandal and lawsuit. The visitor died at sea. A second visitor broke his leg just before departing. A third was captured by pirates. Three years had passed before a fourth arrived intact in 1762. Two months later this visitor concluded that Lavalette should be removed, sent back to Europe, and excommunicated. Lavalette's response was to plead guilty, but not to evil intent, only to poor judgment. He forth-

rightly placed all the burden on himself, exonerating all others including his Jesuit superiors, saying his confession had not been prompted
by "force, nor threats, nor caresses or other tricks." Lavalette then fled
to refuge in England to avoid almost certain lengthy imprisonment.

By then events in Paris had spun out of control. In 1760 the defrauded
investors won a judgment from the courts for a staggering three
million livres—several tens of millions in today's dollars. In what
turned out to be two gross miscalculations, Father Pierre-Claude Frey
de Neuville who was the provincial of the Paris Jesuits took a firm
stand against the idea of his Paris province having to make payments to
cover Lavalette's losses. He argued for the traditional legal interpretation that each local house was solely responsible for its debts. That was
rejected by the courts. Then Frey de Neuville made things even worse.
He believed that an appeal to Parlement would be a show of good
faith, especially given its perception that the Jesuits enjoyed excessive
privileges. Peculiar logic. He could have appealed directly to Louis, but
that too would have been a risky proposition given the shaky political
ground the king was on. The Seven Years' War with England was
going badly and the mortifying Treaty of Paris would soon heap shame
on him. In his appeal to Parlement, Frey de Neuville was really throwing himself at their mercy. He seems to have known that. But it was a
catastrophic mistake, a complete misread of the political climate. He
found no mercy. Instead, not only did parlement decide for the plain-
tiffs, but it also upped the judgment to five million livres.

Lacouture writes that at this time Diderot was directing "all his brilliant fury at these [Jesuits]" who were in Diderot's words into
"intrigue . . . politics and occupations alien to their condition and
unworthy of their [priestly] profession," which profession Diderot
despised to begin with. The Lavalette affair had met the criteria of
"intrigue, politics, and occupations alien." The perfect storm!

Meanwhile, Parlement's agent, Abbé de Chauvelin, a man well connected to the *philosophes* and the Jansenists, issued a harrowing report
on the Jesuits calling them a

> . . . war machine, a cunning instrument of oppression, a tool in
> the hands of a foreign potentate [the pope] . . . and a fifth column.

He then launched into the two-century-old canard of "regicide" as an
example of Jesuit "morality." The public approved. Surprisingly, this
time Louis had the courage to overrule Parlement and to appoint his
own more moderate committee to handle the case. This committee

recommended a large reduction in the monetary judgment but added, crucially, that the French Jesuits should be integrated into the French Church. The French Jesuits would report to the French bishops, not to the general in Rome (a *quid pro quo*?). Then a general assembly of the French bishops concluded by a vote of forty-four to seven that, among other things, the Jesuits should continue to report directly to the pope through their general. The bishops must have understood that if the Jesuits were to be sacrificed, they themselves could not avoid being caught up in the ensuing maelstrom.

Meanwhile, other enemies of the Jesuits had joined the fray. They included the Marquise de Pompadour, paramour of Louis. Joining her were his powerful First Minister Etienne-François de Choiseul, better known as the Duc de Choiseul, and a number of bishops with self-serving motives. The enmity of the Marquise de Pompadour towards the Jesuits resulted from the fact that her and Louis' Jesuit confessors were unwilling to forgive their intimacy. Gradually the king's lassitude cooled their passion anyway. In 1757, after they apparently separated, a separation that included the entry from her boudoir to the royal chamber being walled-up, their confessors remained unforgiving for reasons that are unclear. So she appealed to the pope to overrule them. After the Vatican rejected her entreaty, she angrily threw her support behind the Jansenist Jesuit-baiters. The Jansenists themselves had been reanimated by the engaging and subtle Pasquier Quesnel, who built up an ardent Jansenist spirit in France's parliaments.

French Jesuits Surrender, Pope Reacts Rudely

French Chancellor Guillaume de Lamoignon, a Jesuit sympathizer, publicly agreed with Louis' committee's conclusion that the Jesuits must move in the direction of Gallicanism and place themselves under the French Church. In the process they would become answerable to the French bishops. At this point, December 1761, the French Jesuit leaders reacted with a most stunning surrender, what Lacouture calls a "Jesuit Munich." They agreed to do so! He writes that the reaction in Rome was quite another matter. Clement XIII and Jesuit General Lorenzo Ricci rejected any kind of accommodation with "venomous disdain." He continues that Clement "retorted with superb hauteur" to the French envoy who had brought the proposal, "Let them [the Jesuits] be what they are or let them not be." No compromise!

Bangert writes that Ricci had been a "teacher of rhetoric, philosophy, and theology . . . [who] manifested a quick and clear intelligence . . .

[who had] never been a superior . . . and [had] no practical administrative experience." He was a Florentine nobleman, gentle, cultivated, broad-minded, and modest—the kind of man who would not stand up to Clement. He was fifty-eight at this point. He would become one of the most tragic figures in Church history.

Clement's "no compromise" reaction was taken as a challenge. It provoked many in Parlement. In February 1762 members published a pamphlet *Extracts of Dangerous and Pernicious Assertions of All Kinds, Which the So-called Jesuits Have at All Times and Most Stubbornly Maintained and Taught and Published in Their Books with the Approval of Their Superiors and Generals.* Its success was as huge as its title. Co-editor of *L'Encyclopédie*, Jean Le Rond d'Alembert, wrote that the pamphlet "furnished the benefit the nation asked of it—the annihilation of the Jesuits." On the other hand Wright points out that it contained nothing new, just the "full gamut of hackneyed anti-Jesuit accusations—that they were king killers, sorcerers, and dispensers of shameful moral advice." The last crime alleged had, no doubt, the hidden hand of the joyless Jansenists behind it. For almost a century they had accused the Jesuits of "lax moral theology . . . a consequence of the Society's rosy view of human nature." The Jesuits had even gone so far as to argue that humans were worthy of "taking communion quite often."

Some months before this, d'Alembert wrote to Voltaire, ". . . let the Jansenist rabble rid us of the Jesuit blackguards. Do not put anything in the way of these spiders gobbling one another up." This time the Protestants were not even involved. It was Catholics against Catholics; they were doing his work for him.

Expulsion from Paris and then France
In August 1762 the Paris Parlement delivered the final blow, declaring:

> . . . the Society [of Jesus is] inadmissible by its very nature . . . contrary to natural law . . . a political body whose essence is continual activity aimed at attaining . . . absolute independence and...the usurpation of all authority."

That left little to the imagination. France's 2,900 Jesuits were scattered, and the order's assets were seized. The parliaments of Alsace and Lorraine (and several other parliaments in the provinces) did not go along with Paris. They and several smaller provinces allowed the Jesuits to remain. Many fathers placed themselves as secular priests under their local bishop. Some went to other countries. Surprisingly for the venom unleashed against them, the Jesuits were allotted a modest daily stipend by most French parliaments. Thus were consciences salved.

In October 1763 the archbishop of Paris, Christophe de Beaumont, issued a pastoral instruction condemning Parlement's action. He saw it for what it was—the beginning of the end for the official Church in France. Parlement had his paper burned and ordered him to appear before it. To protect him, the king temporarily banished him from Paris. One more retreat by Louis. We will hear more from Beaumont in 1773, right after the suppression of the Society by the pope.

Despite whatever deep belief the king might still have harbored in favor of the Jesuits, by mid-1762 he had surrendered to Parlement's wishes. He showed his true character: He was indolent, timorous, bored by everything and everybody, suffering from ennui; he holed up in the Palace of Versailles. Then in November 1764, under intense pressure and resigned to the inevitable, he liquidated the Jesuit order across the realm.

Ironically, the most visible refuge for France's Jesuits was in Canada, newly won by Protestant England. The order was permitted to thrive there, ministering to the French in Quebec and to the Algonquin Indians in Canada and the northern portions of the sprawling Louisiana Territory.

Leave it to Voltaire with his contradictory, peculiar affection for his former teachers, to offer a final drollery when he responded to d'Alembert's concern that there were still some Jesuits around:

> The Jesuits are not yet destroyed; they remain in Alsace; they are preaching in Dijon . . . there are twelve of them at Versailles, and one who says Mass for me.

Two years later Clement issued a papal Bull, *Apostolicum* (*pascendi*) (The Ministry of Nurturing), declaring:

> The Company of Jesus breathes piety and holiness of the highest degree, even though there are men who, after disfiguring it with their malicious interpretations, dared characterize it as irreligious and impious, thus insulting the Church of God in the most outrageous manner.

Too little, too late!

It was over for the Jesuits in Portugal and now in France, but the main event was yet to come in Madrid twenty-eight months later.

CHAPTER 16

Spain Turns On Her Favorite Sons— The Main Event

On February 27, 1767, an enraged Carlos III (Charles III), king of Spain, once an admirer of the Jesuits, ferociously turned on them, signing an order expelling them from Spain and its worldwide empire. Any person opposing the king's Expulsion Decree or even failing to cooperate in its execution was to "suffer the penalty of death" under orders for Spain, signed *"Ca R"* (Carlos Rey). Charles' warning to his administrators was even more ominous, if that is possible: "If after the embarkation [the expelled Jesuits boarding transports for exile] there should be found in that district a single Jesuit, even if ill or dying, you shall suffer the penalty of death." How could this possibly come to be?

Spain's Favorite Sons

When we imagine the Society of Jesus, we should think of Spain as its epicenter. Its headquarters might have been in Rome but most of its energy and zeal and the largest contribution of priests and brothers from any country were from Spain. Spain's pride in the Jesuits was well justified since six of the seven founders of the order were born there including Ignatius of Loyola, the order's founding father, and Francis Xavier, the globe-trotting evangelist who introduced Christianity to India, southeast Asia, and Japan. Spain's Jesuits, with their missions and schools, circled the earth with a thousand more missionaries than came from any other country. In addition, Spaniards considered themselves as Catholics without equal in the world. The intensity of their Catholicism came from the cauldron of 700 years of battling Muslim Moor invaders from north Africa, until Ferdinand and Isabella completed the effort to drive them back to Africa in 1492.

It seemed inconceivable to anyone that Spain would ever turn against the spiritual successors to the Jesuits' Spanish founders. But turn it did, with an almost maniacal vengeance emanating from His Most Catholic Majesty. Even after he expelled them in 1767 from Spain and its empire, his hostility continued for another six years, long after the monarchs of France and Portugal lost interest in persecuting them. Charles was not fully satisfied until 1773, when the Society of Jesus was liquidated by the intimidated Pope Clement XIV in what became known as their "Suppression." Even Charles' son and successor Charles IV perpetuated his father's policies towards the order, although by then the Jesuit priests and brothers had been largely scattered throughout Christian Europe. Because the Spanish part is central to the story of the Jesuit Republic of the Guaraní, the political, religious, and social events precipitating the expulsion from Spain and its possessions need to be described.

Louis XIV's Grandson Becomes Philip V of Spain (1700)

Charles II, the last of the inbred line of Hapsburg Spanish kings, the son of Philip IV by his niece Mariana of Austria, mentally retarded, physically handicapped, and monstrously homely, died childless on November 1, 1700.

In his will Charles named Philip, Duke of Anjou (a French province) and a grandson of France's Louis XIV, as his heir by "the right of the closest relative." Philip would be Spain's first Bourbon monarch.

Later that month, Louis presented his seventeen-year-old grandson to the gathered nobility and ambassadors in the French court at the palace of Versailles, saying: "Gentlemen, here is the King of Spain! His birth has called him to this crown; the Spanish nation has asked for him and has eagerly begged me for him; I concede to this with pleasure, actuated by the decrees of Providence." Turning to Philip he added: "Be a good Spaniard; that, from this moment, is your first obligation; but remember that you were born French to preserve unity between both nations so as to make them both happy and to keep the peace in Europe."

Then the Spanish ambassador to France sent chills down the spines of the ambassadors of France's many opponents by proclaiming: "What happiness! Now there are no Pyrenees! They have sunk into the ground, and we form only one nation!"

Not long after this ceremony, Philip entered Madrid to rapturous crowds who were glad to be rid of the Hapsburgs whom they rightly blamed for Spain's decay. And now to have the grandson of a Spaniard, Maria Teresa, crowned as Philip V—how could it have turned out better?

War of the Spanish Succession

Immediately the two great Catholic dynasties, the Austrian Hapsburgs and Bourbons of France, went to war over Spain. Charles' will had upset the balance of power in Europe. Austria and its main allies, England, the Dutch Republic, and Prussia, would not tolerate a Spain—with its immense colonial possessions around the world, from the Philippines to the Americas, and large parts of Italy and north Africa—to be under French hegemony. Today we would call the War of the Spanish Succession "a preemptive war," waged to prevent a dangerous and suddenly too powerful France from radically changing what had been a delicate balance of continental power.

The war was a lengthy one, lasting thirteen years with neither side willing to concede much on such a profoundly important matter. France, though exhausted, finally prevailed. In the end Louis had to make concessions—by Spain. However, his first priority was gained: Philip was securely seated on the Spanish throne. With Louis' approval, Spain had to surrender Belgium and its possessions in Italy to Austria and to cede Gibraltar to England, a recurrent national angst.

A subtle but profoundly important shift in autocracy had also occurred in Spain. Government administration under a Bourbon monarchy was more centralized, uniform, and absolutist than under the Hapsburgs. This strengthened the idea of the nation-state and would help lead to conflict between the monarchy and the Jesuits a half-century later.

Philip V's first marriage to María Luisa Gabriela of Savoy (now in southeastern France) when he was eighteen and she thirteen, produced two sons—Luis and Ferdinand. The second, born in Madrid in 1713, would eventually become King Ferdinand VI. María Luisa died early in 1714, at age twenty-five.

Philip's mourning was brief; he married Elizabeth Farnese of Naples later that same year .In those times life was often so short and death so capricious that such brief mourning was commonplace. Elizabeth was a strong-willed, robust, blue-eyed woman with an oval, pock-marked face. She became the dominant member of the family, fully compensating for Philip's bouts of crippling introversion; she was an extrovert. She was a horsewoman and huntress. Intellectually gifted, she spoke several languages. She supported music and the arts. Her strong personality was attested to by her brusqueness and occasionally violent mannerisms. She bore seven children including her first son Charles in 1716. He was small but promising as far as his ambitious mother was concerned. She saw him as a contender for the throne even though his two half-brothers, sons of Philip and María Luisa, placed Charles third in the line of succession.

In the early 1720s Philip V suffered bouts of extreme neurosis, which he feared was a prelude to madness—a genetic predisposition in the Bourbon line, as it was with the inbred Hapsburgs. Yet he was sufficiently aware of himself and his surroundings to have enough sense to abdicate in 1724 in favor of his eldest son Luis. Luis died of smallpox eight months later. Charles was now second in line. Philip, barely able to manage his problems at this point, remounted the throne at the insistence of Elizabeth. Given Philip's mental state, Elizabeth became *de facto* head-of-state and remained so throughout his reign. Her main priority during these two decades was to ensure that Charles would remain positioned to become king should Ferdinand not live and produce an heir.

In 1729 the sixteen-year-old future Ferdinand VI was married to María Barbara, daughter of Portugal's King João V (John V). Her exceeding homeliness—pock-marked skin, large mouth, small beady eyes (later, she became grossly obese)—made her repulsive at their initial meeting, but she had such a wonderful way about her that he soon became and remained deeply in love and submissive to her for the rest of his life.

Although Philip V's reign was long (1700-1746) and it restored Spain to the financially strong and respected power it was before his Hapsburg predecessors, it was unremarkable in relation to the Jesuits. He maintained crown support for the missions and did not have to deal with difficult issues in Paraguay.

Upon Philip's death in 1746, thirty-three-year-old Ferdinand ascended to the throne as Ferdinand VI with María Barbara as his queen. María Barbara was a great patron of music. At court in Madrid she sponsored the great Domenico Scarlatti and Carlo Broschi (also known as Farinelli) a castrato who was the most famous and widely acclaimed as the best singer in eighteenth century Europe. Farinelli sang exclusively for the king for much of his two decades in Madrid. His singing had a beneficial effect on Ferdinand's melancholia to the point that the king was often able to function somewhat normally. His Jesuit confessors also helped reduce his depression, but only somewhat. His terrible insecurity led to procrastination in decision making that proved inadvertently beneficial in keeping Spain neutral between warring France and England. Meanwhile he favored the latter's interests in return for several British favors. At one point England's prime minister, William Pitt, even offered to return Gibraltar, a huge psychological issue for Spain—if Ferdinand would join England against France. But Ferdinand demurred.

Four years into Ferdinand's reign, Spain and Portugal signed the Treaty of Madrid (Chapter 13) affecting seven Jesuit missions in the Guayrá region of southern Brazil. Ferdinand's personality and mental handicap together with his Portuguese wife's domineering personality combined to help make that treaty the disaster it was for the Guaraní and the Jesuits of Paraguay.

After María Barbara died of fever in 1758, Ferdinand, already sick from tuberculosis and now emotionally devastated, retired to a castle near Madrid where he went completely mad. Reduced to a skeleton and bed-ridden in his own filth, he died almost a year later at forty-six, childless.

During Ferdinand's final years, Charles remained in Naples despite entreaties from Spain's ministers for him to assume the throne. The entire government of Spain felt that Ferdinand would readily abdicate if asked to. To his great credit Charles resisted those entreaties and, in spite of many officials' frustration, his humility in doing so was universally admired. In late 1759 he would be crowned Charles III, king of Spain.

What Charles III's Early Years Were Like

Charles as a teenager was studious, thoughtful, and energetic. When his father Philip V was functioning, he was an effective role model. Charles was a quick study and developed rapidly under his English Jesuit teachers in Madrid. In 1733 Philip appointed Charles at the age of only sixteen to be Duke of Parma. Parma, in fragmented northern Italy, had recently been acquired by Spain. Thanks to his Italian mother, Elizabeth Farnese, Charles was warmly welcomed by the Parmasans.

Charles had arrived at the right place at the right time. Through additional warring in Italy—this time the War of the Polish Succession, with Spain and its allies defeating Austria—Charles was able to prove himself. Though he was a teenager with an exceedingly youthful and rather unattractive and unregal appearance, he always showed extraordinary leadership and courage at the head of his forces. At the Battle of Bitonto in 1734 Duke Charles, still just a teenager, won an important victory over the Austrians. A decade later in the Italian Campaign of the War of the Austrian Succession, he would reach the pinnacle of his battlefield career. Demonstrating confidence and bravery under fire, he personally rallied his demoralized, retreating troops to repel the attacking Austrians, while benefiting from a secret alliance under which the British navy played a pivotal role in his success. This experience, combined with his happy early years with his English Jesuit teachers, deeply influenced his attitude toward England later on.

The Polish war victory led to his rule over much of central and southern Italy including Naples and Sicily, a large area known as The Kingdom of the Two Sicilies. Later, after seizing some papal lands, the young Charles showed impressive statesmanship for his age as he cleverly ingratiated himself with the aggrieved pope, resulting in a papal Bull from the now-flattered pontiff confirming Charles' territorial acquisitions. Another coup for the young man!

On the domestic front Charles had his work cut out for him, as the Kingdom of the Two Sicilies was backward and disorganized by almost every measure. Injustice, social and civil, was rampant. There was no infrastructure. It had been a virtually feudal society run by self-serving nobles and popes. Here too, even from the outset Charles showed wisdom beyond his years. Rather than confront the nobles head-on, he cleverly played to their pride and empowered them through appointments to positions in his new government. In doing so, he discovered a rare treasure in the form of Justice Minister Bernardo Tanucci, eighteen years Charles' senior. He stood out among his peers, quickly winning Charles' confidence and favor. Their relationship became the closest of Charles' political life—the eager, able, and respectful student together with the wise and learned teacher and mentor. The mutual admiration lasted into their old age. Together they introduced reforms into every aspect of Italian life.

By 1755 Charles had made Tanucci minister of state (prime minister) placing him above all the other ministers and nobles, de facto head of state. Tanucci no doubt studied the works of the French philosophes because he had become "enlightened" in his social and economic policies. He was also mildly anti-clerical, an attitude formed from the absolute control the Church exercised over the Papal States of central Italy. This control led to a ubiquitous clergy who were in numbers grossly disproportionate to the population and thus a major economic burden.

Tanucci's reforms under Charles included rationalizing finances and taxes in ways that stimulated trade and fattened the treasury. Great construction works could now be funded in both civil infrastructure and the arts including a grand palace, museums, monuments, libraries, and the excavation of the ruins of Pompeii and Herculaneum near Mt. Vesuvius. The Church's landholdings were shrunk along with those of the increasingly subservient nobles. In 1741 Charles, with Tanucci's support (or at his instigation), had encouraged the immigration of Jews, widely known for their business acumen and plentiful capital. Sadly for all, popular opposition was so intense that after six years his Jewish policy had to be withdrawn. The populace had come to believe that their various sufferings at the time resulted from divine anger over the Jews' presence. Discontent then turned to street violence compelling Charles to revoke his welcome to the Jews. His excuse was that, after all, they had contributed little to the economy. Privately he later admitted that he was embarrassed by both the reversal and the excuse.

Charles Marries María Warburg

In 1737 the exceedingly worldly, self-confident, and mature twenty-one-year-old Charles became eager to marry. He brushed aside family pressure aimed at his marrying for an alliance's sake. Instead, this most-eligible bachelor lit upon María Amalia Warburg, the daughter of Frederick Augustus, king of Poland, and the Archduchess María Josepha of Austria. Her physique suggested good breeding stock despite her tender age, only thirteen. She was taller than Charles and was a typical fair, blue-eyed, robust German maiden. How she viewed him is not known, but his appearance notwithstanding, he had great charm and charisma.

A year later Charles and María Amalia were married twice amid sumptuous pomp and circumstance, characteristic of royal Catholic weddings. First she was married by proxy in her baroque home town of Dresden in a fairy-tale ceremony with her brother, the Prince of Saxony, standing in for Charles. Six weeks later the marriage was affirmed with Charles, in person this time, at a grand reception in Naples. The marriage delighted not only the Neapolitans, but also the many defeated Austrians who had remained in Charles' Kingdom of the Two Sicilies. María soon contracted smallpox which left her scarred. As mentioned, Charles was not much to look at himself and his own case of smallpox had worsened his already mousy appearance, moving the British ambassador to say that they were the ugliest couple in the world.

Appearances aside, their marriage was blessed. Charles and María Amalia complemented each other in every way. James Gray, the British ambassador, reporting to London in the 1750s wrote:

> The King of Naples is of a very reserved temper; a great master of dissimulation, he has a habitual smile on his face, contracted by a constant attention to conceal his thoughts; has a good understanding and a surprising memory, as his father had; is unread and unlearned, but retains an exact knowledge of all that has passed within his own observation, and is capable of entering into the most minute detail. He is in many things his own [Prime] Minister, passing several hours every day alone in his cabinet . . . and is so positive and obstinate that he is seldom induced to alter his resolutions. . . . The queen . . . has a great influence over the king who is very fond of her.

Queen María Amalia Dies at Thirty-six

Their life together was idyllic. They had thirteen children, although only eight reached adolescence—not unusual for the times. While Charles had been exuberant about returning to Spain and seeing his mother in Madrid for the first time in thirty years, his exuberance was not shared by María, at least not in her letters to Tanucci. She would soon find her first winter in Spain to be cold, rainy, and gloomy, in sharp contrast to her many happy years in sunny Naples. Her health declined and her mood became darker. She was living in the drafty, damp Buen Retiro palace and, before anyone fully appreciated her dire condition, it was too late to save her. On September 27, 1760, after months of exhaustion and depression and after twenty-two years of marriage, María Amalia died from pleurisy. She was only thirty-six. It was just nine months after moving to Madrid and just weeks after Charles was crowned King of Spain.

María Amalia was a temperamental but intelligent woman, and considerably more astute than most consorts of her day. She would have been of inestimable help to Charles in the troubled years ahead. She opposed Spain's involvement in disputes on behalf of either Bourbon France (his ancestry) or Hapsburg Austria (hers). Instead, she favored a strong isolationist foreign policy. Subsequent events would prove her to be right.

Charles never remarried and is believed to have remained celibate ever after, a tribute to his high notion of love and fidelity. Some believe that this notion might have been a major factor in his explosive reaction in 1767 to the escalating allegations of Jesuit disloyalty. He had always been loyal to them, especially their men in Paraguay.

Charles in Naples Protests the Treaty of Madrid (1750)

In 1749, after bitter infighting among Ferdinand VI's ministers, a treaty with Portugal was proposed to deal with questions surrounding ownership of Sacramento, also called Colonia—that part of what is now Uruguay bordering on the north shore of Río de La Plata opposite Buenos Aires. Spain wanted to remove any threat to that vital harbor and the navigable rivers running deep into northern Argentina and Paraguay. In return Spain would cede to Portugal part of the up-river Jesuit territory, the Guayrá containing seven prosperous Guaraní missions east of the Uruguay River in what is today's huge, fertile Brazilian state of Rio Grande do Sul. In addition, Portugal gained most of the Amazon basin.

The Treaty of Madrid, sometimes called the Treaty of Limits and Treaty of 1750, was signed in January 1750 (Chapter 13). The treaty terms were broad and imprecise, soon becoming a major source of friction between the two countries. This friction was partly due to Portuguese aggressiveness in interpreting the treaty terms and partly because of the mission Jesuits' opposition to Spain's immoral and impractical selling out of the Guaraní in the seven missions. Charles, still in Naples during the signing, protested that he was not involved. Its disadvantages to Spain were obvious. Nine years later, when he mounted the Spanish throne, he would have much to make him unhappy about it.

Charles Ascends the Throne

Late in 1759 Charles left Tanucci and a lamenting Naples behind. He had become a hugely popular "people's king." Charles and his family sailed to Barcelona and then made an arduous journey by carriage, entering Madrid in December to a tumultuous welcome. Along with the royal entourage were several trusted Italian aides, including Finance Minister Marchese di Squillace who would soon be a source of disenchantment. Charles was crowned Charles III in Madrid in the summer of 1760.

After María Amalia's death, Charles immersed himself in projects. The Alcázar in Seville, renowned for its Moorish architecture, was expanded and improved to be his grandest palace; various reforms were initiated; and magnanimous amnesties were given. In the provinces, some autonomy was restored; nobles were allowed to display their once-forbidden family coats of arms; and many creditors with long-past-due claims were paid. These actions were wildly popular.

At this time, the Seven Years' War was raging, with France gradually losing its Canadian and East Indian colonies to England. Charles, remembering the French-Spanish "family compact"—a personal agreement for mutual aid between the French and Spanish monarchs, an alliance that the French called an *affair du Coeur*—harbored hopes for his cousin Louis XV. For a while he wisely stayed out of the war and tried to mediate. He knew that his own sprawling global empire was vulnerable to England's peerless navy. And he still harbored fond memories of his English Jesuit teachers and England's aid during his battles in Italy.

Spain had only minor political differences with England. France's first minister, the Duke of Choiseul, told Charles that he had been rebuffed by the English when he promoted Spain's issues with them. The scheming Choiseul had exaggerated the issues to widen the gulf between Spain and England to draw Spain into the war. Then Choiseul let on that Louis XV would feel offended if cousin Charles did not join him and take up arms against England. At this point Charles made an uncharacteristically foolish decision. He declared war on England. His reasons are obscure. The best guess is that it was driven by several factors: resentment over two centuries of British pirate and naval attacks on Spanish shipping, the occupation of Gibraltar, and loyalty to Louis based on past family compacts.

France was virtually defeated by the time Spanish forces under the aging general Sarria made their first move in 1762, invading Portugal which was England's ally. Sarria soon got bogged down and was replaced by Aranda, to no benefit. Then Havana and Manila quickly fell to England's navy. The battle in the eastern theatre was not going well for another English ally, the small but militaristic Prussia which was battling Austria and Russia. Czar Peter III snatched defeat out of the jaws of victory, deciding to withdraw and leave the field to his personal hero, Frederick the Great. Concurrently, England's George III felt he had won enough (in those days, total defeat and unconditional surrender were not essential outcomes) and was keen to lock in his substantial conquests with a peace treaty. That was lucky for Charles. With France virtually prostrate, he likely would have lost much of his empire to England.

The resulting Treaty of Paris in 1763 was surprisingly generous to Spain. In a dizzying round robin of deals, France was the only real loser. It ceded to its ally Spain its vast American lands known as "Louisiana." Spain lost Florida to England, gaining back Havana and Manila. More relevant to this narrative, Spain had to return Sacramento on Río de La Plata, gained under the Treaty of Madrid, back to Portugal.

Charles then settled down to improving Madrid and the administration of Spanish government. The ministerial and civil service meritocracy that was begun under his father in 1705 was greatly expanded and improved. The losers in this situation were college-educated plutocrats, usually minor nobles often from Jesuit schools. This group would become a thorn in his relationship with the Jesuits. They were elitists who constantly and underhandedly caviled at his new civil service and pressed for a comeback. Charles turned a deaf ear to the criticism but probably harbored irritation that would come into play later. He had a long memory.

Madrid Riots Threaten Monarchy

In the middle of the 1760s, Spain experienced a severe bout of inflation in the cost of food. It resulted from two years of poor harvests and the reopening of the sea lanes after the war, thus allowing the inflow of large amounts of bottled-up gold and silver from the Americas. At the same time, under Charles' direction, one of his imported Neapolitan ministers attempted to clean up Madrid's poorly paved, filthy streets which were roamed freely by pigs. But many poor, slovenly Madrilenos were quite satisfied with the streets as they were. They liked to toss slop and garbage from their upper balconies. It would come raining down on the streets below with the cry of warning—"*agua va*" (water's coming). The improved sanitation was unappreciated.

As though they did not have enough to deal with, Charles and his Italian ministers then decreed that the popular Spanish fashion of broad-brimmed hats, covering half the face as protection from the sun, and a long cloak must be replaced with more modern European dress. Its justification was that the hat, pulled down, could cover the face sufficiently to conceal a known criminal and the cloak could cover-up illicit weapons. It was seen as government interference in daily life. From the royal decree of January 22, 1766, aimed initially at officials:

We are sending directives . . . especially to those in his Majesty's service in and around Madrid . . . that in [the] future royal officials should wear proper dress, i.e., jacket or riding coat with a wig or appropriate hair style, and with a cocked hat in place of the wide-brimmed hat, the coat to be worn in such a manner so as not to conceal anything. We hereby give warning that orders have been issued to arrest anyone in the king's service henceforth found wearing the forbidden style of dress.

The king's order made no difference to commoners. However, on March 10, just seven weeks later a new proclamation was posted in all public squares. It required all citizens, not just royal officials, to observe the code. Two weeks later some soldiers tried to enforce the code. All hell broke loose. Thousands rioted in the streets. The Neapolitan ministers were blamed by the mob. Finance Minister Leopoldo de Gregorio, Marqués de Esquilace (better known as Squillace in his native Italian), bore the brunt of it.

In April more riots broke out in many neighborhoods of Madrid and in several other cities. The king's elite guards were carefully picked Walloons from the Spanish Netherlands, a former Spanish possession. More foreigners! Under attack, the guards fired at some of the worst rioters, killing two women whose bodies were borne through the streets, further inflaming the mobs; they became "martyrs." Rioters overwhelmed some of the guards and decapitated and mutilated them. The savagery escalated to even more grisly scenes. Guards' heads were carried on pikes as the mobs rampaged on; some had their eyes gouged and tongues torn out, and their corpses dragged through the streets and finally burned. The full import of all this was not lost on the king. Soon a huge crowd assembled outside his palace with a list of demands including the expulsion of Squillace, a rolling back of the new dress code, and a reduction in food prices. Thanks to the mediation of a Franciscan who led a saying of the Rosary, the crowd finally went home for the night, illustrating once again the overwhelming power of Catholicism in Spain. The royal family fled Madrid, going some twenty-five miles south to the royal residence at Aranjuez. They stayed there for eight months, an act for which many accused him of cowardice. What is clear to almost all is that had he not fled he probably would have ended up on the guillotine like his cousin's son, Louis XVI.

The mobs attacked Squillace's house rather than the palace, doing so just after he had fled. He would certainly have been killed if caught.

Ruling from Aranjuez, Charles fired Squillace. The minister immediately returned to Naples. Other Italian officials who came with Squillace in 1759 soon followed him home. All were replaced by Spaniards who met the rioters' demands.

The riots appeared to have been too coordinated to have been spontaneous. Some alleged that Jesuits had been seen passing out money to the mob. As unlikely as that may be, the idea found currency among the many Jesuit-haters, especially those within the government.

The riots were in all likelihood provoked, but not by the Jesuits. The anti-Jesuit Duke of Alba reportedly made a deathbed confession that he and others had helped organize the riots in order to attribute them to the Jesuits. Mörner asks:

> Who in fact started this whole affair that led to the king fleeing for his life? The answers seem fairly clear, today [mid-twentieth century]. The riot was a political bomb cleverly laid by a group of "philosophers" led by the Duke of Alba. The calmness of the principal nobles at the moment when a general massacre was dreaded, the comings and goings of the crowd, of mysterious persons with a distinguished mien and self-possessed air, the ample funds and food the crowd never lacked, finally the Duke of Alba's own death-bed confessions prove that the riot was organized in order to frighten the king into expelling the Jesuits.

Papal historian Pastor wrote, "The reports which adhere most closely to events . . . contain no hints of the Jesuits being responsible for the uprising." He goes on to say that, from Aranda's pen, the rioters' intent was to "slaughter" Squillace who was by his machinations preventing the complaints and petitions of the people from reaching the ear of Charles.

Charles Appoints Aranda as Prime Minister

A month later, in April 1766, Charles appointed Pedro Pablo de Abarca y Bolea, Conde de Aranda or simply "Aranda," as president of the council of ministers. Aranda, age forty-six, was a strong choice. He was a reformer yet a centrist, with impressive credentials from military achievements and from a brief period as a Spanish diplomat to Frederick the Great and as an ambassador to Poland. Most importantly, when he later resided in Paris he often met with the *philosophes*, becoming their disciple.

Charles' Anti-Jesuit Feelings Grow, the Teaching of Suarez and the Palafox Case

As for the king, his anti-Jesuit feelings were growing. The riots had cast doubt over the loyalty of the Jesuits. He valued fidelity highly; he was still celibate since María Amalia's death. Further, did not the Jesuits place the papacy's interests above those of the crown? Making matters still worse for Charles and the regalists, Jesuit schools expounded the enlightened humanist philosophy of Jesuit Francisco Suarez, a man "hostile to the throne." Over a century and a half earlier Suarez had taught that while rulers received their authority from God, it was only through the mediation of the people. By the mid-eighteenth century, this had become the message of Rousseau and others in the Enlightenment.

The experiences of Portugal and France weighed heavy on Charles' mind as did the drumbeat of accusations and outright calumnies against the Jesuits from the current *philosophes*, including Spain's own—the Franciscans, and other religious orders. He himself was a tertiary of the Franciscans. (Tertiaries generally go through some of the education and prayer requirements of full members and contribute to the order's mission, such as education and charitable works in a serious but reduced way. They do all this from the outside, remaining in their own occupation, often married and living in the secular world.) And there were many government leaders who resented the Jesuits' "interference." Standing up for the Jesuits of Paraguay had been the right thing to do, but it was costly in his relations with Portugal. He must have second guessed himself.

Charles also had several relatively minor prejudices, some long-standing, that affected his attitude towards the Jesuits. One concerned the canonization of the Spanish-born bishop, Juan de Palafox y Mendoza, Bishop of Puebla in Mexico, from 1640 to 1649. Palafox had come in conflict with all of the religious orders in Mexico, especially the "crafty machinations" of the Jesuits. He resented their independence and "privileges," demanding that they be answerable only to himself. Still, until 1641 he had good relationships with the Jesuits, even having one as his confessor. Then, after a dispute with the Jesuits over the ownership of a farm, he ordered that no property could be transferred to any religious order unless the order paid tithes to him as bishop. He went so far as to go public with his complaints by writing to Pope Innocent X, alleging that the power-hungry Jesuits had forced him to go into hiding for fear of assassination, that they controlled the wealth of Mexico, and that they made their schoolboys perform lewd, blasphe-

mous dances on the feast of St. Ignatius. The pope declined to interfere, providing only a comforting ear but no relief. Further disputes
with the Jesuits led to Rome's formation of an ecclesiastical commission, a regular procedure for resolving such problems at the time. The
commission decided for the Jesuits. Soon thereafter, his performance,
especially with respect to the Jesuits, became megalomanic. Among
other peculiar maneuvers, he excommunicated the Jesuits of Mexico,
an action ignored. In 1649 his return to Spain put an end to his bizarre
incumbency.

Charles, piously Catholic and fiercely Spanish, took up Palafox's case
for canonization. The Jesuits were blamed by some of their adversaries
for the Vatican's inaction on the case. Whether that was true is uncertain. Two things are certain: First, Charles' confessor at the time was a
Franciscan who reportedly was anti-Jesuit. Second, Charles suspected
the Jesuits as being behind the stalemate. Moreover, members of other
orders including the Dominicans, Capuchins, and Augustinians joined
in finding fault with the Jesuits over the Palafox canonization, making
themselves popular with Charles while reinforcing his belief in the
righteousness of his cause.

Charles Angry at Vatican over Censorship

In another issue with the Jesuits, Charles took a page out of Pombal's
book. He forbade the publication of a papal brief condemning a
catechism by French abbot François Philippe Mésenguy. The catechism
promoted a version of Jansenist doctrine that had become popular in
Spain due to its being interpreted in a way that appealed to Spanish
nationalism. To Charles' frustration and anger, the papal brief was
published anyway. He had become the censor but had been ignored. He
suspected that the Jesuits were behind the brief and its publication.
Nevertheless, there was no evidence suggesting they had any role in its
publication, especially not in Spain.

One of the most important influences on the king at this time was
Bernardo Tanucci, his former minister of state in Naples and his
mentor. Tanucci had maintained warm, open, and regular correspondence with his student whom he had sought to turn into the model of
an enlightened despot. Tanucci wrote often about the Jesuits presenting
them as intriguers. Once he said, "I shall regret having to pass into the
next world with the knowledge that I was leaving behind me this
poison in the house of my honored lord [Charles]." These too were
having their effect.

Fallout Lingers From Charles' Rescinding the Treaty of Madrid

For Charles the fall-out from the Treaty of Madrid became a continuing irritant. It was an open sore in Spain's relationship with Portugal and troubled the Spanish conscience for selling out their loyal and valued Guaraní. The Jesuits' constant pressure on Madrid from 1750 until Charles rescinded the treaty in 1761, along with the embarrassing military setbacks at the hands of Indians, allegedly led by Jesuits, caused a royal discomfort not helpful to their cause. Meddlesome priests, advocating the admittedly right path when one was constrained by foreign policy considerations, were irritating. When he eventually took the right path, it would be costly in his relationship with Portugal.

Aranda Takes Charge

Immediately after the harrowing experience of the April 1766 riots, Charles appointed Aranda, forty-seven, first minister, head of the judiciary, and chief of the military with the all-powerful title, Captain General. Aranda had been known as a "tough soldier." He did not take long to bring matters under control. He did so by ordering 10,000 elite troops into Madrid in an intimidating show of force preventing further riots.

Aranda was charismatic, friendly, vigorous, and highly popular. His was an old noble family of great wealth. He had been a Jesuit pupil and had close relatives who were members of the order. Hargreaves writes that he possessed great independence, self-assurance, and an uninhibited sense of humor—an example of which comes from Petrie who describes a cabinet meeting in which Aranda was pressing a point, causing Charles to say, "Conde de Aranda, you are more obstinate than an Aragonese mule." To that Aranda replied that he knew one even more stubborn. When the king demanded, "Who?" Aranda responded with deference, "His Sacred Majesty, Don Carlos the Third, the King of Spain and the Indies." Charles laughed and repeated this story over and over. It was one of his favorites. Hargreaves writes that Aranda was "dark . . . his nose always stained with snuff, thick and curved . . . large grey eyes, the right one squinting, a toothless mouth and a hoarse voice . . . incredulous, a philosopher, obstinate, a discreet epicurean, a gallant sensualist, a proud aristocrat, moody, irascible, quarrelsome . . . a crank. He lacked tact . . . was generous in spirit, rough . . . beloved by the common people whose wishes he listened to with patience." He was a friend of French deists and was close to Spain's own *encyclopédists*—Fernán-Nuñez, the Marqués de Mora, and others—

who in turn remained in contact with Voltaire, Diderot, d'Alembert, and the other French *philosophes.*

He did much to change Spain's hidebound economy. Even given the fact that he was a trade protectionist who resisted imports and thereby protected certain inefficient domestic industries, he would be considered economically progressive by today's standards. He stabilized Spain's currency and sharply increased agricultural and manufacturing output.

Aranda was eerily similar to France's Choiseul and Portugal's Pombal in his talent for intrigue, yet he was nothing when compared to Pombal in terms of bloodletting. Unlike the other two, Aranda had a strong king with his own agenda. In policy-making, especially concerning the Jesuits, it was Charles, not Aranda, who set the agenda. Thus so constrained, Aranda understood his task was to set the stage so that Charles' own conscience—including his devout Catholicism, respect for the papacy and fear of its "keys to the kingdom"—could be reconciled with the destruction of the Jesuits. Some Catholic monarchs, especially Charles, still had an abiding fear of the pope's ability to decide the fate of their souls.

Had it not been for Aranda's rudeness toward peers and his insufferable ego, he might well have survived as the king's favorite far later than 1773. That year Charles had enough of his behavior, including insults aimed at the king himself and frequent threats to resign if not given his way. The king packed Aranda off to be ambassador to France as a face-saving way out. That Spain had lost the Falkland Islands (Malvinas) to England did not help Aranda's position with Charles. The ambassadorial assignment lasted fourteen years.

Meanwhile First Minister Aranda, like Charles, was unhappy with the unpredictable and still powerful Spanish Inquisition. Contrary to today's popular impression, the Jesuits were also its frequent adversary. From the Inquisition's founding in the thirteenth century, the dominant order associated with it had always been the Dominicans. Indeed, the fifteenth century's infamous inquisitor general, Cardinal Tomás de Torquemada, was a Dominican. Aranda and Charles felt unable to eliminate it due to its broad support from a superstitious public concerned with witches and witchcraft. Instead they settled for limiting it. (It is worth noting that burning at the stake was not unique to Spain. It continued in England eight years after it ended in Spain.) Freedom for authors resulting from the elimination of the bishops'

imprimatur and a generally liberal attitude towards censorship charac-
terized the Aranda government's human rights policy. Aranda was
gradually steering Spain in a liberal secular direction.

Ricci's Letter Alleges Charles' Illegitimacy

One of the most bizarre and murky stories, fitting the crafty Aranda, is
a letter, probably forged, in which Jesuit General Lorenzo Ricci alleged
that Charles was a bastard, the product of a liaison between his mother
Queen Elizabeth Farnese and Cardinal Giulio Alberoni. The allegation,
if believed, would have invalidated Charles' kingship! Ricci's letter
might have provided Aranda with the necessary ammunition in case
the pious Charles was not yet sufficiently committed to expelling the
Jesuits. The letter needed to be infuriating or terrifying for Charles. It
apparently was both.

Ricci's letter has been lost to history; perhaps buried in some archive in
Madrid or the personal archives of a descendent of a participant in the
affair; perhaps it never existed, as some historians argue. That it did
exist, however, is a reasonable explanation for Charles' sudden rage.

Historians who dismiss the existence of the letter often cite Pastor, a
papal historian, who called its existence "baseless" on the argument
that there is no known meaningful documentary support for it. The
nineteenth century monarchist historian, Cretineau-Joly who, being a
Jesuit, was not necessarily disinterested, disagrees with Pastor based on
what he believes is reliable hearsay. Lacouture quotes Cretineau-Joly:

> It would need extraordinary motives to drive [Charles] to an
> act of such unprecedented harshness. The most plausible, the
> only one that would truly infuriate him, was to violate the royal
> escutcheon with the stigma of bastardy.

It is common knowledge that a number of documents concerning the
Jesuits' expulsion from Spain, known to have existed, have been lost to
history. The most important of these is the first part of Charles' Expulsion Decree itself. Lack of a copy of Ricci's letter does not mean it did
not exist. Furthermore, Charles and Aranda would have had good
reason to destroy it.

The letter in question was sent by Ricci to the Jesuit rector of the
Imperial College of Madrid and was dated a year or more before the
riots. Suspiciously, it was delivered and then almost immediately
discovered out in the open on the rector's desk during an amazingly

coincidental police raid. The raid occurred at a time when it was known that the rector would be elsewhere. The police had been armed with a search warrant thus indicating advanced knowledge of what they might find and ensuring the search would be legal. They apparently had little difficulty finding it. The letter was soon shown to Charles who might have panicked. Charles then asked Aranda to develop a strategy which would lead to the expulsion of the Jesuits. (Of course, there is another explanation, though not as good, for Charles' rage. As mentioned in connection with the death of his young wife, he had a high notion of personal fidelity. Perhaps it had been just one more falsehood about the disloyalty of Jesuits, men whom he had once dearly loved, that was the last straw.)

The obvious questions have never been answered: Would such a document have been treated so casually by the Jesuits? How could and why would the police arrive at precisely the right time to expose it—with a warrant no less? Cretineau-Joly wrote that the Duke of Alba, an ally of Aranda and a co-conspirator on the council of ministers, gave a written deathbed admission to the bishop of Salamanca that the letter was forged and that he helped write it. If that is true, where is the admission? Is it also true that when pro-Jesuit Pope Clement XIII demanded proof and was shown the document that a nearby priest, later Pius VI, observed the watermark on the paper as showing that the paper was not of Italian manufacture but Spanish. The watermark also was said to have been made well after the date on the letter. How and why did such an important document disappear? And why did Pius not expose the document during his reign? Was it because he had been forced by the cardinals at his election (it was unanimous) in 1775 to maintain a complete silence (which he did) about the Jesuits' liquidation? And what would speaking out have accomplished—more Bourbon hostility toward his Church? Better to let sleeping dogs lie? There are numerous unanswered questions in this fascinating story.

Might the allegation in the letter of Charles' illegitimacy have been true? (This would, of course, point to Ricci's culpability.) This question is worth considering. If he were illegitimate, the finger should be pointed at Cardinal Alberoni.

Giulio Alberoni, born in 1664 in Piacenza, Italy, was the son of a gardener and had a certain earthiness to him. He was Jesuit-educated, a raconteur, a ribald joker, sometimes a buffoon, and a chef of some note. As an altar boy he caught the attention of an archbishop who ordained him a priest and took him to Rome to study French among other things.

There he met the great French Marshal Vendome. The marshal was so impressed with his personality, his French fluency, and his specially prepared plate of macaroni which Vendome declared was the best he ever had, that he became Alberoni's mentor. Taking him back to Paris, he even introduced the young man to Louis XIV—heady stuff.

Insinuating himself into royal society, Alberoni was in a position to help arrange the marriage of the Italian Elizabeth Farnese to Charles' father Philip V. Thanks to her support and his own innate cleverness, Alberoni rose to become Spain's first minister in 1715 and a cardinal two years later. However, his intrigues and double-dealing with foreign powers eventually caught up with him. Following failed military adventures in Italy in 1720, he was expelled back to that country by Philip acting under pressure from England and others who had been duped. He remained there until his death in 1752 at eighty-eight.

Philip had spent much time on hunting outings including during the period when Charles was conceived. However, Elizabeth often accompanied him. Of course, Philip did not have it all together. Might she have found comfort in another man's arms? As early as her inauguration, Elizabeth had regularly socialized with Alberoni who regaled her with stories in Italian, often when they were alone. He became her confidant. They clearly enjoyed each other's company. Whether their relationship went beyond that is unknown. Charles bore no physical resemblance to Alberoni, for whatever that is worth.

Aranda Initiates the Secret Trial of the Jesuits

By mid-1766 Aranda's Council of Ministers was comprised of four other Jesuit opponents including the king's Franciscan confessor and one other uncommitted. (Some reliable sources think this last member might have been the Jesuit-educated Duke of Alba who over time had become anti-Jesuit, but his membership is not certain.) The council placed two (some say one) of these ministers in charge of a secret investigation into the riots and other alleged Jesuit offenses. The investigation was actually a court, a supreme court, with the misleading name, the "Extraordinary Council of Castile." The ministers in charge were: Manuel Roda y Arrieta, a committed Jansenist and a friend of the general of the Augustinians who was openly opposed to the Jesuits, and the attorney general of Castile, Pedro Rodríguez de Campomanes, the council's president. The outcome was predetermined.

Some 1,500 witnesses gave their opinions. Their testimony was long on hearsay, unsupported allegations, and preposterous suppositions while suffering from a lack of any incriminating facts. Most of it was ludicrous. From Mörner: "A certain Fray Marco Sanchez claimed to know on hearsay evidence of a Jesuit who had said that an association with a popular preacher [named] Calatayud as its president had been informed in Pamplona with the object of murdering the King" and that the Jesuits had secret printing presses producing numerous "lampoons against the government." From Reiter: One witness said the Jesuits had tortured him with satires; another said their vicious influence over his wife had ruined his marriage; one told of a Jesuit who had interpreted the appearance of a comet as an omen of the king's imminent death (regicide again). On and on it went: The news of the 1766 street riots had caused the Jesuits' faces to be filled with joy as they went from tavern to tavern buying the rioters food and drinks; seditious pamphlets could not be traced back because they had no watermarks—typical Jesuit craftiness. Sex and murder sold well. One witness said that it was "common knowledge" that the Jesuits were behind the Távora attempt on the life of Portugal's Joseph I and behind the rumors of adultery between Charles and Squillace's wife, because her closely spaced offspring could not all have come from the sickly Squillace by himself. The best was from a Dominican who had had conversations with people in France and Italy who were convinced that Ferdinand VI and his first wife Queen Barbara had died of a Jesuit poisoning.

Court Issues Formal Charges, Paraguay Jesuits Singled Out

The secret investigation produced a brief that laid out the collective responsibility of the Society of Jesus as a despotic body that could not co-exist with the monarchy. It included a lengthy analysis of Jesuit crimes. Their exploitation of the Guaraní and other crimes in Paraguay were given prominent coverage. The Indians had been treated as slaves. Their ancestral lands had been appropriated and the products of their labor had been taken for the sole purpose of accumulating riches for this insatiable order. These lands contained gold mines that were worked to benefit the Jesuit headquarters in Rome. The Guaraníes' spiritual needs were neglected. The Jesuit claim of spiritual conquest in the thirty missions of the Republic was a fraud because the Guaraní had been conquered and pacified by Governor Hernandarias and converted by Franciscan Fray Luis de Bolaños years before the Jesuits were even founded! (There was a grain of truth to this point. Franciscans helped found Asunción in 1537. The Jesuits were formally founded in 1540 and arrived in Paraguay fifty years later. Bolaños' work among the Guaraní began in 1575, and the Jesuits honored him for valuable proselytizing and organizing eighteen villages of Christian Indians by the end of the century.)

Continuing, the Jesuits prevented the Guaraní from paying their fair share of taxes to the crown. (True, but done with the crown's permission, in return for their military service to the crown in the form of an effective defense force against the encroaching Portuguese and invading mamelucos.) Bishops did not receive the tithes due them. (Also true, but the bishops had concurred, since by their own admission they were ill-prepared to take over the missions, a necessary precondition for tithing.) The Jesuits in Paraguay had sabotaged the 1750 Treaty of Madrid in open defiance of the two kings. (Sabotaged? The Jesuits there had only exercised every subject's right to appeal to the king, in this case to negate the treaty). They had directed the Guaraní rebellion against the treaty. (One or two out of 150 *might* have participated indirectly by giving secret encouragement. There was never any sustainable evidence.)

Many of these accusations were from Bishop Cárdenas' infamous 1644 sermon in Paraguay. Cárdenas' seven accusations were:

- The Jesuits prevented the Guaraní from paying taxes to the crown.
- They withheld tithes due to the bishops (for example, Cárdenas).
- They had rich mines worked by their Indians for the benefit of their headquarters in Rome.
- They violated the secrecy of the confessional.
- They used these secrets to their own enrichment.
- They had deceived the king by getting him to award the mission lands to the Jesuits, lands that rightfully belonged to the Spaniards because of their conquests.
- The Jesuits had created a great republic over which they alone ruled.

This was powerful stuff, and from a bishop no less, at the right time and place—seventeenth century Paraguay—to satisfy the prosecutors.

Bangert writes of a document, published in 1977, that covered the 746 charges against the Jesuits made by Campomanes. Its most prominent charges were that the Jesuits incited the Madrid riots and that they were plotting with aristocrats, with whom they traditionally had close ties, to overthrow the king. These reasons are not terribly convincing as the reasons for Charles' imminent explosion, as they could not have been news to him.

Other prominent charges made against the Jesuits included their teaching of regicide, the "despotic behavior" of their General Acquaviva, the Society's constitution itself, their defense of probabilism (if certainty is unattainable then the probability of an outcome is sufficient to govern faith and practice), Molinism (consent must be given before God awards divine grace), and the Malabar rites under which Jesuits allowed converts in India to add their own customs and practices to Catholic rituals. These last three typify the complaint of Erasmus that the Church focussed too much on doctrinal trivia at the expense of the fundamentals of the Gospel. These charges, when augmented by so many others, gave Charles and Aranda the list they wanted in order to remove any doubt about the right verdict.

Individual members of other orders—especially the Benedictines, Franciscans, Dominicans, Capuchins, Augustinians—weighed in with many additional denunciations.

Trial Finds Jesuits Guilty

In its summary, the trial brief found the Jesuits to be the center of discord and a constant danger to the public order. Their preaching, teaching, and disloyalty had reached such scandalous proportions that, in order to safeguard the sacred person of King Charles and the security of the kingdom, they must be expelled.

As luck would have it, the last well-positioned Jesuit supporter, Queen Mother Elizabeth, died in July. With strong winds blowing few others would risk leaning into them. Meanwhile Tanucci, having that special relationship with Charles, continued his messages from Naples. In a letter to José de Azara, a member of Spain's embassy in Rome, Tanucci wrote, "The Jesuits are always the same, everywhere seditious, enemies of sovereigns and nations, public thieves, full of vices, and generally atheists."

To obtain the support or at least the non-opposition of the Spanish Church, Roda sent a confidential letter to its bishops stating his conclusions. He received back what he was hoping for: support from a majority and silence from the rest.

The secret investigation of the Extraordinary Council was now complete and its conclusion, also a secret, was sent to the king on January 29, 1767.

Charles Expels Jesuits

The king's ensuing Royal Decree was in two parts: The first gave the reasons for the expulsion, and the second contained the details for its implementation. The first part disappeared in the early nineteenth century, like some other documents important to this story—strangely so, as Spanish archivists were among the best in the world. Its disappearance might be explained by the ridicule it received among Europe's intellectuals or by the embarrassment of those who produced it or to whom it was addressed.

The king hesitated for a month before signing it. Perhaps he feared the release by Jesuit General Ricci of the letter asserting his illegitimacy. Perhaps it was an inner struggle over taking such a drastic step, knowing he was going to have to deal with an angry pope. Perhaps he feared for his soul—many European royals, Charles included, still believed that the pope had the keys to the kingdom.

Finally, on February 27, 1767, Charles signed the *Real Decreto de Execucion*, the Royal Decree of Expulsion.

Expulsion Is Carried Out

As shameless as the expulsion was, the manner of its execution was vicious. Everything was planned in the utmost secrecy for fear of reactions from the public, especially in Madrid. After all, it was to be done just twelve months after the street riots of 1766 that almost toppled the government. Charles had not read the mood of the people correctly then, and he would take no chances now.

The date of the expulsion was set for April 1, 1767. Only Charles, Aranda, the Duke of Alba, Roda, Campomanes, and a few of their fellow ministers were in on the arrangements. The first part of the Decree declared the expulsion and its reasons. Aranda wrote the procedures to be followed in expelling the priests and brothers. They were specified in minute detail and restated the bracing admonition that anyone opposing the edict or failing to cooperate with its implementation would suffer the penalty of death.

Copies of the procedures were secretly printed on presses by children who could not read. The copies were kept under guard. Even until the last days of March, all government functionaries were kept in the dark. Secrecy was so well maintained that not a single Jesuit of the 2,641 in Spain was aware of the impending doom.

On March 6, orders relative to the proscription, *Real Directo de Execucion*, were placed in sealed envelopes and sent to the colonies in the Americas and the Philippines with the admonition, "Not to be opened, on pain of death, until the evening of April 2, 1767." Of course, it reached many colonies well after that date. The decree read:

> I invest in you all my royal authority . . . that you . . . hasten under arms to the house of the Jesuits. You will seize all of the Religious and you will convey them as prisoners to the port herein mentioned within twenty-four hours. There they will embark for the destinations indicated. At the very moment of execution of this order, you will seal the archives of the house and the papers of individuals, not allowing anyone to take with him any but his prayer books and the linen strictly necessary for the crossing. If, after their embarkation a single Jesuit, even sick or dying, remains in your department you will suffer death.
>
> Myself, the King

Back in Spain, when the appointed hour arrived late in the evening of March 31, all six Jesuit colleges in Madrid were surrounded by troops. The next day the scene was replicated in other major cities across Spain where there were Jesuit facilities. In Madrid, entry was gained by troops and police in the early morning of April 1. Immediately, the chapel bells were secured to prevent an alarm that might attract a crowd. All the fathers and brothers were awakened; they assembled in the college meeting halls, and the decree was read to them. Then each was taken to his room and allowed to pick up his meager possessions including chocolate, prayer books, and breviaries (containing psalms, hymns, lessons, and prayers for daily use). No books or documents that might be examined later by officials searching for seditious material could be taken. An accounting of all funds was made; what little there was could be kept by the fathers. The novices were told that they could leave the order. Most demurred even though they were not to receive the small annual pension that Charles had authorized for each Jesuit—ninety to a hundred pesos, each worth about a day's wage for a common laborer. Charles' reason for the pension is not known. It might have been to lighten the financial burden on the papacy from all these priests being forced on it. But it might also have been out of sincere concern for the fathers' welfare. After all, as Reiter puts it, Aranda had made it perfectly clear through his expulsion procedures that the king wanted the fathers to be treated with the "greatest decency, humanity, and assistance." Or the reason might have been both.

Around daylight, the fathers were loaded into carriages and taken to the nearest port of embarkation. There they waited to be placed on ships for the Papal States port of Civitavecchia, fifty miles northwest of Rome. Jesuits from other Spanish cities followed a day later. The overcrowding was an ordeal for these bewildered men, especially for the old and sickly, since the ports were not equipped to house and care for 2,641 refugees arriving all at once with no notice.

Great pains were taken to account for every Jesuit given Charles' threat that "if there is left behind a single Jesuit, either sick or dying, you shall suffer death." One can only imagine the pall of fear overlying the proceedings.

Pope Rejects the Jesuits; They Become Refugees Stuck at Sea

After some ten days of waiting, the priests were packed onto transport ships. They arrived 750 miles and several weeks later in mid-May outside Civitavecchia. With relief now at hand, the exhausted men fully expected to be welcomed by the Pope Clement XIII's emissaries. Instead, an astonishing rejection occurred. Clement would not let them disembark. He feared that to do so might imply papal approval of the expulsion. In addition, the port was already overcrowded with refugees, including some left from the French and Portuguese expulsions a few years earlier.

After much discussion between Clement and the Spanish ambassador, the now fetid ships with their pathetic cargo set sail for the port of Bastia on the island of Corsica, some 150 miles to the northwest, arriving there in late May. Incredibly, at Bastia there was yet another delay. Corsica was in rebellion at the time. Its French commander claimed he could barely feed his own troops much less feed and house these refugees whose numbers swelled to 3,000 when those from Spain's north African colonies were added.

The now stinking ships rode at anchor at Bastia for several weeks before their cargo could permanently disembark. Until then, the French commander had taken the pitiful figures to heart and let them leave ship for a few hours each day. After disembarking, the squalid conditions they found ashore were worsened by the fighting going on around them. Many weeks later, as reports of their situation reached Spain and Italy, food and other supplies began to arrive.

The barely tolerable exile in Corsica continued through the second half of 1767, but conditions worsened in early 1768 as huge numbers started arriving from Spain's overseas empire, as far away as Mexico, Paraguay, and the Philippines.

Jesuits Finally Land in Italy

In the spring of 1768 all sides agreed to allow the pathetic refugees to "escape" to the Papal States, but added a final insult: They had to do so clandestinely. Their agonizing journey had taken over a year. Several hundred had died en route. Now they were at least safely ensconced in Italy. Yet even there they were not completely free, because they were under a strict prohibition from Charles against speaking or writing in their own defense. If even one exile were to do so, the pensions of all of them would be forfeited.

History Judges the Expulsion, the Aftermath

How did Charles fare in the judgement of those whose approval he would have wanted? Not very well it would appear.

There was universal cynicism over Charles having said that his reason for expelling the Jesuits was

> to spare the world great scandal [and that] he [Charles] would keep forever in his heart the abominable conspiracy that had necessitated his harsh actions . . . that his life's safety demanded of him profound silence on this affair.

Hollis says that the scoffers at religion in the Enlightenment, like d'Alembert, now scoffed at Charles for his explanation. When Charles appeared on his balcony on November 4, 1768, his patron saint's feast day, to receive the plaudits of his people, he was greeted with an uproarious demand of, "Send us back the Jesuits." Charles suspected it had been instigated by the cardinal archbishop of Toledo, the primate of Spain, and promptly banished him from the capital.

Picking apart Charles' words could reasonably lead one to the conclusion that he *believed* the Jesuits *had* spread rumors about his legitimacy. Yet, when the belittlers ridiculed the king for his ineptitude and were insulted by his explanation, considering it effrontery, they made the Jesuits popular by comparison.

As for Spain, it had lost the vast majority of its best educators. It would pay for more than two centuries.

Tanucci, Charles' mentor still back in Naples, promptly followed his monarch's example and expelled the Jesuits there. The Duke of Parma, ruler of that Spanish dependency, followed Naples, though reluctantly. Italy would become more backward, paying like Spain.

The other Catholic orders—Benedictines, Franciscans, Dominicans, Capuchins, Augustinians—had gotten even for prior insults, the Jesuits perceived superior attitude, and the exalted positions the Jesuits had obtained at their expense. Many of them were gratified, although some feared for their own future.

Francisco Xavier Vázquez, the general of the Augustinians, still carrying a grudge from earlier Jesuit attacks, strongly welcomed their departure. He called for a hymn of praise to God for Spain's purification from the Jesuit "reptiles." He impatiently awaited these exiles coming to the Papal States with their gods of avarice, ambition, slander, and regicide. Other Augustinians weighed in: Bishop Francisco Armañá y Font of Lugo publicly defended the expulsion, terming the Jesuit order a "rotten tree," "teachers of perverse morality and deceitful maxims," and their colleges "chairs of pestilence." One Augustinian monk echoed the accusation of contemporary French Jansenists that the Jesuits had sown the seed of natural religion and of the impieties of Voltaire and Rousseau. The frightened, jealous bishops of Spain had overwhelmingly endorsed Charles' action even before he took it. Now they re-endorsed Aranda's earlier confidential draft proposal on the subject.

Roda, the Jansenist and intimate of the Augustinian general, wrote to French Prime Minister Choiseul, expressing the Spanish government's mood, "We have killed the son. Now nothing remains for us to do but to carry out like action against the mother, our Holy Roman Church."

For the Indians of the Americas, especially the Guaraní and the Mexican Indians, the expulsion of their revered teachers and protectors was a catastrophe. The Guaraní reacted with unmitigated disbelief which turned to grief as their society, so painstakingly and lovingly built out of the jungle over a period of 160 years, gradually faded away. They lost the only opportunity to move, as a people, intact into the modern world. In the old Guaraní Republic and its nearby lands, many of them never recovered, remaining in oppressive ignorance and palpable poverty even to this day.

As for the Jesuits of Paraguay, the words of the Scots Presbyterian Labourite, Cunninghame-Graham, cannot be improved upon. He lived in and explored Paraguay in much of the last quarter of the nineteenth century. He wrote in March 1900:

The [Jesuit] order did much good and worked amongst the Indians like apostles, receiving an apostle's true reward of calumny, of stripes, of blows, and journeying hungry, athirst, on foot, in perils oft, from the great cataract [Iguazú] of the Paraná to the recesses of the [jungle] . . . the Jesuits' rule acted upon the Indians themselves . . . it made them more happy than those Indians who were directly ruled from Spain or through the Spanish Governors. . . . That the Jesuits rendered the Indians happy is certain. . . . All that I know is I myself, in the deserted missions [ruins c. 1890], often have I met old men who spoke regretfully of Jesuit times, who cherished all the customs left by the Company and though they spoke at secondhand, repeating but the stories they had heard in youth, kept the [image] that the missions in the Jesuits' time had been a paradise. Into the matter of the Jesuits' motives, I do not propose to enter, holding that the origin of motives is too deeply seated to be worth inquiry. . . . Yet it is certain that the Jesuits in Paraguay had faith fit to remove all mountains, as the brief stories of their lives, so often ending with a rude field-cross by the corner of some forest and the inscription *hic occissus est* (here he lies) survived the show. . . . I believe that Father Rúiz Montoya—whose story I have told . . . and with how little justice to his greatness, none knows better than myself . . . was a good man . . . that is, a man without ulterior motives, and actuated by his love [for] the poor Indians with whom he passed his life. . . .

In the great controversy which engaged the pens of many of the best writers of the world, after the Jesuits were expelled from Spain and her colonial possessions, it will be found that amongst all the mud so freely flung about, the insults given and received, hardly anyone but a few ex-Jesuits had any harm to say of the doings of the order during its long rule in Paraguay. None of the Jesuits were ever tried; no crimes were charged against them; even the reasons for their expulsion were never given to the world at large. Certain it is that but a few years after their final exit from the missions between the Uruguay and the Paraná, all was confusion. In twenty years most of the missions were deserted, and before thirty years had passed, no vestige of their old prosperity remained. . . .

The semi-communism which the Jesuits had introduced was swept away, and the keen light of free and vivifying competition, which beats so fiercely in the paradise of the economist, reigned in its stead. The revenues declined, all was corruption, and . . . the secular priests sent by the government were brawlers, drunkards, and strikers, carrying arms beneath their cloaks; robbery was rife; and the Indians daily deserted and returned by hundreds to the woods.

All the reports of riches amassed in Paraguay by the Jesuits . . . proved to be untrue. [At their expulsion] although they stood to the Indians almost [as] gods and had control of an armed force larger by far than any which the temporal power could have disposed of, they did not resist, but silently departed from the rich territories which their care and industry had formed.

Rightly or wrongly . . . they strove to teach the Indian population all the best part of the European progress of the times in which they lived, shielding them sedulously from all contact with commercialism, and standing between them and the Spanish settlers, who would have treated them as slaves. These were their crimes. . . . When all is said and done, and now their work is over, and all they worked for is lost . . . what crime so terrible can men commit as to stand up for near upon two centuries against that slavery which disgraced every American possession of the [Europeans]. . . .

Nearly two hundred years they strove, and now their territories, once so populous and so well cultivated, remain, if not a desert, yet delivered up to that fierce-growing subtropical American plant life. . . . For a brief period those Guaranis gathered together in the missions, ruled over by their priests, treated like grown-up children, yet with a kindness which attached them to their rulers, enjoyed a half-Arcadian, half-monastic life, reaching to just so much of what the world called civilization as they could profit by and use with pleasure to themselves. A commonwealth where money was unknown to the majority of the citizens, a curious experiment by self-devoted men . . . [kept] alive a population which would otherwise soon have been suffocated . . . was doomed to failure by the very nature of mankind. Foredoomed to failure, it has disappeared, leaving nothing of a like nature now upon the earth.

As for Clement XIII, he was in extreme distress which historians believe led to his death in 1769. Clement, seeing the expulsion already underway, wrote a humble and tenderly phrased protest to Charles on May 16, 1767. It was too late to affect the course of events, and it certainly would not have changed the outcome even if written earlier. The long letter, excerpted here, is both interesting and moving.

Is it possible that you too, my son, want to distress your father?

Is it possible that the Catholic king that we love so tenderly, wants to fill the cup of bitterness to overflowing and submerge in tears and pain our miserable last years and plunge us to the grave with this final act?

But what most deeply wounds our heart is to see the wise and pious King Carlos III who would not commit the slightest injustice against any of his vassals, endanger his own salvation by exterminating a religious institute consecrated to the service of God and mankind without a hearing, an investigation, an opportunity to defend itself, depriving it of its good name, its fatherland, and its legitimate property. . . . If this terrible measure can never be justified before God, of what use to you will be the approval of your ministers when you appear before the supreme Judge? If we are to understand from Your words "for the peace and tranquility of our peoples" that a member of the Order caused in March [the riots of March 1766, the year before], why are the guilty not punished and the innocent left in peace? We testify before God and man that the Society as a whole, its Institute, and its spirit are completely guiltless, and are not merely not guilty, but pious, useful, and holy. . . . Its foes . . . at most have been able to broadcast lies and calumnies. . . .

In the name of sweet Jesus, which has always been the device of the sons of St. Ignatius, by the name of the ever-blessed Virgin Mary, whose immaculate conception [to which Charles had a particular attachment] they have always defended, by the sufferings of our old age, we beg and implore your Majesty to take back the order, or at least to suspend it and subject the whole affair to a regular examination, and to hearken to the counsel of the Bishops in a matter affecting the State and the Church, the salvation of souls and the conscience and the eternal happiness of Your Majesty. We are convinced your Majesty will realize at once that the punishment and annihilation of a whole body are neither just nor befitting the offense, if only a few are guilty.

Charles wrote back on June 2:

My heart is filled with grief and anguish at receiving the letter of your Holiness. . . . What son would not be melted when he saw a respected and beloved father overwhelmed with affliction and bathed in tears? I love the person of your Holiness, in whom I observe the most exemplary virtues ever united in the vicar of Jesus Christ. . . . The reasons [for the expulsion] are too strong and indubitable . . . to expel only a small number of Jesuits. [Then Charles added a financial point, believing that was the pope's real issue] . . . No aid due to men . . . should be wanting for the expelled Jesuits. . . . Your Holiness may be tranquil on this subject since it appears to be that which gives you the greatest cause of complaint.

Aranda Dies, Charles Dies

During his fourteen years as ambassador to France, Aranda cut a truly sorry figure. Charles banished him there after he wrote a letter to a third party insulting Charles and the letter was shown to the king by an Aranda adversary. Initially he had been welcomed with enthusiasm by the *encyclopédists*. They wrote that here is "the Spanish Hercules who cleansed the Augean stables" — the manure being the Jesuits. Hargreaves writes that the delight "turned to disappointment, then to irony as they beheld this yellow-complexioned courtier, squinting and toothless, who nearly always remained silent. . . .When he did speak [he offered] no more than the odd phrase gracelessly spoken."

Aranda's contribution to American history, however, is noteworthy. He was a driving force behind Spain's substantial financial support for the American colonies starting in June of 1776. After he met with Benjamin Franklin and other American commissioners in Paris in December 1776 and January 1777, Spain would have become allied with the colonies and declared war on England if he had had his way. Charles' restraint caused him to reject that reckless idea, understanding the example it would set for Spain's own colonies. In 1780 Aranda became a master of the Grand Orient Lodge of Freemasons, consistent with his anti-clerical beliefs.

Pedro Pablo de Abarca y Bolea, Conde de Aranda, died from a fall in 1798. He was eighty years old.

In the fall of 1788 Charles developed a severe chill and went to bed for the first time since he was crowned almost three decades earlier. In November he was overwhelmed with grief by the sudden deaths of his favorite son Gabriel at age thirty-six and Gabriel's wife María Ana of Portugal. In December a fever worsened to the point that his death was obviously near. Petrie writes that, as his will was being read, Chief Minister José de Moñino y Redondo, the Count Floridablanca, became emotional, to which Charles replied, "Did you think I was going to live forever?" A bishop asked Charles whether he had pardoned his enemies. Charles asked rhetorically, "How should I wait for this to pass before forgiving them? They were all forgiven the moment after the offense." Forgiveness, however, appears not to have been given to the Jesuits. Charles died in Madrid at dawn on December 14, 1788, at age seventy-two.

Petrie writes that Charles was one of the best and most patriotic monarchs Spain has ever known. His "greatest achievement was that he brought about, if only temporarily, a national revival in all spheres of activity." All historians are in agreement on that, especially given who preceded and followed him. There is also much agreement that the expulsion and its manner of implementation were a blot on his memory and legacy, and a major contributor to Spain's long decline, not reversed until the late twentieth century.

.

CHAPTER 17

Jesuits Expelled from Paraguay and Brazil

"A mystery of iniquity." So said Pope Pius VI in 1780 about the expulsion of the Jesuits from Spain and its empire in 1767 by Charles III, and what came to be called the "Suppression," the abolition of the Society of Jesus six years later by Pius' predecessor, Clement XIV.

If the expulsion and Suppression were iniquitous, the manner in which they were carried out was abominable. While the main event was being played out in Europe, the events that follow are as they were seen by the Spanish administrators in Paraguay and by the submissive Jesuits and hapless Guaraní in the Republic. Also covered here, purposefully out of sequence in order to better keep the flow of the story, is the expulsion from Brazil by Portugal.

Anti-Jesuit Governor Bucareli Arrives in Buenos Aires

While the expulsion from Spain was scheduled to start on April 1, 1767, on March 6 secret, sealed orders from Madrid were put on the fastest ships for the colonies, from Mexico and Peru to Paraguay and the Philippines. The orders arrived at their destinations many months later.

The new governor in the viceroyalty of Buenos Aires, Marqués Don Francisco de Paula Bucareli y Ursua, replaced the pro-Jesuit, pro-mission Cevallos late in 1765. Bucareli apparently was highly regarded and trusted by the Spanish court and could be counted on to do whatever was asked of him. That was unlike Cevallos who seemed to Madrid to be less compliant when it came to doing the crown's bidding—meaning he was excessively restrained by a decent respect for facts and honest conclusions that could be drawn from them.

Cunninghame-Graham called Bucareli "no ordinary man," one who had a "distinguished career of public service" in Europe and who held to the slanderous views extant at home that the "Jesuits of Paraguay possess great wealth, had bodies of trained troops and would resist all efforts at expulsion to the death . . . [Bucareli} seems to have been a timid, but honest and upright man. . . . O'Neill has less good to say:

Yes to "timid," but otherwise "obstinate, a liar, a hypocrite and a thief . . . showed a silly credulity [to] every tale circulated about the Jesuits' treasures, a childish dread of their power and of their possible vengeance, complete indifference to veracity in his long-winded reports, heartless cruelty to his victims, and limitless tyranny in misapplying the royal decree." Caraman calls him a "capable hypocrite [who] sent the king endless, long-winded reports exaggerating the dangers and difficulties of his commission." He was "cruel and inept," wrote Mörner. The truth may be all of the above at different times. And it certainly is true that Bucareli's verbose, hyperbolic memorandums to Madrid show a pandering, obsequious, self-promoting, bureaucratic survivor in a government that was full of such courtiers. Yet, after he arrived in Vera Cruz on August 23, 1771, as the forty-sixth viceroy of New Spain (Mexico), Engelhardt reports, "the term of his rule was the happiest that New Spain experienced" and his death eight years later "was justly regarded as a heavy blow to the missions."

In any event, the plan for executing the royal decree in the Spanish colonies was developed by First Minister Aranda, as we saw, a man as able an executive as he was an accomplished schemer. His plan left few details to the imagination of Spain's colonial administrators.

Bucareli Arrests Buenos Aires Jesuits

The heavily sealed pouch of expulsion instructions arrived for Bucareli in Buenos Aires on June 7, which means that it must have been put on a fast ship from Spain right after the king's signing on February 27. On July 2, two other ships arrived from Spain with the now-common knowledge of the expulsion. Bucareli had to act fast to implement plans already made. The implementation in Buenos Aires itself was set for that night, July 2-3. Immediately, all fifty-two Jesuits of the three colleges in the city were imprisoned in one of their own buildings. Bucareli, the able bureaucrat, took to heart the king's unambiguous warning in the expulsion documents that anyone, regardless of rank, interfering in the slightest way or providing aid or comfort to the Jesuits, would suffer the punishment of *death*. Bucareli, becoming alarmed at how his citizens' lamentations and complaints over the expulsion might reflect on him, ordered that "no sign of mourning should be noticeable anywhere, that all business should go on as usual, that soldiers should enter any house whence sound of lamentations proceeded and threaten the householder with fines, prison, and exile unless such manifestations ceased." Nevertheless sounds of support and lamentations were indeed heard. In response, Bucareli had the streets cleared and all shops closed for eight days. He arrested a number of Buenos Aires' leading citizens—suspected Jesuit sympathizers. One of them, Miguel García de Tagle was immediately condemned to death without so much as a hearing. Fortunately, cooler heads prevailed, and Tagle was sent off to Spain in chains where he languished for years until his innocence was established.

Jesuit College of Córdoba Closed

After dealing with Buenos Aires, Bucareli's next step was to decapitate the Paraguay Jesuits by moving on the center of Jesuit learning, the University College of Córdoba, some 400 miles to the west. In the early days of July, an army contingent of five junior officers and eighty soldiers, led by Bucareli-confidante Major Fernando Fabro, force-marched to Córdoba, arriving at the University College in the early morning hours of Sunday, July 12. Using a ruse about the need for a priest to assist a dying man, they got the attending brother to open the door at which point they barged in. They seized Rector Father Pedro Juan Andreu, ordering him to assemble the entire community. The religious were herded into the main dining hall where Bucareli's orders were read to the now bewildered and frightened priests: You are to be deported forthwith to Spain; you can take no property other than your prayer books, personal possessions (typically they had only a few shirts, two cassocks, some underwear, socks, and a bit of chocolate), money (they had little), and your snuff, "the only relic of their luxurious mission life." Many Jesuits sniffed this powdered tobacco—the narcotic equivalent of today's unfiltered cigarettes—to help sustain them during the crushing boredom of the Atlantic crossings.

As in Spain, a detailed inventory of all personal and college assets was made. The residents of the other Jesuit houses in the city, including the Seminary of Montserrat, were also arrested and packed into the same hall, with their property also inventoried. The fabled Jesuit wealth was tallied: 5,900 pesos, soon reduced to 1,900 after the rector while giving his accounting mentioned 4,000 pesos of debt owed to the Córdoba cathedral. The 1,900 peso liquid net worth was equal to eight times the annual wage of an ordinary laborer.

The crowd of fathers locked-up in the hall reached 135, including twenty-seven sixteen- and seventeen-year-old novices. Insufficient mattresses were laid on tables and floors. Doors were nailed shut, except for one guarded by soldiers to let the residents briefly tend to personal needs. The residents were penned up in these ghastly conditions for ten days in spite of the king's explicit instructions for decent, humane, considerate treatment. Meanwhile the novices, each privately given the opportunity by Fabro to desert the order, as called for in the king's instructions, declared their loyalty. This loyalty was despite intense coaching to the contrary by family and friends.

The Jesuits' situation became known throughout Córdoba, but the other clergy were timid and helpless as is so often the case for those under despotic authority. In a surprising exception, the prior of the Dominicans who often contended with the Jesuits on scholastic and theological battlefields, gathered his members to pray for them and held a solemn public service of supplication. Similar demonstrations were made by nuns from the city's convents.

Córdoba Jesuits Expelled

On July 22, all the Jesuits with their meager possessions were carted off to Ensenada, over 350 miles away on the coast, thirty-five miles southeast of Buenos Aires. It was a gut-wrenching, bone-jarring trip over rough roads through hostile Indian country. They were jammed into all sorts of conveyances, mainly high-wheeled carts, supplied to transport only half their number. The prisoners received one inadequate meal each day. Father José Peramas, maintaining a sense of humor, penned that perhaps because of "Fabro's piety," he had given them nothing to eat the whole day thus "generously allowing them to fast." En route, they were rarely given the chance to celebrate Mass, so important to Jesuits. No Mass or Communion was allowed on the feast of St. Ignatius, a gratuitous insult.

The caravan had begun in July and passed the outskirts of Buenos Aires one midnight in September, a time and route chosen to maintain as much secrecy as possible. Nevertheless, large numbers of prominent, well-regarded citizens came out to greet the refugees and offer them sympathy. None of the well-wishers were local diocesan priests, however, as the city's bishop, Manuel Antonio de la Torre, not a friend of the Jesuits, had forbidden them to approach the Jesuits under pain of excommunication. At Ensenada on September 29, the men were loaded onto the frigate La Venus, and they were sent off to Spain. LaVenus was one of a five-ship flotilla carrying a total of 224 Jesuit fathers and brothers. In February and March 221 of them reached Cadiz; three died en route. Four months of imprisonment followed the trip so that fathers from other regions as far away as the Philippines could be gathered for shipment to the Papal States and the further agony yet to come.

Back in Córdoba, a rigorous search was undertaken for incriminating evidence. Irreplaceable archives at the University College, covering much of South America's early history, were destroyed by soldiers, acting like the ruffians they were. Cunninghame-Graham writes: "Nothing seems to have been preserved, except material which the ravagers thought might prove incriminating to the Jesuits, it being a well-known practice to judge and condemn a man and then search for evidence against him." Such had been the modus operandi in the trial of the Jesuits in Spain.

New Jesuits Arrive, Are Imprisoned, Expelled

In the weeks following the imprisonments in Buenos Aires, a group of thirty-six Jesuit recruits arrived from Spain at the port of Montevideo (in today's Uruguay) on Río de La Plata opposite Buenos Aires. They did not know of the expulsion, the secret having been kept so well. They probably left in February as the king was signing the decree, since their crossing took six months. Provisions had run out and four had died at sea while the others were starving. One more died upon arrival. As the ship approached the port, its captain had hoisted the distress flag. For twenty-four hours it was ignored as the ship was quarantined by Bucareli, fearing the king's admonition. The next day he boarded the vessel and read the decree. At the insistence of the captain, however, Bucareli reluctantly allowed them to disembark, but immediately arrested them and threw them into the prison in Buenos Aires with the others already there. Five weeks later they were transported back to Cádiz. With them went the chance to further evangelize and pacify the vast, wild Chaco northwest of Asunción.

Bucareli Afraid to Attack the Missions, Fears "Clouds" of Guaraní Warriors

As the expulsion was in progress in the summer and fall of 1767, word got out that it was not going down well in some other colonies. Petrie reports that in New Spain, soldiers had to use the butt-end of their muskets to force their way through large crowds gathered to watch the departing carriages taking the Jesuits from their numerous missions and colleges to the port of Vera Cruz for transport to Spain. The operation was so unpopular that there were uprisings in several towns for which ninety residents were executed. Such news must have spread like wildfire throughout the Americas and might well have played a role in Bucareli's caution in moving against the missions of the Republic where the potential for resistance and deaths dwarfed that in Mexico. In spite of the fathers' obvious submission to the king's wishes, Bucareli took many months, even into 1768, to begin a march to arrest the Jesuits in those distant missions. His flood of ink to Madrid described the hazards from recalcitrant Jesuits in the heartland, adding that they could unleash "clouds" of superb horsemen and guerrilla warriors into the field. It is likely that Aranda was not buying these lies, as he wrote at the time to a fellow conspirator, "The Jesuits will accept the decree with resignation and not give any reason for [further] royal displeasure."

In any event, Bucareli schemed to outflank the mission fathers. He ordered the Indian *corregidores* (mayors) of each Guaraní mission to a conference in Buenos Aires. In an impressive building designed by the renowned Jesuit architect, Juan Bautista Prímoli, he welcomed them in the ostentatious outfit of an emperor. A solemn High Mass followed. Then a banquet was held with flattering assurances given to the Indians. They would be totally freed of the Jesuits and their domination; a university would be established at Candelaria, the Jesuits' headquarters, to teach them European arts and sciences—effective campaign promises. He polished it off with a formal signing ceremony in which he had all thirty *corregidores* dressed up in regal costumes and then persuaded them to sign a letter to the king full of calumnies against the Jesuits. It resurrected all the old charges made by Bishop Cárdenas 115 years earlier: hoarded Jesuit riches, their enslavement of the Guaraní, keeping the Indians in ignorance and from intermingling with Spanish traders and settlers. The *corregidores'* letter included a thank you to the king for sending Viceroy Bucareli " to carry out... all the just orders of your Majesty," language so obviously contrived as to be laughable. Yet it served its purpose well in this theater of the absurd.

Still Bucareli procrastinated in delivering the final blow, the one to annihilate the missions themselves. He was driven by fear that the loss of the Jesuits and the absence of replacements for them would create a void that would end in chaos. The Dominicans, Franciscans, and Mercedarians, the largest orders there, begged off, saying they could not spare priests to replace the Jesuits. The few local diocesan priests who were suggested by the bishop tried hard to excuse themselves, successfully so. Perhaps they felt unwelcome since many reports and rumors from the upcountry predicted that the Indians would resist any replacements. They knew too, that the Indians were used to speaking with the Jesuits in Guaraní, and few of these diocesan priests had even a rudimentary knowledge of the language—not a recipe for a good start. A letter to Bucareli from mission San Luis, one of the thirty missions of the Republic, reveals the Guaraníes' dislike for priests other than Jesuits and their growing despair over losing their fathers. The mission's February 28, 1768, letter reads in part:

Senor Gobernador,

May the Lord protect you who are our father. This we say to you, the *cabildo* and all the *caciques* and the men and women . . . of San Luis. The *corregidor* . . . asked for parrots . . . to send [to] the king. We are sorry but we cannot send them because those birds live in the wild forests where God created them, and they fly away from us when we try to catch them. Still we are servants of the Lord and of our King . . . [and] our soldiers have marched three times against Colonia [near Montevideo, winning it for the Spaniards], and we work hard and pay tribute. We ask that God may send the most beautiful of birds, the Holy Ghost, to you and to our King to enlighten and protect you.

Therefore we say to you . . . with tears in our eyes we humbly beg you to let the sainted fathers of the Compañía, the sons of San Ignacio, live among us forever. . . . We don't like to have curas [diocesan priests] or [Dominican or Franciscan] friars . . . who have no love for us . . . the *padres* of the Compañía took care of us since the time of our ancestors; they taught us, baptized us, and conserved us for God and for the King. So we don't want under any circumstances, friars or clerics as our priests.

Hear the plea of us poor ones . . . we are not slaves and we don't like the ways of the Spaniards who work, everyone for himself, instead of aiding each other in their daily work.

This is the pure truth. . . . If the contrary is done this mission will soon be lost as will be the other missions . . . and we shall fall into the hands of the devil . . . in the hour of our death who will help us? Absolutely no one."

Perhaps the *cabildo* and *caciques* had some help with the letter, but the thoughts were no doubt their own. And clearly, their fears were to be proven real. Needless to say, the letter had no effect.

Meanwhile, thirty priests from sundry minor orders in Spain about to embark in Cádiz for Buenos Aires to help fill in behind the departing Jesuits were seized by panic and scattered. The word was getting around.

Bucareli Finally Invades the Republic of the Guaraní, Jesuits Surrender Peacefully

Timid as he was, Bucareli took no chances when in April 1768, after obtaining replacements for the Jesuits, he finally sallied forth from Buenos Aires headed for the thirty missions of the Republic. Up along the Uruguay he went with a large force of 60 cavalry and 1,400 infantry—he was ready for a big fight. But the Jesuits spoiled his outing, for when he arrived at Yapayú, the southern-most mission, some 400 miles upriver, the fathers there came out to meet him. They handed over the keys to every building with a lock while surrendering their vehicles and ample supplies available since Yapayú was the Republic's commercial headquarters. Despite all the outright lies and swirling rumors, their submission should have been foreseen. Earlier in his machinations, Bucareli had sent his legal agent with the king's decree to the Jesuit provincial, the aging Father Manuel Vergara, widely known and admired for his saintliness. When Vergara accepted the decree with the words, "In my own name and that of the missioners . . . I submit absolutely . . . to the king and bow my head . . . in homage," the lawyer lost his composure and tearfully responded, "Father Provincial, we expected nothing less from your Reverence." Vergara and his priests had honored his word.

Ruffians in the army showed no respect for the subjugated missions, pilfering everything of value, as each one in turn surrendered in obedience and resignation to "higher authorities." Bucareli reached the Jesuit provincial capital Candelaria at the end of August. His conquest had been completed in four months.

Caraman describes Bucareli's prolix and boastful dispatches to Aranda, turning quotidian events into sixteen pages of monumental challenges—terrible weather, incessant rains (the campaign was during the reliably dry season), savage Indians surprising his men, provisions scarce.

In September the Jesuits from all thirty missions were sent by boat down to Buenos Aires and imprisoned there. Eighty-two sailed for Spain on December 8, taking over four months crossing the stormy

Atlantic for imprisonment at Puerto de Santa María. There they buried their Provincial Vergara. In January 1769, 151 sailed on the Esmeralda for Spain; sixteen died at sea. Caraman writes that these exiles included the legendary Bohemian, Martin Dobritzhoffer. He wound up in Vienna near his birthplace, entertaining Empress Maria Theresa and her court with his stories. At her prompting, he documented them for posterity. Caraman continues: Florían Paucke wound up nearby in a monastery in Zwettl, Austria, where he produced a book on the Mocobíes tribe and sometimes "snuck into the kitchen to prepare boeuf à la mode sauvage for the community." Thomas Faulkner, originally from Manchester, wound up home in England as a chaplain in several villages.

Other Tribes Resist

Two hundred miles north of Asunción in the Chaco region, the newer converts, the previously unruly Guaycurú, threatened to kill Bucareli's commissioner in response to the imminent removal of their father, Sánchez Labrador, from their mission in Belén. The commissioner had to promise the father's eventual return in order to save his own skin. Southwest of Asunción, the Abipones, also frequently warlike and relatively new converts, burned their San Fernando mission to the ground when their father, José Klein, was arrested. Their *cacique* rode some 400 miles south to Santa Fe to demand his release and returned, unsuccessful. Further south, the Mocobíes gave their priest, Florían Paucke, two alternatives: They would destroy the Santa Fe mission or retreat with him deep into the wilderness where they could not be reached. Paucke was able to persuade them to acquiesce to their (his) fate.

Armed uprisings occurred 600 miles northwest of Asunción in the Bolivian *altiplano* silver city of Potosí. The Jesuits being expelled there had to be immediately readmitted into their college until the insurrection could be brought under control.

Old, Sick Jesuits Trek Long Distances into Exile

The dutiful Bucareli, adhering to the king's warning that there were to be no exceptions for Jesuits who were aged, sick, infirm, or moribund, permitted no delay or special treatment for such missionaries. Father Ignacio Chomé, was seventy and had been bedridden for months in the remote Chiquitos region some 600 miles northwest of Asunción. He had become famous for his written works in the Chiquitos dialects (which, upon his departure, were permanently lost). He was carried in a hammock by two of his flock, directed by a Bucareli officer, west-ward 400 miles over the Andes for the Pacific coast and Lima. It was a puzzling choice of direction because the route to Buenos Aires would have been all downriver after Asunción. High in the Bolivian *altiplano* in the remote village of Oruro, with 800 miles still to go to complete his impossible journey, he expired.

Bohemian Father Juan (Hans) Messner's trek in the Chiquitos was even more like torture. Seventy-seven and asthmatic, he was dragged on a travois-like sled behind a horse for 225 miles, west from San Ignacio to Santa Cruz, en route to Lima. That region, known for its fire-ants, did not disappoint, and with the horses growing violent from being stung the ride on the sled became all the more jarring. The high *cordillera* beyond Santa Cruz was impassable due to snow, leading to a five-month wait in the thin air. His asthma worsened daily. With the snowmelt, his journey continued, now on mule-back. At a rest break, Messner asked to be left behind and allowed to die. The guard, unmoved, hoisted him back on the mule and had an attendant continually support him to prevent his falling off. A bit later, while passing over particularly rough terrain, the attendant, while making an extra effort to keep his charge mounted, discovered that Messner was now a corpse.

The seventy-three-year-old Swiss, Father Martin Schmid, spent five months on a mule traveling from the Chiquitos Guaraní tribe in today's southern Bolivia to Panama. Eleven Jesuits who started out with him died on the trail.

An Italian, one Father Pallozzi, seventy-two years old, endured a 700-mile ride on horseback to Lima and then embarked also for Panama. Crossing the isthmus, overcome by exhaustion from the tropical climate, he expired just before embarking for Spain. On and on it went.

Reiter reports that of the 2,276 Jesuits in the Americas, more than 500 died during the expulsion. In Paraguay, only one is documented to have remained—the octagenarian, paralyzed, helpless, Hungarian physician, Father Zsigismund Asperger. He died ten years later, at age ninety-one in Apóstoles—the last Jesuit of Paraguay.

Southey wrote that the expulsion

> . . . occurred just as the Guaraní missions were beginning to
> recover from the evils brought upon them by the Treaty of
> Madrid. . . . Every motive which was pretended for the expul-

sion of the Jesuits was founded upon malicious misrepresenta-
tion, or gross calumny."

Spain deprived itself of

. . . its most faithful and meritorious subjects in America . . .
who were ready to live or die in its service . . . had extended
the Spanish territories in the interior . . . and thereby prevented
the Portuguese from [taking even more of the continent] . . .
had protected the cities from . . . the most formidable of
[Spain's] enemies [England and Portugal] . . . when the Spaniards were calling on their saints for protection.

Reiter wrote that:

The administrators following the Jesuits' departure . . . worked
for their own benefit. . . . No books were kept, the products,
the cattle, even the [mission] lands were misappropriated. The
Guaraníes, used to the leisurely rhythm of work which produced relative abundance under Jesuit guidance, experienced
want for the first time in more than a century. The new
"curas," inexperienced and unprepared for the task of caring
each for several thousand Indians, limited themselves to
parochial matters and closed their eyes to the abuse they
witnessed.

In 1801 while Spain was struggling, unsuccessfully, to resist Napoleon,
Portugal annexed the land of the Guayrá containing the seven missions
contested after the Treaty of Madrid. These were destroyed in the
coming decades by neglect and bloody wars among the new, nineteenth
century, South American republics.

Brazilian Jesuits Expelled to Portugal

The expulsion of the Jesuits from Brazil nine years earlier was no less
heinous. Orders for the expulsion had come from Pombal in 1759 to
confiscate their property and secure all members of the order.

In 1751 Pombal, then minister of foreign affairs, appointed his brother
Francisco Xavier de Mendoça Furtado to be governor of the captaincy of
Grão-Para. Pombal's secret instructions were to adjust the boundary of
Amazonas and enlarge it at the expense of Spain, while "reforming" the
region's socio-economic framework. Reform was a code word mainly for
secularizing the Jesuit mission towns by stripping the Jesuits of all
vestiges of temporal power and authority over the Indians living there.

In 1757 Pombal published his ominous sixty-eight page history, *A Brief Account of the Republic Founded by the Jesuits in the Spanish and Portuguese Dominions of the New World and Their War Against the Armies of the Two Crowns.* He had it translated into several languages; copies were circulated throughout Europe. The title said it all: He placed blame for the Guaraní War squarely on the fathers there. The Brazilian fathers would soon pay the price.

Twenty-eight of the most well kept Brazilian Jesuit missions were situated along the Madeira river, a tributary of the Amazon, in the huge, centrally-located Amazonas state. The Jesuits also had seven missions in Pernambuco including Paraíba and Ceará, nine in Bahia, five in Rio de Janeiro, six in São Paulo, and one in what is now the large interior port city, Manaus. By 1759 the bishop of the sprawling state of Pará in northern and central Brazil, Don Miguel de Bulhoens, had suspended all Jesuits in his diocese. Bishop Antonio de São Jozé of Maranham to the east of Pará abandoned his bishopric in São Luiz to avoid participating in the evolving persecution of which he strongly disapproved. Bulhoens acted on his behalf.

The order of expulsion itself was executed with heartlessness and sometimes cruelty. Confined below decks in fetid holds and stowed together like slaves, 115 Jesuits left São Luiz in one ship for Lisbon. Four died on the trip from unwholesome food, confinement and thirst. Conversely, fathers from the Ceará and Paraíba provinces on the east coast were transported to the port of Recife, treated humanely and with respect by governor Luiz Diogo Lobo de Silva and the bishop of Olinda. The captain of their transport ship, one that had been seized from the Jesuits, was not so benevolent. Under the most deprived conditions and denied adequate sustenance, five of the fifty-three expired en route. More than 300 others traveled in many other ships.

Southey describes the actions of some men of decency and courage in the face of potentially murderous revenge from Pombal: Brazil's primate, the cardinal archbishop of Bahia, Don Jozé Botelho de Mattos, obeyed the order to send all the foreign Jesuits to Lisbon because of their "evil-doing." However, when it came time to render an account of his investigation, he sent home the candid attestation that he found them not only to be blameless but highly useful and meritorious. He got eighty of the most respected persons in Bahia to countersign his attestation. He had received instructions to substitute secular priests for the Jesuits in the missions, but it was difficult to find priests who would accept the assignment even though the property of the Jesuits was to be given to them along with a small fixed salary. And, in addition, they were to have fees at christenings, marriages, and burials, whereas the Jesuits had taken none. Thus the Indians looked upon the Jesuits' successors as mercenary interlopers and were even more unhappy than the unfortunate priests who had been inserted into the missions. At some missions the Indians rose up, and their priests had to flee to save their lives. Five years earlier, the archbishop had asked for permission to resign as primate while remaining in Brazil since he was too old to undertake the long voyage to Portugal. At the time, his request had been denied, but now it was accepted. He was given no pension and this venerable man, now over eighty, was left dependent upon charity to survive.

In São Paulo and its environs, Jesuits were treated with humanity and respect. Bishop Antonio de Madre de Deos, a Franciscan, said publicly that the expulsion of the Jesuits would result in the ruin of religion first and the overthrow of the government afterwards. Rio de Janeiro was to be the site of embarkation for the 145 São Paulo fathers. They were stowed in one ship below decks and treated like the others who were exiled, as slaves, possibly thanks to Rio's bishop.

Bishop Don Antonio de Desterro of Rio de Janeiro acted very much differently than Madre de Deos. Southey writes that he too was a Franciscan but seemed to endorse the envy and dislike that his order commonly had for the Jesuits. Desterro "issued the most virulent pastoral epistle that ever was so misnamed, wherein he called the Jesuits the inventors and instigators of the attempted assassination [of King Joseph I]." He suspended them from all functions and enjoined all persons from having even the slightest intercourse with them lest "they should be infected with the deadly contagion of their pestiferous opinions." Then he published the circular from the king which charged them with "treason and intended regicide." This was followed by "a proclamation accusing the Jesuits of having concealed their relics, church-plate, and ornaments." He ordered "any persons to whose keeping they had been entrusted to deliver them up under pain of excommunication."

By the end of 1759 all 500 Jesuits from Brazil's cities and 55 missions had sailed for Europe. As in Paraguay almost all of the missions gradually withered away.

The system that replaced the Jesuits had one overriding drawback—it would no longer be in the hands of devoted men. The administrators were extortionists, the new priests ineffective, and whatever laws there were for the protection of the Indians were constantly evaded. The remaining Indians' behavior suffered from the removal of all moral discipline. Their houses degenerated into sties, their lives into orgies of drunkenness, and their society collapsed.

In 1930 the Portuguese historian, João Lúcio de Azevedo, wrote a fitting epitaph for the missions:

> Throughout the vastness of the American continent, the only place where Indian communities prospered . . . was Paraguay where the Jesuits established their missions. After the indescribable cruelties in Mexico and Peru and at the time when the oppression of the colonists rapidly proceeded in its destructive work in the Portuguese territory, the missionaries of the Society managed to establish, in neutral terrain, a harbor for the remainder of the race.

PART THREE

Pope Abolishes Jesuit Order Forever; It Is Rescued and Reestablished

CHAPTER 18

Pope Abolishes the Society of Jesus

It was July 21, 1773, some 233 years after the founding of the Jesuits and five after their expulsion from Paraguay when the Society of Jesus was abolished by the pope himself, Clement XIV. That year Clement wrote:

> . . . we abolish and suppress [the Society] . . .we take away and abrogate each and every one of its offices . . .schools, colleges, ministries . . .houses. . . . We do away with the statutes, customs, [their] constitution even if [they] were formulated with legal safeguards. . . . The name of the Society is to be completely removed and suppressed.

He continued:

> . . . we order and command each and every ecclesiastical person . . . especially members of the Society . . . not dare to defend, attack, write about, or even speak about [this] suppression and of its causes and motives.

Thus, 23,000 men who had given him and preceding popes their total loyalty, obedience, and boundless energies were being swept away forever. Forever. Or so he thought.

Jesuits Survive the Expulsions

For years, the majority of Jesuits from the Bourbon and Bragança monarchies—France, Spain, Portugal, and Spain's Naples and Parma dominions—had been subsisting in exile in the Papal States. Many others, however, still remained actively engaged as Jesuits in the Austrian Empire, the fourth great Catholic power, and in smaller numbers elsewhere in northern Europe, especially in Poland, where some 2,000 remained active as Jesuits in their own communities. Still smaller numbers became priests in secular (diocesan) churches in their native Bourbon countries. Some lived as Jesuits in semi-independent provinces like Alsace in France or retired in monasteries to end their days suffering in silence. Significant numbers were welcomed for their teaching skills by Lutheran Prussia and Orthodox Russia.

For over a decade, Pope Clement XIII, Clement XIV's immediate predecessor, had been their besieged though worthy, if unbending defender. For example, in December 1761 the French Jesuits had effectively surrendered to the Paris Parlement and offered to place themselves under the authority of the compliant French bishops if their general, Lorenzo Ricci, would not oppose it. But in Rome, Clement XIII and Ricci, unyielding, summarily rejected the idea, seeming to view it as a slippery slope that would do grave harm to both the papacy and the Jesuits. With a compromise being refused, the Jesuits were expelled from France in 1764.

In Portugal (1759), in Spain (1767) and its dominions Naples (later in 1767) and Parma (1768), the expulsions had been immediate and complete. Their monarchs did not suffer the same self-doubt and occasional remorse displayed in France by both its people and its king, Louis XV.

Bourbons Demand Complete Suppression

In late 1767, the first ministers of France, Spain, and Naples (The Kingdom of the Two Sicilies) began to badger Clement XIII, a naturally timid and often indecisive man, to eradicate the Jesuits completely. Clement, buttressed by his strong secretary of state, Cardinal Luigi Torrigiani, vacillated but did not capitulate. Then in early 1768 a relatively minor incident brought matters to a head. The Duke of Parma in northern Italy, a Bourbon duchy, directed a series of local, relatively minor ordinances against the Church, ordinances that moved the line dividing temporal and religious matters. Clement promptly issued a papal brief declaring the ordinances null and void. The crowns rallied around the duke and accused Clement of insulting them over a temporal matter. French troops seized two papal towns including Avignon, and Neapolitan troops seized two others. It was a shot across the papal bow.

Jesuit Defender Pope Clement XIII Dies

At the beginning of 1769 the monarchs, presenting a united front, insisted that Clement accede to several demands, especially the liquidation of the Jesuits. The distraught pope replied with a blunt "no," adding that he would rather have his hands cut off than suppress the Jesuits. A few days later he suffered a fatal heart attack. Some say a stroke. He was seventy-six.

Now there was a *tabula rasa,* and the kings and ministers would make the most of it. The conclave to elect a new pope began on February 15. It immediately became contentious, pitting the pro-Jesuit and anti-Jesuit factions against one another, often bitterly so. The anti-Jesuits were led by the court cardinals beholden to the monarchies. France's Choiseul and Spain's Charles III, along with the court cardinals from Paris and Naples, led the charge. Their burning desire was the selection of a pope who would do their bidding and finish off the Jesuits world-wide.

Not surprisingly, the Spanish cardinals, given Charles' obsessive hatred of the Jesuits, urged that any future pope commit in writing to suppress them. That was just too much for some, especially the pivotal cardinal, François-Joachim-Pierre de Bernis, French ambassador to the Vatican. He argued that such a promise would be a kind of simony, violating canon law, and therefore would be a blot on the honor of the monarchs. Charles III responded that he was willing to bear the responsibility, that canon law had no standing when it was opposed to reason, and that reason required the abolition of the Jesuit order for the peace of the world.

The maneuvering continued with great emotion. This was truly a struggle for the soul of the Catholic Church, and all combatants knew it. The Bourbons even made threats to blockade Rome and instigate popular uprisings in the city. Unfortunately for the Jesuits, a potentially powerful ally, the devout Empress Maria Theresa of Austria, once a Jesuit pupil as were her children, had appointed her son Joseph to be emperor and co-regent. A few years before, Joseph who was head-strong and rebellious had become a religious skeptic and an admirer of Voltaire and Frederick the Great. He considered himself "enlightened." In 1770 he wrote to Choiseul about the Jesuits, "I know the pains they have taken to spread darkness over the surface of the earth and to dominate and confuse Europe." To make matters worse, the empress' daughter Marie Antoinette was betrothed to France's future Louis XVI—it was called the best match in Europe, an important connection given other European alliances that could militarily threaten Austria. Soon the empress would reverse her earlier position when she prom-ised one of her teachers that the Jesuits "had nothing to fear" as long as she was empress. Thus the huge, influential, and very Catholic Aus-trian Empire would not help the Jesuits at the risk of alienating the Bourbons, especially Louis.

The debate ground on and on, generating much heat and little light. Then some anti-Jesuit cardinals took it upon themselves to sound out Cardinal Lorenzo Ganganelli about his willingness to give the desired commitment without reservations. Ganganelli was a Franciscan, an order that was still not on friendly terms with the Jesuits; yet he had been a Jesuit student and it was said that he owed his red hat to General Ricci's support. During the conclave he had tried to please both sides, just as one might expect from a man who was intelligent, kind, scholarly, charming, but weak in character, unskilled in diplomacy, and with a timidity that was bent more on pleasing others than doing the right thing. He had another major deficiency for a pope: He had an "insufficient faith in God."

Clement XIV Elected

Ganganelli might have signed a paper in which he made the vague representation: "I recognize the right of the Sovereign Pontiff to extinguish in good conscience the Company of Jesus, in accordance with canonical rule, and that it is to be desired that the future pope deploy every effort to fulfill the wish of the Crowns." He "might" have signed it, because there is no physical evidence of it today. If true, Ganganelli was a master politician in currying favor with the Spaniards. Perhaps there were also oral codicils aimed at both sides, because both sides viewed him as acceptable.

Finally, after three months of lobbying, on May 18, Ganganelli was elected by forty-six votes out of forty-seven, the forty-seventh being his own vote which he gave to a cardinal who was a nephew of Clement XIII. Ganganelli took the name Clement XIV.

Immediately the new pope took many steps, both substantial and symbolic, to make peace with the Bourbon monarchs, thus stemming the fragmenting of his Church, and to respond to the assaults of the Enlightenment which were undermining his religion everywhere. While these "show-of-good-faith" steps bought time, the monarchs would put up with only so much of it. Clement, timorous as he was, needed to proceed with great caution due to pressure on the pro-Jesuit side as well. The Jesuits still had many friends located in the German states, Poland, Austria, the Italian princes and states, and even in French provinces far from Paris, with its wavering and conscience-stricken King Louis.

Just two months after the pope's election the French ambassador to Rome, the same Cardinal Bernis, gave Clement a memorandum stating that the Bourbons "still believe the destruction (of the Jesuits) to be useful and necessary" and renewed their request for the pope to act. Clement temporized and on September 30 made a vague promise to Louis who, being the dove of the monarchs, was unwilling to press the issue further.

Charles III Pressures Clement to Liquidate the Jesuits

More stalling by Clement led to more intense admonitions from Madrid and a demand from the hawk, Charles III, for the "absolute extinction" of the order, since the Jesuits "disturbed the peace" wherever they were firmly established. A major concession was needed. It came in a letter Clement wrote to Charles on November 30, 1769, promising to suppress the Jesuits. But he gave no deadline. His stalling tactics now ranged from the symbolic to the profound: from prohibiting non-Italian Jesuits from hearing confessions in the Papal States to suggesting that "perhaps such an important issue requires convening a formal Vatican Council" to consider the charges against the Jesuits (that could take years). But the monarchs, knowing a trap when they saw one, would have none of that.

In mid-1772 Charles III appointed a new ambassador to the Vatican, José de Moñino y Redondo, with instructions to take a hard line on the liquidation of the Jesuits. Moñino was a heavyweight; he was the fiscal of the council of Castile and a lawyer. From Naples, Charles' mentor, Tanucci, approved, writing that Moñino was the only Spaniard who knew how to manage affairs in Rome. Later Moñino would become Spain's first minister and a count—Conde de Floridablanca—in large part due to his key role in convincing the pope to suppress the Jesuits.

Clement dreaded Moñino's tactics, especially his threat that Spain would crush all religious orders if Clement continued temporizing. The ambassador "shrank from no method of achieving his purpose, whether it was bribery of the pope's confidants or threats against the head of the Church himself." At an audience on November 22, 1772, he threatened the pope with a complete rupture with Spain, Naples, France, and Portugal. In frustration over Clement's delays, Moñino wrote: ". . . the Holy Father, under frivolous and contrived pretexts, keeps postponing its (the Suppression's) execution." On and on it went. Another token sanction came from Clement; this time it was prohibiting the use of the Jesuits' Lenten catechism. In another sop to his adversaries, Clement elevated to cardinal Paulo de Carvalho, Pombal's brother, to no effect since the new cardinal died twelve days before the consistory when his elevation would have been made official. An issue dear to the heart of Charles was belief in the immaculate conception. Charles wanted the pope to make it official Church doctrine. Clement stalled. He was still trying to buy time and avoid the order's capital punishment. But this issue would not go away.

Pastor writes:

> Meanwhile every courier from Madrid brought further urgent and insistent instruction. Moñino could think of no other course but to bribe the pope's associates . . . with Spanish gold

The key would be Clement's secretary, confidant, and an *eminence grise*, a Franciscan friar named Innocenzo Buontempi. Moñino wrote to Madrid that Buontempi had incurred debts of 40,000 scudi. (One scudo was a bit more than a day's wages for a Roman laborer.) Madrid's response was, "Buontempi shall have his jingling reward, but not until the deed is done." In addition, the province of Avignon was to be returned by the French to papal control, although this representation was worded somewhat ambiguously, facilitating a French renege. As part of the deal, three minor Italian states were also to be returned to the pope.

At the end of 1772, the anti-Jesuits had a political windfall when Frederick the Great wrote to d'Alembert as editor of *L'Encyclopédie* saying:

> Amid all these various movements the order of the Jesuits is to be destroyed at last and the pope, after wriggling for a long time, has yielded at last, so it is said, to the importunities of the first-born sons of his Church. I have received an emissary of the general of the Ignatians, who urges me to proclaim myself as the protector of this order. . . I did not consider myself entitled to intercede on its behalf, and that the pope was sufficiently master in his own house to undertake any reform that he found to be right and fitting, without any heretics [like me] meddling in the business.

Frederick's intention was simply to remain a member in good standing of the Enlightenment but it quickly circulated among the Jesuits' adversaries igniting a firestorm. They saw at once what a powerful weapon the letter was. The Jesuits were intriguing with a heretic against the Catholic monarchs and the pope himself.

In the meantime, Clement was worn down, distraught and out of excuses for further delay. Matters were coming to a head. On November 29 in an audience given to Moñino, Clement repeated his promise to suppress the Jesuit order, "adding that he would bring the matter to a speedy end." In a similar vein Clement said to Bernis:

> It is true that three and a half years of my pontificate have passed [Moñino and Bernis had repeatedly made an issue over how much time had elapsed with no papal action taken on the Jesuit matter.] but I have been continually active and I have already succeeded in destroying the Jesuits' prestige in Rome with the nobility, the prelates, the Curia and the people."

In December, Clement took a gratuitously mean-spirited action, "depriving the Jesuits expelled from Portugal of the pension given them by Clement XIII, which he had already reduced from 12,000 scudi to 9,000 scudi."

Moñino, elated by the most convincing promises yet from Clement, increased his pressure on the pontiff to draft a Suppression document, successfully so. The drafting was assigned to a politically astute Spanish priest at the Vatican, one Francisco de Zelada, recently commissioned titular bishop of Petra. Zelada took his cue from Moñino and his collaborators, the Spanish leaders of the Dominicans and the Franciscans. To help move things along, Moñino awarded a bribe of 8,000 scudi for Zelada, not that it was needed. Zelada and Buontempi became the ultimate authors of the brief of Suppression. At the same time, threatening Neapolitan troops were withdrawn from the frontier of the Papal States to help set a reassuring tone.

In March, a draft of the brief arrived in Madrid for Charles' review. He was highly satisfied with the fulfillment of all his wishes. Immediately, Charles wrote to Louis and Maria Theresa, both compliant, and to the hawkish Joseph I of Portugal. The empress wrote back that despite her "high esteem" for the Jesuits who had merited it by their "zeal and good conduct" in the Austrian Empire, "she would put no obstacle in the way" of their Suppression "if the pope considered it expedient and profitable for the unity of their holy religion." Her Lord High Steward Khevenhüller privately told her "she would rue this step till her dying day." Seven years later, shortly before her death in 1780, while regretting her abandoning the Jesuits, she said to Khevenhüller, "If only I had taken your advice and listened to your remonstrances." Pastor writes, "Her regret would have been greater still had she known the fate that awaited her daughter in France, for the sake of whose marriage [to the

Dauphin, the future Louis XVI] she had sacrificed the Jesuits." She had been the only one who had a chance to stop the Suppression, since its only other opponents left were a few small independent states in Italy such as Florence and the bishops of Germany who carried little weight. Pastor writes that "Clement XIV had hoped in vain that the sincerely pious empress who had inherited from her forebears a liking for the Jesuit. . . would never agree to their suppression." But she would not take this bitter cup from him.

At this point the momentum leading up to the Suppression became overwhelming. In spite of that, even at this late date, he harbored hopes "that something might intervene to prevent its consummation." On April 19, 1773, Clement rewarded Zelada with the red hat.

On June 3, Clement's temporizing caused Moñino to confront him with more threats and reproaches. The pope, now "deeply depressed, asked him not to worry and frighten him so much." The two-hour audience produced nothing. Fearing that even at this late date, the agreement on the Suppression might still fall apart, Moñino called for more bribes. Zelada had become deeply in debt. Moñino asked Charles for 6,000 to 7,000 scudi. Charles sent 8,000. Louis XV gave Zelada an abbey producing benefices of 2,000 scudi annually and Charles then added another 3,000 annually. Buontempi's 10,000 scudi promised earlier, would be withheld until the brief of Suppression was published.

Clement Issues Brief of Suppression

Finally, on June 8, Clement issued the brief of Suppression. It was entitled *Dominus ac Redemptor (noster)* (Our Lord and Redeemer). Curiously, it was dated July 21. Was he still temporizing, hoping the problem would somehow go away during the intervening six weeks? And why was it a "brief" rather than the more formal and solemn "Bull"? Was it to minimize the consequences of his act and thereby help relieve his soul of this awful burden?

Even then, the document did not go public. Instead, the agonizing Clement formed a commission of five cardinals to announce the brief. He met with them on August 9 in the strictest confidence, under pain of excommunication. He then set the public announcement for August 16. On that date, the cardinal-secretary of the commission, accompanied by soldiers and police went to the Jesuit residence at Gesú and told General Ricci that the Society of Jesus was no more. Two days later it was announced to the world.

Pastor writes, "On reading the Brief, Ricci was amazed, but he retained full control of himself and, when asked, on the Pope's orders, if he accepted the Brief, he replied that whatever the Pope decided must be sacred to everyone; it did not need his concurrence."

Why the further delay? Why did Clement not have the courtesy or the courage to summon Ricci and tell him face to face? Was it the pain and awkwardness of it all? Was it shame? Lacouture vividly describes Clement's mental anguish in signing the brief. He says we have it from Pope Gregory XVI that Clement fainted onto his palace's marble floor immediately after the signing. According to Cardinal de Simone, Clement's auditor, he wandered through his papal chambers sobbing, *"Compulsus feci!"* (I did it under duress!) "Hell is my abode. . . . I am doomed."

Dominus ac Redemptor was a lengthy document of forty-five paragraphs, replete with many charges but with not a shred of evidence to support them. Its tone starts off gently enough, masterfully laying the groundwork for what was to come thirty paragraphs later, no coincidence given the brief's provenance with Moñino, Charles III's smooth lawyer and politician par excellence directing Zelada. Lawyerly like, it reviews several papal precedents in dealing with wayward orders. Then it eases into the real issue—the Church's political exigency and the role of the three crowns. The operative paragraph was two-thirds the way through. Threats against any opposition to the brief or even any comment about it, closed the matter. The following excerpts speak for themselves. It starts off:

> Our Lord and Redeemer Jesus Christ, the Prince of peace announced by the prophet, when he came into this world first proclaiming peace to the shepherds through the angels . . . he also gave the apostles the ministry of conciliation and entrusted to them this world of reconciliation so that, serving as envoys of Christ, who is not the God of dissension, but of peace and love. . . . In cultivating God's vineyard and in preserving the house of the Christian religion . . . we root up and we destroy we dispose and we scatter and we build and we plant. . . . Similarly, when the same bond of charity requires it, we should be ready to uproot and destroy anything even if it be most pleasant and gratifying to us and even if doing without it would cause the greatest distress and mental anguish. . . .

> In deciding and carrying out all these measures [destruction of other orders in past centuries], our predecessors always judged

it better to use prudent consultation. . . . Hence they bypassed the unpleasantness and troublesome procedures that characterize judicial trials. . . . They solved every case without giving the regular orders destined for suppression leave and opportunity of exercising their rights or refuting the very grave charges. . . .

. . . one clearly gathers that in the Society [of Jesus] almost from its beginning, seeds of dissension and rivalry grew. The discord was not only among members but also with members of other religious orders, with the secular clergy, with academies, with universities . . . and even with princes in whose realms the Society had been received.

. . . further the Spanish Inquisition raised a hue and cry against . . . the Society, its form of government, and disputed [many] topics on which . . . the Society held positions.

. . . the clamor and complaints against the Society [were such] that very unpleasant wrangling spread throughout the world about the Society's teaching which very many represented as repugnant to orthodox faith and good morals.

. . . More and more charges were made against the Society for excessive greed and worldly goods.

. . . No comfort for the Apostolic See [or] the Society, and no good for the Christian public resulted from the most recent apostolic letter of Pope Clement XIII. . . . The letter was more extorted than requested [here Zelada dismisses those who might use Clement XIII's words against the brief].

. . . During Clement XIII's reign . . . loud complaints against the said Society grew more numerous each day . . . there were very dangerous seditions, tumults, dissentions, and scandals. . . . They inflamed the minds of the faithful with partisan zealotry, hatred and enmity. . . . But now the kings were forced to send away and expel members of the Society from their realms possessions and provinces . . . that it was absolutely necessary to keep Christian people in the bosom of Holy Mother Church from challenging, provoking and lashing out against one another.

. . . Our aforementioned dearest sons [the kings] in Christ thought the remedy could not be sur . . . unless the Society itself was utterly eliminated and completely suppressed.

. . . Further we have noticed that the Society of Jesus is no longer able to produce the very rich fruits and usefulness for which it was founded . . . the true and lasting peace of the Church [can not] be restored as long as the Society is intact.

. . . From sure knowledge and fullness of apostolic power, we abolish and suppress the oft-mentioned Society. We take away and abrogate each and every one of its offices. . . . We do away with the statutes, customs, usages decrees, constitutions. . . .

. . . The name of the Society is to be completely removed and suppressed. . . .In addition, we order and command in virtue of holy obedience that each and every ecclesiastical person . . . especially . . . members of the Society . . . not dare to defend, attack, write about, or even speak about [this] suppression and of its causes and motives. . . .

Given at Rome at St. Mary Major under the Ring of the Fisherman. 21 July 1773, the fifth year of our pontificate.

The only omissions were Charles' threats of "the penalty of death" for non-compliance; perhaps that was because Clement could not enforce it. How did the Guaraní react? There is no record that they had ever been given an opportunity to see any of it.

The archbishop of Paris, Christophe de Beaumont, replied to the brief with scorn, ignoring Clement's prohibition against attacking it or writing against it. Beaumont recalled that Clement's predecessor had, just ten years earlier, declared the "sanctity" of the Jesuit order in a formal Bull, but now

. . . this brief . . . is nothing other than an isolated . . . judgment, pernicious, reflecting little honor on the papal tiara and deleterious to the glory of the Church.

He went on to say that he would not be wretch enough to lend his support to it. The archbishop's reply greatly upset Clement.

In Lisbon, however, the brief was welcomed with the greatest jubilation. A *Te Deum* service was held on September 29 chanted by the patriarch before the king and his court. A royal decree called for three days of rejoicing. The country obeyed.

Buontempi's payoff was increased to a life pension of 1,500 scudi, annually. It was paid from a secret account with anonymity protected.

Louis XV's return of Avignon to the papacy took almost a year, marked by convoluted, acrimonious negotiations. It was not consummated until after Louis died. A French spokesman described Tanucci, a mediator in the negotiations, as the most mischievous, mendacious caviler that had ever walked the earth. Charles was so displeased with his mentor's performance that the minister had to beg, in a letter, for his pardon. Some thought the return of Avignon would never happen, and cynics in Rome observed that the pope was swindled even over the price to be paid for the Suppression. Clement's efforts to avoid having the public see any linkage between the two events had fooled no one.

Bangert writes that some 23,000 Jesuits, seventy-five percent of them priests and twenty-five percent brothers were "torn . . . [from] all those . . . ties of affection which bound them to one another in a spiritual brotherhood and saw disappear the . . . landmarks which steered their course to eternity. . . ." The novices and brothers were dismissed, and the priests were free to live as secular clergy or enter other religious orders.

Clement Imprisons General Ricci, Puts Him on Trial

Six weeks after publication of the brief, the now former general, seventy-year-old Lorenzo Ricci and five fathers who were closest to him were taken to a papal prison in Castel Sant'Angelo to await trial by a papal tribunal. While there Ricci was kept in a cell for a period that wound up lasting until his death two years later. During this time he was denied permission to communicate with his fellows, to light a fire in cold weather, to open the window, or even to say Mass—it was solitary confinement. His isolation was such that he did not learn of the death of his closest assistant in a nearby cell until months after the event.

The threatened trial of Ricci turned into a farce. The tribunal was comprised of the same prelates who advised Clement on the brief. Ricci was guilty even before the presentation of any charges to the tribunal. The fact that no misdeeds were being proven resulted in the proceedings languishing for two years, never reaching a conclusion. Lacouture writes that at one point the anti-Jesuit Cardinal Marefoschi, had to withdraw, "sickened by the irregularities committed." The trial ended only with Ricci's death.

Meanwhile, the treasure hunt for Jesuit riches, rumored at fifty million scudi (several billion in today's dollars) turned up mostly debts. Ricci had pointed to the Society's books and the fact that the Society could not even support its Spanish and Portuguese exiles. Any funds sent out were to support the foreign missions. Other assets included 500,000 volumes in Jesuit libraries in Belgium; three-quarters of them were sold by local officials as trash paper. However, they did have some thirty paintings by Flemish masters. These were shipped off to Vienna.

What was the trial's purpose? The real verdict, abolishment, had been declared earlier. Might the tribunal simply rubber-stamp the decision to imprison Ricci, thereby endorsing the decree of July 21 and helping to take some of the burden off Clement? Perhaps it was just to postpone the finality of this pathetic and sinister episode while keeping the kings satisfied. We may never know.

Clement Dies in Agony, Ricci Dies in Prison

When Clement died on September 22, 1775, at age sixty-nine, rumors circulated, helped along by the Spanish, that the Jesuits had poisoned him. But when the doctors opened the body in front of many witnesses, they attributed his death to longstanding scurvy and a hemorrhoid condition, aggravated by intense emotional distress labeled at the time as "artificially induced perspiration," a term unknown today. Although the rumors of his poisoning persisted, no credible historians took them seriously.

Ricci died on November 24, 1775, two months after Clement, from age-related illness aggravated by the conditions of his confinement. He was seventy-two.

Clement's successor, Pius VI, despite intense opposition from the first ministers and especially from King Charles and no doubt knowing of Ricci's grave condition—he had been given the last rites well before he died—ordered the release of the remaining fathers. Yet, because of the opposition, Pius delayed releasing Ricci, then took action too late. Death came just before the pope's decree of release arrived at Castel Sant'Angelo.

What the Real Issue Was

Bangert addresses the ultimate issue that was at stake here—the very *survival* of the Catholic Church. He writes that France's Choiseul advised Cardinal de Bernis during the interregnum between Clement XIII and Clement XIV that, if the former pope had reigned another ten years, a schism would most likely have occurred in the Church. Choiseul wrote, "Without question the pope must be a man with understanding of the spirit of the courts and the mood of our age, so completely different from that of the previous century." Bangert, putting a positive spin on the events, writes, "The sacrifice of the Society, removing as it did a serious irritant to Bourbon relations with the Vatican, helped to keep important countries linked to the Holy See until a better day. Even in their death the Jesuits continued true to their vocation of service to the Church." Given the century of events leading up to this outcome, perhaps it was the best the Jesuits could have hoped for. Perhaps.

Vatican Has Medallion Struck to Commemorate the Abolition of the Jesuits

The medallion pictured here and on the front cover of this book is one of five very similar medallions all struck at about the same time, in the fifth year of the pontificate of Pope Clement XIV, between May 19, 1773, and May 18, 1774 to memorialize the Suppression of the Jesuits. According to Dr. Clemens Brodkorb, director of the archives of the German Province of the Jesuits in Munich and the source of the photographs, the cover's medallion—45 millimeters in diameter and made of silver—in their possession is one of the five struck outside the Vatican and without any known involvement by the Curia. At least one additional medallion was struck by the Holy See itself and another was struck separately by a third party with Holy See approval. It is unclear whether these last two were prototypes for the other five.

Professor Mathes has a bronze example in his personal collection. He believes that there were seven struck by the Vatican and points to the definitive catalogue by A. Patrignani, *Le Medaglie Pontificie da Clemente XII 1730 a Pio VI 1799* (Bologna: Forni Editore, 1939), for corroboration. His and the Munich Jesuits' version are the only ones that I have been able to locate after several contacts with dealers in such artifacts.

The front side of the medallion (left) contains a profile of a bust of Clement XIV. It reads: *CLEMENS XIV PONTIF · MAX* (Clement XIV Supreme Pontiff).

The reverse side of the medal in the German archives is shown on the next page and on the front cover. To the left of the tableau are three characters reported by Professor Mathes to be St. Paul (extreme left), St. Peter (center, holding the keys) and to his right is Christ (with the sunburst halo) pointing at three sinister-looking Jesuits as he casts them out of heaven. The Jesuits are wearing their order's signal cassock and biretta. Also, according to Mathes, they are Saints Ignatius, Francis Xavier, and Francis Borja—three founders of the Society of Jesus.

Around the upper circumference are the words: *NUMQUAM NOVI VOS DISCEDITE A ME OMNES* ("I never knew you: depart from me all of you." [Matthew 7:23]) At the bottom are the letters *EXAUG·SOC·IESU·MEMOR* colloquially translated as "Eradicate the Society of Jesus from Memory" above the date MDCCLXXIII. At the very bottom is PS CXVII referring to Psalm 117: "By the Lord has that been done and this [is] a wonder in our eyes." In today's Christian Bibles it is Psalm 118.

CHAPTER 19

Frederick and Catherine:
The Great "Heretics" Rescue the Jesuits

Politics makes strange bedfellows, religious politics not excepted.

It could not have been more improbable. At the time when the Society of Jesus was "abolished and suppressed" by the very papacy it had so faithfully served, when its general had died in the pope's prison, and when the great Catholic kings had done everything possible to ensure that there would be no resurrection, who should come to the rescue but two "heretics." Both were Germans—one was nominally a Lutheran, although a non-practicing one; the other was a Lutheran convert to Russian Orthodoxy. Both were enlightened autocrat monarchs who managed to attain greatness after suffering through miserable formative years.

Their personalities and attitudes were formed in that crucible of teenage traumas that scarred and steeled them, planting private demons and melancholy in their psyches lasting throughout their lives. Those early years had a profound effect, making them less judgmental and more empathetic to others who also suffered persecution and rejection, like the outcast Jesuits.

Frederick the Great, King of Prussia

King Frederick II, "the Great," of Prussia was not what one would expect from his early years. Born in 1712, he was a frail and sickly child. His father, King Frederick William I, was a domineering, physically abusive, cold, and demeaning parent. Frederick rarely measured up to his father's expectations. By the age of sixteen, his foppish, sissified ways exacerbated his father's abuse, resulting in jeers and derisive laughter that often turned to rage. On one occasion the king tried to strangle him, and on another he threw a plate full of food at the boy in front of other people. Even one of the king's daughters, Frederick's favorite sister, was brutally beaten, possibly because she came to Frederick's defense. It was at this time that Frederick was tasting philosophical fruit forbidden by his father—that of Voltaire, Diderot, d'Alembert, Locke and others, sowing in him the seeds of the Enlightenment. They would eventually blossom in him with beneficial consequences for the Jesuits.

At eighteen, the increasingly unhappy Frederick, now a colonel, collaborated with a friend, possibly a lover eight years older, in the same prestigious cavalry regiment as the crown prince, to flee to England. Their plan was discovered. Frederick and the friend, Lieutenant Hans Hermann von Katte, were court-martialed for desertion and sentenced to life in prison. The king, enraged at the "light" sentence, upped it to capital punishment for Katte. His son's prison term remained but turned out to be a brief one, followed by lengthy house-arrest, thanks to the son submitting to the father and begging forgiveness. While incarcerated in a castle tower overlooking the execution site, the crown prince was forced to watch as his friend was put on the chopping block. As the executioner's sword came down on Katte's neck and blood gushed, Frederick failed to see it, thus missing his father's intended lesson. He had fainted moments before. Many contemporaries and historians have seen in these traumatic experiences a reason for Frederick's later character traits of sensitivity and aloofness.

As it sometimes turns out, the father's treatment of the son in this case would strengthen, energize, and enlighten him, such that he became a brilliant general—one who possessed rare diplomatic skills as well. Sometimes such a son emulates his father. In Frederick's case he seems to have learned from his father what not to do.

At the age of nineteen, Frederick fell in love with Louise Eleanor, the strikingly beautiful and poised twenty-three-year-old wife of army Colonel von Wreech. This was one of the few passionately happy episodes of his life, perhaps the only one. While there is some dispute over how far their relationship went, it is likely that he fathered a daughter with her. In any event, she soon became bored and ended the relationship.

When Frederick was twenty-one, his father arranged his marriage to an attractive, tall, blue-eyed blonde, Princess Elizabeth Christina from the German principality of Brunswick-Bevern. Even before the wedding, Frederick found little to like in her, pronouncing her to be "stupid, silly, and silent." Of course that she was his father's choice did not help her. The closer the wedding date came the more she lost any appeal. Frederick began speaking openly about the poor seventeen year old, telling intimates that sex could not come from duty and that he loved sex but only in a fickle way. He and his wife spent little time together early on, and although their written communications were tender they rarely saw each other in their later years. They had no children. She had never even been to *Sans Souci*, his small pink and white whimsical palace. For the rest of his life he showed little interest in women.

Frederick became an able flutist, wrote many pieces for the instrument, much poetry, and some thirty books. As crown prince he began a long correspondence with Voltaire, which he filled with such excesses of praise for the latter that by today's standards it would be considered shameless pandering. Voltaire's ego must have been sufficiently stroked because later, when Frederick became king, he was able to entice Voltaire to spend three years with him, from 1750 to 1753. Voltaire lived at *Sans Souci* for much of that time. This ended when a clash of the two inflated egos caused an angry rupture. In 1764 their relationship was renewed by Frederick, but only in correspondence, until Voltaire's death in 1778. Other *philosophes* such as d'Alembert and Diderot also joined his circle. Under the influence of Voltaire and the others, Frederick signed on fully to the Enlightenment. He came to oppose all organized religions, especially Catholicism because of what he saw as its allegiance to the pope rather than the state. His revised General Directory of laws added an egalitarian judicial code to protect the weak, although it continued financial discrimination against Jews. While he praised the goodness in the Gospels, his true beliefs are hard to discern since he was all over the philosophical map at one time or another. He might be called a deist or a secular humanist or agnostic but not quite an atheist. He did not believe in the immortality of the human soul.

A German website, friedrichdergrossezitateaphorismenbonmots, offers some of the king's philosophy:

- The foremost virtue of every honorable human being and, according to my belief also of every Christian, must be humanitarianism. The voice of nature, which is the basis of humanitarianism, wills that we all love one another and foster our mutual well-being (Frederick to Cardinal von Sinzendorff).

- Should you be present when I die, you will see that I shall go calmly, for I believe that after death everything is at an end.

- But apart from that I am firmly convinced that one must leave to everyone the freedom to believe what he considers believable.

Thus human beings may believe in immortality; I do not object provided that they not persecute me.

- All religions must be tolerated, and the state must keep an eye out so none of them does harm to another, for here everyone should become blessed in accordance with his own wishes.

- In every society tolerance must assure to every citizen the freedom to believe what he wishes (Frederick to Voltaire).

Nevertheless, this agnostic rejected atheism.

Upon his accession to the throne in 1740, Frederick built a new palace in Potsdam near Berlin, that he designed himself in great detail, revealing much about himself in the process. Its name, *Sans Souci* (carefree), its small size, its music room, its library, and its adjacent Chinese Tea House say a lot.

Frederick's commitment to advancing the influence and expansion of Prussia, transforming it into a modern nation-state, was unrelenting. Education and militarism (the idea of the latter, a sharp departure from Enlightenment principles) were the centerpieces of his reign. It soon came to his attention that the Jesuits, the universally recognized premier teachers of his time, were becoming available to accomplish the education part. After the Jesuits were expelled from Portugal and France, he proposed to Jesuit General Lorenzo Ricci that they be sent to Breslau in Silesia, a land he had recently won in the Seven Years' War. Many would go there.

Frederick Welcomes Jesuits, Delights in His "Heresy," Tweaks Pope

At the time of the Suppression in 1773, Frederick was at the peak of his power on the international political stage, especially among the enlightened. It was then that he flexed his political muscles in a most nuanced way, not needing his iron-mailed fist. One of the strangest aspects of Pope Clement XIV's brief of Suppression was its provision for implementation. The Vatican had stipulated that the bishops in all Catholic dioceses would be required to publish the brief to their flock before it would become effective in their respective districts. A master at gamesmanship, Frederick forbade his Catholic bishops from doing so "under pain of stern punishment." This, of course, was a clever way around the brief without confronting Clement head-on. The Catholic bishops, mainly in Lutheran Prussia but also in adjacent more heavily Catholic conquered lands like Silesia, had nowhere to turn for help and obeyed. Never again would the Vatican refer to Frederick as the "mere heretic, Margrave of Brandenburg" as Benedict XIV once did. Now and hereafter it would always be "the King."

Well after the expulsions and prior to the Suppression, Frederick, now a committed secular humanist, wrote to Voltaire wanting it clear among the *philosophes,* that he intended to:

> . . . keep my Jesuits, who are everywhere persecuted. I shall hoard the precious seed (the Jesuits) in order to redistribute it one day to those who may wish to cultivate this rare plant in their own land.

After the Suppression, while further wallowing in his heresy, Frederick took mischievous delight in tweaking the papacy on its own rules. Lacouture writes that Frederick did indeed start to interfere by saying that, while the pope might be "master in his own house," he had no authority in Prussia. He adds that Frederick sent a personal note to Clement that was "the most insolent and gleeful lesson in virtue that a heretic can ever have had the pleasure of inflicting on the leader of the Roman Church."

> On the matter of the Jesuits, my mind is made up to preserve them. . . . I have never known better priests. . . . Since I belong to the class of heretics, the pope [you] may not dispense me of my obligation to keep my word nor my duty as an honest man and a king.

Then he wrote to the Prussian and Silesian Catholic bishops:

> We, Frederick, by the grace of God King of Prussia . . . We have resolved that this recently executed destruction of the Society of Jesus shall not be promulgated in our States. We graciously command you to render null and void the said Bull [he meant brief] of the Pope . . . [we] expressly forbid, on pain of stern punishment, [you] to publish the said papal Bull doing away with the Society of Jesus.

After the expulsions Frederick wrote to Voltaire:

> My brothers the catholic, most faithful and most apostolic kings, have expelled the Jesuits. And I, most heretical, am taking in as many as I can. Thus I keep this race alive.

In another letter to Voltaire, shortly after the Suppression, Frederick wrote:

> In our domains there is no educated Catholic except among the Jesuits; we had no one capable of holding classes . . . other kinds of monks are of crassest ignorance; we have therefore to preserve the Jesuits or allow our schools to die . . . all of these good reasons have made me the Lancelot of this order.

Frederick also defended the order when there were rumors circulating that Clement XIV had died of Jesuit poisoning, writing to d'Alembert:

> Nothing [is] less true. . . . When they opened him up they found not a trace of poison . . . but he had often reproached himself for [sacrificing] the Jesuits. . . . In the last days of his life his mood was sorrowful and cantankerous, which helped cut short his existence.

In 1772 Frederick collaborated with Catherine of Russia (her modesty led her to eschew "the Great," so it came into widespread use only after her death) to invade and partition Poland, a country much larger than it is today, with its millions of devout Catholics and some 2,000 Jesuits. A year after Poland's partition and soon after the Suppression, an embryonic movement developed for a Nordic Company of Jesus to include Prussia and Poland among others. However, the local bishops became so opposed to it, they threatened to refuse ordinations and to prohibit priests from carrying out their routine priestly duties. Once again the Catholic Church was on the verge of a schism and on familiar ground since the Jesuits were again the eye of the storm.

This was all too much for Clement and his successor, the pro-Jesuit Pius VI, as they capitulated to Frederick and released the Jesuits of Prussia and Poland to carry on to the extent desired by "higher [meaning his] authority." The Catholic kings were dismayed by these papal concessions to this Lutheran heretic. The concessions led to a new, subtle compromise: The Jesuits' prominence in day-to-day life would be reduced but they could still keep their all-important communal groups, thus retaining their identity as an order.

Bangert writes that by the end of 1775, Pius was willing to allow the Jesuits to continue their "corporative" work in church and school, and even to accept new recruits—not as members of a religious order, but as individuals under the local bishop. As for Frederick, he was never able to understand why Pius was so insistent on removing the Jesuits' character as a religious order. The subtlety was lost on this man of action.

Frederick Prussianizes Jesuits

In 1776 Frederick ordered that the Jesuit order be dissolved in his realms and "Prussianized"—part of his efforts to build national identity—giving them the title "Priests of the Royal Schools Institute." This Institute lasted until 1800 when King Frederick William III (Frederick's great nephew) created a new system for controlling Catholic schools in Silesia. This system of socialized religion eventually eliminated the Jesuits as such by removing their sources of income. Some of them remained under their local bishops. Many others went east to Russia to serve under Catherine. But most importantly, Frederick and then Catherine had bought the order vital time during which the Catholic Church began to recognize the error of its ways and pave the way for the Jesuits' revival a generation later.

Catherine the Great, Empress of All the Russias

Catherine the Great was born Sophia Augusta Frederika of Anhalt-Zerbst, a minor principality in eastern Germany, in 1729. Her father was a high-ranking Prussian officer and thus well-connected among Prussian nobility. At that time there was much intermarriage among German and Russian nobility.

In 1741 Elizabeth Petrovna, daughter of Czar Peter the Great, became Empress of Russia in a coup. She soon brought her nephew, Peter Ulrich of Germany's Holstein-Gottorp principality and sole surviving male heir of Czar Peter, to St. Petersburg. She promptly declared him to be Grand Duke and future Czar Peter III. Although Peter was just fourteen, it was not too early to begin the search for a bride, and where better to find one than in the German principalities. The Prussian ambassador to Russia mentioned the beautiful, baby-faced, fair, blue-eyed Sophia's name to Elizabeth. Early in 1744 an invitation was sent to Sophia and her mother to come to St. Petersburg. Sophia's father was uninvited because his strong Lutheran beliefs might cause him to oppose a marriage in which his daughter would be required to convert to Russian Orthodoxy. En route to Russia, Sophia and her mother visited with Frederick the Great, now thirty-two and four years into his forty-six year reign. This must have been a heady experience for the fifteen-year-old maiden to be with the monarch of the greatest of German states and a major player on the world stage. No doubt seeds were planted in her mind for great things later.

Sophia studied Russian and Orthodoxy with such gusto and success, delighting the Empress Elizabeth so much that later the same year she was betrothed to Peter. Sophia as Grand Duchess took her mother's name, Catherine (Ekaterina in Russian), as it was the custom to take a parent's name. Shortly thereafter Peter contracted the measles and possibly smallpox, leaving him pitifully repulsive to his sixteen-year-old bride to be. His personality also became scarred.

The teenagers' wedding in 1745 was followed by disaster, as the marriage could not be consummated due to Peter's illnesses. Catherine went into years of frequent despondency and melancholy. She became a voracious reader, and like Frederick became persuaded by Voltaire's works and those of other *philosophes*. For her too, the seeds of the Enlightenment were planted.

After nine years of her isolation and misery and with the intervention of physicians, the royal couple was able to produce a son. The Empress Elizabeth took it upon herself to name him Paul. He was to be Catherine's only family.

In 1756 the Seven Years' War broke out with England, Prussia, and Hanover (the large northwestern German state) aligned against France, Russia, Austria, Sweden, and Saxony (the large eastern German state) with Spain joining France in the last year of the war. The war grew out of the colonial rivalry between England and France, and out of the struggle between Austria and Prussia for supremacy in Germany.

The fighting descended into a war of attrition with dominance gradually gained by England and Prussia such that by 1762 the exhausted powers were ready to sign a treaty. By the Treaty of Paris in 1763, Europe was restored basically to the *status quo ante.*

In Russia the most important outcome of the war followed the law of "unintended consequences" and the maxim "no good deed goes unpunished." Russia, typically for her, suffered massive human losses. The Russian military became infuriated when, at the time they had defeated Prussia and even occupied Berlin, Czar Peter capriciously withdrew his forces because of his admiration for Frederick. Soon, Russia's generals joined with many nobles and other admirers of Catherine in plotting to replace Peter and make her the empress. Her support snowballed throughout the entire officer corps, so that by late June 1762 she was acclaimed by all as Empress Catherine II. Concurrently, Peter was deposed. A few days later, while in custody, Peter was murdered, apparently by those guarding him. Catherine's complicity and that of her biggest supporters—the Orlov brothers, army officers devoted to her—is unclear. One, Gregory Orlov, had become her lover some months before. He was one of many to follow. Her sexual escapades became legendary.

In 1772 Catherine and Frederick put aside earlier differences and annexed portions of Poland and the then-sprawling Lithuania with Russia taking the lion's share. It would not be long before additional partitions would remove Poland from the map. Russia went on to defeat the Turks and seize the Crimea. Catherine was at her military and political zenith. How fortunate for the Jesuits, now at their nadir.

Catherine at Her Zenith Welcomes Jesuits

Yet Catherine would proceed carefully. Peter the Great had expelled the Jesuits a half century earlier partly from his fear that their loyalties were with Catholic Austria and because of their advice to the Chinese on a border dispute, to Russia's disadvantage. But Catherine fully appreciated their value as teachers to the educationally backward Russia just as Frederick did and began to pursue them as soon as the news of their Suppression reached her.

When *Dominus ac Redemptor* arrived in St. Petersburg in October 1773, two months after its pronouncement in Rome, Catherine declared it null and void. She threatened severe punishment for anyone publishing or preaching it. Like Frederick, there was no mincing of words. Understanding that Clement had required that the Suppression would go into effect in a diocese only after the brief was formally presented by its bishop, her and Frederick's approaches became identical.

Meanwhile, after the annexations, the astute Jesuits of Poland and Lithuania, overlapping with today's Belarus—together known as White Russia—were the first to rally to Catherine's side. They brought with them the nobles and the people. She became indebted to them. When the *de facto* Roman Catholic primate of her empire, Stanislaus Siestrezenciewitz, received disapproval from the Vatican over her disdain for Clement's brief, the primate answered the Vatican as follows: "The most high will is unmovable in (her) decrees. . . . I have received the order to leave the Jesuits as they are. Her majesty must be obeyed."

After a conference with Catherine, Austria's anti-Jesuit, pro-*philosophe* Joseph II told his entourage that the empress was stubborn (about the Jesuits) and that by "maintaining [them] in a flourishing condition" she would ensure their eventual reestablishment.

Catherine Warns Pope Not to Interfere

A few years later the one-sided debate resumed, now between Clement's successor Pius VI and the empress. He too should have known better than to oppose her. When his papal nuncio to St. Petersburg, Giovanni Andrea Archetti, tried to obtain some concessions from her, she threatened to remove the free practice of Catholicism in Russia and to abolish all Catholic institutions. She warned Pius not "to seek the intercession of favor, friendship, or prayer from anyone. . . . It would serve nothing." Pius quickly capitulated. In response, she wrote a most profoundly insightful and strategically beneficial (for the Jesuits) letter to Pius:

> I know that Your Holiness is most disturbed, but fear ill suits him. . . . My motives in granting my protection to the Jesuits are founded on reason and justice [and] the hope that they will be useful to [Russia]. This band of peaceable and innocent men shall live in my empire because, of all the Catholic societies, theirs is best fitted to instruct my subjects and inspire in them feelings of humanity and the true principles of the Christian religion. I am resolved to support these priests against any power whatsoever; and in this I do but fulfill my duty, since I am their sovereign and consider them loyal, useful, and blameless subjects.

Pius would surrender to her with three approvals given to her messenger: "I approve of the maintenance of the Society of Jesus in White Russia. I approve it, I approve it."

The Jesuits would thrive in Russia throughout her long reign and far beyond it. What a paradox that these heretics—Frederick and especially Catherine, who were disciples of the same Enlightenment that had done so much harm to the Jesuits in Catholic countries—should have given them so much aid in Lutheran and Orthodox countries.

Catherine's Son and Grandson Support Jesuits

After Catherine died in 1796, her son Paul I continued her policies towards the Jesuits, even strengthening them by granting them the Church of St. Catherine in St. Petersburg and approving a Jesuit college to be started there. In 1801, he was assassinated by disaffected nobles. His son Alexander I also favored the Jesuits until 1814 when, ironically, the Society of Jesus had been restored worldwide. After that, the Jesuits' prestige and influence in Russia rapidly declined.

Shortly before his assassination, Czar Paul was persuaded by his former tutor, Jesuit Father Gabriel Gruber (who became the vicar-general in St. Petersburg from 1802 to 1805, the highest ranking Jesuit in the world) to write to the newly elected Pope Pius VII:

My Most Holy Father,

The Reverend Father Gruber, superior of the religious of the Society of Jesus established in my states, having conveyed to me the desire of the members of this Society to be recognized by your Holiness, I have decided that it would not be fitting for me to refuse to request for this [Jesuit] order, in which I have a special interest, your Holiness's formal approval, hoping that I shall not have wasted my efforts in taking this step.

The most affectionate friend of your Holiness, Paul

On March 7, 1801, Pius issued the brief, *Catholicae fidei*, (For the Catholic Faith) formally restoring the Society of Jesus as an order, but only in Russia. There was still too much opposition to the Jesuits in the Vatican itself and elsewhere in Catholic countries to make the restoration worldwide.

Epilogue

Pius VII Reestablishes the Society of Jesus Worldwide, an Emotional Aftermath

After the collapse of Napoleon's empire in April 1814, there was a political clean slate in Europe such that seventy-six-year-old Pius VII was now able to reestablish the Society of Jesus worldwide. Pius had been Napoleon's captive in Fontainbleu, forty miles south of Paris. The pope reentered Rome on May 24 and began preparing a papal Bull to reestablish the Society of Jesus. He hoped to complete it by the Feast of St. Ignatius, July 31, but several cardinals insisted on their input, delaying its release for a week.

Bangert describes a touching scene as follows: On August 7, 1814, at the altar of St. Ignatius in the Gesù, the Jesuits' Mother Church in Rome, Pius VII offered the Sacrifice of the Mass. Then, before an immense crowd of cardinals, royalty, and about 150 Jesuits, Monsignor Cristaldi read the short, flowery papal Bull, *Sollicitudo Omnium Ecclesiarum,* (Care for the Whole Church), restoring the Society of Jesus. It stated:

> The Catholic world unanimously demands the reestablishment of the Society of Jesus. . . . We should consider ourselves culpable in the sight of God . . . if we should fail to use the help which the special Providence of God now puts at our disposal; if, seated as we are in the Barque of St. Peter, we should refuse the aid of the tried and vigorous mariners who offer to face the storms which threaten us with shipwreck. . . . We have decreed, in the virtue of Our Apostolic power, that all the concessions and faculties accorded by us to the Russian empire . . . shall . . . be . . . extended in perpetuity to all other countries of the world.

It was an explicit admission of Catherine's and her descendents' role over four decades.

When the reading was finished the pope gave the Bull to one of the Jesuits, the aging Luigi Panizzoni. One by one the old men who had experienced the sorrows of the Suppression, having suffered in imposed silence while leading lives of quiet desperation for forty-one years, now knelt before their smiling pontiff to receive a few kind words. When Pius left, it was to cheering throngs.

Two monarchs, not present, were King Charles IV and Queen María Luisa of Spain, who had been expelled by a revolution in their country. Some days later the few remaining Spanish Jesuits in Rome met with them in the Gesù to pay their respects. "The son of the king who had expelled the Society from Spain wept."

Acknowledgments

For a retired executive with a passion for history, writing this book turned into a labor of love. This may be unique for a person with a BSEE from the days when vacuum tubes were still common. I hope you found reading it to be as interesting as I found researching it.

While pursuing my long-standing curiosity about the Spanish missions of the seventeenth and eighteenth centuries on the internet, I discovered the California Mission Studies Association (CMSA), a non-denominational organization of people whom I found to be extraordinarily accomplished and friendly—academicians, historians, archaeologists, architects, preservationists, explorers and others of different beliefs and ethnic backgrounds. After I attended a CMSA convention, CMSA member Dr. W. Michael Mathes, emeritus professor of the University of San Francisco and perhaps the leading authority on Hispanic-American history, religion, and culture, proposed a thorough tour of the thirty Jesuit mission ruin sites that remain in southern Paraguay, northern Argentina, and southern Brazil. These comprised what was known to many as the "Jesuit Republic of the Guaraní". Mike planned all aspects of the mid-2003 trip in detail. His invitation was too enticing. I joined several CMSA members, including Edward W. Vernon, the author of a stunning photo essay of the Baja California missions, on the trip hoping to produce my own photo-essay of the Jesuits' "Republic" missions. To my surprise and discouragement there were several fine books on the subject available in Argentina including a masterpiece published by UNESCO as part of its World Heritage series. While studying everything available in English and some material in Spanish, I learned that the South American part of the story of the Jesuit Republic had been told from different perspectives many times. Nevertheless, as far as I could determine, no one has ever connected all the pieces to the complete story, especially how and why the missionaries' labors in Paraguay, combined with eighteenth century religious upheaval in Europe, resulted in the expulsion of the Jesuit fathers by the Bourbon monarchs of Europe, France, and especially Spain, in addition to Portugal's Bragança king; why and how the pope abolished the Jesuit order in 1773; and finally why two "Great" monarchs, Frederick and Catherine, born Lutherans, rescued enough Jesuit exiles to form a nucleus when the pope reestablished Society of Jesus in 1814.

After I described the limitations of prior histories, some challenged me to not just cavil, but write the whole story myself. The challenge was too much, and the story too awesome and moving to refuse.

In summary, that is the story I have tried to tell: How did it come to be that all of the labors of the Jesuits of Paraguay, for God and the Guaraní, was turned around and used to help destroy them?

This book could not have been accomplished without Mike's passion for and encyclopedic knowledge of the subject; his lectures during the long, bumpy bus rides between backcountry ruin sites; rap sessions over late night dinners of sweet Argentine beef washed down with flagons of Mendoza malbec; and his and Ed Vernon's constructive criticism of my manuscript. Mike also introduced me to the fascinating medallion on the cover of this book, memorializing the Suppression of the Jesuit order.

Thanks to Mike's network of friends in South America, we Norteamericanos were welcomed like royalty by the citizens of Santo Tomé, Argentina, a staging point for our tour. They treated us to generous receptions and feasts. Special mention must be made of the hospitality of the Casa de la Cultura "Concepción Centeno de Navajas" de Santo Tomé and its presidente, Profesora Elba Elisa Batalla de Vignolo. Her daughter, Silvia René Vignolo, our principal tour guide, made it all work and taught us the proprieties for the yerba maté pipe. Silvia also obtained interesting facts about the pre-Columbian Guaraní, included in the text.

This book would be lacking if it had not been for the help of John Wrynn, S.J., of St. Peter's College. His comments, especially on translations of Latin were helpful. More importantly, he used his European Jesuit contacts to direct me to the North German Province of the Society of Jesus, in Munich, where the 1773 medallion commemorating Clement XIV's abolition of the Jesuits could be found. Sure enough, the Archivist of Archiv der Norddeutschen Provinz SJ in Munich, Dr.

Clemens Brodkorb, was not only able to locate the medallion, but he also researched its provenance and generously provided a complimentary selection of high quality photographs of it. The dark and painful image on the medallion of three sinister-looking Jesuits being cast out of heaven by Christ was an initial and extra incentive for me to proceed with the book.

I owe much to our long-time family friend, Helmut Leuffen, for handling the communications with Dr. Brodkorb in German, and for his many hours spent researching material, both American sources and the German internet, especially about Frederick the Great and Catherine the Great.

I am particularly indebted to a friend of thirty-five years, Carl T. Hagberg, who spent dozens of hours editing the manuscript. Carl's extraordinary communications skills and knowledge of European history, especially about religion at the time of the Reformation and the Enlightenment greatly improved the organization, completeness, and accuracy of this book.

I wish to thank William T. Dentzer, Jr., my boss and mentor for twenty years, for reviewing the text and for clarifying certain fine points of Protestant theology.

Most of all, I am indebted to my wife, Betty, for her excellent linguistic and editing skills which helped make this book more colorful and easier to read. She also cleverly came up with the title of the book. Her only greater contribution was to maintain good humor and patience during my long periods of exasperating research involving multiple sources that contained conflicting "facts" requiring much cross-checking and rewriting.

Bibliography

Primary Sources

Bangert, William V., S.J., *A History of the Society of Jesus*. St. Louis: The Institute of Jesuit Sources, 1986.

Caraman, Philip, *The Lost Paradise*. London: Sedgwick & Jackson Ltd., 1975.

Cheke, Marcus, Sir, *Dictator of Portugal*. Freeport, New York: Books for Library Press, 1969 (original 1938).

Cunninghame-Graham, R.B., *A Vanished Arcadia*. New York: Haskell House Ltd., 1958 (original 1901).

Durant, Will and Ariel, *The Age of Voltaire*. New York: Simon and Schuster, 1965.

Hull, Anthony H., *Charles III and the Revival of Spain*. Washington D.C.: University Press of America, 1980.

Lacouture, Jean, *Jesuits: A Multibiography*. Washington D.C.: Counterpoint, 1991.

Mathes, W. Michael, *Lectures on tour of Jesuit mission ruins*. Argentina, Brazil, Paraguay: July 2003 .

Mörner, Magnus, ed. *The Expulsion of the Jesuits from Latin America*. New York: Alfred A. Knopf, 1965.

Mörner, Magnus, *The Activities of the Jesuits in La Plata*. Stockholm: Peterson, 1953.

O'Neill, George, S.J., *Golden Years on the Paraguay*. London: Burns Oates and Washbourne, 1934.

Pastor, Ludwig von, *The History of the Popes. Translated by Peeler*. London: Kraus Reprint, 1967 (original 1950).

Reiter, Frederick J., *They Built Utopia: The Jesuit Missions of Paraguay*. Potomac , Maryland: Scripta Humanistica, 1995.

Southey, Robert, *History of Brazil. vols. I-III*. New York: Greenwood Press (original 1822).

Secondary Sources

Abou, Sélim, *La "República" jesuítica de los Guaraníes (1609-1767) y su herencia*. Buenos Aires: Zago, 1996.

Addison, Joseph, *Charles III of Spain*. London: Simkin, Marshall, Hamilton, Kent & Co. 1900.

Adorno, Rolena, *Álvar Núñez Cabeza de Vaca*. Lincoln, Nebraska: University of Nebraska Press, 1999.

Asprey, Robert B., *Frederick the Great: the Magnificent Enigma*. New York: Ticknor & Fields, 1986.

Bainton, Roland, *Hunted Heretic; Life and Death of Michael Servetus*. Boston: Beacon Press, 1953.

Barton, Simon, *A History of Spain*. New York: Palgrave Macmillan, 2004.

Bertrand, Louis, and Petrie, Charles, *The History of Spain*. London: Eyre and Spottiswoode, 1934.

Carvajal, Gaspar, de, *Discovery of the Amazon, Edited by H.C. Heaton*. New York: American Geographic Society, 1934.

Cheetham, Nicolas, *A History of the Popes*. New York: Dorset Press, 1982.

Cronin, Vincent, *Catherine, Empress of All the Russias*. New York: William Morrow and Co., 1978.

Davis, David Brion, *Inhuman Bondage: Rise and Fall of Slavery in New World*. New York: Oxford University Press, 2006.

Eakin, Marshall C., *Conquest of the Americas Parts I & II*. The Teaching Company (audio tapes).

Engelhardt, Zephyrin, *The Missions and Missionaries of California vols. II-IV*. San Francisco: J.H. Barry, 1916.

Fraser, David, *Frederick the Great*. New York: Fromm International, 2000.

Fülöp-Miller, René, *The Power and Secret of the Jesuits*. New York: The Viking Press, 1930.

Furneaux, Robin, *The Amazon*. London: Hamish Hamilton, 1969.

Gagliano, Joseph A., *Jesuit Encounters in the New World*. Rome: Institutum Historicum S.I., 1997.

Gómez, Luiz Palacin, S.J., *Jesuit Encounters in the New World*, Rome: Institutum Historicum S.I. 1997.

Groh, John E., "Antonio Ruíz de Montoya and the Early Reductions" in *The Catholic Historical Review*, October 1970.

Hanke, Lewis, *The Spanish Struggle for Justice in the Conquest of America*, Philadelphia: University of Pennsylvania Press, 1949.

Harenberg, *Harenberg Lexikon der Sprichwörter & Zitate*. Dortmund: Harenberg Kommunikation, 1997.

Hargreaves-Mawdsley, W.N., *Eighteenth Century Spain*. Totowa, New Jersey: Rowman and Littlefield, 1979.

Hargreaves-Mawdsley, W.N., *Spain under the Bourbons*. London: The Macmillan Press Ltd., 1973.

Heaton, H.C., *The Discovery of the Amazon*. New York: American Geographical Society, 1934.

Herr, Richard, *The Eighteenth-Century Revolution in Spain*. Princeton, New Jersey: Princeton University Press, 1958.

Hollis, Christopher, *The Jesuits A History*. New York: The Macmillan Company, 1968.

Kamen, Henry, *Empire: How Spain Became a World Power*. New York: HarperCollins Publishers Inc., 2003.

Kamen, Henry, *The Spanish Inquisition*. New York: American Library, Inc., 1965.

Kirchberger, Joe H., *Zeugen ihrer Zeit (Witnesses of their Time)*. Munich: Piper, 1983.

Livermore, Harold, *A History of Spain*. New York: Grove Press Inc., 1968.

Lowney, Chris, *Heroic Leadership: Best Practices From a 450-Year Old Company*. Chicago: Loyola Press, 2003.

MacDonogh, Giles, *Frederick the Great*. New York: St. Martin's Press, 1999.

Mann, Charles C., *1491*. New York: Alfred A. Knopf, 2005.

McCoog, Thomas M., S.J., *Promising Hope*. Rome: Institutum Historicum Societatis Iesu, 2003.

McNaspy, C.J., S.J., *Conquistador Without Sword*. Chicago: Loyola University Press, 1984.

McNaspy, C.J., S.J., *Lost Cities of Paraguay*. Chicago: Loyola University Press, 1982.

Madariaga, Isabel, de, *Catherine the Great*. Yale University Press, 1990.

Mitchell, David, *The Jesuits, a history*. New York: Franklin Watts, 1981.

Mitford, Nancy, *Frederick the Great*. London: Rainbird, 1970.

Mousnier, Roland, *The Institutions of France Under the Absolute Monarchy, 1598-1789*. Chicago: University of Chicago, 1979.

Mousnier, Roland, *The Assassination of Henry IV*. London: Faber and Faber, 1973.

O'Malley, John W., S.J., *The Jesuits: Cultures, Sciences and the Arts, 1540-1773*. Toronto: University of Toronto, 1999.

O'Donnell, James J., *Augustine: A New Biography*. New York: HarperCollins, 2005.

Petrie, Charles, *King Charles III of Spain*. New York: The John Day Company, 1971.

Price, Richard, *Augustine*. New York: HarperCollins, 1997.

Profesores de la Universidad Católica Argentina, *Documento Histórico*. Buenos Aires, date unknown.

Ranke, Leopold von, *The History of the Popes vol. II*. London: George Bell and Sons, 1908.

Ruíz de Montoya, Antonio, *The Spiritual Conquest*. St. Louis: Institute of Jesuit Sources, 1993 (original 1639).

Saraiva, José Hermano, *Portugal, a Companion History*. Manchester: Carcanet Press, 1997.

Solsten, Eric, *Portugal: A Country Study*. Washington D.C.: Library of Congress.

Stankiewicz, W.J., *Politics and Religion in Seventeenth-Century France*. Berkeley, California: University of California Press, 1960.

Thomas, Hugh, *Rivers of Gold: The Rise of the Spanish Empire*. New York: Random House, 2003.

Thompson, Jesse E., "Sagittectomy – First Recorded Surgical Procedures" in *New England Journal of Medicine*, December 27, 1973.

Wild, Peter, *Álvar Núñez Cabeza de Vaca*. Boise, Idaho: Boise State University Press, 1991.

Wood, Michael, *Conquistadors*. Berkeley, California: University of California Press, 2000.

Wright, Jonathan, *God's Soldiers*. New York: Doubleday, 2004.

Notes

In order to provide effective citations without the distracting clutter of cumbersome footnotes or endnotes, I have employed the increasingly common use of identifying sources by stating the main references for each chapter followed by citing individual sources for quotations and historical facts not commonly known.

Prologue
P 16 "Among the numberless calumnies. . . " Southey, v. II p362-364
P 19 ". . . their superiors [in Europe]. . . " Ibid 362-364

Chapter 1 Why the Europeans Went to the Land of the Guaraní
Main references: Southey, Cheetham, Davis and Thomas
P 29 ". . . horrified ships' crews." Southey, v.I p35
P 29 ". . . valuable Brazil wood. . . " various sources. Brazil wood, rich red in color, was highly prized, especially for its use as a dye, in pre-Columbian Europe as early as the Roman Empire. The country we know as Brazil got its name from the vast quantities of the wood in its dense forests. The word is derived from the ancient Spanish *brasa*, their word for the red color of glowing charcoal.
P 31 ". . . South America to Portugal." Ibid 35
P 31 ". . . received the 'red hat'. . . " Cheetham , p187-188
P 33 ". . . consulted Columbus. . . " Thomas, p145
P 33 ". . . 370 leagues. . . " Ibid 144
P 34 ". . . journey to India." Ibid 186, et al
P 34 ". . . during his papacy." Cheetham, p191
P 35 " Davis writes that the race. . . " Davis, p86
P 35 ". . . coast south of Mali." Davis, p84
P 36 ". . . sugar monoculture. . . " Ibid 84
P 36 ". . . second voyage." Ibid 84
P 38 ". . . resembling an agribusiness. . . " Ibid 109
P 38 ". . . fabled Asian spice trade." Ibid 109
P 38 ". . . strategist on the international political stage." Southey, v.I p222, 233
P 39 ". . . in front of a large crowd." Ibid 225

Chapter 2 Who *Were* These Jesuits?
Main references: Wright, Bangert, Cunninghame-Graham, Kamen and Lowney
P 40 ". . . tremendous wild fowl. . . " Cunninghame-Graham, pviii
P 40 ". . . shattered by a cannonball. . . " Wright, p17
P 40 ". . . clever and irreverently witty. . . " Lacouture, p35
P 41 ". . . keen eye for talent. . . " Wright, p23, et al
P 41 ". . . come forth to engage in toils." Wright, p50
P 41 "Archibald Bower. . . " Ibid 13
P 41 ". . . loneliness of the gathering storm. . . " Mitchell, p8
P 43 ". . . spiritual malaise and moral crisis." Wright, p25
P 43 ". . . often chose Jesuits. . . " Ibid 38
P 44 ". . . popes in mental servitude. . . " Cunninghame-Graham, p260
P 44 ". . . from the pen of Rousseau. . . " Mörner, *Expulsion of the Jesuits*, p10

P 45 "... Dominicans who controlled the Inquisition. . . " Kamen, p155
P 45 "... opposition came to nil.." Ibid 88,89
P 45 "... summoned before the Inquisition, although with no consequence." Ibid 88,89.
P 45 "... clinched its (the Inquisition's) victory over the religious orders." Ibid 156
P 46 "... the Glorious Virgin Mary." Ibid 128
P 46 "... Ignatius had become a deep and sincere spiritual Semite." Ibid 128
P 46 "... Laínez, the second General, was a converso." Lacouture, p51
P 46 "... examine prospective priests for Jewish ancestry." Kamen, p128
P 46 "... more virtue than among Old Christians." Ibid 128
P 46 "... no distinction between persons, between Greek or Jew." Ibid 129
P 47 "... up to 7000 in the Province of Peru alone." Bangert, p385
P 47 "... 1000 Negro slaves at Córdoba and Asunción." Mörner, *Political and Economic Activities*, p76, 208
P 47 Peter Claver at Cartagena. Wright, p112
P 47 "... three quarters, priests and one quarter, brothers." Wright, p49
P 48 "... facilitate phonetic spelling. . . or providing the required Hispanic ring" Mathes lectures and Caraman, p56
P 48 "... Dominicans lived off the faith while the Jesuits died for it." Bangert, p272
P 48 "... paper condemned even by the Inquisition, but not by the Jesuits." Caraman, p110
P 48 "... no social promotion. . . " Wright p54
P 48 "... Jesuit schools were usually free." Ibid 55
P 49 "... In France. . . Jesuits had as many as 40,000 students." Ibid 53
P 49 "... eloquent if they were to be effective." Ibid 55
P 49 "... Jesuit. . . wished the new publication well. . . " Bangert, p304
P 50 "... Jansenism was grafted onto nationalistic Gallicanism. . . " Ibid 302
P 50 "... Jesuits conduct. . . their argument in off-putting Latin." Ibid 308
P 50 "... quarrel over Jansenism concerned the main conduct of Christian life." Wright, p162
P 50 "... the most considerable matter faced by Catholicism. . . " Ibid 162
P 50 "... Jansenism. . . was reheated Calvinism." Bangert, p355
P 50 "... Augustine. . . champion of predestinarian Protestants." Wright, p166
P 50 "... Jansenism. . . an opponent of. . . Richelieu." Ibid 168
P 50 "... Jesuits. . . lax moral theology. . . rosy view of man's nature and prospects for redemption." Ibid 168
P 51 "... Quesnel (calls) pope Clement. . . a doctor of lies." Bangert, p303
P 51 Paris Parlement restive against Jesuits. Wright, p184
P 51 The Enlightenment and Jansenists attack Jesuits from opposite sides. Lowney, p232
P 52 Rome's solution to Jesuit crises was penance and ever-more prayer. Bangert, p305
P 52 Jesuits' reputation included intellectual arrogance. Lowney, p232
P 53 Recognition that Jesuit works in Paraguay should have received. Cunninghame-Graham, p197
P 52 Raynal's "Maybe never so much good has been done for mankind with so little evil." Reiter, p355

Chapter 3 Who Were The Guaraní before the Europeans Invaded?
Main references: Southey, Cunninghame-Graham, Davis and Profesores de la Universidad Católica Argentina
P 54 "... 3000 miles south to the pampas of Argentina." Cunninghame-Graham, p19
P 54 "Yerba plants. . . " *Yerba* is Spanish for "herb." *Maté* is from the Quechua Indian word "*máti*" meaning "gourd" from which the tea is drunk
P 56 "... *La tierra sin mal*." Profesores de la Universidad Católica Argentina
P 56 "... never sparing a [enemy] man in battle." Southey, v.I, p64,65
P 57 "... name of the butchered victim, a signal honor." Ibid 125
P 57 "... consumption at the most nutritionally or ritually advantageous time." Ibid 227
P 57 "... *saca de moza* in Spanish or kidnap the girl, deadly intra-village fighting..." Profesores de la Universidad Católica

P 58 ". . . perpetually at war with their neighbors." Davis, p28
P 58 ". . . cat-and-mouse. . . allowing a frantic slave to escape. . . " Ibid 28,29
P 58 ". . . but not all native Brazilians were cannibals." Southey, v.I, p232,233
P 58 ". . . infants who were consumed by their own parents." Ibid 400
P 59 ". . . Guaycurú and. . . Agaces were the extreme in their hostility. . . most primitive."
Ibid 126
P 59 ". . . all deformed and illegitimate babies were killed. . . " Ibid 128
P 59 ". . . Guaycurú women were the most promiscuous..." there is no agreement among
sources on this allegation

Chapter 4 Portuguese Defeat French and Dutch in Brazil, Introduce Slavery

Main references: Southey, Gomez, Wright, Thomas and uk.encarta/Portuguese empire
P 61 ". . . he (Cabral) claimed the land for Portugal. . . " Thomas, p186, et al
P 61 ". . . sank both, along with their entire crews." Southey, v.I, p37
P 63 ". . . harsh rule over the colonists destroyed their morale." Ibid 315, et al
P 63 ". . . partnership of Mem de Sa and Nóbrega. . . responsible for Brazil remaining
Portuguese." Ibid 314
P 63 ". . . governor. . . limited forces, stretched thin." Mörner, *Political and Economic
Activities*, p59
P 64 ". . . we lose authority in the entire pagan (Indian) world. . . " Gómez, p248
P 64 ". . . obliging them to walk beneath the banner of Christ." Ibid 250
P 64 ". . . Jesuit missionaries would be brought in to teach them." Southey, v.I, p323
P 65 ". . . a system. . . compatible with pious fraud." Ibid 323
P 66 Vieira: what better way to remove burden of slavery from backs of (Indians) than to
increase African slaves. Wright, p112
P 66 ". . . Vieira: Portuguese fifth monarchy might require spilling of Muslim and heathen
blood. . . " Ibid 112
P 66 Acosta railed against idea of mestizo priests. Ibid 114
P 67 Hans Stade and the Tupinamba cannibals. Southey, v.I, p184-220
P 70 Portuguese decimate English near Rio de Janeiro. Ibid 314
P 70 French court too busy burning and massacring Hugonots to think of Brazil. Ibid 314

Chapter 5 Jesuit Missionaries Find Danger at Every Turn

Main references: Southey, Caraman, Cunninghame-Graham and Bangert
P 72 ". . . fifteen Jesuits on board. . . ten. . . were captured and devoured by cannibals."
Bangert, p254
P 73 Sores butchered, beheaded, Jesuits and threw them overboard. Lowney, p184
P 73 Jesuit novice escapes by being in layman's habit. Southey, v.I, p321
P 73 ". . . one of original group of seventy-three survived he having been left ashore in
Mexico." Ibid 321,322
P 74 Europeans encourage cannibalism. . . Jesuits give the Devil the whole merit for it. Ibid
226,227
P 75 Old Tupí woman asks Jesuit for hand of Tapuya boy to eat. Ibid 226-232
P 75 Some Indians eat those they slay in battle, make flutes from their shinbones and mugs
from their skulls. Lowney, p184
P 75 Montoya find remains of his former altar server in stew. Southey, v.I, p291, Caraman,
p240
P 75 Legend of lust as Timbues chief falls in love with Lucia Miranda. Southey, v.I, p 65
P 76 Vast numbers of jaguars attack ferociously. Dobritzhoffer via Caraman, p151
P 77 Novena drives away jaguars but they return and eat villagers. Ibid 151
P 77 Dobritzhoffer's close call with a jaguar. Ibid 152
P 77 Sepp loses Indian aides to jaguars. Ibid 152
P 77 Indians drive off jaguars by urinating in their eyes. Ibid 153
P 77 Faulkner's greasy hat eaten by wild dogs. Mitchell, p192

Notes

P 78 Indians drive off alligators with mirrors held in front of their eyes. Southey, v.II, p166
P 78 Indians keep snakes away from campgrounds. Ibid 365
P 78 Electric eels and sting rays. Cunninghame-Graham, p39
P 78 Ticks, flies and ants that soften mission foundations. Southey, v.II, p366, v.I, p142 and Caraman p137
P 78 Mosquitoes, giant flying bed bugs, aggressive wasps, vampire bats; and maggots cause excruciating death. Southey v.I, p143,144, v.II, p366 and Lowney, p182
P 79 Small pox kills tens of thousand of Indians and many Jesuits. Bangert, p351

Chapter 6 Spain Begins to Settle Paraguay

Main references: O'Neill (esp. pages 1-49), Southey, Cunninghame-Graham (esp. pages 13-23) and Caraman
P 80 Cabot sails up the Paraná and Paraguay rivers. Cunninghame-Graham gives possible etymologies for the names Paraguay and Guaraní, p23.
P 80 Cabot seeks rumored riches of Peru, seven years before Pizarro. Ibid 19
P 81 "Cabot remained. . . with friendly Guaraní for two years." Southey, v.I, p63, 64
P 84 Ayolas hopes to find the still-legendary gold and silver of Peru commonly mislabeled "El Dorado". The imaginary kingdom obtained the name, El Dorado (or in English, "The Gilded One") from its barbarian lord whose body was anointed every morning with a certain fragrant gum, and gold dust was blown on him through a tube until he was covered head to foot. The whole covering was washed off each night, only to be repeated the next day. Ibid 395
P 85 Spaniards found Asunción, abandon Buenos Aires after Indian attacks. Mörner, *Political and Economic Activities* p46

Chapter 7 Spain Occupies Paraguay: The Middle Years (1537-1630)

Main references: Mathes, Southey, McNaspy's *Conquistador* and Caraman
P 88 Pet cricket rattle saves ships from Brazilian shoals. Southey, v.I, p115
P 88 Cabeza de Vaca treks 2000 miles across Brazil and Paraguay to Asunción. Caraman, p24
P 90 Cabeza performs heart surgery on Indian. Thompson, New England Journal of Medicine, December 27, 1973, p1403
P 90 Cabeza exits wilderness at San Miguel de Culiacán on Sea of Cortés. Mathes lectures
P 91 Samuel Eliot Morison eulogizes Cabeza. Texas State University Center for the Study of the Southwest
P 93 Debate over nationality of Thomas Fields. Southey, v.II, p252 and Caraman, p27
P 93 Jesuits in Paraguay rebel over Acquaviva's decision to abandon Guaraní in favor of riches of Peru. Caraman, p28,29
P 94 Jesuit synod in Asunción calls for Indians to be gathered into mission settlements. Ibid 28,29
P 94 Mission idea arguably originated with Paraguay Jesuits. Groh, p504,505, footnotes
P 94 ". . . Guillermo Furlong argued. . . " Groh, p505
P 94 Acquaviva relents as Martín Ignacio de Loyola argues for new Jesuit Chile-Paraguay Province. McNaspy, *Conquistador* p51
P 98 Guayrá was the Guaraní name for a cacique helpful to Irala. Southey, v.I, p264,265
P 98 Guayrá's borders. Ibid, 264,265 and Caraman, p36
P 98 Guayrá missions expand rapidly. Groh, p509
P 99 Ortega's close call with an anaconda during flood. Southey, v.I, p255
P 100 González develops economic foundation for missions. Mörner, *Political and Economic Activities of the Jesuits* p73
P 100 The mission's name was derived from the fact that February 2 was the 40th day after the traditional birth of Christ when Catholics celebrated the "purification" of the Virgin Mary by a rabbi under Mosaic law. The Mosaic ritual included the blessing of candles, which were then carried in a procession in the temple.
P 101 González and aides killed by Ñezú's followers. McNaspy, *Conquistador* p156

P 101 "Let the jaguars devour him." Ibid 159
P 101 González killed ". . . to preserve our way of life and ancient songs." Ibid 155
P 101 Ñezú celebrates by unbaptizing mission children. Southey, v.II, p296
P 102 Ñezú slain by wandering bands. Ibid 296
P 103 Indians astonished at Jesuits exalted by martyrdom and soon joined missions from their example. Ibid 299

Chapter 8 What the Jesuit Missions Were Like

Main references: Mörner's, *Political and Economic Activities of the Jesuits*, Hanke, Caraman and Cunninghame-Graham

P 107 Deaths from epidemics. Bangert, p351
P 108 Jesuit imprisoned after allowing excessive punishment and General Retz orders, "any missionary who was excessive in punishing Indians should be removed instantly from the missions." Caraman, p164
P 109 Comparison of savagery of English law with that of Paraguay. Cunninghame-Graham, p65
P 109 Description of the Council of the Indies. Mörner, *Political and Economic Activities of the Jesuits*, p22
P 109 Spain copies Portugal's *Casa de la Contratación* or House of Trade to regulate monopolies. Kamen, p289
P 110 Spanish political and judicial arrangements. Mörner, *Political and Economic Activities of the Jesuits*, p26
P 111 Council of the Indies approves mission's yerba business. Ibid 100
P 113 Up to one third of yerba harvesters die from poisonous snakes, jaguars and sickness. Caraman, p126
P 114 Economics of yerba harvest. Cunninghame-Graham, p194 and Caraman, p125
P 114 Exports of agriculture and animals and animal products. Mörner, *Political and Economic Activities*, p167
P 121 In 1499 Columbus' administrators impose *encomienda*-like serfdom on the Indians. Hanke, p19
P 121 Isabella protects Indians asking "By what authority does the Admiral (Columbus) give my vassals away?" Ibid 20
P 121 Scottish Protestant historian Robertson wrote of the Spanish crown's struggle for justice for the Indians, "nothing similar occurs in the history of human affairs." Ibid 3
P 121 Under Philip II's law, "offenses committed against the Indians should be punished with greater severity than those committed against Spaniards." Cunninghame-Graham, p71
P 121 Montesino's 1511 call for justice for the Indians was "a voice crying in the wilderness. . . they had rational souls" Hanke p17,18
P 121 In 1512 Ferdinand signed Laws of Burgos. . . precise and humane. . . ignored by Spanish settlers, convicts. Ibid 24-27
P 122 Spaniard's attitude summarized by Cortés. . . "I came to get gold, not to till the soil like a peasant." Ibid 71
P 122 Spain's emphasis on plunder causes it to earn less from trade than France earned from Martinique alone. Kamen, p458
P 122 Dominican Bartolomé de Las Casas appeals to king to end *encomienda* system. The New Laws have little effect. Mörner, *Political and Economic Activities*, p35
P 123 ". . . encomerderos accounted for only a small proportion of the white population." Ibid 35
P 123 Angulo compared encomenderos to the dreaded Turks, "from birth to death, fathers and sons, men and women labor. . . for the. . . enrichment of their masters (not) receiving a garment in return or even a handful of maize." Caraman, p32
P 124 Royal commission investigates slavery. . . every Indian is a free man. . . Alfaro and Torres win for Indians. Caraman, p35

Chapter 9 Slave Hunters Invade theGuayrá; Desperate Guaraní Escape (1630)

Main references: Cunninghame-Graham, Southey, Caraman, O'Neill, Reiter and Carvajal (via Heaton)

P 125 Millions of Guaraní souls to be saved together with those of pygmies and strapping Amazon women living in war all their lives. Caraman, p70

P 127 ". . . mamelucos. . . warrior-slaves of the emirs in Baghdad, Syria and Egypt." O'Neill, p76, et al

P 128 ". . . attackers. . . smashed everything to pieces." O'Neill, p78

P 128 Maceta rescues Guiravera on death march. ". . . Guiravera. . . would titillate their palates with a roast Jesuit." Caraman, p59

P 128 Maceta, van Suerck and Indian captives on death march to São Paulo. Southey, v.II, p310

P 129 Indians sold to planters. . . no concern for keeping families together. They were split up as often as not. Mathes lectures

P 129 1,500 slaves arrive in São Paulo. Several times that number had started the trip from the Guayrá. Southey, v.II, p310

P 129 . . . mameluco reposted with a version of Jansenist dogma, "I shall be saved. . . for to be saved a man has only to believe." Cunninghame-Graham, p56

P 129 Montoya's anti-Lutheran bias. Groh, p515

Martin Luther's words in 1517 must be read in the context of his revulsion for the sale of indulgences as the means to salvation. The theology of over-emphasizing belief and discounting the need to be worthy of God's grace is based on a selective reading of St. Paul's epistles and St. Augustine's writings. It is basic to a number of sects today (Chapter II).

P 129 . . . slavers reenact captures dressed as Jesuits. . . a source of much amusement – in Montoya's mind even more damnable than the actual crime. Cunninghame-Graham, p56,57

P 129 Maceta and van Suerck seek justice in Brazilian courts. Disagreement on details. Caraman, p60, O'Neill, p79

P 130 Brazilian priests approve slave raids. . . Maceta writes, ". . . what can be expected from a people among whom are found priests that encourage and direct such criminal raids? Not among Turks or Moors are done such things. . . " O'Neill p80

P 131 Sorcerer puts on caricature of Catholic Mass, Baptisms. Many Indians follow. Caraman, p61

P 131 Montoya and Guiravera retake mission Jesús María. Sorcerer punished and converts. Ibid, 62

P 131 New, larger invasion by mamelucos led by plantation owner. Mörner, *Political and Economic Activities*, p89

P 132 Jesuit Taño seeks help from Governor Céspedes. Caraman, p62

P 132 Céspedes married to daughter of Portuguese official, possibly acquired plantation in Brazil. Mörner, *Political and Economic Activities*, ibid

P 132 Céspedes made no bones about it. Southey, v.II, p314

P 132 Céspedes said to Taño, "Leave these poor Portuguese to help themselves as best they can in their poverty." O'Neill, p80

P 132 Céspedes said, "May the devil take all the Indians. Write that to your missioners." Reiter, p42

P 132 Audencia in Charcas tries Céspedes, he's found guilty, punished mildly. Mörner, *Political and Economic Activities*, p91

P 132 Jesuit Provincial Trujillo calls Guayrá strategy meeting at Jesús María. Caraman, p63

P 133 Jesuits decide to abandon the Guayrá starting with San Ignacio Guazú and Loreto. Ibid 64

P 134 Montoya and Indians begin huge exodus. Dead priests disinterred and taken on exodus. O'Neill, p82,83

P 134 Silence of jungle broken by symphony of tree-dwellers. Ibid 83

P 135 "Guayrá Falls... perpetual shower... such drenching force... that they who visit the place strip themselves naked to approach it." Southey, v.II, p315

P 135 "... rafts smashed to bits on the rocks at the bottom." Caraman, p65

P 136 Mendoza and Indian escorts ambushed by Gualpalache, horse stuck in swamp, Mendoza and Indians killed. O'Neill, p86

P 136 "Your ancient martyr (Mendoza), fallen out of fashion and favor by the Christians of today... " Cunninghame-Graham, p91

P 136 Of 50,000 to 100,000 mission Indians in the Guayra, only 4,000 survived. Caraman, p67

P 137 Frustrated mamelucos destroy Villarica and Ciudad Real. Southey, v.II, p316

P 138 Amazon story... from Quito, Spaniards set out for cinnamon and gold in Amazon basin.. Southey, v..I, p395

P 139 "... fed to attack dogs... " Carvajal (via Heaton), p51

P 139 troops sign petition. Carvajal (via Heaton), p77

P 140 Spanish kill Amazons. Carvajal (via Heaton), p214

P 140 Spaniards see "... women marching in front of their fighting squadrons." Carvajal (via Heaton), p26

P 140 Male Indians who wavered in battle were beaten to death by these female tyrants. Southey, v.I, p105

P 141 Amazons would turn "... a boy into an old man... " Carvajal (via Heaton), p222

P 141 Heaton quotes Balée about Amazons. Mann, p285

P 141 Amazon women force men into their own country for their "carnal desires... multiplying their own race." Southey, v.I, p437 and Carvajal (via Heaton), p220

P 142 Portuguese Luiz de Mello da Sylva acquires lower Amazon grant, ships wrecked, goes broke, becomes wealthy in India, disappears en route to his Amazon grant. Southey, v.I, p112,113

Chapter 10 Guaraní and Jesuits Fight Back – Savage Battle at Mbororé

Main references: Southey, Caraman, Reiter, O'Neill and Groh

P 143 Mamelucos return with 25,000 captives from Guayrá and Tape in 1638. O'Neill, p88

P 144 Montoya and Taño sail for Madrid and Rome seeking permission to arm the Guarani. Philip IV approves. Pope Urban VIII issues papal brief , *Commissum Nobis*, censuring slavery. Ibid 90

P 146 Montoya returns to Lima... 1640 Portuguese Revolution causes break with Spain... Viceroy Mancera starts arming Indians. Mörner, *Political and Economic Activities*, p116

P 147 Mameluco invasions become lawful warfare in Brazil. Southey, v.II, p329

P 147 Alfaro releases mamelucos on own recognizance. Caraman, p76

P 147 Alfaro, musket in hand, shot dead by same mamelucos. Mörner, *Political and Economic Activities*, p96, Caraman, p79

P 148 Huge invasion by mamelucos and Tupí allies begins in 1641. Mörner, *Political and Economic Activities*, p97

P 149 Guaraní and Jesuits ambush invaders. Slaughter follows. Reiter, p45, O'Neill, p91

P 149 Jungle silence broken by murderous interludes of screaming, shooting, moans from dying. Caraman, p79

P 149 No mercy for invaders. One third of mamelucos and most of Tupí killed. Ibid 79

P 150 Gualache cannibals set upon survivors, mutilate them, fix heads on poles. Ibid 79

P 150 Casualty count for victors is small. Southey, v.II, p330

P 150 More than 2,000 Guaraní captives already en route to Sao Paulo are rescued. Ibid 330

P 150 News of the victory spreads. Large numbers of Guaraní enter missions. Governor of Paraguay sees Guaraní as his army against mamelucos and Portuguese incursions. Golden Age of the Republic begins. Great celebrations held. Ibid 331,332

P 151 Montoya never returns to his missions...remains in Lima advising viceroy...dies there. Cunninghame-Graham, p100

P 152 Epitaph on Montoya. Groh, p533

Chapter 11 A Rapscallion Bishop Persecutes the Jesuits for 125 Years

Main references: Caraman, Cunninghame-Graham, O'Neill, and Reiter

P 153 Jesuits considered him a "gifted and pernicious clown." Caraman, p82

P 153 Franciscans "held him up as one who fought through his life for the honor of (their) founder." Cunninghame-Graham, p168

P 153 Indians "loved and revered him. . . and considered him a saint." Ibid 168

P 153 "half crazy." Southey, v.III, p537

P 155 Disciples believe he was St. Thomas Aquinas reincarnated. Caraman, p85

P 155 He collides with Governor Gregorio de Hinestrosa. Mörner, *Political and Economic Activities*, p115

P 156 He converts Guaycurú who then burn down Spanish town." Caraman, p86

P 157 sermon at Yaguarón lists Jesuit crimes. . . became by 1767, 'known facts' to all... Cunninghame-Graham, p139

P 157 List of seven accusations. Caraman, p88,89, et al

P 157 Cárdenas said bishops were under orders to expel Jesuits but only he had the courage to actually do it. Ibid 89

P 159 ". . . tincture of civilization they possessed to the calumniated Jesuits." Cunninghame-Graham, p143

P 160 Bienaventura alleges Jesuit mines. . . condemned to death. . . Jesuits secure his release on grounds of insanity. Caraman, p94

P 161 Mosquera, gives deathbed confession that Cardenas had forced him to promote lies against the Jesuits. O'Neill, p115,116

P 161 León finds Cárdenas arrayed in pontifical vestments, seated on bishop's throne and crowned by his miter. Ibid 119

P 161 Dying King Philip, in pity, appoints 88-year old bishop to diocese in Charcas. Cunninghame-Graham, p169

P 162 León restores Jesuit properties and recalls them from exile. O'Neill, p119

P 162 European lawyers ". . . were the only persons to derive unquestioned benefit" from the Cárdenas affair. Caraman, p96

P 162 One of Cárdenas' accusations proved to be intractable. . . that of vast Jesuit hidden treasure, especially gold. O'Neill p122

P 162 Cárdenas' allegations of Jesuit gold delays German Jesuits and mission expansion for forty years. Caraman, p97,98

Chapter 12 Jesuit Republic's Golden Years of Prosperity and Growth (1651-1721), Then Civil War and Communist Revolt (1721-1736)

Main references: Southey, O'Neill and Caraman

P 165 Portuguese invade Mato Grosso. Disaster follows. Southey, v.III, p381

P 165 Victorious Indians trade six pounds of gold for Spaniards' pewter plate. Ibid, 381, O'Neill says five pounds.

P 166 Bolivian Amazon missions thrive. Caraman, p185,186

P 166 Indians kill Arce, Zea and Blende deep in Bolivian jungle. Ibid 187

P 167 Pro-slavery cabal rebels. . . audencia appoints Antequera to investigate...he joins rebels. Southey, v.III, p317, O'Neill p163

P 168 Antequera expels Jesuits. . . attacks Indians. . . plans for "King of Paraguay". Southey, v.III,p215,

P 169 New Franciscan bishop, Palos, in Asunción praises Jesuits to Philip V. O'Neill, p170

P 169 Zabala seizes Antequira who is shot dead on scaffold. . . angry mob shot into by soldiers. Southey, v.III, p233

P 170 New rebellion in Asunción under Governor Barua. O'Neill, p174

P 170 Angles writes king The Fathers of the Society of Jesus are the only competent persons of the province of Paraguay. Ibid 178

P 170 Communists under Mompó seize Asunción. O'Neill, p182, Southey, v.III p233

P 171 Three religious leaders support Communists. O'Neill, p184

P 172 Governor Ruibola overthrown and killed by Communists. . . they proclaim their leader, Bishop Arregui, governor. Ibid, 190

P 172 Zabala defeats Communists. . . appoints Echauri, governor. Ibid 192

P 173 Echauri burns Communist documents. . . Jesuits restored, exonerated and vindicated. Ibid 195

P 173 Palos writes king "If this province were deprived of the Fathers I am certain it would sink into ignorance and vice." Ibid 204

P 173 ". . . caused me shame. . . Christians in our land who would do well to go amongst these Indians to learn from them." Ibid 204

Chapter 13 Spain and Portugal Try to Resolve Their Paraguay Dispute, Treaty of Madrid and the Guaraní War, The Beginning of the End

Main references: Southey, O'Neill, Cunninghame-Graham, Reiter and Mörner

P 175 as you now possess. Mörner, *Expulsion of the Jesuits*, p114

P 175 England as Portugal's ally. Ibid 114

P 176 having many Portuguese Jesuit missions near its banks. Ibid 113

P 177 San Juan and San Luis. Caraman, p314

P 178 apostles and pastors of the people she was expatriating. O'Neill, p214

P 179 the Treaty but also that they induce the Guaraní to accept it. Ibid 216

P 179 impeding. . . "transfer of the missions would do so under pain of mortal sin." Ibid 221

P 181 one avenue open – try to get the Treaty modified. Ibid 218

P 181 Paraguay Jesuits insubordinate. . . do not feel safe in obeying the civil law. Ibid 219

P 182 king's confessor offers sympathy and consolation. Nothing more. Ibid 223

P 182 Jesuit Visitor Altamirano convinced Jesuits of Paraguay actively opposing the Treaty. Caraman, p243

P 182 imposing . . . painful, difficult and dangerous tasks on his temporary subjects. O'Neill, p227,228

P 183 Andrade calls Treaty "mi gran negocio." Ibid 216

P 183 Altamirano fails to find "any trace of it (hidden Jesuit hand). Ibid 229

P 183 Jesuits were going to follow their conscience not their general's orders. Ibid 229

P 184 he had no more proof than he had the year before. Caraman, p244,245

P 184 probably Taddeo Ennis offered to mediate. Cunninghame-Graham, p247,248, 251

P 185 armed with artillery and led by Jesuits! O'Neill, p231

P 185 Altamirano's most terrific set of fulminations ever issued in the Society of Jesus. Ibid p233, quoting Astrain

P 185 fathers. . . returned to their seven missions. Caraman, p246

P 186 As supplies and morale ran down, they retreated. Southey, v.III, p471

P 188 corregidor asks governor to spare church. . . even infidels would not do it any harm. Cunninghame-Graham, p257

P 189 Cevallos charges Altamirano and accomplices gross liars, strong language. O'Neill, p236

P 190 Everything was to be returned to the *status quo ante*. Ibid 236

P 190 Cevallos earned the gratitude of Jesuits not only in Paraguay but around the world. Ibid 236

P 191 Cevallos defeats English ships. . . commissioned by Portuguese in Lisbon. Southey, v.III, p561

P 191 MacNamara let go of his hold and sunk. Ibid 362

Chapter 14 Portugal's Jesuits – The First to Fall

Main references: Cheke, Bangert, Mörner, Lacouture and Saraiva

P 198 gold added about $30 billion. . . the diamonds, several billion more. Saraiva, p75,76

P 199 José I. . . surrounded by beautiful women and musicians. Fülöp-Miller, p375

P 199 Pombal's superior intelligence. Bangert, p367

P 199 music and hunting..a passion of his Spanish wife, Queen Marianna Victoria. Cheke, p59

P 200 he came to appreciate "enlightened autocrats." Saraiva, p78

P 200 starting as minister of foreign affairs. Bangert, p353
P 201 ". . . rob corpses in the street." Cheke, p65
P 201 He was deeply moved. Ibid 66
P 201 Almighty. . . spared the city's street of brothels. Ibid 111
P 201 "Sire, we must bury the dead and feed the living." Ibid 66
P 201 Spain sent "four wagon loads of money." Ibid 73
P 202 "Do not call me king, call me sinner." Ibid 91,92
P 202 fair haired with a flowing white beard even in his early years. Ibid 89-92
P 202 the image which the king kept in his bedroom. Ibid 90-92
P 202 They were soon exiled by Mendoça. Mörner, *The Expulsion of the Jesuits*, p124
P 203 Pombal viewed with a "grim eye." Cheke, p93
P 203 Pombal was beginning to get Jesuits on the brain. Cheke, p93, Bangert, p353, Mörner, p124
P 203 their "continual intrigues" against him. Cheke, p105
P 204 Superiors of the Augustinians and the Carmelites. Ibid 105
P 204 three months after they had left Lisbon. Mörner, *The Expulsion of the Jesuits*, p133
P 204 prices of which Pombal personally fixed. Ibid 122
P 204 Pombal immediately sent him into exile. Cheke, p58,59
P 205 General Company. . . formed in 1756. Saraiva, p78
P 205 Pombal accused of exploitation. Cheke, p84
P 205 aggrieved tavern-keepers. Ibid 86
P 205 promise to abolish the Company. Cheke, p86
P 205 first taste of Pombal the tyrant. Ibid 87
P 205 crime was that they had complained. Mörner, *The Expulsion of the Jesuits*, p124
P 205 distributed complimentary copies. Cheke, p95
P 206 the prince was a heretic. Mörner, *The Expulsion of the Jesuits*, p125
P 206 Paraguay. . . an obsession. . . work burned by Castile's executioner. Lacouture, p266, Bangert, p353
P 206 "The Jesuit Kingdom in Paraguay". Bangert, p354
P 207 litany of accusations. . . reviving and recruiting animosity against them. Cheke, p106-108, Bangert, p367
P 207 "good-natured man of no exceptional competence or endowments." Bangert p367
P 208 bribed the two with cases of Brazilian sugar supplied by Pombal. Cheke, p109,110
P 208 charges were as "silly as they were false." Southey, v.I, p226
P 209 by being "in strict mourning" from the death of his sister. Cheke, p114
P 209 Her fame was sung by poets. Ibid 112
P 210 The king returned to the palace without delay. Lacouture, p266, Cheke, p114
P 210 What happened is "shrouded in mystery and obscurity." Cheke, p115
P 210 planning to place the Duke. . . on the throne. Lacouture, p267
P 210 threats and denunciations against the government. Cheke, p118
P 211 trial conducted in secret. . . evidence without fear. Ibid 121
P 211 Aveiro confessed that four Jesuits were involved. Mörner, *The Expulsion of the Jesuits*, p125
P 211 Malagrida was also arrested with nine other Jesuits. Bangert, p371
P 211 Ferreira told him that he was in service of the Duke. Cheke, p117
P 212 compelling alibis from unimpeachable sources. Ibid 124
P 212 their "colonies' in Paraguay were being destroyed. Ibid 126
P 212 His Majesty's faithful vassals. Ibid 124
P 212 Death sentences. . . passed out. Lacouture, p267
P 212 a cold drizzle was falling on the Plaza. Reiter, p259
P 213 executions. . . nunnery were permitted. Lacouture, p267, Cheke, p127,128, Mörner, *The Expulsion of the Jesuits*, p126
P 213 They are the only ones who teach it. Lacouture, p268
P 214 Malagrida found guilty. Bangert, p370
P 214 burned to death in a wok-shaped device. Mathes lectures, Mörner, *The Expulsion of the Jesuits*, p123
P 214 Pombal celebrated the triumph over "Jesuit wickedness." Mörner, *The Expulsion of the*

Jesuits, p123

P 214 Voltaire called Malagrida's execution "infamy. . . combination of ridiculous and horrible." Lacouture p267, Cheke, p209

P 214 Pombal's personal hatred for Jesuits considered "grotesque" by European society. Cheke, p209

P 215 death to anyone who harbors a Jesuit. Mörner, *The Expulsion of the Jesuits*, p127 et al

P 215 after 15 years. . . 60 survivors emerged gaunt and confused. Bangert, p371

P 215 pope would not seem to agree with their expulsion. Lacouture, p267

P 216 Pombal becomes de facto head of the Portuguese Church. Cheke, p204

P 216 second attempt on life of King Joseph. Ibid 216

P 216 "If there still (in 1938) clings to Jesuits a sinister reputation. . . fact attributed to Pombal." Ibid 216,217

P 217 demonstrators clamor for Pombal's death. . . pelt his coach with stones. Saraiva, p68

P 217 Pombal destroyed all relevant documents. Cheke, p129

P 217 Pombal's trial exonerates Aveiros. Ibid 129

P 217 he claimed Aveiro's companion wore white breeches. Ibid 122,290

P 218 Jews and white hats. . . one is for you and one is for me. Ibid 205 et al

P 218 Pombal left a full treasury upon the death of the king. Sources are in disagreement on this point. It is uncertain..

Chapter 15 The Enlightenment Overwhelms France's Jesuits, They Fall

Main references: Bangert, Lacouture, the Durants, Stankiewicz, Mousnier and Wright

P 219 by far the most crushing was the Enlightenment. Bangert, p273

P 221 the "French Court was too busy burning and massacring Hugonots to think of Brazil. . . " Southey, v.I, p314

P 221 withdrawal of France from Brazil was unfortunate for the Guaraní. Stankiewicz, p45

P 222 dispose of the Huguenots, "once and for all." Ibid 22

P 222 A huge cost for France. Ibid 26

P 223 Catholics in effigy. . . Protestants in actuality. Bainton, p3

P 223 significant currents of the sixteenth century. Ibid 4

P 223 Francis I. . . whose religion sat lightly. Ibid 75

P 223 Calvin would refer to Servetus "as a satan." Ibid 144

P 224 "I will not suffer him to get out alive." Ibid 145

P 224 Servetus "exposed by certain brothers from Lyon." Ibid 168

P 224 "Papists persecute the truth. . . should we refrain from repressing error." Ibid 169

P 224 "future trifles and impious ravings." Ibid 184,185

P 224 Calvin preferred the sword to the stake. Ibid 207

P 224 As he was burned he cried out. Ibid 212

P 224 "to spare Servetus would have been to endanger the souls. . . " Stankiewicz, p7,8

P 225 Castellion for tolerance across the board. Ibid 7

P 226 Edict of Nantes. . . a compendium of prior edicts. Ibid 30,64

P 226 Châtel attempts to kill Henry IV. . . Châtel executed. . . Jesuit instructor Guéret exiled. Wright, p37, Mousnier, p223

P 226 Jesuit Guignard hanged. Wright, p37

P 226 Jesuits exiled by Parlement. . . attending Jesuit colleges outside France considered high treason. Mousnier, p222

P 227 Jesuits surrounded with myth of duplicity, tortuous intrigue, double-dealing and cruelty. Ibid 228

P 227 Ravaillac assassinates Henry IV. . . Jesuit confessor had told him to go home. . . lead quiet life. Ibid 34

P 228 Ravaillac tortured to death. Ibid 51

P 230 "Santarelli Affair." Jesuit argues papal supremacy over crowns. Richelieu opposed. Bangert, p200,201, Stankiewicz, p121

P 231 On dying bed Mazarin warns king against Jansenists. Stankiewicz, p150

P 231 Louis XIV facilitates rise of Enlightenment. Bangert, p297

P 232 Edict of Fontainebleu exiles Huguenots. Stankiewicz, p240

Notes

343

P 233 Huguenots support Louis' divine right principle. Ibid 68
P 233 Louis approves minor interpretations of Edict of Nantes against Huguenots. Ibid 183
P 233 he must expiate his amorous liaisons. Ibid 191
P 233 France's trade vitiated. . . colonies lost. Ibid 240,241
P 234 Pompadour wields influence over Louis XV. Ibid 301
P 234 *"Aprés moi le déluge."* Ibid 299
P 236 Montaigne and "cultural relativism." Washington State University site montaigne
P 237 Voltaire would become the standard bearer for French humanism. Durants, p4
P 237 Voltaire on Father Porée. . . the care they took of us. . . there is not one who would belie my words. Ibid 4, Bangert, p306
P 237 Voltaire. . . "thin, long and fleshless, without buttocks." Durants, p34
P 237 dismiss half the asses that crowded his Highness's court. Ibid 34
P 237 fluttering and rhyming. . . always cleverly. Ibid 34
P 237 Voltaire begging for release from the Bastille. Ibid 37
P 238 "our priests learning depends on our credulity." Ibid 37
P 238 "I do not recognize in this disgraceful picture of God. . . I should dishonor him." Ibid 39
P 239 "a pitiless Jansenist. . . or an ambitious pope. Ibid 39
P 239 quotes from *Candide* ridiculing the Jesuits. Lacouture, p231
P 239 Voltaire quote on the missions of Paraguay. Cunningham-Grahame attributes this quote to Voltaire, taking it from *Histoire Politique et Philosophique des Indies* vol. i., p289 Genève, 1780. O'Neill, p60, "correcting" Cunninghame-Graham attributes it to Raynal, taking it from *Histoire Politique et Philosophique des deux Indies* with no further identification. Research turned up no copy of either in the U.S.
P 240 Diderot was educated by Jesuits. Bangert, p308
P 240 Jesuit editor welcomes first edition of *L'Encyclopédie.* Ibid 304
P 240 Jesuits expose *L'Encyclopédie's* plagiarism. Voltaire's scorn shrinks Jesuit Journal. Ibid 305
P 240 Jesuits respond to deists with older ways of earlier generations. Ibid 305
P 240 their language was still Latin. . . barely understood by ten out of a thousand. Ibid 308
P 241 salons of Paris. . . vivacious, witty and refined language. Ibid 298
P 241 Father Tournemine believes everything he makes up. Ibid 298
P 242 Rousseau's "pursuit of happiness" and his social contract. Washington State University site, Rousseau
P 242 Damien attempts to kill Louis XV. . . had been Jesuit servant. Bangert, p372
P 244 Treaty of Paris would heap shame on Louis. Ibid 375
P 244 Lavalette affair. . . intrigue, politics and occupations alien. . . Lacouture, p362,363
P 244 Parlement agent, Abbe de Chauvelin, connected to *philosophes* and Jansenists, attacks Jesuits. Bangert, p374, Lacouture, p274
P 244 Chauvelin accuses Jesuits. . . war machine. . . fifth column. . . regicide is Jesuit morality. Bangert, p374
P 245 bishops reject Gallicanizing Jesuits. Bangert, p381, Lacouture, p275
P 245 Vatican rejects Pompadour. . . she joins Jansenists. Lacouture, p270
P 245 Quesnel reanimates Jansenists. Bangert, p301
P 245 French Jesuits agree to Gallicanization. Lacouture, p275
P 245 pope rejects approach. . . "let them be what they are or let them not be." Ibid 275, Cheetham, p238
P 246 description of General Ricci. . . no practical administrative experience. Bangert, p363
P 246 he was 58 at this point. Ibid 363, Lacouture, p288
P 246 Parlement pamphlet attack Jesuits. Ibid 275
P 246 d'Alembert calls for annihilation of Jesuits. Ibid 276
P 246 humans worthy of "taking communion quite often." Wright, p168
P 246 d'Alembert writes "let the Jansenist rabble rid us of the Jesuit blackguards. . . spiders gobbling one another." Bangert, p380
P 246 Parlement delivers final blow. Lacouture, p277, Bangert, p377

P 246 Jesuits scattered, assets seized. Bangert, p379
P 247 Paris archbishop protests. . . is banished. Lacouture, p279
P 247 Jesuits survive in English Canada. Bangert, p383
P 247 pope issues Bull *Apostolicum* praising Jesuits. Lacouture, p280

Chapter 16 Spain Turns On Her Favorite Sons – The Main Event

Main references: Petrie, Bangert, Lacouture, Hargreaves-Mawdsley, Hull, Pastor, Hollis, Mörner, Wright, Cunninghame-Graham, Herr and Bertrand-Petrie

P 248 "you shall suffer the penalty of death." Lacouture, p286 et al
P 248 Catholics without equal in the world. Bangert, p61
P 249 heir by "the right of the closest relative." Hargreaves-Mawdsley, *Spain Under The Bourbons*, p15
P 249 ". . . we form only one nation." Hargreaves-Mawdsley, *Eighteenth Century Spain*, p16
P 251 Charles third in line of succession. Ibid 45
P 251 Ferdinand not live and produce an heir. Ibid 55-65
P 254 Charles expels Jews. Hull, p79
P 255 British ambassador quoted, describes Charles favorably. Hull, p59
P 255 Queen sickens in Buen Retiro palace. Hargreaves-Mawdsley, *Eighteenth Century Spain*, p100
P 255 Queen dies. Hull, p97
P 255 Queen's isolationist policy was proved right. Ibid 97,98
P 256 Charles, in Naples, complains about Treaty of Madrid. Hargreaves-Mawdsley, *Eighteenth Century Spain*, p94
P 258 severe inflation from poor harvests and reopening of sea lanes. Bangert, p385
P 258 Madrilenos toss slop onto streets. . . "agua va." Hull, p107
P 259 royal decree on forbidden dress. Ibid 110
P 259 king flees riots in Madrid. Petrie, p119,120
P 260 Duke of Alba's death-bed confession on the riots exonerates Jesuits. Lacouture, p285, quoting Crétineau-Joly
P 260 Riot was a political bomb to frighten the king into expelling Jesuits. Mörner, *The Expulsion of the Jesuits*, p38
P 260 from Aranda's pen the rioters' intent was to slaughter Squillace. Pastor, v.XXXVII, p62-146
P 261 Jesuit philosopher Suarez, a man "hostile to the throne." Mörner, *The Expulsion of the Jesuits*, p43
P 261 Suarez. . . rulers' authority is from God through the mediation of the people. Bangert, p384
P 261 Palafox in conflict with the Jesuits in Mexico. Mörner, *The Expulsion of the Jesuits*, p142
P 262 Palafox excommunicates Mexico's Jesuits. . . returns to Spain. Ibid 36,37, Wright, p160 et al
P 262 Tanucci regrets leaving this poison (Jesuits) behind. Pastor, v.XXXVII, p38
P 263 Aranda, a "tough soldier". Bangert, p384
P 263 Aranda the Jesuit pupil, has Jesuit relatives. Mörner, *The Expulsion of the Jesuits*, p145
P 263 Aranda, uninhibited sense of humor. Hargreaves-Mawdsley, *Eighteenth Century Spain*, p114
P 263 Charles repeats Aranda's "the king is even more stubborn." Petrie, p151
P 263 Aranda friend of French deists. Bangert, p384
P 265 existence of Ricci's bastardy letter about Charles is "baseless". . . no evidence of it. Pastor, V.XXXVII, p143-150
P 265 Ricci's letter most plausible reason for Charles' being infuriated. Lacouture, p285, quoting Crétineau-Joly
P 266 Ricci letter found in open during police raid. Petrie, p129
P 267 Alberoni introduced to Louis XIV. Hargreaves-Mawdsley, *Eighteenth Century Spain*, p43
P 267 Alberoni intrigues. . . expelled back to Italy. Ibid 50

Notes

P 267 "Extraordinary Council of Castile" formed to secretly investigate Jesuits. Mörner, *The Expulsion of the Jesuits*, p139

P 267 1500 witnesses give opinions. Addison, p68

P 268 Jesuit printing presses produce "lampoons against the Government." Mörner, *The Expulsion of the Jesuits*, p140,141

P 268 Witnesses testify to multiple Jesuit crimes at their trial. Reiter, p321

P 269 1977 document lists 746 charges by Campomanes against Jesuits. Bangert, p386

P 272 Expulsion Decree sent to colonies. Lacouture, p286, Mörner, *The Expulsion of the Jesuits*, p146

P 272 annual pension for each Jesuit, 90 to 100 pesos. Pastor, v.XXXVII, p151

P 274 pensions of all would be forfeited. Bangert, p388

P 275 Tanucci and Duke of Parma follow Charles' expulsion. Bertrand-Petrie, p426

P 275 General of Augustinians calls for hymn of praise for Spain's purification from the Jesuit "reptiles." Herr, p23

P 275 awaits these exiles with their gods of avarice, ambition, slander and regicide. Bangert, p387

P 275 Spanish bishops re-endorse expulsion. Herr, p22

P 275 " We have killed the son. . . carry out like action against. . . our Holy Roman Church." Mörner, *The Expulsion of the Jesuits*, p50

P 277 long quote from Cunninghame-Graham, pix-xiii

P 278 Clement XIII letter to Charles, May 16, 1767. Pastor, v.XXXVII, p152

P 279 Charles to Clement, June 2, 1767. Petrie, p132,133

P 279 "spoke [he offered] no more than an odd phrase gracelessly spoken. . . " Hargreaves-Mawdsley, *Eighteenth Century Spain*, p123

Chapter 17 Jesuits Expelled from Paraguay and Brazil

Main references: Caraman, O'Neill, Cunninghame-Graham, Southey, Mörner and Reiter

P 281 "A mystery of Iniquity." So said Pope Pius VI. O'Neill, p238

P 281 Bucareli. . . timid, but honest and upright man. Cunninghame-Graham, p262

P 282 "obstinate, a liar, a hypocrite and a thief. . . heartless cruelty. . . " O'Neill, p241

P 282 "sent the King endless long-winded reports exaggerating the dangers. . . " Caraman, p276

P 282 He was "cruel and inept." Mörner, p164

P 282 his rule in New Spain was the happiest. Engelhardt, v.II, p295,296 quoting others

P 283 lamentations threatened with fines, prison and exile. O'Neill, p249

P 283 snuff, the only relic of their luxurious mission life. Cunninghame-Graham, p281

P 284 Fabro "generously allowed them to fast." O'Neill, p247

P 284 "Nothing seems to have been preserved." O'Neill, p248 quoting Cunninghame-Graham. The latter seems to be unaware of what was preserved, as Mathes says that much relevant material was sent to Rome as the years went by, an understandable oversight given the author's limited time perspective.

P 286 ninety residents executed after uprising in Mexico over Jesuit expulsion. Bertrand-Petrie, p147

P 286 Jesuits could unleash "clouds" of superb horsemen. Caraman, p279 et al

P 286 Aranda says the Jesuits will accept the Decree with resignation. O'Neill, p252

P 286 corregidores thank king for sending them Viceroy Bucareli. Caraman, p278

P 287 San Luis mission letter to Bucareli "We shall fall into the hands of the devil." Reiter p343

P 288 Father Vergara surrenders missions to Bucareli's agent. O'Neill, p255

P 289 imprisonment at Puerta de Santa Maria. No two sources agree on the ships' names, the dates and the number of Jesuits.

P 289 Thomas Faulkner returns to England. Caraman, p282

P 290 Father Chomé expires high in the Andes. Ibid p281

P 290 Father Messner's attendant discovers him to be a corpse. Ibid 281

P 290 Father Schmid and 11 others die on trail in Bolivia. Ibid 281

P 290 Father Pallozzi dies in Panama. Ibid 281
P 290 500 Jesuits from the Americas die during expulsion. Reiter, p347
P 290 Asperger, the last Jesuit in Paraguay, dies in Apóstoles at 91. Caraman p284
P 291 Southey's post mortem on the expulsion. . . Spain's most faithful servants. Southey, v.III, p603,604
P 291 Reiter's post mortem. . . new priests closed their eyes to the abuse they witnessed. Reiter, p349
P 291 Guayrá missions destroyed by neglect and wars. Ibid 350
P 292 Pombal's 1757 pamphlet on the war of the Jesuits against the two crowns. Lacouture, p266
P 292 bishop of Maranham abandons bishopric to avoid persecuting the Jesuits there. Southey, v.III, p542
P 292 Four Jesuits of São Luiz die en route to Portugal. Ibid v.III, p542
P 292 Five Jesuits from Ceará and Paraíba die en route to Portugal. Ibid v.III, 543
P 293 bishop of Rio de Janeiro "issues most virulent Pastoral Epistle ever so misnamed. Ibid v.III, p545
P 293 Rio bishop threatens those helping Jesuits. Ibid v.III, p545
P 294 Jesuit missions. . . only place in the American continent where Indians prospered. Mörner, p182, quoting Portuguese historian.

Chapter 18   Pope Abolishes the Society of Jesus
Main references: Bangert, Pastor, Lacouture, Fülöp-Miller and McCoog
P 297 Translation of *Dominus ac Redemptor*. McCoog, p296
P 298 Clement XIII and General Ricci oppose Gallicanization of French Jesuits. Bangert, p365
P 298 Clement vacillates but does not capitulate. Ibid p364
P 298 crowns accuse pope of insulting them. Petrie, p133
P 298 troops seize papal towns. Ranke, p492 et al
P 298 Clement XIII has fatal heart attack. Bangert, p345
P 299 French cardinal opposes future pope not to agree to abolish Jesuits. Ibid 396
P 299 it would be simony. Petrie, p134
P 299 Austria's emperor Joseph. . . Jesuits spread darkness and dominate and confuse Europe. Fülöp-Miller, p384
P 299 Louis XVI and Marie Antoinette, the best match in Europe. Ibid 383
P 299 Maria Theresa reverses support for Jesuits. Ibid 382
P 299 Austria fears alienating the Bourbons. Reiter, p351, Cheetham, p239 et al
P 300 Ganganelli tries to please both sides at papal conclave. . . intelligent, kind, scholarly, charming. Bangert, p395
P 300 Ganganelli has insufficient faith in God. Hollis, p152
P 300 Pope proceeds with caution. . . Jesuits have many friends. Pastor, v.XXXVII, p245
P 301 Charles III demands extinguishing of Jesuit Order. Bangert, p396
P 301 a Vatican Council could take years. Lacouture, p293 et al
P 301 Moñino, the only Spaniard who knew how to manage affairs in Rome. Pastor, v.XXXVII, p244
P 301 convincing the pope to suppress the Jesuits. Hargreaves-Mawdsley, *Eighteenth Century Spain*, p120 et al
P 301 pope dreads Moñino's tactics. Bangert, p398
P 301 Moñino's tactics include bribery and threats. Pastor, v.XXXVII, p244
P 301 Pombal's brother, a cardinal, dies before his elevation. FIUcardinalslist
P 302 bribe with Spanish gold. Pastor, v.XXXVII, p244
P 302 Buontempi bribe. . . not until the deed is done. Pastor, v.XXXVII, p250
P 302 Frederick writes d'Alembert. . . without heretics like me meddling. Lacouture, p303
P 302 Jesuits were intriguing with a heretic, Frederick. Pastor, v.XXXVII, p250,251
P 303 pope will bring matters to a speedy end. Pastor, v.XXXVII, p248
P 303 "I have already succeeded in destroying the Jesuits". . . Ibid 248
P 303 pope deprives Portuguese Jesuits of pensions. Ibid 249

P 303 Spanish Dominicans and Franciscans collaborate with Moñino. Hargreaves-Mawdsley, *Eighteenth Century Spain*, p120
P 303 Zelada accepts 8,000 scudi bribe. Bangert, p398
P 303 Neapolitan troops withdrawn. Pastor, v.XXXVII, p253
P 303 Charles III satisfied with fulfillment of his wishes. Ibid 255
P 303 Maria Theresa would put no obstacle in the way. Ibid 260
P 303 Maria Theresa told that she would rue this step. Ibid 261
P 304 Maria Theresa had sacrificed the Jesuits. . . fate awaiting her daughter. Ibid 261
P 304 pope had hoped empress would oppose suppression of Jesuits. Ibid 261
P 304 pope hopes something might intervene. Ibid 265
P 304 pope asks Moñino not to frighten him so much. Ibid 274
P 304 Ricci arrested. . . announced to the world. Cheetham, p240 et al
P 305 whatever the pope decided must be sacred. Pastor, v.XXXVII, p255,286
P 305 "Hell is my abode. . . I am doomed." Lacouture, p293
P 305 quotes from Dominus ac Redemptor. McCoog, p302-312
P 306 pope forbids any form of comment on his brief. McCoog, p310
P 307 Paris Archbishop Beaumont declares brief pernicious and deleterious to the Church. Ibid 295
P 308 Tanucci called a mendacious caviler. Pastor, v.XXXVII, p307
P 308 pope swindled by Tanucci over price paid for abolishing Jesuits. Ibid 306
P 308 three-quarters of Jesuits were priests, one-quarter, brothers. Wright, p49
P 308 novices and brothers free to live. . . Bangert, p400,401
P 308 Ricci awaits trial in solitary confinement. Lacouture, p296
P 308 closest assistant dies in nearby cell. Bangert, p402
P 308 cardinal withdraws "sickened by irregularities committed." Lacouture, p296
P 310 even in death the Jesuits served the Church. Bangert, p400
P 311 John Wrynn, S.J., writes an interesting footnote to the medallion story. Until the end of the last century there were two ways to number the psalms: one followed the Greek translation of the Old Testament, the Septuagint, and the other the Hebrew text. During the schism that accompanied the religious changes of the 16th century the Catholics chose to follow the Greek version and the Protestants the Hebrew. In the mid-20th century a papal document issued by Pius XII (*Divino afflante Spiritu*) approved the use of the Hebrew text as the basis for translations of the Bible and Catholics began following the same numbering system as did the Protestants.

Chapter 19 Frederick and Catherine: The Great "Heretics" Rescue the Jesuits

Main references: Asprey, Lacouture and Bangert
P 312 Frederick's cold and demeaning parent. Asprey, p12-15
P 312 king tried to strangle him. Ibid 51 et al
P 312 she came to Frederick's defense. Ibid 16-21, 34
P 313 Crown Prince to flee to England. Ibid 51-53
P 313 Katte's sentence. Preussen-Chronik.de. Section 1713-1786, Fluchthelfer des Kronprinzen
P 313 He had fainted moments before. Asprey, p62-71
P 313 she became bored and ended the relationship. Ibid 83,84
P 314 communications were tender. Mitford, p84
P 314 he showed little interest in women. Ibid 84 et al
P 314 wrote poetry and some thirty books. Asprey, p21 et al
P 314 Frederick signed on to the Enlightenment. Ibid 116,117, 395-405
P 314 discrimination against Jews. Ibid 356-362
P 314 did not believe in immortality of the soul. Kirchberger , p289
P 314 nature will that we all love one another. Ibid
P 314 after death everything is at an end. Ibid

P 315 provided they do not persecute me. Ibid
P 315 all religions must be tolerated. Ibid
P 315 tolerance must assure freedom. Frederick to Voltaire. Harenberg, p1200
P 315 Jesuits available to. . . education part. Lacouture, p263
P 315 Jesuits. . . sent to Silesia. Asprey, p608
P 315 Frederick forbade catholic bishops "under pain of stern punishment." Bangert, 405 et al
P 316 I shall hoard the Jesuits. . . cultivate this rare plant. Lacouture, p303
P 316 On the matter of the Jesuits my mind is made up to preserve them. Ibid 303
P 316 we forbid you to publish the papal bull. Ibid 303
P 316 I am taking in as many (Jesuits) as I can. Thus I keep this race alive. Ibid 304
P 317 no educated Catholic except. . . Jesuits. . . other kinds of monks are of crassest ignorance. Ibid 305
P 317 on Jesuit poisoning of Clement XIV. . . nothing is less true. Ibid 296
P 317 Frederick and Catherine partition Poland. MacDonogh, p598
P 317 papal concession to Frederick. . . Jesuits retaining their identity as an order. Bangert, p406
P 318 Jesuits become "Priests of the Royal Schools Institute." Ibid 406
P 318 new system for Catholic schools in Silesia. Ibid 406
P 320 Jesuits' value to educationally backward Russia. Ibid 413
P 320 as Frederick did. Lacouture, p263
P 320 Catherine was indebted to Jesuits for bringing nobles and the people. Ibid 307
P 320 leave the Jesuits as they are. Her majesty must be obeyed. Ibid 309
P 320 she would ensure their (the Jesuits) eventual reestablishment. Ibid 310
P 321 Catherine considers (the Jesuits) loyal, useful, and blameless subjects. Ibid 311
P 321 pope approves of maintaining Society of Jesus in White Russia. I approve it, I approve it. Ibid 312
P 321 Catherine's successors support Jesuits. Bangert, p427,434
P 322 Czar Paul obtains pope's recognition of Jesuits in Russia. Lacouture, p313

Epilogue

P 323 cardinals insist on input. . . delay Bull restoring Society of Jesus. Bangert, p428
P 324 Spain's Charles IV weeps at meeting with old Jesuits. Ibid 429

Index

Index   351

Black Robes in Paraguay

Saint-Cyran, Abbé de, 50, 231
Salazar, Diego de, 128
Saldhana, Francisco de, 207-209, 214-216
Salvatierra, Viceroy, 161
Sánchez, Francisco, 45
Sánchez Labrador, José, 166, 289
Sánchez, Marco, 268
Sancho, King, 88
San Francisco, (the ship), 142
San Martín Xavier, Francisco de, 96, 99
San Pedro, (the boat), 139
Sans Souci, 314, 315
Santa Clara, Joachim de, 217
Santarelli, Antonio, 229, 230
São José, Antonio, 292
São Lorenço, Count, 201
Sarajevo, 18
Sarria, Carlos José de, 192
Sarria, General, 257
Scarlatti, Domenico, 251
Schmid, Martin, 290
Seábra de Silva, José, 216
Sepé Tiarayo, 184, 186
Sepp, Antonio, 77, 117, 118
Servin, louis, 230
Servetus, Michael, 222-224
servicio personal, 122
Seven Years' War, 192, 193, 234, 244, 257,
    313, 319
Siestrezenciewitz, Stanislaus, 320
Silíceo, Martinez, 45
Silva de Fonseca, Vicente, 191
Silva, Luiz Diogo Lobo de, 292
Simone, Cardinal de, 305
Sinzendorff, Cardinal, von, 314
Siripus (chief), 76
Smith, Adam, 199
Society of Jesus, 11, 13, 39-42, 49, 170, 184,
    193, 215, 216, 248, 249, 268, 281, 297,
    300, 304, 305, 310, 319-321
Sollicitudo Omnium Ecclesiarum, 323
Solano, Francisco, 92-94
Song of Paraguay, 15
Sophia Augusta Frederika (see Catherine II)
Sophocles, 238
Sores, Jacques, 73
Soroeta, Ignacio, 170, 172
Sousa, Tomè de, 38, 39
Squillace, Marques di, 256, 259, 260, 268
Stade, Hans, 67-70
Stroessner, Alfredo, 20, 87
Suarez, Francisco, 261
⬛erck, Joost van, 47, 128, 129, 159
⬛pression, The, 17, 249, 281, 304, 307,
    313, 314

T

Tagle, Miguel García de, 283
Taño (see Diaz Taño)
Tanucci, Bernardo, 253-256, 262, 270, 275,
    307
Távora(s), 199, 209-213, 217, 218, 268
Techo, Nicolás del, 47, 150
Teixeira, Pedro, 217
Thirty Year's War, 220, 229, 231
Thou, François August de, 229
Tibirica (chief), 64
Toit, Nicolas du, 47
Torquemada, Tomás de, 45, 264
Torre, Manuel Antonio de la, 284
Torre Rezzonico, Carlo della, 208
Torres, Diego de, 75, 95
Torres, Domingo, 149
Torres del Bollo, Diego de, 124
Torrigiani, Luigi, 298
Tournemine, René-Joseph, 241
Treaty of Madrid, 18, 98, 174, 175, 190,
    193, 203, 252, 256, 258, 263, 269, 290,
    291
Treaty of Paris, 192, 234, 244, 258, 317
Treaty of San Ildefonso, 193
Treaty of Tordesillas, 30, 31, 33, 34, 60, 62,
    70, 81, 96, 98, 126, 174, 197
Trujillo, Vásquez, 132, 133

U

Ulrich, Peter, (see Peter III, Czar)
Unigenitus dei Filius, 49, 50
Urban VIII, Pope, 144, 145, 230
Utopia, More's 11, 94

V

Valdelirios, Marquis de, 183-187
Vallejo, Juan, 171
van Suerck (see Suerck)
Vansurque, (see Suerck)
Varade, Father, 226
Vaudois, 221
Vázquez, Francisco Xavier, 275
Vendome, Marshall, 267
Vera, Martín de, 160
Vergara, Manuel, 288, 289
Vespucci, Amerigo, 29
Victoria (Orellana's ship), 140
Victoria (Sarria's ship), 192
Victoria, Francisco de, 92
Vieira, Antonio, 48, 64, 65
Villanueva, Francisco, 46
Villasante, Tomás de, 171
Villegagnon, Nicholas Durand de, 63, 71
Visconti, Ignacio, 179, 182, 189
Vitelleschi, Muzio (also Mutio), 107, 125,